THE MATERIAL CULTURE OF THE BUILT ENVIRONMENT
IN THE ANGLO-SAXON WORLD

EXETER STUDIES IN MEDIEVAL EUROPE
History, Society and the Arts

SERIES EDITORS
Simon Barton, Anthony Musson,
Yolanda Plumley and Oliver Creighton

The Material Culture of the Built Environment in the Anglo-Saxon World

Volume II of
The Material Culture of Daily Living in the Anglo-Saxon World

edited by
Maren Clegg Hyer and Gale R. Owen-Crocker
with contributions by
John Baker, Stuart Brookes, Elizabeth Coatsworth,
Erik Grigg, Christopher Grocock, Jeremy Haslam, Paul Hindle,
Kevin Leahy, Michael Lewis, Gale R. Owen-Crocker, Sarah
Semple, Michael Shapland, Damian Tyler, Howard Williams
and Margaret Worthington Hill

LIVERPOOL UNIVERSITY PRESS

First published 2015 by
Liverpool University Press
4 Cambridge Street
Liverpool
L69 7ZU

© 2015 Liverpool University Press

The right of Maren Clegg Hyer and Gale R. Owen-Crocker to be identified as editors of this work has been asserted by them in accordance with the Copyright, Designs and Patents Acts 1988.

No part of this volume may be reproduced, stored in a retrieval system or transmitted, in any form or by any means, electronic, mechanical, photocopying, recording or otherwise without prior written permission of the publishers.

British Library Cataloguing-in-Publication Data
A British Library CIP record is available

ISBN 978 1 78138 265 3

Typeset by Carnegie Book Production, Lancaster.
Printed and bound by CPI Group (UK) Ltd, Croydon CR0 4YY

With profound thanks to J. Halvor and Miriam W. Clegg,
and Paul V. and Karen Hyer,
for journeys across landscapes, and lessons learned.
M.C.H.

For David James Richard Crocker and Emma Jane Bateman,
married 30 August 2014.
G.R.O.-C.

In Memoriam: David Hill, colleague and friend

Contents

List of Figures ix
List of Tables xiii
List of Contributors xv

Introduction 1
    Gale R. Owen-Crocker

1 *Enta geweorc*: *The Ruin* and its Contexts Reconsidered 13
    Christopher Grocock

2 Roads and Tracks in Anglo-Saxon England 37
    Paul Hindle

3 Domestic Dwellings, Workshops and Working Buildings 50
    Kevin Leahy and Michael Lewis

4 Place and Power: Meetings between Kings in Early
Anglo-Saxon England 76
    Damian Tyler

5 The Cuckoo and the Magpie: The Building Culture of the
Anglo-Saxon Church 92
    Michael Shapland

6 Landmarks of Faith: Crosses and other Free-standing Stones 117
  Elizabeth Coatsworth

7 Landmarks of the Dead: Exploring Anglo-Saxon Mortuary
  Geographies 137
  Sarah Semple and Howard Williams

8 Boundaries and Walls 162
  Margaret Worthington Hill and Erik Grigg

9 The Landscape of Late Saxon *Burhs* and the Politics of
  Urban Foundation 181
  Jeremy Haslam

10 Signalling Intent: Beacons, Lookouts and Military
  Communications 216
  John Baker and Stuart Brookes

Notes 235
Suggested Reading 281
Index 284

Figures

1.1	Bath: the end wall of the main hall	15
1.2	Chesters Fort, Hadrian's Wall: the fort's bath house	16
1.3	Richborough, the remains of the main walls	21
1.4	Remains of the Roman bridge at Piercebridge, south of Hadrian's Wall	22
1.5	Wroxeter: the 'Old Work'	26
1.6	Leicester: the surviving wall of the Jewry Wall baths	28
1.7	Birdoswald	30
1.8	Greensted church	31
1.9	Wearmouth: the west tower of St Peter's church	32
1.10	Brixworth church	35
2.1	The network of main Roman roads	39
2.2	Ermine Street, running south from Lincoln to London	40
2.3	The massive agger of Ackling Dyke on Bottlebush Down, south-west of Salisbury	41
2.4	Roman roads and other older tracks still in use in medieval times versus post-Roman routes	45
3.1	Building remains at Flixborough, Lincolnshire	51
3.2	*Grubenhaus* at Catholme, Staffordshire	53
3.3	Small 'Hall' at Catholme, Staffordshire	58
3.4	Hall at Cowdery's Down, Hampshire	60
3.5	Woodworking tools from Flixborough, Lincolnshire	62
3.6	Reconstructed Anglo-Saxon buildings at West Stow, Suffolk	63

3.7	Anglo-Scandinavian building remains at Coppergate, York	65
3.8	Building in the Bayeux Tapestry	68
4.1	Great Hall (A4), Yeavering, Northumberland	82
4.2	The 'Theatre', Yeavering (building E)	84
5.1	The early seventh-century church of Saints Peter and Paul at St Augustine's Abbey, Canterbury	96
5.2	The excavated putative seventh-century timber church and cemetery on an existing cult focus at the royal Bernician site at Yeavering	97
5.3	The late seventh-century church at Escomb (County Durham), viewed from the south-east	99
5.4	The slow development of two great Anglo-Saxon monastic churches	
	5.4a St Augustine's Abbey, Canterbury	102
	5.4b Glastonbury, which incorporated an early hypogeum and timber church, or *vetusta ecclesia*	103
5.5	Cowdery's Down, Hampshire, plan of the seventh-century hall (building A1)	107
5.6	Eighth-century royal mausoleum at St Wystan's church, Repton	
	5.6a plan	108
	5.6b photograph	109
5.7	Late tenth-/early eleventh-century church and Roman lighthouse in Dover Castle, Kent	112
5.8	Two Anglo-Saxon lordly tower-nave churches, both with prominent pilaster strip work, both of probable early eleventh-century date	
	5.8a Earl's Barton, Northamptonshire	114
	5.8b Barton-upon-Humber, Lincolnshire	115
6.1	Map showing pre-1974 boundaries of counties in England, the West Riding in solid black	119
6.2	The Parish of Dewsbury	121
7.1	A visual reconstruction of an Anglo-Saxon funeral capturing how such events may have involved the gathering of family and mourners	143

7.2	The surviving burial mound at Taplow, Buckinghamshire: a seventh-century princely grave	144
7.3	View of a reused prehistoric barrow on Painsthorpe Wold, East Yorkshire	152
7.4	Ripon Cathedral in its landscape setting: Ailcy Hill hidden in the clump of trees to the right of the cathedral	155
7.5	Reconstruction of a late Anglo-Saxon gallows site, positioned on an old earthwork	157
8.1	Features found on Anglo-Saxon dykes	163
8.2	The southern end of Offa's Dyke on Rushock Hill, Herefordshire	164
8.3	Devil's Ditch near Newmarket	166
8.4	West Wansdyke	178
9.1	The two *burhs* of Maldon (shaded half tones) in their immediate landscape setting	185
9.2	Maldon – reconstruction of the extent of the *burh* of 916 on a background of the Ordnance Survey 1:500 map of 1873–75	186
9.3	A reconstruction of the interlocking burghal territories of three areas in central Wessex	190
9.4	The extent of the *burhs* (shaded) at Axbridge, Bridport, Buckingham and Langport	194
9.5	The extent of the *burhs* (shaded) at Christchurch, Lewes and Lydford	195
9.6	The extent of the *burhs* (shaded) at Lyng, Malmesbury and Shaftesbury	196
9.7	The extent of the *burhs* (shaded) at Wilton, Watchet, Southampton and Barnstaple	197
9.8	The extent of the *burhs* (shaded) at Guildford, Kingsbridge and Marlborough	198
9.9	The extent of the *burhs* (shaded) at Oxford (second *burh* of *c*.911), Stamford (two *burhs* on each side of the river) and Worcester	199
9.10	The extent of the *burhs* (shaded) at Newport Pagnell, Beccles and Woodbridge	200
9.11	The extent of the *burh* (shaded) at Totnes	201

10.1	Distribution of Old English *weard* and **tōt(e)* place names in England	219
10.2	Excavations under way on the Yatesbury beacon platform in 1994	223
10.3	Map of beacons in Kent, by William Lambarde	224
10.4	Photograph showing the relationship between St Mary-in-Castro church (left) and the Roman *pharos* (right)	226
10.5	Photograph of Wickham tower-nave	227
10.6	Map of the Avebury landscape	231
10.7	Map of the south-east Midland lookouts along the Icknield Way	233

Tables

6.1 Sites with sculpture in the area of Dewbury Parish/Manor of Wakefield   124
9.1 Characteristics of *burhs*   202–3

Contributors

Editors

Maren Clegg Hyer is Associate Professor of English at Valdosta State University, Georgia. She specialises in researching textiles and textile imagery in Anglo-Saxon culture. Her recent publications include *The Material Culture of Daily Living in Anglo-Saxon England* (with Gale R. Owen-Crocker) (University of Exeter Press, 2011); 'Recycle, Reduce, Reuse: Imagined and Re-imagined Textiles in Anglo-Saxon England', *Medieval Clothing and Textiles* 8 (2012): 49–62 and 'Material Culture in Teaching *Beowulf*', *Teaching Beowulf in the Twenty-First Century*, Medieval and Renaissance Texts and Studies 449 (2014): 177–84.

Gale R. Owen-Crocker is Professor Emerita and until recently was Professor of Anglo-Saxon Culture at The University of Manchester, and Director of the Manchester Centre for Anglo-Saxon Studies. She has published extensively on dress and textiles, especially the Bayeux Tapestry, and on Old English literature. She directed the AHRC-funded research project which created the medieval cloth and clothing lexis database (http://lexisproject.arts.manchester.ac.uk/) on the semantics of cloth and clothing terminology and was co-investigator on a Leverhulme Trust-funded project which produced (with L.M. Sylvester and M.C. Chambers), *Medieval Dress and Textiles in Britain: A Multilingual Sourcebook* (2014). She co-founded and co-edits the international, cross-disciplinary journal *Medieval Clothing and Textiles* and is a general editor of the Boydell series Medieval and Renaissance Dress and Textiles. She is a Fellow of the Society of Antiquaries of London.

Contributors

John Baker is Senior Research Fellow at the Institute for Name-Studies at the University of Nottingham. He is especially interested in multi-disciplinary approaches to questions of social and cultural change in medieval England. He was part of the research team on the *Beyond the Burghal Hidage* and *Landscapes of Governance* projects, and is currently working on *The Place-Names of Shropshire*.

Stuart Brookes is Research Fellow in the History Faculty, University of Oxford, and Honorary Senior Lecturer of the UCL Institute of Archaeology. He specialises in comparative landscape studies and the archaeologies of state formation in early medieval Europe. His recent work has concentrated on the landscape archaeology of Anglo-Saxon civil defence and the structure of governance and administration in early medieval states, published as *Beyond the Burghal Hidage: Civil Defence in Anglo-Saxon England* (with J. Baker, 2013), *Landscapes of Defence in the Viking Age* (with J. Baker and A. Reynolds, 2013) and *Landscapes of Governance: Legal Geographies and Political Order in Anglo-Saxon England* (in preparation). He is currently working on travel and communication in Anglo-Saxon England as part of a major Leverhulme Trust-funded project.

Elizabeth Coatsworth was until 2014 an Honorary Research Fellow based in MIRIAD (Manchester Institute for Research and Innovation in Art and Design), at Manchester Metropolitan University, where she was formerly a Senior Lecturer in the Department of History of Art and Design. She is author of volume 8 of the *Corpus of Anglo-Saxon Stone Sculpture, Western Yorkshire* and co-author of *The Art of the Anglo-Saxon Goldsmith* and *Medieval Textiles of the British Isles c.450–1100: An Annotated Bibliography*.

Erik Grigg has recently submitted his PhD thesis on early medieval dykes to the University of Manchester. He works at The Collection in Lincoln where he heads the education programme, delivering workshops on various archaeological and historical themes. He lives in Lincoln (where he is a member of various historical and archaeological groups) with his wife and two children.

Christopher Grocock is Head of Classics at Bedales School, Hampshire. He studied at both Royal Holloway and Bedford Colleges, University of London, reading Latin and French, and finally specialising in Medieval Latin studies. He is the editor of critical editions of the *Ruodlieb* (1985),

Gilo of Paris's *Historia Vie Hierosolimitane* (with Elizabeth Siberry, 1997), and *Apicius* (with Sally Grainger, 2006), as well as numerous articles and papers. With Professor Ian Wood, he has edited an Oxford Medieval Text volume entitled *Abbots of Wearmouth and Jarrow*, containing Bede's *Historia Abbatum, Homily* 1.13, the (anonymous) *Life of Ceolfrith* and Bede's *Letter to Ecgbert* (2013). He combines these interests with a fascination for the practical aspects of ancient and medieval social life and reconstruction archaeology; he was Project Director of the *Bede's World Museum* from 1993 to 1996, and was until 2015 the Chairman of the Friends of Butser Ancient Farm.

Jeremy Haslam is a Senior Research Fellow, Institute of Historical Research, University of London. His research interests and publication output lie at the boundaries between archaeology, geography and history, and in particular concentrate on the development of towns and *burhs* in the early medieval period in England. He has edited *Anglo-Saxon Towns in Southern England* (1984) and has published detailed studies of the development of the Saxon towns of Cambridge, London, Oxford, Bedford, Ilchester, Christchurch, Worcester and Maldon, and separate analyses of the Anglo-Saxon towns of Wiltshire, Devon and Somerset, in the contexts of their political, strategic, geographical and historical landscapes. He recently published *Urban–Rural Connections in Domesday Book and Late Anglo-Saxon Royal Administration* (BAR 571, 2012). Other research includes King Alfred, the late ninth-century Burghal Hidage and its context, late Saxon architecture (in particular the eleventh-century chapel at Bradford on Avon) and the archaeology of early medieval industries (ceramics, glass and iron-making).

Margaret Worthington Hill is a freelance tutor and archaeologist specialising in the early medieval period. She has co-directed excavations and surveys in France, Greece and the Welsh Marches, where she also owned and directed a study centre for ten years. She has a long involvement with continuing education at The University of Manchester where she developed and taught a three-year part-time certificate course in Celtic Studies.

Paul Hindle was a Senior Lecturer in geography at Salford University until taking very early retirement in 2000. His research interests began with a study of the road system in medieval England and Wales and broadened into the history of roads in general, from the Romans to the present day. Alongside this was a keen interest in historical cartography, beginning with roads shown on medieval maps, and again broadening into the study of old maps. The principal output was the publication of two books by Phillimore: *Roads and Tracks for Historians* (2001) and *Maps for Historians* (1998), while Shire Archaeology published *Medieval Roads and Tracks* (1982) and *Medieval Town Plans* (1990). He is Honorary Secretary of the Manchester Geographical Society.

Kevin Leahy is an archaeological finds specialist who works as the National Adviser, Early Medieval Metalwork for the Portable Antiquities Scheme. Before going into archaeology he trained as a foundry engineer which gave him a deep interest in metals and materials. For twenty-nine years he was the archaeologist at the North Lincolnshire Museum, during which time he excavated some important Anglo-Saxon sites including the Cleatham cremation cemetery ('Interrupting the Pots. The Excavation of the Cleatham Anglo-Saxon Cemetery', CBA Research Report 155, 2007) and published a number of books on Anglo-Saxon archaeology including *Anglo-Saxon Crafts* (2003) and *The Anglo-Saxon Kingdom of Lindsey* (2007). He is a Fellow of the Society of Antiquaries of London and is an Honorary Visiting Fellow at the University of Leicester.

Michael Lewis is Head of Portable Antiquities and Treasure at the British Museum and an Honorary Research Associate at the University of York. He also has an Honorary Research Fellowship at the University of Reading. He has a particular interest in the material culture of medieval England, and has written extensively on medieval and post-medieval small finds and the Bayeux Tapestry. His doctorate was on the archaeological authority of the Bayeux Tapestry, published by British Archaeological Reports (BAR 404), and he co-organised the British Museum symposium on the Bayeux Tapestry in 2008, of which the proceedings were published in 2011. He is a Fellow of the Society of Antiquaries of London and a Member of the Chartered Institute of Archaeologists.

Sarah Semple is a Reader in Archaeology at Durham University. Her research interests and recent publications focus on early medieval funerary ritual and its landscape context, with a primary focus on Anglo-Saxon England, as well as landscape as a means of articulating political affiliation, religious ideas, ideology and identity, which, via a variety of grant-funded projects, is addressing the archaeology of power and politics in early medieval societies in the British Isles and more widely in northern Europe.

Michael Shapland is a Senior Buildings Archaeologist at UCL's commercial field unit, Archaeology South-East. His PhD was on Anglo-Saxon towers and tower-nave churches, and his research interests include the archaeology and architecture of the Anglo-Saxon church, and elite power structures of the early Middle Ages. Recent publications include *Trees and Timber in the Anglo-Saxon World* (2013), *Churches and Social Power in Early Medieval Europe* (in press) and a paper on 'Anglo-Saxon Lordly Towers and the Origins of the Castle in England' in a forthcoming volume on the *Archaeology of the Norman Conquest* (Society for Medieval Archaeology).

Damian Tyler studied for a BA in history at The University of Manchester followed by an MA in medieval history and a PhD on the impact of Christian conversion on early Mercian kingship. His research interests focus on early Anglo-Saxon England and include kingship, religion and conversion, warfare and violence, and ethnicity and identity; he is completing a monograph on kingship and conversion. He has taught at The University of Manchester and currently lectures at Manchester Metropolitan University.

Howard Williams is Professor of Archaeology at The University of Chester. His research interests and publications centre on mortuary archaeology, archaeologies of memory and the history of archaeology, with a focus on the study of the British Isles and Scandinavia in the early Middle Ages (*c.*AD 400–1100). He has also published on the theory of mortuary archaeology, exploring case studies from later Prehistory, the Roman world, as well as the later Middle Ages and modern times.

Introduction

Gale R. Owen-Crocker

It is related that there was so great a peace in Britain, wherever the dominion of King Edwin reached, that, as the proverb still runs, a woman with a new-born child could walk throughout the island from sea to sea and take no harm. The king cared so much for the good of the people that in various places where he had noticed clear springs near the highway, he caused stakes to be set up and bronze drinking cups to be hung on them for the refreshment of travellers.[1]

This book sets out to examine how man-made structures impinged on the natural landscape of Anglo-Saxon England. Its individual chapters demonstrate an increasing degree of co-operation, of planning and of royal control over the territory and social structures of Anglo-Saxon England as well as the widely visible power and influence of the Church.

Twenty-first-century human beings take a built environment for granted. Most people in Europe live and work in towns or their suburbs. These places are reached by roads and bridges and supplied with water, electricity and, in some countries, piped gas. They are lit at night. Our environment is totally mapped, with literacy and numeracy taken for granted: as we move from place to place we are guided by signs that identify places and structures. Street names are labelled and, even as we cross bridges, rivers are identified for us by name. The system of zones which was invented in the nineteenth century to cope with increasing postal deliveries in big cities has now been refined to the point that we can key a combination of letters and numbers into a computer or mobile phone and it will direct us to a specific building. There are still wild and uninhabited places in England, but to reach them we generally take transport, and we usually visit them for recreational activities such as walking, cycling, fishing or shooting which are purposeful only for the pursuit of pleasure. Few people live or work in wilderness.

To travel from coast to coast in Anglo-Saxon times without company, like Bede's putative female traveller in the opening quotation, was, however, an adventure, a potentially dangerous one. Bede's vulnerable mother and child are of course proverbial, created to demonstrate the peaceful nature of King Edwin's reign,[2] but many people did travel, and we might ask how they found their way and what they saw.

Bede, a Northumbrian writing in the early eighth century, takes it for granted that his journeyers used a 'highway' (Colgrave and Mynors' translation of *publicos uiaram transitus*, literally 'public passages of the roads')[3] and that it was one that the king himself had travelled: kings, by the nature of their role, lived a peripatetic existence in order to hold assemblies in different places, meet with other kings in alliance or hostility and generally to exert their influence over a range of areas both within and outside their own realms. This 'highway' known to King Edwin was probably an old Roman road. Roman surveyors and road builders had built a network of direct routes between fortresses and towns during their four-century occupation of Britain. Roman roads were raised and metalled, that is they were constructed with an underpinning of stone and surfaced with smaller stones or gravel which still survived into Anglo-Saxon times. It was probably safest to use these public and well-known routes, at least in Bede's day. As far as we know the Anglo-Saxons erected no signposts, no equivalents to the milestones the Romans had created for the roads in Britain in the third and fourth centuries AD.[4] There were no street lamps, no roadside cafés, as far as we know, apart from Edwin's drinking bowls. The Romans had established way stations, *mansiones*, one day's travel by ox-cart apart, for the rest and refreshment of military travellers and beasts. These had attracted civilian catering places around them; but there is no evidence that the Anglo-Saxons had such an organised system.

A traveller would need to reach a destination before darkness, and if that destination were a town, the gates in the walls might close by nightfall. Journeys would have to be planned so that a safe haven was reached in good time for each night. In Christian times monks travelled from monastery to monastery to study and work, in itineraries that became well-tried. Bishops had to journey to Rome to collect their pallium – the insignia of their office – in person. The itinerary of Sigeric (archbishop of Canterbury 989–994) on his return from his Roman visit of 989 or 990, recorded in British Library MS Cotton Tiberius B. fols 23v–24r, establishes that he made eighty stops on his journey from Rome through Italy, Switzerland and France.[5] By the tenth and eleventh centuries the annual journeys of Anglo-Saxon kings were regular and predictable, with the monarch presiding at assemblies at the great Christian festivals and other occasions on royal estates and in towns large and small throughout southern England.[6] The routes travelled by the king and his entourage would be well-known, and the royal convoy would be large and adequately guarded. Though the Anglo-Saxons continued to use and value Roman roads, and possibly older trackways too, they never established paved roads themselves. Rather, a dense network of land routes developed during the Anglo-Saxon era, fulfilling new needs. As Roman bridges fell into disrepair, roads diverted to alternative crossing places. As the Anglo-Saxons built planned towns, routes of communication inevitably developed, too. As a settlement on a river and or coast grew into a trading port, the tracks along which goods were transported into and out of the port evolved into established routes between port and hinterland. Elsewhere, frequency of use for specific purposes led to the recognition of 'saltways' and 'army paths'. Whereas Roman roads were raised above the landscape, in many cases the passing feet of the Anglo-Saxon period carved pathways into it, making so-called 'hollow ways'.

The inhabited area of England was smaller in Anglo-Saxon times than it is today. Its fens were undrained, and its settlers naturally chose to farm the areas with the most fertile soil, only gradually spreading to less hospitable areas. The original Anglo-Saxon settlements were probably family farms, which only gave way to nucleated villages surrounded by open fields in the centuries after the settlement. This development probably arose because of a combination of factors, including the invention of the heavy plough making it possible to cultivate heavier soils but requiring co-operation to finance and operate, and the desirability of living in proximity to a church as Christianity became the universal religion. Manor estates developed in the Middle Saxon period, and towns, originally constructed for defence against the Vikings, had become a major feature of Anglo-Saxon society by the tenth and eleventh centuries. Tracts of largely uninhabited countryside remained (though monastic buildings were sometimes deliberately placed away from civilisation, which gave reason for people to visit and for the surrounding lands to be farmed).

Today we may drive through the country and see only one solitary tractor as evidence that humans are exploiting that landscape. Since the Industrial Revolution of the eighteenth and nineteenth centuries, machinery has replaced man- and woman-power. Interior lighting, whether it be from large windows of clear glass or electric light, means that most of our work is done indoors. Anglo-Saxon travellers would, in contrast, have crossed a busy landscape where the people were visible working out of doors. There was a great deal of woodland, but it was far from being primitive forest since it was heavily exploited. The grazing of domesticated pigs and cattle, as well as wild boar and deer, kept the undergrowth down. Woodland was evidently managed: trees were a valuable resource that would only have been felled when necessary for major architectural or ship-building projects. Otherwise they were regularly coppiced or pollarded to provide wood for various purposes such making stakes for walls and fences, with larger branches providing planks for furniture and carts. Wood was important for fuel, both for domestic cooking and warmth, but also for a range of industrial purposes ranging from metalworking to boiling and evaporating salt, and it was transported in carts pulled by men or oxen.[7] The woods would have been busy with people cutting, loading and transporting timber. Around settlements there would have been many cart tracks and drovers' routes along which beasts were herded. Arable farming would have taken a great deal of human time, ploughing, planting, weeding and harvesting, and people would have been very visible working in the fields and transporting tools and produce. More fragile crops which needed protection from the wind would have been grown in gardens,[8] and animals would have been kept out of the gardens and fields – or kept in their designated enclosures – by thorn hedges, fences, ditches and possibly by dry stone walls, all of which had to be constructed and maintained. Flocks of sheep and fowl would have needed guarding against predators and people would have taken portable work – such as spinning – with them while they attended to their animals. Given the lack of light within buildings (since windows were small and glass was either unavailable or available only as small quarries – small pieces of glass – for setting into leaded windows of churches), people would have been visible at doorways or possibly in open-sided shelters doing craft work which required some protection from rain and wind.

There must have been many more settlements than are obvious today from surviving remains or even from the evidence of place names. Recent decades have been productive archaeologically: field walking has produced finds of pottery which demonstrate habitation; aerial photography and geophysical surveys have proved the existence of dense and long-lived settlement on areas where it was not before suspected.[9] Metal detecting has produced not only prestigious finds like the Staffordshire Hoard, but a wealth of unpretentious objects such as horse-harness fittings, which have amplified knowledge of the extent to which the Anglo-Saxons rode about their country.[10] Of particular importance are the many finds of coins, since coins are datable, and they often carry inscriptions giving the names of current kings, the moneyers who made them and the kingdom of their origin, or the mint where they were struck. Moneyers operated, by royal authority, at mints located in towns, so the evidence of coin finds is an important testimony in the study of Anglo-Saxon towns.

The so-called *adventus Saxonum*, the 'coming of the Saxons', once viewed as the start of an entirely new era, today only represents a new beginning for certain kinds of Anglo-Saxon specialists, particularly those concerned with the origins of the English language. Though we count the Anglo-Saxon period of English history as beginning when waves of migrants crossed the North Sea from Scandinavia, north Germany and Frisia, it is clear that these fifth-century Germanic settlers came to a land already inhabited and a landscape well-exploited. The coasts of Britain still bore evidence of the former presence of the Romans: there were many shore forts round the east and south-east seaboard and two Roman lighthouses at Dover. Inland, the country was already criss-crossed with roads and tracks as well as the famous Roman roads. The forts, cities and bridges to which these roads linked dated back to Roman times, and other built structures in the landscape such as barrows and dykes were even more ancient. Old English poetry would have us believe that the Anglo-Saxons considered such structures 'ancient works of giants', a poetic formula used, for example, in *The Wanderer*, where a ruined (probably Roman) building is testament to the transience of man-made splendours in God's continuing world,[11] and in *Beowulf* for the stone-built barrow from which a dragon has emerged, challenging the flimsy glory of contemporary mankind;[12] but it is unlikely that any but the philosophical and highly religious wasted much time on such thoughts. In practice, the Anglo-Saxons exploited and re-vivified older structures in many different ways, burying their dead in Bronze Age barrows, using ancient earthworks for lookout posts and beacons, plundering Roman buildings for dressed stone, brick and metal, building within Roman structures (as King Edwin had his baptistery constructed at York) and eventually rebuilding Roman fortified cities as new *burhs* in opposition to the Vikings as King Alfred and his West Saxon and Mercian children were to do.

The Anglo-Saxons inevitably made new landmarks on the horizon, changing the nature of the vista with built constructions of their own, which were meant to be seen, in some cases from great distances. New barrows commemorating dead ancestors demonstrated the power of living Anglo-Saxon kings. New earthworks marked their boundaries and helped in the defence of their territory. Free-standing crosses illustrated and symbolised the doctrine and power of Christianity. Great buildings, both secular and ecclesiastical, testified to the success of the English aristocracy and the English Church. The sheer quantity of their building work populated the English landscape as Anglo-Saxon society evolved – both secular (villages, towns and great manorial estates) and ecclesiastical (the parish system, estate churches and cathedrals and monasteries). We have little evidence of the appearance of their wooden buildings, but surviving remains of stone churches such as the decorated tower at Earls Barton, Northamptonshire, the arcaded walls of Bradford on Avon, Wiltshire, and the beast-head sculptures originally on the outside of Deerhurst, Gloucestershire, testify that, although of modest size in comparison to some later medieval churches, these were impressive and handsome structures.

If the Anglo-Saxons lacked Roman milestones, routes became well-established in the course of the Anglo-Saxon era, and there were plenty of landmarks, natural and built, old and new, for the traveller. Place name studies show an acute awareness of natural features which were reflected in vocabulary, so that hills and valleys of different shapes, and woods of different characteristics, were called by different names.[13] To these were added preaching crosses and commemorative barrows and boundary ditches which could act as guides for a traveller, while gruesome execution sites with decapitated or hanging bodies on display (see Chapter 7) ensured that he (or she) was aware of the power of the king through whose realm he passed on his way to his destination, farmstead, village, monastic estate, secular estate or town. The Anglo-Saxons did not generally build high structures, and domestic dwellings were at most two storeys, but the introduction of church and secular towers towards the end of the period provided new landmarks, and the domes and towers of great cathedral churches, the latter surmounted by weathercocks, must have provided focal points for miles around.

The 600 years of the Anglo-Saxon era, from the gradual transition from Roman-British landscape to Anglo-Saxon in the later fifth century to the enforced development from Anglo-Saxon/Anglo-Scandinavian culture to Anglo-Norman in the later eleventh century, were energetic in terms of building. There was constant change, though two major events may be identified as transformative. The first was the conversion to Christianity, which took place largely in the seventh century, and had long-term effects in every area of life, not just on the religious beliefs of the population. To relate the conversion in particular to the physical appearance of the English landscape, it caused the construction of new buildings to bring together worshippers and to house the monks and nuns who chose the monastic life, an entirely new vocation for the Anglo-Saxons. It introduced and patronised new art forms, not least stone crosses, and it created the literacy that is attested on some of the surviving sculptures. It may even, as Debby Banham has persuasively suggested, have introduced a new taste for white bread, which promoted wheat farming, transforming the appearance and contributing to the relocation of arable fields, and thus of some farming communities, in Anglo-Saxon England.[14] The second event, or rather series of events, was the Viking invasions which provoked, among other innovations, the renovation of Roman towns and the building of new ones, and the necessary development of more routeways. The increased development of signalling systems was probably also a defensive measure, though the Vikings themselves may have also exploited beacons. Early Anglo-Saxon England may have been characterised by family-run farming settlements, but late Anglo-Saxon England was a rich and sophisticated kingdom, with a civilised urban economy, a well-equipped army, rapid internal communications and citizens well-accustomed to cross-country as well as overseas international trade and travel.

This book presents ten specialist essays which illuminate our knowledge of built features of the Anglo-Saxon landscape in very different ways. Several inevitably consider buildings – domestic, ecclesiastical and industrial. Christopher Grocock (Chapter 1) discusses the Roman heritage, initially examining the architectural details of buildings from a former civilisation as enumerated in the Old English poem *The Ruin*. The text presents the crumbling edifices with a sense of awe, coupled with regret; the buildings described are seen as alien to the poet's own social experience. Grocock then contrasts the view presented in the poem with evidence from historical and archaeological sources. He demonstrates that some Roman buildings fell into disuse, that some were even demolished well before the end of the Romano-British period and, conversely, that there was continuity of use of some Roman sites into the post-Roman period, as *The Ruin* demonstrates.

Kevin Leahy and Michael Lewis (Chapter 3) are concerned with secular, largely domestic buildings. While we are faced with the limitations of archaeological evidence for structures that were built of wood, wattle and daub and thatch, and the unreliability of evidence from art, Leahy and Lewis note the usefulness of metalwork finds such as locks and keys and explore the differences between Roman building materials and Anglo-Saxon and the architectural differences between continental Germanic dwellings and Anglo-Saxon ones. They examine the sunken featured buildings known as *Grubenhäuser* and the controversies concerning their structure and use. They consider the evolution of small and large halls at several individual sites, including the manor complex at Goltho, Lincolnshire, and urban buildings in Anglo-Scandinavian York. Leahy and Lewis focus on evidence for basements, upper storeys, flooring materials, the placing and practical usage of hearths, doorways and windows, storage space, water supply and drainage and hard and soft furnishings in houses. The authors also discuss evidence for ancillary buildings, workshops, cooking places and latrines.

While Leahy and Lewis give detailed evidence of individual buildings, Damian Tyler (Chapter 4) offers an oblique and imaginative way of approaching the issue: he considers documentary evidence for the meeting together of kings in the seventh and eighth centuries, a period when there were multiple rulers in Anglo-Saxon England.

Jeremy Haslam (Chapter 9) considers urban design. The walled town with a formal layout of straight, internal streets was a new phenomenon of middle and late Anglo-Saxon England. The new *burhs* of Wessex and Mercia were either re-formed from pre-existing Roman towns or were new builds. The author focuses in particular on towns with spinal 'High Streets', which differed from the Roman rectilinear street plan, analysing Maldon, Essex, as a case study. He suggests that such a town, protected by an encircling wall, was, from the start, divided into burgage plots which were assigned to thegns and other landholders by the king. Controversially rejecting suggestions that such *burhs* evolved from refuges and fortresses, he sees the linear-designed towns with their associated infrastructures of mills, fields and bridges as planned and planted, elements in a political and strategic strategy which encompassed Wessex, Mercia and East Anglia, visible manifestations of royal control.

Michael Shapland (Chapter 5) focuses on churches and associated Christian buildings, emphasising the eclecticism of Anglo-Saxon ecclesiastical architecture. He identifies two strands in early church construction: those which reused Roman sites or building materials (brick or stone), thus assuming a heritage from the Roman past, and those which expressed allegiance to the Celtic Church by continuing the Romano-British tradition of timber construction. Architecture, too, followed different paths: continental patterns or the model of the secular hall. Rebuilding of timber churches or new building in stone is seen here as a political act following the victory of the Roman party at the Synod of Whitby in 664 and the construction of stone churches in the tenth and eleventh centuries as giving authority to secular patrons. The author detects an unwillingness among Anglo-Saxon churchmen to destroy old buildings, suggesting a preference for integrating the old, with its historic and sacred associations, into the new. The article also discusses the construction and function of mausolea, church towers and tower nave churches, all of which dotted the mid- and late Anglo-Saxon landscape.

Moving away from architectural structures, two other chapters consider built constructions associated with belief and ritual. Although the English may have erected wooden monuments before the conversion, Christianity introduced a new art form in the shape of stone carvings, especially crosses. Elizabeth Coatsworth (Chapter 6) considers the contemporary significance of these carved and/or painted monuments in the landscape, focusing on the parish of Dewsbury, which is rich in high-quality sculpture but entirely without surviving contemporary evidence in documentary form. She demonstrates the complex biblical iconography of two crosses, each represented by several fragments, which were probably erected outdoors within the monastery precincts and which could have been used as teaching aids or for theological meditation by a monastic community. Dating to the eighth or ninth centuries, these crosses demonstrate the interchange of ideas between Dewsbury and major religious centres. A later, Viking Age cross probably stood inside a church, where it might have been seen by the laity; and a wealthy, religious and perhaps literate lay population in the parish is also attested by several memorial sculptures, some with dedicatory inscriptions. Other sculptures in the area were probably boundary markers or were deliberately placed as highly visible landmarks or reminders with multiple functions, social, political and religious.

Most of our knowledge of early Anglo-Saxon material culture comes from cemetery archaeology. Inevitably, attention has focused on the disposition of the grave goods on and around the corpse and most scholars have, in their imaginations, looked down to the final appearance of the grave or burial chamber before it was covered with earth, as it remained for centuries until excavation in modern times. In their study of mortuary geographies, Sarah Semple and Howard Williams (Chapter 7) make us look upwards, as they demonstrate the visible, above-ground presence of burial sites and their role as continued *memoria* to the dead throughout the pre-Christian and Christian periods. Many burials were attached to landmarks that were already visible, both natural and built. The authors argue that although each funeral involved procession and performance, the effect of utilising existing landmark sites was cumulative, their meaning for the living augmented by memory of the past and suggestive usage. The rare evidence for above-ground markers on Anglo-Saxon burial grounds suggests 'monumentalised terrains'.

The appearance and period of usage of Anglo-Saxon burial sites is enormously varied, and the cemeteries themselves demonstrate a range of layout from the apparently haphazard to the closely planned, almost theatrical scene. While some burial sites were isolated, some evidently had close association with dwelling places of the living, and while some rapidly fell out of use others had a prolonged existence or even afterlives as meeting places.

Two chapters discuss features which cut across the Anglo-Saxon landscape. Dykes, unlike cemeteries, have produced very little in terms of artefacts for the excavator. Yet these earthworks testify to an enormous investment of labour on the part of those who dug them, and good organisation on the part of those who planned them. Margaret Worthington Hill and Erik Grigg (Chapter 8) acknowledge that many dykes and ditches were in existence prior to Anglo-Saxon times but note that Anglo-Saxon earthworks are distinctive and identifiable. They consider the possible functions of the very large structures, Offa's and Wat's Dykes in the west and the Cambridgeshire Dykes in the east, concluding that they were more likely to have been built for defensive purposes rather than as boundary markers. They also discuss the functions of the more modest earthworks still evident in the landscape today: estate markers, town walls and monastic enclosures; and utilitarian built structures such as hedges, walls and fences round fields to separate animals from crops, deer fences and sheepfolds. They discuss the likelihood of continuity of practice from Roman times, both the rare possibilities of Roman villa estate boundaries taken over by the Anglo-Saxons and the extent to which field boundaries may have continued from Romano-British times, even if the farming within the fields was different.

Paul Hindle (Chapter 2) examines evidence for roads and tracks, considering, but largely dismissing, the continued use of pathways from prehistoric times. He discusses in detail the network of Roman roads which the Anglo-Saxons inherited, including the survival, shifting and abandonment of various routes. He suggests the various categories of travellers who would have used land routes and the documentary, onomastic, archaeological and later cartographic evidence for tracks and routeways developed during the Anglo-Saxon period by regular use for commercial and military purposes.

One further chapter considers another aspect of the built environment of the Anglo-Saxon landscape, the communication systems which enabled the rapid transmission of news, particularly the threat of invasion, across an extensive land where transport of people and supplies was relatively slow. John Baker and Stuart Brookes (Chapter 10) examine archaeological, onomastic and other documentary evidence for fire-beacons and lookout sites, paying particular attention to the intervisibility which evidences an established system of signalling. Beacons utilised raised positions, both natural and built, such as towers. They also consider the roles of some beacons that did not interconnect with other Anglo-Saxon beacon sites, including the possibility that buildings were burnt as *ad hoc* signalling fires, and the continuing role of a Roman lighthouse incorporated into Anglo-Saxon built structures at Dover, for its original purpose, or some other.

As in the landscape, none of these topics is a truly isolated entity. These subjects unsurprisingly overlap. Kings would inevitably meet to engage in warfare or to discuss strategy in places where routeways met, as well as visiting each other in residences which were in themselves strategically placed. Towns were the destination of many roads, both remaining features of a Roman landscape and the new builds, new tracks of an increasingly sophisticated and integrated Anglo-Saxon population. Barrows that were primarily burial mounds may have been used as beacons; carved stone crosses, Christian emblems, could function as way-markers and grave-markers. Church towers which had a primary religious function and secular towers which marked lordly prestige could be used as lookouts and signalling places. Anglo-Saxon burial sites include both earthen structures and ecclesiastical buildings. Roads, ditches, barrows and crosses could all act as boundary markers. Beacon sites related to routeways as well as to the towns where the population clustered. Roman heritage included roads, churches and towns. The reader will find many more connections.

1

Enta geweorc:
The Ruin and its Contexts Reconsidered

Christopher Grocock

> Wrætlic is þes wealstan, wyrde gebræcon;
> burgstede burston, brosnað enta geweorc.
>
> *The Ruin*, ll. 1–2
>
> Splendid this stone wall is, though fate destroyed it, the stronghold fell apart, the works of giants crumble.[1]

Introduction

The Old English poem *The Ruin* expresses a variety of feelings about the remains of Romano-British buildings which could be encountered in the landscape during the early medieval period. These achievements of the 'giants of the past' invoke a sense of awe and admiration, coupled with regret; the detail in the description of the buildings is typified by a sense of wonder which implies that they are in some way outside the writer's own usual socioeconomic context. This study examines the views expressed in the poem in the context of some other evidence from historical and archaeological sources, focusing on a range of locations: Winchester and its immediate environs; Wroxeter, on the borders of Anglo-Saxon (Mercian) and Welsh territories; and Wearmouth-Jarrow, in the context of the Hadrian's Wall frontier. Archaeological evidence points to a variety of ways in which Anglo-Saxons related to the sub-Roman remains which they could encounter in the landscape at various periods. This evidence enables us to suggest a historical context in which different expressions about such remains could develop, and further points to contrasts between the poetic expression of *The Ruin* and actual practice in Anglo-Saxon society from the eighth century onwards.

Textual tradition

'*The Ruin* is an Old English poem whose mystery may never be solved, and which will always be difficult to translate'. This comment by R.F.S. Hamer encapsulates the two main issues which have been the focus of discussion and comment by specialists in Old English since the publication of a definitive text and commentary by R.F. Leslie in 1961. Sîan Eckhard likewise notes that her 'working translation ... is suggestive (even speculative) rather than definitive'.[2] *The Ruin* is the final poem in *The Exeter Book*, and as such it received more damage from the fire which caused such injury to the volume than texts which precede it.[3] Hamer goes on to note William Johnson's view that 'some of the difficulty in translating is caused by the "largely unique" language' in *The Ruin*, and Christopher Abram notes, with interesting comparisons set out in tables, the peculiarities of both vocabulary and syntax of the poem, together with its idiosyncratic quirks of poetic style.[4] As the title of Johnson's article suggests, most of the studies in Old English philology and literature on *The Ruin* have tended to move from discussion of the meaning of the poem itself to wider issues, such as the genre to which it should be assigned, or whether the text as we have received it has any overall unity, structure or theme, as the articles by Abram and J.F. Doubleday indicate; the value of the poem as literature had already been stressed by Leslie in his edition.[5]

The poem: a statement of wonder and regret?

The poem opens with a statement of wonder and awe at the scale and grandeur of a building from a previous age and culture:

> *Wrætlic is þes wealstan,   wyrde gebræcon;*
> *burgstede burston,   brosnað enta geweorc.*
> *Hrofas sind gehronene,   hreorge torras,*
> *hrungeat berofen,   hrim on lime,*
> *scearde scurbeorge   scorene, gedrorene,*   5
> *ældo undereotone.   Eorðgrap hafað*
> *waldend wyrhtan   forweorone, geleorene,*
> *heardgripe hrusan,   oþ hund cnea*

Fig. 1.1 Bath: the end wall of the main hall covering the naturally hot water. Note the fine stonework on a monumental scale and the triple arches. The roof of this hall was a barrel vault, perhaps a 'high curved wall' (photograph: C. Grocock).

```
werþeoda gewitan.        Oft þæs wag gebad,
ræghar and readfah,      rice æfter oþrum,                10
ofstonden under stormum; steap geap gedreas.
```

Splendid this stone wall is, though fate destroyed it,
the stronghold fell apart, the works of giants crumble.
ruined are the roofs, tumbled are the towers,
broken the barred gate, frost in the plaster,
all the ceilings gape, torn and collapsed
and eaten away by age. And the grasp of earth holds
the master-builders, long dead, long departed,
the fierce grip of earth, until a hundred generations now
of people have passed by. Often this wall
stained red and grey with lichen has stood by
surviving storms while kingdoms rose and fell,
and now the high curved wall itself has fallen.

Leslie notes that the literary merit of this and other Old English elegies 'lies precisely in the balance struck between delineation of character and situation on the one hand, and the evocation of an elegiac mood on the other'.[6] The final extant lines of the poem may indicate Bath as an original inspiration (Figure 1.1), but there have been suggestions that it might be Chester or Hadrian's Wall (Figure 1.2), or even a non-specific location.[7] In among the awe and admiration there are considerable specific details mentioned: *hrofas sind gehrorene, hreorge torras / hrungeat berofen*, 'ruined are the roofs, tumbled are the towers, broken the barred gate', which implies the recognition of roofs, towers and a barred gate (perhaps a city gate or a monumental door), while *hrim on lime* indicates an awareness of materials and weathering; 'frost in the plaster' might not have been unknown in the daub used in Anglo-Saxon wooden constructions.

That the building clearly belongs to a past age is shown by the phrase *Eorðgrap hafað / waldend wyrhtan* with its reference to the 'the dead departed master-builders', mirrored later in line 27 by *Betend crungon* 'its repairers fell'. *Waldend wyrhtan* is sometimes interpreted as a compound *waldendwyrhtan*;[8] Abram thinks that this means 'lords and makers' or possibly 'master-builders', but that it is also an epithet for Almighty God in a Christian context, and the poem may thus address the inevitability of the fall of a pagan shrine in a hubristic manner.[9] However, *hund cnea / werþeoda gewitan* 'a hundred generations now of people have passed by' (lines 8b–9a) is clearly poetic exaggeration (five generations per century would make a total of 2,000 years), or else it shows a total lack of awareness of the time which elapsed between the end of Roman Britain and the composition of the poem, an unawareness shared by other authors, as we shall see.

Fig. 1.2 Chesters Fort, Hadrian's Wall: the fort's bath house, with the stoke-hole or *praefurnium* in the foreground and the raised floor or hypocaust behind it (photograph: C. Grocock).

The next section of the poem returns to more detail of the construction:

mod mo[nade,   m]yne swiftne gebrægd;
hwætred in hringas,   hygerof gebond
weallwalan wirum   wundrum togædre. (ll. 18–20)

The heart inspired, stimulated swift action;
ingenious circles and long-lasting foundations
with iron bonds endured, holding together wonderfully.

The *weallwalan wirum* or 'iron bonds' may refer to the iron cramps or ties which are used to fasten pieces of stone together in classical buildings. Iron nails and other items have been found at Wearmouth-Jarrow, but the stone construction there appears to make no use of iron ties to link the masonry together, and it seems not to be in evidence in later Roman structures either.[10] The reference to 'ingenious circles' may refer to circular, or possibly octagonal, buildings, which are not unknown in the Roman period (though rectangular designs are more common), or perhaps to barrel-vaults and arches. At any event, such structures were alien to Anglo-Saxon construction in timber, and this is a further reason why the remains discussed in the poem are thought to be the 'work of giants'. This point is further discussed below (see pp. 30–31).

Then follows a contrast between the ruined building's heyday and its decline and fall:

Beorht wæron burgræced,   burnsele monige,
heah horngestreon,   heresweg micel,
meodoheall monig   [mon][11]*dreama full,*
oþþæt þæt onwende   wyrd seo swiþe.
Crungon walo wide,   cwoman woldagas,   25
swylt eall fornom   secgrofra wera;
wurdon hyra wigsteal   westen staþolas,
brosnade burgsteall.   Betend crungon,
hergas to hrusan.   (ll. 21–29a)

Bright were the public halls with bathing halls a-plenty
and lofty gables, great the cheerful noise,
and many mead-halls filled with human pleasures,
till mighty fate brought change upon it all.
Slaughter was widespread, pestilence was rife,
and death took all those valiant men away.

> The martial halls became deserted places,
> the city crumbled, its repairers fell,
> its armies to the earth.

There are references in these lines to three apparently distinct types of architectural features, *burgræced*, *burnsele* and *horngestreon*, 'public halls', 'bathing halls' and 'gables', which may represent the different parts of a Roman bathing complex (or include a building such as a *palaestra* or exercise yard (so Leicester), or even an adjacent basilica (as at Wroxeter) or temple complex (for example, that at Bath, with its famous 'male gorgon' in the tympanum).[12] The terms which the writer uses to describe the ruined buildings are significant, as the bathing halls (which clearly have a Roman social function) are interpreted in terms which make sense in his own milieu. This is a fascinating illustration of the ways in which the observers of a later generation convey their own thought-processes as they try to make sense of the works they encountered as they went about their daily travels trying to make sense of their landscape.[13] The reasons for the 'end' are nicely expressed, and mirror both Celtic and Anglo-Saxon accounts of the change from Roman Britain to Anglo-Saxon England, although these accounts are not necessarily supported by archaeology, as will be discussed below. The absence of 'repairers', *betend*, on which the poet comments, is a realistic reason for the decline of Romano-British styles of building, however; in the case of Bath:

> From c.AD 350 onwards ... much of the colonnade and stylobate of the outer precinct were demolished ... then followed a period of deliberate demolition affecting the entablature of the reservoir and its buttresses ... apparently in search of the iron cramps and their lead sealings. Thus weakened, this would be the logical point at which the reservoir collapsed ... it has been argued that this occurred in the sixth or seventh century, after which the site remained derelict.[14]

So the focus turns to the sad state of decay in which this ancient building now exists:

>   Forþon þas hofu dreorgiað
> and þæs teaforgeapa   tigelum sceadeð   30
> hrostbeages hrof.   Hryre wong gecrong
> gebrocen to beorgum   þær iu beorn monig
> glædmod and goldbeorht   gleoma gefrætwed,

wlonc and wingal   wighyrstum scan;
seah on sinc, on sylfor,   on searogimmas,   35
on ead, on æht,   on eorcanstan,
on þas beorhtan burg   bradan rices.   (ll. 29b–37)

                And so these halls
are empty, and this red curved roof now sheds its tiles,
decay has brought it to the ground,
smashed it to piles of rubble, where long since
a host of heroes, glorious, gold-adorned, gleaming in splendour,
proud and flushed with wine shone in their armour,
gazed on gems and treasure,
on silver, riches, wealth and jewellery,
on this bright city with its wide domains.

The 'red curved roof' suggests either tiles or brick-and-lime barrel vaulting, both of which were alien to the native types of Anglo-Saxon architecture; the indication of 'decay which has brought it to the ground' led Barry C. Burnham and John Wacher to identify Bath with *The Ruin*, further noting that 'enough must have survived into the sixth century, however, for the Saxons to inherit it in the aftermath of the Battle of Dryham in AD 577'.[15]

Stanhofu stodan,   stream hate wearp
widan wylme;   weal eall befeng
beorhtan bosme   þær þa baþu wæron,   40
hat on hreþre.   Þæt wæs hyðelic.
Leton þonne geotan   ...
ofer harne stan   hate streamas
u[nder]...   ...
[o]þþæt hringmere   hate ...   45
...   þær þa baþu wæron.

Stone buildings stood, and the hot stream cast forth
wide sprays of water, which a wall enclosed
in its bright compass, where convenient
stood hot baths ready for them at the centre.
Hot streams poured forth over the clear grey stone,
to the round pool and down into the baths.

The past tenses add to the sense of loss. The building seems to represent something distant; its construction does not form part of the writer's world except to gaze in wonder at it (and there is also a sense of regret, building on the Christian theme, that nothing earthly can endure).[16] Abram regards the poem as a form of *encomium*, and notes in a very pertinent comparison with some verses from Alcuin's *Bishops, Kings and Saints of York*, ll. 15–23, and the Old English poem *Durham* that 'in these two texts, as well as in *The Ruin*, it is only stone-built, Roman cities, which are lauded. Native Anglo-Saxon habitations, built in wood, do not seem to have attracted the attentions of such poets'.[17] As to the date of the poem, *The Exeter Book* is regarded as a product of the late tenth century, though, on the basis of discussion of 'when the ruins could have been observed in the state described by the poet', Leslie concluded that 'it may be considered with some probability that *The Ruin* describes the scene as it must have appeared no later than the first half of the eighth century'.[18]

The context of the *adventus Saxonum*: the earliest years of Anglo-Saxon settlement

A range of models for the pattern of Anglo-Saxon settlement – or, in its early interpretation, conquest – may provide some archaeological context for the poem, and for its reaction to the 'work of giants' of which the writer speaks. During the past sixty years or so, the very earliest stages of Anglo-Saxon presence in Britain have been understood in very different ways, but all of them raise issues about the ways in which the first Anglo-Saxons might have interacted with the Romanised landscape they encountered. A 'traditional' view, not much accepted now, may be found in Sir Frank Stenton's *Anglo-Saxon England*; here, the narrative constructed is based largely on Gildas and Procopius, the traditions recorded in the *Anglo-Saxon Chronicle*, found also in Bede, and place name evidence.[19] According to this interpretation, the continental Anglo-Saxons, invited to be mercenaries assisting the Romanised Britons, turn on their paymasters and, over a century and a half, take control aggressively of the whole of southern Britain, beginning in the far south and east. In paragraphs which Stenton himself summarised as showing 'consistency of tradition about the conquest', he wrote that 'Gildas, Procopius, and the early traditions of the West Saxon Court agree in suggesting that the English conquest of southern Britain was accomplished in two phases ... the greater part of southern England was overrun in the first phase of the war'.[20] This view was largely followed by John Morris, in early work, such as the 1959 article 'Anglo-Saxon Surrey',[21] and by his controversial study *The Age of Arthur* and a review article he wrote in 1974 entitled 'The Chronology of Early Anglo-Saxon

Archaeology'.[22] This approach is echoed by D.J.V. Fisher, who speaks of 'evidence of heavy Germanic settlement in England before the departure of the Romans'.[23]

More recent scholarship pursues a different line. In 1992, Nick Higham, for example, while admitting the necessarily hypothetical nature of his discussion, moved away from the idea of 'conquest', and offered a 'solution ... that allows for massive ethnic continuity from late Roman Britain to Anglo-Saxon England',[24] and elsewhere sees the *adventus* in terms of a 'War of the Saxon Federates' won by 'small numbers of Saxons ... who imposed their will on the mass of a civilian, diocesan population'.[25] In similar vein, Michael Jones, at the end of a very detailed review of the arrival of the Anglo-Saxons in Britain in terms of both *adventus* and 'invasion', notes that the impression gained from the archaeology of rural areas is very different from one of mass migration and invasion: 'Instead of a vista of Anglo-Saxon pioneers and a virgin landscape, Romano-British and Anglo-Saxon settlement areas in southern Britain largely coincide' and concludes that 'without the long accepted contrast between the general settlement patterns of Celt and Saxon, a warrant for a large-scale extraordinary settlement by the invading Anglo-Saxons disappears'.[26] Most recently, Guy Halsall has suggested an alternative model of Saxon migration and conquest, one which saw barbarian mercenaries employing their military strength in a series of civil wars which culminated in their seizure of power in the frontier of the villa zone, in central areas of southern Britain, and moving eastwards at the same time as the historically documented migration and settlement occurred from east to west.[27] At this stage, there would have been considerable evidence of Roman remains in good condition, some standing to a considerable height, as Figures 1.3 and 1.4 show.

It is still possible to consider the fifth century as a period of major changes, particularly in the case of towns, which will constitute the

Fig. 1.3 Richborough, the remains of the main walls – the sheer scale of the surviving masonry makes them truly like *enta geweorc* (photograph: C. Grocock).

Fig. 1.4 Remains of the Roman bridge at Piercebridge, south of Hadrian's Wall – evidence for the survival of more masonry on a monumental scale beyond the Roman occupation period (photograph: C. Grocock).

'ruins' in the landscape to which later writers could react; Higham considers that 'it would be a mistake ... to argue for any survival of urban life, as opposed to life in what had been towns, in sub-Roman Britain'.[28] This view has been qualified by Adam Rogers, who, in an extensive review of the types of buildings extant in late Roman towns, notes that:

> the changing structural nature of public buildings in the later Roman period, including the partial demolition of some sections of them, can be seen across the Empire ... Although late Roman phases of buildings are increasingly being documented ... there is seldom much debate regarding the length or the importance of use of the buildings in the late Roman period.[29]

Rogers helpfully points out that continued occupation of sites is actually 'symbolic of the continued significance of the sites and even of generation and vitality'.[30] An examination of some sub-Roman and early medieval sites might help shed some more light on the actual experience Anglo-Saxons might have had of the built environment they encountered, and point towards a context for the poetic expression found in *The Ruin*.

Winchester

The old Roman town of *Venta Belgarum* is an interesting site to consider in relation to *The Ruin*, as recent archaeological study seems to indicate that there was a 'decline' in the quality of its domestic buildings from the fourth century onwards: 'Flickerings of urban existence in Winchester continued perhaps until AD 400. Archaeology shows clearly that the city of the second and third centuries underwent comprehensive change'.[31] Late Roman evidence from 'The Brooks', an area at the centre of Winchester now redeveloped as a shopping mall, was interpreted by John M. Zant as indicating that:

> The second half of the fourth century saw the decay and eventual demolition of the large, well-appointed townhouses which had been constructed earlier in the century. All four of the fully or partially excavated houses which lay within the site (VIII.1, VIII.9, XXIII.3, and probably XXIII.2) went out of use during this period. The east–west street and its associated ditches also eventually ceased to be maintained, though precisely when this happened is very difficult to determine.[32]

Writing in 1960 about the St George's Street excavations, Barry Cunliffe could assert that 'For the period from the middle of the fourth century to the latter part of the tenth century the area covered by the excavation has produced very little evidence of occupation ... documentary sources are likewise completely lacking'.[33] Against this negative view, Paul Booth et al. note that 'these changes do not appear to represent abandonment as much as a change in the nature of occupation. The area of occupation, as reflected in the distribution of pottery and coins, actually seems to have increased at this time'.[34] Tom Beaumont-James summarises the changes which can be identified in late Roman and sub-Roman *Venta Belgarum*.[35] There was an extension of the city to the west (hardly a sign of decay) and increased industrial activity, particularly in ironworking.[36] Bastions were added to the town walls.[37] Finally, there was a marked expansion of cemeteries around the city itself. Beaumont-James comments that these developments 'could indicate the weakening of imperial bonds and the development of a new military culture in the shell of the old Roman city ... or, alternatively ... a strengthening of connections with Rome with the added military presence and even the establishment of a Roman diocese based in Winchester, c.AD 350–500'.[38]

The curious phenomenon known by archaeologists as 'dark earth' also made an appearance here: Beaumont-James describes it as 'a black clayey soil usually 15 cm (6 in.) thick but sometimes up to 0.7 metres (2 ft) containing sherds of broken Roman pottery, and indicating that vegetation covered the remains of Roman buildings for a very considerable period'.[39] In his discussion of 'The Brooks', Zant comments that 'in a few cases masonry walls stood higher than the surrounding deposits and cannot have been truncated',[40] and concludes that:

> By whatever process, or combination of processes, the 'dark earth' at The Brooks may have been formed, its accumulation marks, in all likelihood, the end of intensive occupation on the site for several centuries. The latest deposits below the soil were of late 4th–early 5th century date, while the earliest dateable features cutting the deposit belonged to the mid-9th to 10th centuries.[41]

Such limited ruins do not seem to match any building which could have inspired our poem; an explanation for the rapid demise of buildings here comes from the presence of so many cemeteries located around *Venta Belgarum*, which has led to the suggestion that it became the focus for burials for a much wider area than the city itself.[42] A key site for Winchester burials is the cemetery at Lankhills, extensively excavated in 1967–72 and revisited with the benefit of much more sophisticated scientific analytical techniques in 2000–05.[43] Here, the 'use of the cemetery probably commenced early in the 4th century and continued at least to the end of the century, but ... the degree of use of the cemetery after AD 400 remains uncertain'.[44] Evidence from other cemeteries in the suburbs of Winchester is in line with the findings from the Lankhills site, save that the authors push the terminus date into the 'early fifth century'.[45] The growth of the cemeteries may also be linked to the removal of domestic structures in much of the Roman town: 'The appearance of building materials as grave linings in the late 4th and 5th centuries especially at St Martin's Close ... leads to the suspicion that town houses standing empty at this time were robbed for the construction of new graves'.[46]

Beaumont-James concludes that:

> it is possible to suggest the extension of town life in Roman Winchester by half a century or so into the early 440s by use of these military and industrial scraps of evidence ... even so, the arguments for continuance beyond 400 or 'urban' Winchester are more difficult to sustain, not least because cemetery evidence, our major source for the key indicator – the population concentration

– diminishes. There seems to be a 50-year period in the fifth century for which there is remarkably little evidence.[47]

Most readings of the *adventus Saxonum* would place Winchester, in the north-eastern part of the modern country of Hampshire and only 20 kilometres (11 miles) from the south coast, firmly in the area of Britain which came under Saxon control at a fairly early stage – early enough for some survival of Roman remains to be noticeable to the incomers, as the place name evidence suggests:

> In Saxon times the Roman name *Venta Belgarum* gave way to *Wintaceaster*. The 'ceaster' element in Old English indicates a place recognised by the Saxons as a Roman walled site – the walls were among those Roman features which pierced the 'dark earth'. The survival of the 'Venta' element in the name indicates contact – of an unknown nature – between Saxons and natives, and hints at continuity in some form from the Roman period. However, no dates can be assigned to these contacts between natives and invaders.[48]

Events of later centuries were to have a major impact on Winchester, particularly the Viking attack in 860, followed by Alfred's restoration, which follows a largely fresh plan, as evidence from 'The Brooks' indicates.[49] P.J. Ottaway comments on this latter point that 'There seems little doubt that the street system (of medieval Winchester) was largely planned and executed as a single operation'.[50] However, there was activity on the site in the early Saxon period: summing up the evidence, Beaumont-James comments that 'Before the relaying of the streets and the creation of the ninth-century "burh", at least six estates can be proposed within the town walls from archaeological, topographical and place name evidence'.[51] In this period the city might have been a 'royal centre', perhaps for structural reasons – with established lines of communication and the same landscape which was attractive to the Romans and to the Belgae before them. It had ecclesiastical importance, too. Michael Lapidge notes there is no evidence for a continuous line of bishops from late Roman to Anglo-Saxon times here, 'presumably a reflex of the discontinuity which archaeologists have remarked in Romano-British towns'; nevertheless, as he goes on to observe, according to Bede's account in *Historia Ecclesiastica*,[52] there appears to have been some survival of Romano-British (or Celtic) church organisation at the time, and perhaps therefore some remaining sub-Roman buildings to go with it.

Wroxeter

This 'continuity thesis' is considered by Halsall, who also notes the suggestion that the Roman town of Wroxeter may have been the site of a late post-Roman kingdom/chieftain's residence (Figure 1.5).[53] Wroxeter was the subject of archaeological excavations by Thomas Wright (1859), George Fox (1894, 1896), Dame Kathleen Kenyon (1936–37) and Graham Webster (1955–66) before the latest round from 1966 to 1990.[54] A brief summary of the late Roman evidence is given by John Wacher, though rather imprecisely he comments that 'the Wroxeter buildings ... show a continuation of life in the town, if not of town life, long after the stage had been reached when the last Roman buildings were falling down'.[55] More evidence is provided by the excavation report:

> Between the end of the fifth century and the mid sixth, the basilica fell into disrepair and public access was restricted. The portico roof and colonnades were taken down, possibly as a safety measure. Two buildings, one a bakery, were built across the west portico. The western part of the north portico was floored with a timber boardwalk; at the eastern end two buildings were constructed. The builder's yard took over the eastern end of the basilica; an area of floor was quarried away, hearths built, a lime pit dug, and several wattle buildings erected.

Fig. 1.5 Wroxeter: the 'Old Work'; this wall once formed part of the main hall of the baths-basilica, which might reflect one of the 'lofty gables' envisaged by the author of *The Ruin* (photograph: C. Grocock).

The basilica roof was then taken down and the walls partially demolished. The floor was levelled with earth dumps. Paths made of roofing slates show that the building was open to public use, but the only sign of occupation was a small lean-to structure in the south-west corner.[56]

Further work north of the basilica included 'a massive post-built building set on clay and cobble post-pads', together with levelling and access works and an attempt, it appears, to re-floor the bath with a pebble surface containing water-pipes. This work was dated to the late fourth century and possibly the early fifth.[57]

This was not the end of work at Wroxeter, however. The excavators continue:

The whole site was then redeveloped. This was a highly organised operation, and the original preparation involved demolishing the north wall of the basilica, laying the rubble as building platforms, and digging out a stretch of the east to west street, which was then filled with gravel and earth.

The redeveloped site was dominated by a huge timber-framed building, facing south, and lying across the centre of the north portico, north aisle, and nave, with a narrower timber-framed building attached to its west side. All the buildings of this phase appear to have used the Roman foot as the unit of measurement. To the south were seven lean-to structures of a standard size, and to the west was a masonry lean-to; all were built against the remaining walls of the basilica ... the second phase buildings were more widely spaced and more substantial, possibly two-storeyed, and some had elaborate porched facades.[58]

Elements of the reconstruction carried out during the post-Roman occupation period indicate some kind of market or trading centre, with redevelopment of work in the service area, with 'substantial lean-to buildings and one massive barn'.[59] No evidence was found to indicate dating of this phase of work, though the excavators comment that:

It is thought to have started by the mid to late sixth century, and the number of sub-phases and the wear on surfaces suggests it lasted at least 75 years. All the late timber-framed buildings were carefully demolished and much of the material was presumably

Fig. 1.6 Leicester: the surviving wall of the Jewry Wall baths; as at Richborough and Wroxeter, Roman masonry survives on an immense and impressive scale (photograph: C. Grocock).

salvaged. One last timber building was constructed over the platform of the main basilica building.[60]

The site seems to have functioned as a quarry by the ninth century: St Andrew's church, Wroxeter, incorporates reused stone to a significant degree.[61] The difficulties of interpreting the post- or sub-Roman period work are noted by the excavators: 'The artefactual analysis of the site shows that the inhabitants of post-Roman Wroxeter either continued to use Roman artefacts with little modification other than occasional repair, or were using artefacts made from perishable materials as replacements. In artefactual terms, they are invisible'.[62] However, what seems most significant is the level of continuity of use of the site into the centuries beyond the Roman occupation *per se* and the scale of the works involved; Higham comments that this 'required the use of labour in quantities far greater than the likely number of inhabitants could have provided'.[63] The excavation report concludes that 'Wroxeter thus appears to be the earliest positively identified post-Roman town (or the latest late-Roman town) … The picture that emerges is of an isolated, self-sufficient urban community, holding onto its territory and exploiting it as it had done throughout the Roman period but with few, if any, links with the outside world'.[64] The same may have been true of Leicester, further south, in lands which were to come under Mercian control (Figure 1.6).

Sites further north: Carlisle and Hadrian's Wall

In his *Vita Cuthberti*, Chapter 27, Bede describes some of the remains of Roman Carlisle, Roman *Luguvalium*, which were shown to St Cuthbert in AD 685, when on the occasion of his visit the citizens gave him a guided tour of the site: *ut uideret moenia ciuitatis fontemque in ea miro quondam Romanorum opere exstructum.* Colgrave translates this 'while the citizens were conducting him to see the walls of the city and a marvellously constructed fountain of Roman workmanship';[65] Webb's translation is slightly closer to the Latin: 'the citizens conducted him round the city walls to see a remarkable Roman fountain that was built into them'.[66] The admiration of the fountain may be a minor detail, not developed in the rest of the narrative, but it displays an early interest in antiquarianism, and moreover mirrors the sense of wonder found in *The Ruin*.[67]

Carlisle was certainly not a rare example of surviving Roman constructions in this area, of course. In Bede's day (the early eighth century) much Roman infrastructure was clearly still noticeable in the landscape. As Michael Lapidge notes, 'Bede remarks that the Romans "built towns, lighthouses, bridges and roads" which can be seen "to this day"'.[68] Bede is particularly lucid about the walls left by the Romans, and provides an extensive – and largely erroneous – discussion of their historical origins.[69] However, in a later chapter it becomes clear that he *was* aware of the distinction between Hadrian's Wall and the Antonine Wall.[70] He gives precise dimensions for the structure we know as Hadrian's Wall, and stresses that this detail 'is plain for all to see even to this day'. More to the point, writing about the Antonine Wall, he corrects his source, Gildas, at this point in a manner which indicates that he has made use of his own eyes – or, more likely, is dependent on eye-witnesses from the area, particularly from the monastery at Abercorn.[71] Nevertheless, Bede was as unaware of the details of the historical sequence of building the walls during the Roman occupation of Britain as the author of *The Ruin* appears to have been in respect to the building he describes. What is missing in Bede is the sense of awe – or of sympathy with the tragic fate of the ruins' occupants – which we find in *The Ruin*.

Developments in the sub-Roman period: a change to wood

The post-Roman period did not see all Roman sites abandoned, as A.M. Whitworth makes clear:

Fig. 1.7 Birdoswald: this fort on Hadrian's Wall provides significant evidence for sub-Roman construction in timber: the upright posts show where the fifth-century wooden hall's main supports were placed (photograph: C. Grocock).

Accumulated archaeological and artefactual evidence shows clearly that in the post-Roman period there was continuing occupation within a number of forts on the Wall. From South Shields, Wallsend, Newcastle and Benwell in the east to Vindolanda, Birdoswald and Carlisle in the west, Roman sites continued to function with a civilian or perhaps quasi-military population. Some became strongholds for local warlords or even kings. Anglo-Saxon activity is attested within and around the sites in the 6th and 7th centuries with stone robbing of the former military sites taking place to erect ecclesiastical buildings. Many of the Roman buildings must have remained upstanding as later road alignments appear to take into account their presence.[72]

The evidence of late construction at Birdoswald is one of the clearest examples of this (see Figure 1.7).[73] Here, a series of timber constructions from the late fourth century built in the central area 'have been likened to the post-Roman hall found at Doon Hill near Dunbar in Scotland'.[74]

In the post-Roman period, wood seems to have become the norm, and this mirrors the later practice in the Anglo-Saxon world; there also appears to have been some similarity in designs and methods of construction between Romano-British and Anglo-Saxon buildings,[75]

though original source material and evidence are hard to come by, and literary descriptions are often lacking in precise detail. For example, in the *Historia Ecclesiastica* Bede tells us that:

> Finan ... constructed a church on the island of Lindisfarne suitable for an episcopal see, building after the Irish method, not of stone but of hewn oak, thatching it with reeds; later on the most reverend Archbishop Theodore consecrated it in honour of the blessed apostle Peter. It was Eadberht, who was bishop of Lindisfarne, who removed the reed thatch and had the whole of it, both roof and walls, covered with sheets of lead.[76]

The wooden church at Greensted, Essex, is a fine (albeit partial and much later) surviving example of this tradition of building in timber (Figure 1.8), which seems to have been normative until the importation of skills from continental Europe which are discussed next. A fine example, recently discovered, of a site which exemplifies the preference for timber construction is Lyminge, where a nunnery of the eighth to ninth centuries seems to have been built over the remains of earlier settlements, including a mead hall dated to *c.*AD 600.[77] The rare exceptions of stone structures dating from this period, such as the stone church at Whithorn, probably owe their existence to an Irish or Celtic tradition of religious building construction, not an Anglo-Saxon one.[78]

Fig. 1.8 Greensted church; this is a rare (and probably unique) survivor of an Anglo-Saxon timber building, with split logs set into a grooved sill-beam. The timbers in the nave date from the early eleventh century, though it underwent considerable reconstruction in 1848 (photograph: C. Grocock).

The later change back to stone: Wearmouth-Jarrow and other developments

The church of St Peter at Wearmouth is notable for using the preferred style of its founder Benedict Biscop, *iuxta Romanorum morem*, 'in the Roman fashion', as Bede puts it in his *Historia Abbatum* 5, a work which involved the introduction of masons and glaziers:

Not more than a year passed after the foundation of the monastery before Benedict crossed the seas and headed for the provinces of Gaul. He asked for, engaged, and brought back masons who could build him a church of stone, *in the Roman fashion* which he always liked. Benedict displayed so much energy in carrying out this task for the love of the blessed Peter in whose honour he was doing it, that in less than a year since the foundations were laid the roofs were in place and you might see the solemn rites of the mass being celebrated there. As the work neared its completion, he sent envoys to Gaul to bring back glaziers, workmen unknown to the British up to that time, to put bars and glass into the windows of the church, the porches and in the cells. It was done, and they came; not only did they complete the work asked of them, but in so doing made the English race know and learn this particular skill, a valuable skill not meanly fitted for covering up the windows of churches or making vessels for various uses.[79]

Not all that is currently visible in the west tower of St Peter's, Wearmouth, is Anglo-Saxon, of course, as much re-shaping and restoration has taken place (see Figure 1.9); Rosemary Cramp comments that 'the pre-conquest fabric surviving above ground today consists of the west wall of the nave, and the western porch, with the jambs of its open portal decorated with carvings which are indisputedly accepted as of 7th- to 8th-century date'.[80]

It is worth considering the Latin of Bede's description of the site in some detail:

> cementarios qui lapideam sibi ecclesiam iuxta Romanorum quem semper amabat morem facerent, postulauit, accepit, adtulit.

The specific term for the builders *cementarii*, indicates the way in which stability was to be given to these structures; Bede seems to stress *lapideam ... ecclesiam*, 'stone church' (as opposed to the usual Anglo-Saxon constructions, this was *special*), and the key phrase is *Romano more*, 'in the Roman manner'; the other key point made here is that, according to Bede, the Anglo-Saxons did not have the skills needed to construct sophisticated buildings in stone. These were clearly the fashion in the eighth century: Stephanus' description of the restoration or construction of Wilfrid's churches, including their crypts, at Ripon, York and Hexham are witness to this.[81] By the eighth century, at least in the contexts of minsters, the Anglo-Saxons in general were employing the 'Roman methods' they had learned in building for themselves, though as Eric Cambridge has recently pointed out, the origin of such architectural designs, like that of the builders themselves, was probably more Gallic than Roman; there was likely to be little distinction drawn by the Anglo-Saxons who saw this as an opposition to the Celtic patterns of worship which were firmly rejected in the later seventh century.[82] Such architectural preference extended to a liking for 'Roman culture' in general, as is shown, for example, in the preferred script used in manuscripts.[83] The fact that the poet of *The Ruin* regards masonry structures as 'alien' to his own experience implies a pre-eighth-century origin for the work, that is, before stone churches were a feature of the Anglo-Saxon landscape.

Fig. 1.9 Wearmouth: the west tower of St Peter's church, much of which can confidently be dated to the eighth century if not earlier (Wearmouth was founded in 672/73) (photograph: C. Grocock).

Evidence from rural areas and villas during the period[84]

The extensive villa complex at Bignor, West Sussex, seems simply to have been abandoned at the end of the 'Roman period', and was not to be rediscovered until 1811. The damage to its famous 'Venus mosaic' was caused by the collapse of roof tiles through the floor into the hypocaust, the collapse itself preserving the bulk of the mosaic, which survived unscathed and undisturbed for some 1,500 years.[85] Although the farmland in the area was a valuable commodity, there was no attempt to make use of this rural palace. Observations by Helena Hamerow may explain such abandonment, as she notes that 'early Anglo-Saxon timber buildings generally display little evidence of substantial repair or

Fig. 1.10 Brixworth church, the largest surviving Anglo-Saxon building in England. The scale of this structure, the earliest parts of which date back to AD 680, shows that even in the early medieval period the Anglo-Saxons were capable of producing *enta geweorc* of their own (courtesy of the Friends of Brixworth).

renewal', and indeed that 'the majority of early Anglo-Saxon buildings … were abandoned while still habitable and either dismantled or left to decay *in situ*', regarding this as evidence for a cultural custom of creating 'single generational' buildings for each family unit which passed away as the family unit did.[86] Such an attitude to buildings might explain why – in rural areas at least – Roman villas were left to decay, as a mark of respect for the defunct family which had occupied them. Other factors (such as a lack of knowledge and skill about how to maintain them) might also explain this, of course.[87] Anglo-Saxon sites from the 'middle Saxon' period, such as Flixborough and Higham Ferrers, provide indication that at a later time, in the eighth and ninth centuries, rebuilding and reuse became more commonplace.[88] Not all villa sites were completely abandoned; some, such as Orton Hall Farm and Little Oakley, Essex, provide evidence for continuity, though this may have been by subsequent generations of the proprietors in the late Roman period, and not by Anglo-Saxon incomers; at other villa sites, such as Whittington (Gloucestershire), the presence of very early Anglo-Saxon artefacts on a Roman villa site may be evidence of another cultural practice, of attempting to enhance the claims of new occupiers of the site by associating themselves deliberately with the ancient monuments present in the contemporary landscape, an idea suggested by John Blair.[89]

In this later period, then, it might be argued that the 'work of giants' was being carried out again, under the auspices of the Anglo-Saxon church. At the same time, some buildings were constructed on a small scale, as the surviving timber building at Greensted demonstrates; timber building continued to be an appropriate medium for church structures. On the rebuilding programme of the tenth century, Platt comments that:

> In one church excavation after another, traces have been found of an earlier Saxon building, itself of several phases and almost always completely obscured by the grander building that had later come to replace it. Nor, interestingly, has this grander building always been datable to the post-conquest Anglo-Norman period of reform and renewal … the more important minster church at Hadstock (Essex) was already demonstrably an impressive stone building in the Middle Saxon period.[90]

Brixworth is another notable example of this (Figure 1.10). Blair is more cautious in his comments on eighth- and early ninth-century church building: 'It is hard to say whether basilican churches on the scale of Brixworth and Cirencester were always exceptional, or whether large numbers have been obliterated by the intensity of later rebuilding in central and southern England, but at present they look like relative rarities'.[91] Nevertheless, they were not unknown.

Conclusion

The Ruin clearly conveys a sense of awe and overwhelming admiration for the ruins surviving in the landscape the poet knew – the country villas, the large walls, the palaces at places like Bath – and powerfully communicated his reaction to the evidence of decay and loss using terms which his own people would understand. But the purpose of this chapter has been to explore which circumstances might have been most likely to provoke such a reaction.

At the time of the *adventus*, up to *c*.AD 500, and even into the sixth century, there may have been a significant number of Roman structures still standing, albeit in varying degrees of repair. Despite problems which we have in identifying their precise appearance, it is clear that in many sites, alterations and additions were made in the period beyond AD 400. Early Anglo-Saxons, whether mercenaries, settlers or invaders, could have been familiar with such structures and the construction methods still in existence in some places.[92] Rogers concludes that 'many of the buildings did eventually disappear through structural decay, demolition, and stone robbing in the post-Roman period, although some survived longer, influencing locations of churches and forms of settlement in the medieval period'.[93]

The seventh century provides a more interesting period when it is more likely that a building such as that commented on in *The Ruin* might have become a feature of the landscape. There was a clear 'culture gap' between the Anglo-Saxon elites (including readers and writers of poetry, perhaps) and the sub-Roman past. At this time, such ruins might well have seemed to be *enta geworc*. There was equal hostility towards the Anglo-Saxons from the remnants of the sub-Roman culture and its successors: Christopher Snyder helpfully reminds us that, despite the likely continuity between sub-Roman and Anglo-Saxon periods which is the fashionable (and probably more archaeologically accurate) view held by most current scholars, 'Whatever "peaceful interaction" or "cultural-assimilation" scenarios some scholars have envisaged in order to explain the *adventus Saxonum*, the words of Gildas, Aneirin, Aldhelm, Bede, and Eddius Stephanus leave no doubt that fear and hatred dominated most relationships between Britain and the *Saxones*'.[94]

In the later period, from the eighth century onwards, when the poem has been traditionally dated,[95] major building works using stone and glass had been completed in several areas, and there was no mystery to the means of putting them up any more. The same argument could also be applied to the later *burh*-building programmes carried out under Alfred and Edward. In the earlier period, there might still have been a good level of decayed or ruined Roman building to be seem – as discussed above, Cuthbert's hosts at Carlisle made it an integral part of their guided tour for him in AD 685 – but, in the century after this, Roman structures were seen practically as quarries for new building projects, not as *enta geweorc*. Such a way of regarding ruins may well have become a poetic trope by the eighth century – unless *The Ruin* was composed at an earlier period than hitherto supposed. It may also reveal a marked difference between a secular culture and that which was actively being developed by the Church, which was promoting *enta geweorc* of its own along Roman models (and not just in architecture). Certainly, ruins evoked 'an imaginative nostalgia for a glorious past',[96] but hardly one which originated in the late eighth century. If it is a genuine reaction to an actual building, the poem's origins seem to be better located in a much earlier historical and archaeological setting.

2

Roads and Tracks in Anglo-Saxon England

Paul Hindle

*Ofereode þa   æþelinga bearn
steap stanhliðo,   stige nearwe,
enge anpaðas,   uncuð gelad*

So the noble prince proceeded undismayed up fells and screes, along narrow footpaths and ways where they were forced into single file ledges on cliffs above the lairs of water-monsters.[1]

Introduction

Although there is much evidence for the movement of people and goods in Anglo-Saxon England, the detail of the network of roads and tracks remains something of a mystery. The evidence for both Roman roads before, and medieval roads after, the Anglo-Saxon period is much better. It is clear that many Roman roads remained in use, and new tracks came into being which can be seen in the post-Anglo-Saxon period. But the paucity of Anglo-Saxon documentary, cartographic and archaeological evidence leaves sources such as place names and charters, which can be difficult to interpret. It is clear that many of the roads and tracks in use today were created during the period, related to the establishment and growth of villages, *burhs* and ports, but in most cases putting flesh on the bones is difficult.

The network of roads and tracks during the Anglo-Saxon period is almost impossible to reconstruct, largely because there was apparently no deliberate road construction, and there are few written sources which describe roads.[2] Indeed, most modern books written about the period make little or no mention of roads or communication. One is almost left to agree with G.K. Chesterton that: 'the rolling English drunkard made the rolling English road. / A reeling road a rolling road that rambles round the shire'.[3] Despite the lack of evidence it is highly likely that the road system of England was largely complete (in terms of the number of roads and connectivity) by the end of the Anglo-Saxon period, although the network continued to evolve for another 700 years in response to changing demand. There were not to be any deliberate alterations or additions to the road network, however, until the turnpikes and enclosure roads[4] in the eighteenth and nineteenth centuries, and new roads such as bypasses and motorways in the twentieth.

Origins

Before the Anglo-Saxon period a road system already existed, perhaps partly created in prehistoric times, and certainly during the Roman occupation (Figure 2.1). Much has been written about supposed prehistoric roads, though there is a lack of good evidence for them.[5] There was certainly trading activity (for example, stone axes from the Lake District are found throughout the country), but whether there was enough concentration of traffic to create many distinct lines of travel is unlikely. Most of the speculation has concentrated on the various tracks on the high ridges of Wessex and elsewhere; a few long-distance routes may have become well-used (perhaps the Harrow Way, and the Great Ridgeway, with its continuation the Icknield Way).[6] But most of the suggested routes simply do not connect the prehistoric settlements known today, and, most tellingly, the ridges have little or no water for travellers or animals. Most of these routes are much more likely to have been created and used at a much later date, often as drove roads.[7]

On the other hand, the Romans certainly imposed a totally new network of roads, ranging from great cross-country highways to farm tracks, and their legacy is still very obvious.[8] The Roman road system was planned and carefully constructed, and the typical straightness of the roads shows that a large-scale and detailed system of surveying was used. The major roads were usually surfaced, using whatever materials were available locally. The main Roman roads were built to link the forts and towns in an interconnected control system, built primarily for military use. Thus the Roman army appears to have been heavily involved in road construction, though local labourers were no doubt employed, too. The fact that many Roman roads (or routes parallel to them) were still being used in the Middle Ages, and are still in use today, suggests very strongly that those roads have had continual use for almost two thousand years.

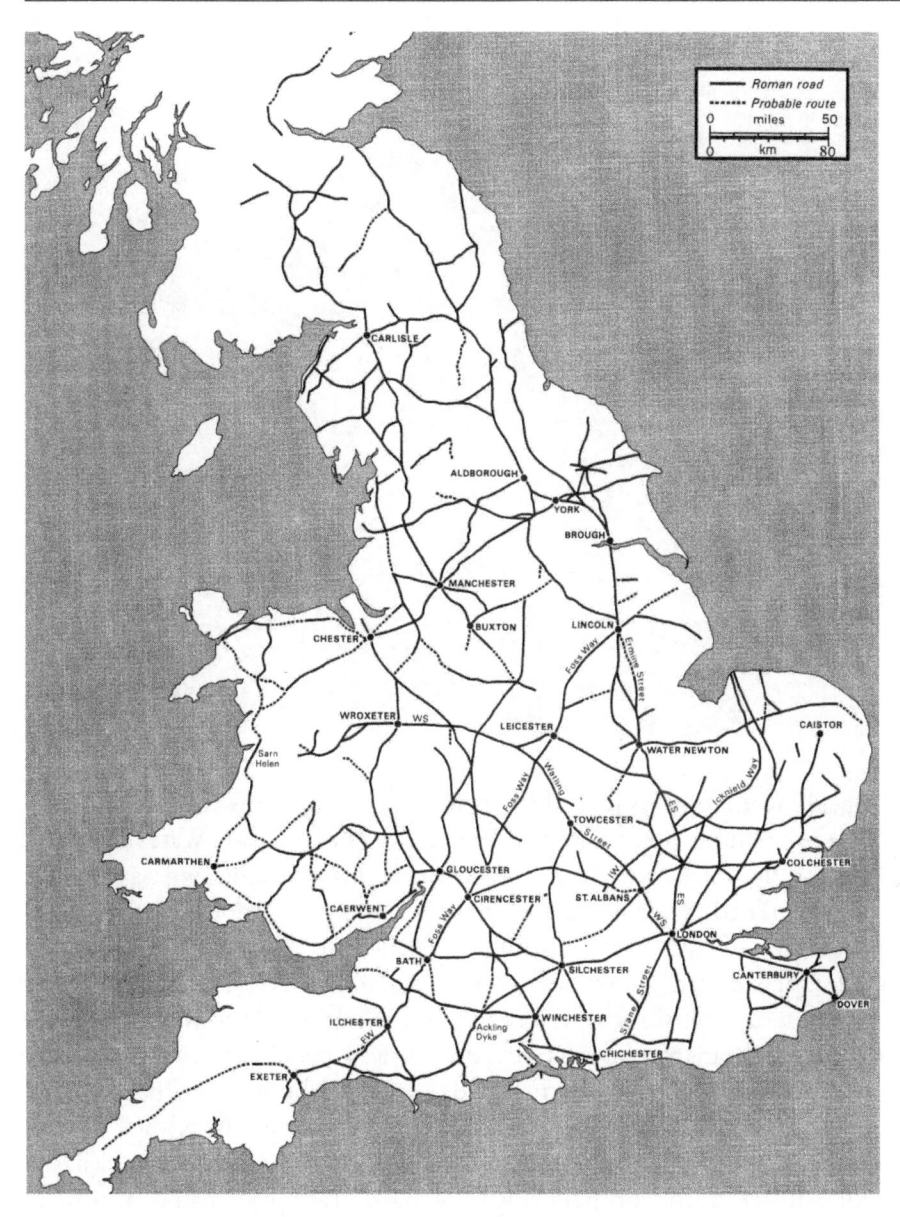

Fig. 2.1 The network of main Roman roads.

But Ivan Margary noted that there would have been difficulties soon after the Romans had left:

> The wooden bridges would be the first to go, and if some local owner did not carry out the repair the road would be broken at that point unless a ford was available nearby; washouts would occur in hilly districts, severing the road at culverts and creating very awkward obstacles.[9]

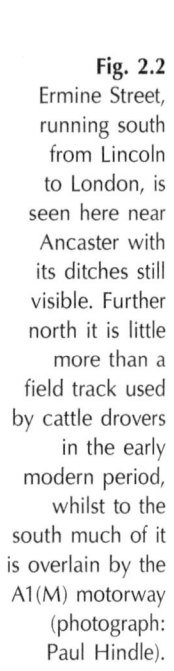

Fig. 2.2 Ermine Street, running south from Lincoln to London, is seen here near Ancaster with its ditches still visible. Further north it is little more than a field track used by cattle drovers in the early modern period, whilst to the south much of it is overlain by the A1(M) motorway (photograph: Paul Hindle).

David Harrison gives several examples of fords replacing Roman bridges.[10] Where Ermine Street crossed the River Nene near Water Newton (Cambridgeshire), the Roman bridge evidently became impassable, and travellers had to cross the river at Wansford, 5 kilometres (3 miles) upstream; a bridge was later built at the ford rather than at the Roman site. Christopher Taylor describes a similar change a few miles further north in Lincolnshire where the same road crossed the River Welland; again the Roman road was abandoned, and people instead forded the river at Stamford, where again a bridge was later built.[11] Another example is where Ermine Street (Figure 2.2) originally crossed the River Ure near Aldborough (North Yorkshire), but the route shifted a kilometre (half a mile) upstream to Boroughbridge. The fairly rare place name 'Stratford' (as at Stratford-upon-Avon) implies that a Roman road bridge had been replaced by a ford.

There are many examples where lengths of Roman routes were abandoned by later travellers, often where the straight Roman road went over a steep hill; thus many modern roads follow but occasionally deviate from the Roman line. Roman roads were often used as boundaries between settlements which later became parish boundaries. This was no doubt because the new settlers wanted to live at some distance from a Roman road, fearing that it would bring only trouble in the form

Fig. 2.3 The massive agger of Ackling Dyke on Bottlebush Down, south-west of Salisbury, is one of the most impressive surviving Roman roads. The dyke is part of the road from Silchester and Old Sarum to Badbury Rings; most of the road is not overlain by modern roads, as those places have not been continuously settled, being replaced by Reading, Salisbury and Wimbourne Minster, respectively (photograph: Paul Hindle).

of invaders or raiding parties. The standard construction of a Roman road with its central, raised area ('agger') and the deep ditches on either side would often have provided a clear and convenient dividing line in the landscape. Perhaps the best example is Ackling Dyke, southwest of Salisbury, which looks more like a disused railway embankment than a Roman road (Figure 2.3).

The complex history of settlement during the Anglo-Saxon period must have involved the creation and use of new tracks as well as the loss of disused routes. The new villages would soon have needed to trade, and new roads must have 'made and maintained themselves', a phrase used by C.T. Flower in relation to the King's Highway in medieval times.[12] The maintenance was certainly not formal, but done by travellers simply going around and avoiding any difficult or waterlogged parts of the road. The same processes must have operated in the Anglo-Saxon period; Sidney Webb and Beatrice Webb describe roads as an 'easement – a right of way, enjoyed by the public at large from village to village, along a certain customary course, which, if much frequented, became a beaten track'.[13] Della Hooke notes that routeways were constantly changing, being adapted to changing circumstances.[14] It is highly likely that the typical winding English country lane, as already described by Chesterton, has its origins in the Anglo-Saxon period, avoiding obstacles and following natural routeways in the landscape. Many still survive, unless altered (and often straightened) when many fields were enclosed in the years around 1800.

Another driving force must have been the creation of *burhs* c.900, which as well as being created for defence must also have been trading centres, not least to feed and clothe their populations; the origins of the later medieval system of towns and trade clearly lie here.[15] Some of these *burhs* were on Roman sites connected by Roman roads (for example, Winchester and Chichester), but others were not (such as Wallingford and Wareham), and new tracks must have come into use to serve them. Taylor outlines some of the changes to the roads leading into Stamford, Winchester and Tamworth.[16]

Travellers and trade

High-status travellers would have included kings and major landowners, whether moving with armies or simply administering estates. Pilgrims would also have been on the move; there is a long list of Anglo-Saxon saints, many of whom were visited and venerated; early shrines included those of St Augustine at Canterbury, St Æthelberht at Hereford, St Swithun at Winchester, St Edmund at Bury and St Alban at St Albans. St Cuthbert's remains were moved from Lindisfarne to Norham, and then to Chester-le-Street before finally coming to rest at Durham. Rich and pious pilgrims also sometimes travelled to Rome or to the Holy Land. There were plenty of other travellers who were not pilgrims, or not solely pilgrims; these would have included ecclesiastics and their entourages going to synods and other Church business, archbishops going to Rome to collect their *pallia*, scholars travelling to study abroad and political travellers such as diplomats. Travellers going to Europe would certainly have used the Roman road from London to Dover via Canterbury to reach the shortest sea crossing; this is reflected in a medieval map of the route from London to Rome and Apulia made by Matthew of Paris in c.1252.[17]

Traders were no doubt the commonest travellers on the roads. Much of the research on medieval trade concentrates on international trade by sea and river, for which archaeological evidence survives. There were important ports at *Eoforwic* (York), Flixborough, Ipswich, London and *Hamwic* (Southampton), with much trade taking place across the English Channel and the North Sea. Both *Hamwic* and Ipswich had an internal rectilinear network of gravelled streets which must have led to routes across country to internal hinterlands. Trade within England must have been increasing; research on medieval towns and trade suggests that access to water, whether sea or river, was important.[18] But some medieval towns, such as Lichfield, Coventry and Marlborough, were not on or near navigable water; the same must have been true for many fledgling towns in Anglo-Saxon times. Even if much trade did go by boat, the first and last legs (at least) of each trading movement must have been by road; roads clearly linked towns to ports and river landing places.

David Hill notes that there is evidence that the roads allowed reasonably rapid progress.[19] Athelstan journeyed with his whole court from Winchester to Nottingham (about 260 kilometres – 160 miles) in eight days, Saint Æthelwold's body was moved 100 kilometres to Winchester in two days and above all King Harold II was able to move his army from London to York (over 320 kilometres) in as little as four or five days in September 1066. Hill has nine regional maps suggesting which roads (mostly Roman) were in use, though he does not explain how he determined which he selected.[20]

Written evidence

An early law of King Ine of Wessex, issued in about 694, says that:

> If a man from afar, or a stranger, goes through the woods off the highway and neither calls out nor blows a horn, he may be considered a thief, to be slain or to be redeemed.[21]

The (so-called) laws of William I refer to four roads being under the king's special protection, namely Watling Street, Ermine Street (both spelt as *strete*), Fosse Way and Icknield Way; the first three were Roman roads, and the last was an older track which had been partly Romanised.[22] The laws were concerned with safety rather than the road surface; anyone committing murder or assault on these roads committed a breach of the King's Peace. This was further extended to all highways in the laws of Henry I (1100–35), which also stipulated minimum widths, namely that the highway should be wide enough for two waggons to meet and pass.[23] This concept of royal roads no doubt extends back into the Anglo-Saxon period. Watling Street was also important as forming part of the boundary between Anglo-Saxon England and the Danelaw at various dates, and is twice named as *wæclinga stræte* and *wæxlingga strate* in a grant of Athelstan in 926.[24]

Charter evidence

Roads and fords are sometimes mentioned in Anglo-Saxon charters as lengths of the boundary of an estate. A very early example which survives in an eleventh-century copy relates to the conveyance of land by Æthelheard, King of the West Saxons, at Crediton in Devon in 739. The boundary description is unusually long and mentions three highways, a green road, a path and no fewer than ten fords; it begins and ends thus:

> First from the Creedy bridge (*brycge*) to the highway (*herpath*), along the highway to the plough ford on the Exe ... to Beonna's ford on the Creedy, thence upstream until Hawk Hollow, thence to the enclosure gate, thence to the old highway (*ealden herepath*) until East Creedy, then along the stream to Creedy bridge.[25]

A charter of King Edgar in 958 mentions a *stræte* (paved road) twice. Della Hooke notes that 15 per cent of boundary features in West Midlands charters are roads, though few are used as major divides for long distances. Watling Street is noted for being used as an estate (and parish) boundary for most of its length, and the same is true of the Fosse Way and parts of Ryknield Way, though lesser Roman roads were used much less frequently as boundaries. She also notes the use of prehistoric ridgeway routes:

> Along one part of the limestone crest on the borders of Warwickshire and Oxfordshire a ridgeway route known as Ditchedge Lane is followed by parish boundaries for almost twenty kilometres, with only one break.[26]

She finds that salt roads (see below) are also often used in the same way.

Archaeological and cartographic evidence

As roads across country were not formally constructed during this period, but simply developed from well-trodden paths, archaeological evidence is almost totally lacking; but as archaeology reveals more of the pre-medieval layout of towns it is at least possible to start to see where roads left the towns and in which direction they were heading. Della Hooke has identified examples of parallel droveways, or livestock roads, in Warwickshire and Kent, which may have been used by cattle and pigs in transhumance movements; one such thoroughfare in Warwickshire was identified as 'the way to the shire wood' in a charter of 963.[27]

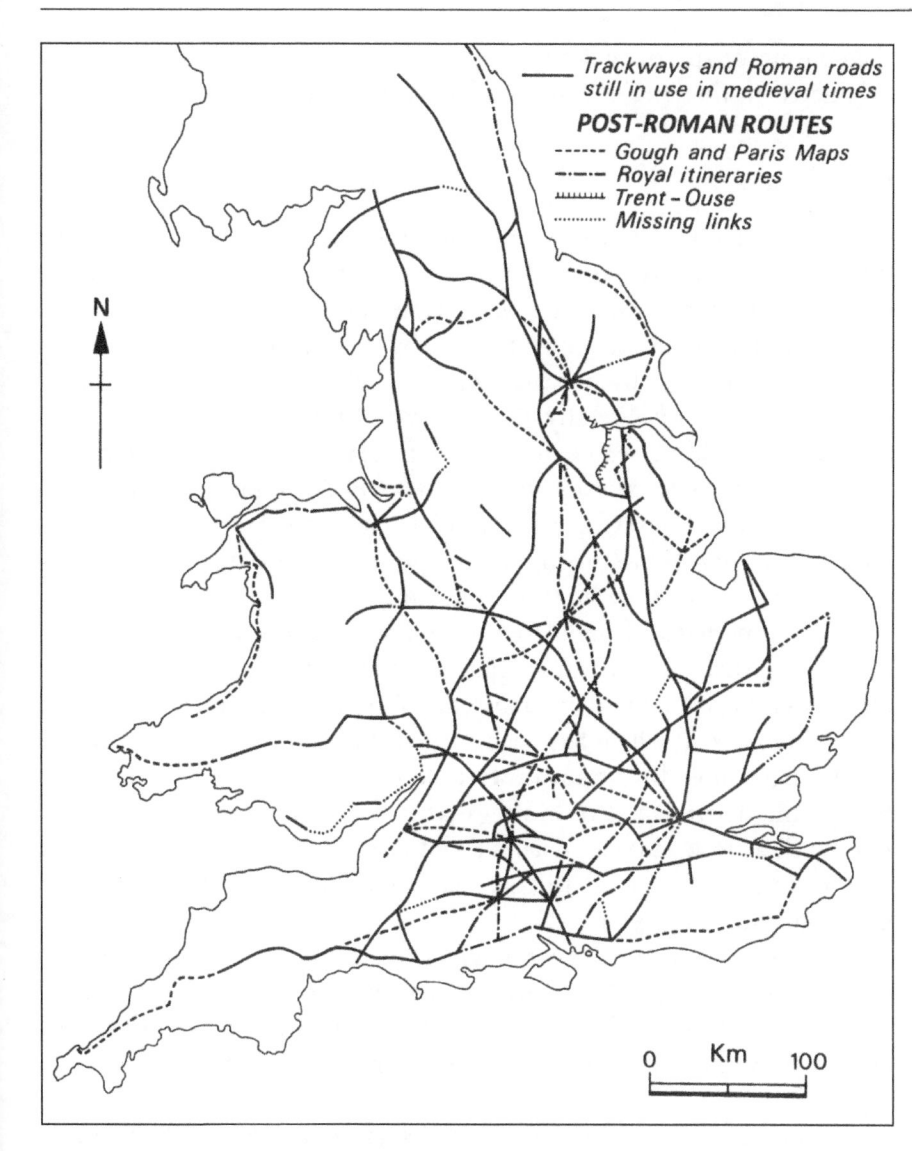

Fig. 2.4 Roman roads and other older tracks still in use in medieval times versus post-Roman routes. Many of the latter no doubt came into use in the Anglo-Saxon period, and are known to have been in use in the medieval period.

There are no Anglo-Saxon maps showing roads, but there are several later maps which may give clues to what happened to the road system in the Anglo-Saxon period. The first is the 'Gough Map' of c.1360, which shows about 4,700 kilometres (2,940 miles) of roads in England and Wales.[28] Most link the main towns, though there are some local roads in Lincolnshire and Yorkshire. It probably shows the more important roads, and about 40 per cent of them are along Roman lines, implying that a mixture of Roman and later roads was in use (Figure 2.4). A much later set of road maps is found in *Britannia*, published by John Ogilby in 1675.[29] Again, the principal roads are shown and side routes indicated, but the value of Ogilby's maps is that a dense network is shown before the coming of the turnpikes; many of the roads shown may well have originated in the Anglo-Saxon period as links between places.

Place names

A number of Old English place names refer to roads.[30] The Latin *via strata* is often rendered as *stræt*, usually referring to a made road, almost inevitably Roman; in modern place names Street is the simplest form, but others include Stretton (settlement by a paved road), Stratford and Streatley (a clearing by a paved road). A reference in *Beowulf* claims *straet waes stan-fah*, literally the road was 'stone-decorated', rendered as a 'paved track' in Seamus Heaney's translation.[31] In Gloucestershire, the Fosse Way is known by its own name in some places, and as *hæn streat* (high street) elsewhere. Other high status descriptions in charters include *via regia* (king's road) and *magna via* (highway).

Weg is a more general term, referring to a way, path or road of any status, perhaps of prehistoric origin; there are several *wegs* in the Cotswolds such as Broadway and Stanway. Ann Cole suggests that many were steep and to be avoided.[32] A special version is *holloway*, referring to a road which has been deepened by the passage of traffic, or more often simply by a track down a slope becoming a stream bed after heavy rain. There are also *stānwegs* (as in Stanway) often referring to a road with a stone surface. A *port* could also refer to a town or market; thus *portway* was a road to that place; Hooke shows that three *port stræts* led into Worcester.[33]

A track of less importance might be referred to as a *pæth* or *stīg*, the latter often a steep path over higher ground (Stye Head, Bransty). *Stíge* is used in *Beowulf* in the passage about the expedition to the mere, quoted at the start of the chapter, and here rendered by Seamus Heaney:

> So the noble prince proceeded undismayed up fells and screes, along narrow footpaths and ways where they were forced into single file ledges on cliffs above the lairs of water-monsters.[34]

A special form is a *herepæth* (army path), suggesting that it had been used by an army or was fit for military use. It is commonly of Saxon origin, though *here* may refer to a group of marauders rather than an army. A well-known example is the Wiltshire Herepath between Marlborough and the prehistoric stone circle at Avebury, traversing Fyfield and Overton Downs. Of course a king or an army may never have travelled a road named after them, but the name suggests a road of special status.

The Old Norse element *gata* can refer to a road, most commonly found in street names in towns in northern England (such as Deansgate or Micklegate). A special variant is *stayngate* (stony road), most famously applied to the early Roman road south of the later Hadrian's Wall. On the other hand, the Old English *geat* usually refers simply to a gate.

Where crossing wet ground or rivers was needed, various solutions could be adopted, depending on the length and depth of the crossing, and the amount of traffic. The sequence might have included a ford or *wath, wade* (often a tidal crossing), causey/causeway, bridge and, *in extremis*, a ferry. In these cases at least the crossing point of a road can be fixed, even if the routes on either side remain elusive. Harrison discusses the fragmentary evidence for the probably numerous Anglo-Saxon bridges.[35] Many places have the element *brycg*, not least Bristol (originally *Brycgstow*); it appears that a *brycg* could refer to any built crossing of water or wet low-lying land. For example, in the Old English poem *The Battle of Maldon*, which commemorates a clash between Vikings who have landed on an island and an Anglo-Saxon army under the ealdorman of Essex who have come to fight them, men are sent to hold the *brycge*, which was probably something between a ford and a causeway.[36] Harrison notes that place name evidence suggests that there were many more fords than bridges; no bridge name is recorded until the late ninth century. He also notes a number of major Anglo-Saxon bridges, discusses the various methods of construction used and shows the importance attached to the repair of bridges. Hill has a map showing 'major bridges' at sixteen places, and has a more detailed map showing the distribution of estates up to 40 kilometres (25 miles) from the Roman bridge at Rochester, which had to supply men to repair the bridge.[37]

In Wales and along the Welsh borders other 'road' elements such as *ffordd, heol* and *sarn* appear, deriving from British (Welsh) rather than English. Cole also suggests that other place names would have been of interest to travellers, including those indicating water, wells, springs and places to stay.[38]

Saltways

The production of salt at the inland centres of Nantwich, Middlewich, Northwich and Droitwich has led several researchers to postulate the existence of 'saltways', though it is unlikely that any road ever carried salt exclusively. Nevertheless, 'salt' place names such as Saltersford and Salt Street are another useful element in tracing some early roads, and those leading from Droitwich have been described by Della Hooke.[39]

A late ninth-century charter describes salt as being carried by packhorse and cartload, the latter implying reasonable road surfaces, especially if the element *stræt* was used. Hooke notes that:

> Many of the major routeways can be traced beyond the Hwiccan frontiers. Two, at least, ran eastwards across Warwickshire into Northamptonshire and northern Oxfordshire, and several ran southwards beyond Gloucestershire into the valley of the upper Thames or south-westwards into Somerset.[40]

Local studies

Hooke brings together the various types of evidence including place names, saltways and documentary sources for several parts of the West Midlands. The Avon valley was served by a number of major routeways:

> On the south bank of the river ... [was] ... a *herepath* ... This seems to have led to Stratford, and a saltway followed the north bank ... towards Warwick ... The Roman road from Alcester ... continued ... into Oxfordshire and is referred to as ... 'the great road' ... Another road ran northwards from Stratford as ... 'the road to the open country'.[41]

In the Vale of Evesham numerous routeways remained in or came into use in the Anglo-Saxon period:

> The Ryknield Street is again referred to as *buggildstret/bugghilde stret* ... and the character of this road led to it being described as ... 'the broad road' ... The Roman road which ran north-eastwards from Hinton-on-the-Green is referred to as ... 'the military way' ... Saltways are also prominent in the area ... The clauses reveal the existence of a *sealtstret* ... A ridgeway route of early origin also entered the area from mid-Gloucestershire ... as the *rīcwege/rugweie/richwege*.[42]

Taylor, a field archaeologist, provides descriptions of the changing routes at places including Stamford, Winchester and Tamworth, and several village studies in Yorkshire, Northamptonshire, Cambridgeshire and Devon.[43] In Cambridgeshire examples he notes how the Saxon villages were aligned along a series of east–west routes rather than the modern north–south roads. In the Peak District, A.E. Dodd and E.M. Dodd, using place names and documents, have traced several portways, notably one from Nottingham to Wirksworth and Bakewell.[44] The route is mainly traced by a series of 'portway' place names, both historic and extant, including Alport (Old Port) and Broad Gate.

Conclusion

The road system inherited by medieval England was made up of a combination of ancient pre-Roman tracks, Roman roads and many new tracks which evolved throughout the Anglo-Saxon period.[45] Taylor concluded that 'the primary layout was there by the time William the Conqueror arrived in England. It was perhaps centuries old by that time'.[46] Richard Muir agreed, adding that it is 'very difficult to extract the Saxon components of this network and distinguish them from those of earlier ages'.[47] The road system clearly evolved to take account of changing demands throughout the Anglo-Saxon period, and this process continued during the medieval and early modern periods. Road repair started to become a problem in the late sixteenth-century, but it was not until the creation of turnpikes and enclosure roads in the eighteenth century that deliberate road building was resumed.

How Anglo-Saxon people saw and related to roads and tracks would have varied with time and place. They inherited Roman and other older roads, and developed more of their own organically for trade and many other reasons. Saxon and Danish invaders would no doubt have used the Roman roads where they suited them as well as creating their own tracks. Settlers establishing new villages would have kept away from routes which invaders or marauding bands might have used, but would have created new tracks between their settlements to use for trade. This creation of tracks would have been simply through continuing use rather than deliberate construction. The distinction between Roman roads and those created by use must have been clear to the peoples of Anglo-Saxon England. As traffic increased between villages and *burhs*, roads must have become increasingly important, though it is difficult to suggest how many people travelled routinely, and how far individuals might have gone. No doubt some villagers never left their village, while those at the top of society might have travelled regularly and much further, including travel overseas. Perhaps, just like today, people regarded roads and tracks as a functional part of the landscape, an important but routine component of everyday life.

3

Domestic Dwellings, Workshops and Working Buildings

Kevin Leahy and Michael Lewis

> You [King Edwin] are sitting feasting with your ealdormen and thegns in winter time; the fire is burning on the hearth in the middle of the hall and all inside is warm, while outside the wintry storms of rain and snow are raging; and a sparrow flies swiftly through the hall. It enters in at one door and quickly flies out through the other. For the few moments it is inside, the storm and wintry tempest cannot touch it, but after the briefest moment of calm, it flits from your sight, out of the wintry storm and into it again. So this life of man appears but for a moment; what follows or indeed what went before, we know not at all.[1]

Introduction

In this celebrated passage, one of King Edwin's retainers describes (if only in passing) the importance of buildings in the Anglo-Saxon period. Not only did such structures provide the setting for domestic life, but they also were a refuge from elements outside: in the words of Le Corbusier, they were 'a machine for living in'.[2] Although most Anglo-Saxon domestic structures were usually less impressive than their ecclesiastical counterparts, particularly later stone churches, they were much more fundamental to life (Figure 3.1). The following will examine these 'machines' and consider how they might have fulfilled the many needs and demands of human existence, including shelter, warmth, security, storage, catering and cultural life and how they served as a workspace.

Fig. 3.1 Building remains at Flixborough, Lincolnshire (photograph: Kevin Leahy).

Climate and environment

A building's form is, to a large extent, determined by the environment in which people live; heat, cold and wet predicated the type of structures needed in Anglo-Saxon times. Britain had enjoyed an equitable climate during the Roman period, as conditions were warmer and drier than those experienced at present and allowed an expansion of agriculture onto low-lying, poorly drained land.[3] This changed during the early fifth century with a fall in mean temperature and increased wetness and flooding. These environmental pressures also affected mainland Europe and played a part in triggering the migrations which brought the Anglo-Saxons to Britain. The climate improved and by the eighth century England seems to have had a more 'continental' type environment, with drier and warmer summers but hard winters. The early tenth century saw the start of the medieval warm period, with temperatures reaching a peak around AD 975, these clement conditions persisting until the climatic deterioration of the fourteenth century. The Anglo-Saxons first settled in the drier eastern side of England, which would have influenced the type of housing needed.

Britain was forested, but, starting in prehistory, wide areas had been cleared and there are indications that large accessible trees may have no longer been available during late Roman and early Anglo-Saxon periods.[4] At this time Britain had more varied wildlife than now. The wolf was common, as were wild boar and beaver, and bears may have survived until the eighth century. Most animals, however, would have learned to stay clear of habitations; human beings, with their canine allies, were a formidable and vengeful force.

Surviving evidence

The first domestic Anglo-Saxon buildings to be recognised in England were found at Sutton Courtenay, Oxfordshire, in 1922. Their discovery came as a shock to the archaeological community, which was expecting something more substantial. The excavation report, a product of its time, describes the Anglo-Saxons as 'living in miserable huts in almost as primitive a condition as can be imagined'.[5] What had been found were *Grubenhäuser*: small buildings, represented by pits, spread with debris. As Tom Lethbridge and Fred Tebbutt put it, 'they had no regard for cleanliness, and were content to throw the remains of a meal into the furthest corner of the hut and leave it there'.[6] Fortunately, the eventual identification of the more acceptable hall-type buildings restored the dignity of the Anglo-Saxons, and henceforth *Grubenhäuser* were relegated to the status of workshops or stores, eventually to be given the opaque and inelegant name of 'sunken featured buildings' or, still worse, 'SFBs' (Figure 3.2).

The discoveries at Sutton Courtenay set a trend. Most evidence for early Anglo-Saxon dwellings and workshops continued to come from archaeology, thanks to improved methods, particularly the development of large-scale, 'open area' excavation. Although Anglo-Saxon buildings are not easy to find (or identify), many have now been investigated and a reasonable body of knowledge now exists. Unfortunately, none of these excavated buildings is sufficiently complete to reveal details of their construction and use, and too few of them are securely dated for a developmental sequence to be defined.[7] Houses in the Anglo-Saxon period were mainly constructed from perishable materials, which (other than on waterlogged sites) have decomposed, leaving only postholes (where the timber uprights were placed) and the trenches that held the foundations. On many sites ploughing has removed the original floor surfaces, along with hearths and signs of how the building was used, including traces of any screen walls subdividing the interior into rooms. Nonetheless, it is possible to look beyond these limitations and, using other sources, to attempt to understand these buildings.

Evidence is more plentiful from the later Anglo-Saxon period, but it is by no means comprehensive. Archaeology remains the main

Fig. 3.2 *Grubenhaus* at Catholme, Staffordshire (courtesy of the Trent and Peak Archaeological Trust).

source of information, and there are surviving structures at some sites. Excavation and research also show how buildings were used, particularly by craftspeople, highlighting the multifunctional use of Anglo-Saxon structures, as in York (discussed further, below). Chance finds found by metal-detectorists and others, now being recorded with the Portable Antiquities Scheme (www.finds.org.uk) – a project to record archaeological finds discovered by the public in England and Wales – highlights the contribution 'stray finds' can make to our understanding of the past, particularly when used in conjunction with excavated data: locks and keys, for example, directly reflect domestic life, and other finds provide a social context in which buildings were constructed.[8]

Anglo-Saxon literature sometimes mentions (or at least alludes to) domestic structures, as in the case of Bede's account of the sparrow flying through King Edwin's hall. In the same vein, Viking Age sagas and epic poems, which, though recorded much later in time, are likely to be based on earlier oral traditions, and therefore can be used with care to help fill out the archaeological evidence.

The late Anglo-Saxon period offers some important artistic sources, especially manuscript illustrations, most from southern scriptoria (which better survived political upheaval, and may have been better endowed), and the eleventh-century Bayeux Tapestry. These suggest the form of contemporary structures, some of apparently domestic use, though it is right to be cautious given their likely dependence on classically inspired sources.[9]

The development of Anglo-Saxon buildings

The Anglo-Saxon period lasted for more than 600 years, and during that time changes took place in the forms and types of buildings used. In view of the difficulty in dating buildings and the probable existence of regional traditions it is not possible to do more than to identify broad trends here, looking at what is likely to be early, middle and late.

The most striking feature of the early Anglo-Saxon period was the disappearance of the building traditions of Roman Britain. That sophisticated building methods like ashlar masonry, hypocaust heating, mosaics and painted plaster should vanish is perhaps not surprising: they were always the prerogative of the elite. Some materials ceased to be available: bricks, tiles and cement (used for floors) depended on an economy that no longer existed. Iron nails, ubiquitous on Roman sites, vanish. Many Roman buildings were wooden, but their walls stood on low stone sills, and were probably timber-framed, consisting of box-like structures infilled to form the walls.

As well as differing from Romano-British houses, most Anglo-Saxon buildings were unlike those of the continental homelands (modern-day north-west Germany and southern Denmark) from which the Anglo-Saxons came. Absent are the large, three-aisled long-houses, such as those at Feddersen Wierde, Germany, and Wijster, in the Netherlands.[10] The lack of such buildings in England may have been due to environmental factors. Continental long-houses sheltered both humans and their livestock under the same roof, which was vital with severe continental winters but less important in the mild British climate where livestock could live outside all year. It is also possible that, during this early period, the Anglo-Saxons lacked the 'social capital' needed to erect such buildings. The collection, preparation and setting up of large quantities of material would have required a considerable labour force and might be equated to an Amish 'Barn Raising', calling on the services of the whole community. However, a possible reason for the change to smaller buildings was that the incomers simply adopted the established agricultural and domestic practices of the Romano-British population, a substantial number of whom remained.[11] A case in point is in Lindsey – one of the three 'Parts' of Lincolnshire – which is well-endowed with Anglo-Saxon cemeteries. However, at any one time these would represent a live population of only around 4,000, too few to maintain a large area of land in cultivation. This suggests that most of the population is missing from the burial record (at the time of Domesday Book, Lindsey had a population of around 60,000). The missing population was probably of British descent and subject to a different burial rite.[12]

A type of building used by the earliest Anglo-Saxons, which was (apparently) imported from northern Europe, is the *Grubenhaus*. These pit huts are found over wide areas of eastern and central England. Their distinguishing feature is their sunken floors, about 0.3 metres to 0.5 metres deep when excavated, usually with a posthole at each end which probably supported the roof's ridge pole. In East Anglia and the south-east, some *Grubenhäuser* have four or six end-posts, suggesting the use of a different type of superstructure. *Grubenhäuser* are rare in central southern England, where chalk subsoils would have made digging a pit more difficult. In these areas other structures must have fulfilled their function.

Interpreting the remains of *Grubenhäuser* has generated much debate, a particular question being whether the base of the pit was the floor, or whether it was planked over. The evidence has been reviewed in Jess Tipper's excellent study.[13] Initially, *Grubenhäuser* were seen as being pit dwellings. However, on the basis of structural, stratigraphic and finds evidence from West Stow in Suffolk, Stanley West suggested that they had planked floors at ground level covering the sunken pit which acted as storage or as an air space.[14] Two of the West Stow *Grubenhäuser* had burnt down, leaving evidence of planked floors (or walls) and thatched roofs. West noted the absence of a trampled floor layer on the bases of these buildings. He also believed that the debris found in the lower layers of *Grubenhäuser* pits was material that had collected under the suspended floor. Later, Tipper was to observe that the pottery pieces in these areas were worn and abraded, suggesting the pits were not their original contexts.[15] More recently, the nature of the material found in the fill of *Grubenhäuser* pits has been reassessed, and it is agreed that most of it was backfill, following the abandonment of the building, most of this being secondary and tertiary material.[16] It is therefore apparent that the Anglo-Saxons did not in fact live in the squalor which so shocked Lethbridge and Tebbutt, but instead the lack of an occupation layer in the base of many *Grubenhäuser* might relate to good house-keeping: during occupation, floors were kept clean, with waste deposited in pits only after abandonment of individual structures.

Like West, Jess Tipper believed that *Grubenhäuser* had suspended floors,[17] although he admitted that certain aspects of this interpretation are problematic. There are a number of arguments for raised floors. Most *Grubenhäuser* pits measure around 4 metres by 3 metres, but their angled sides greatly reduced the area of the base. At West Stow the smallest *Grubenhaus* would have had a 1.8 metre by 1.8 metre base, a tiny, but still usable, area. Trampled surfaces have been observed on the bases of *Grubenhäuser* pits, with, for example, evidence for wear on the pit floor at Wharram Percy, North Yorkshire.[18] There are *Grubenhäuser* in which the pits are lined with stake holes, suggesting some form of revetment. Five of the *Grubenhäuser* at Mucking, Essex, had stake holes around their base, and most of the *Grubenhäuser* at Catholme, Staffordshire, had stakes around their pits, set 15 cm to 20 cm apart. Few *Grubenhäuser* seem to have contained hearths and the evidence for them is far from convincing; in many cases the 'hearths' might be better interpreted as burnt material being dumped in the pits after abandonment. Possible entrances down into the pits were observed at Catholme, but these are rare.[19]

It has been suggested that the function of the cavity in the floor of *Grubenhäuser* was to provide a dry air space beneath,[20] but some pits seem excessively deep for this role. Pits are usually now truncated by the removal of the topsoil and would have extended up to ground level, giving an original depth of around 0.6 metres to 0.8 metres. This seems excessive for an air space and, rather than being warming, might have led to distressing draughts. A planked floor would have been expensive both in time and material and, significantly, any increase in head height gained through the pit would have been lost. Notably, most continental scholars believe that *Grubenhäuser* had sunken floors. West was surely right to keep his options open: some were planked, others were not.[21] Even without suspended floors *Grubenhäuser* are likely to have consisted of more than a simple ridged roof. Walls would have been necessary to raise the thatch off the ground to protect it from the damp. There is evidence for thatch from West Stow, and there was indirect evidence for the use of turf walls at Puddlehill, Bedfordshire, Mucking and West Heslerton, North Yorkshire.[22]

While *Grubenhäuser* were an imported concept, the origins of the small hall-type buildings are less clear. It has been argued that they drew on the pre-existing building traditions of Roman Britain.[23] Certainly, small hall-type buildings are known from rural areas at this time, for example, at Dunstan's Clump, Nottinghamshire,[24] but there are some important differences between these Romano-British structures and those of the early medieval period, in particular, opposed doorways in the long walls, which are rare on Roman structures. These buildings may have had hybrid origins drawing on both Roman and Germanic traditions.[25] The earliest hall-type buildings in England were relatively small (usually less than 12 metres long) and appear to have been symmetrically planned with a length equivalent to twice the width (known as the two-square module). They show a high degree of uniformity throughout Anglo-Saxon England from the fifth to the seventh centuries and were often aligned east–west, with their short gable-ends presented to the prevailing westerly wind, shielding their doors and protecting their long walls from driven rain. Oddly, many of them exhibit what are known as 'weak corners': corner posts, which might be thought to be a vital part of any building, are absent. These simple, one-roomed buildings may reflect the social upheavals of the fifth century and deteriorating climatic conditions: a lack of resources and the need for small, snug dwellings.

During the sixth century, buildings became more varied in size and plan, and towards the end of the century large structures with floor areas greater than 100 m² were being constructed. At this time there was a move towards the wall posts being set in trenches rather than individual holes. This arrangement would have allowed greater flexibility in the alignment of the posts, and in many soils it is also easier to dig a continuous trench than a series of pits. There is little evidence for buildings being constructed in bays, defined by paired posts. Importantly, it is not possible to use a framed structure (commonly seen on surviving medieval buildings and likely on those of Roman date) in conjunction with earth-fast posts, as differences in the levels of the posts make it difficult to align the joints. Earth-fast posts would have been linked at the top of the wall (the wall plate), which was levelled for the roof. At this time the posts or planks used to form the walls of buildings seem mainly to have been of oak, a timber which is durable and readily split to make planks. Where clay was available, the spaces between the posts would have been filled with clay-covered withies (wattle and daub), although there is evidence for fully planked structures in the seventh century at Cowdery's Down, Hampshire.[26] Continuous trenched foundations were common in the seventh century, being used on around 50 per cent of buildings. The end walls of many buildings have very light foundations, pointing to the use of gabled, not hipped, roofs, the weight of which was carried by the long side walls. It is likely that most roofs were thatched, although wooden shingles may have been employed, and the use of grass turves cannot be ruled out. In order to be waterproof, thatch must be at an angle of about 50 degrees, giving buildings large, steep roofs. The use of thatch has implications for quality and strength of a building: a roof covering a 12 metre by 6 metre hall would have weighed four tonnes – a load imposed on the substructure and walls (Figure 3.3). Provision would have to have been needed to prevent the side walls being forced out; the low height of the side walls might make transverse tie beams inconvenient, and it is possible that the rafters were linked by collars, higher in the roof. On other buildings the thrust from the roof was taken by bracing the side walls with buttress-like, raking timbers. The angles of the raking

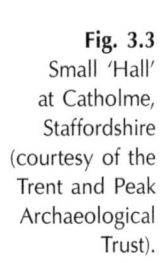

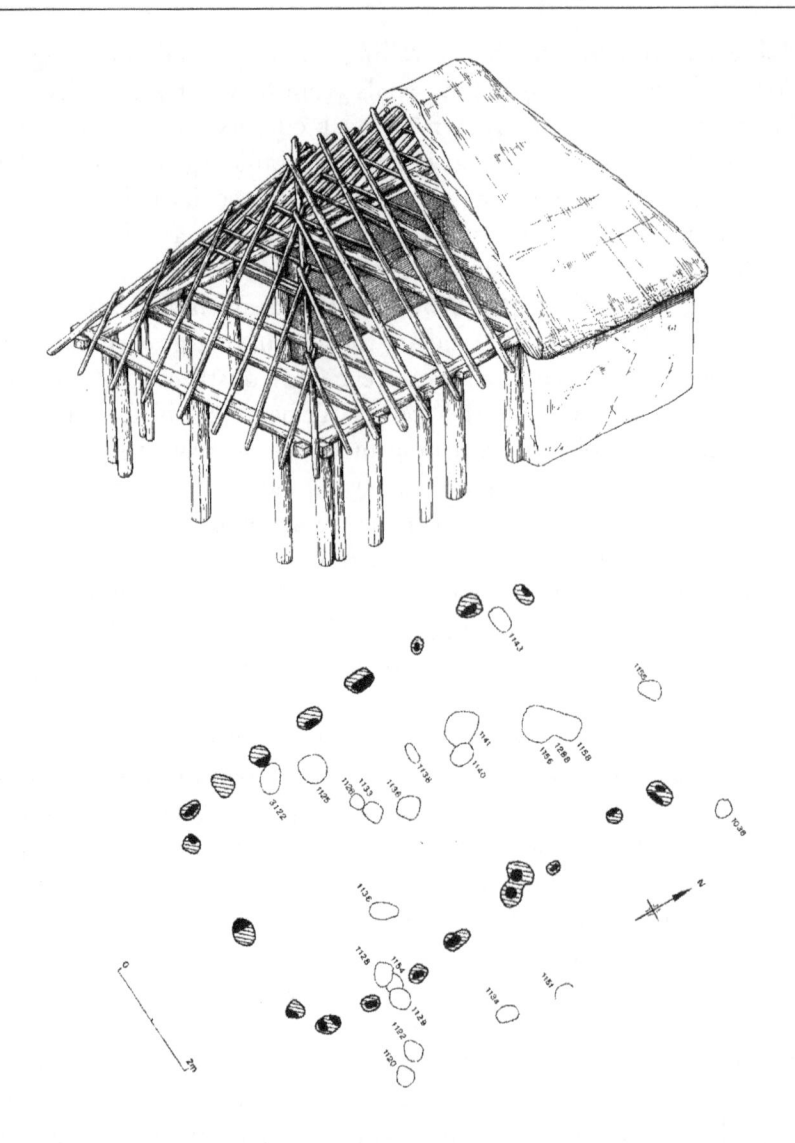

Fig. 3.3
Small 'Hall' at Catholme, Staffordshire (courtesy of the Trent and Peak Archaeological Trust).

side-timbers found on some buildings suggest that the side walls met the roofs below head height.

Most early Anglo-Saxon houses consisted of a single room, although by the end of the sixth century some larger buildings had 'compartments', where one end of the building was divided off, as found at Chalton, Hampshire,[27] or 'annexes' projecting from the gable end as at Cowdery's Down (Building A1), Hampshire (Figure 3.4).[28] Compartments could usually be entered both from outside the building and from within the main room. It is not known what part these narrow 'compartments' played in domestic life. They may have provided private space, but the number of doors might point to a more prosaic function such as a fuel store. 'Annexes', on the other hand, could usually only be entered from within the hall and may therefore have had a different function.

The larger buildings are probably related to the great halls (OE: *heall, reced, sele*) mentioned in Anglo-Saxon texts. Similar buildings were also built on a more humble scale, such as those at Chalton and West Stow.[29] It is difficult to determine if these smaller structures would have been thought of as 'halls' as well, but they must have been at the very least considered a house (OE: *hus*), if not a 'high' house or the 'best of houses' referred to in *Beowulf*.[30] The appearance of larger buildings in the late sixth to seventh centuries may relate to the appearance of a more stratified society, supporting what is seen in the evidence from excavated cemeteries. In the fifth and sixth centuries grave goods are common, and widely distributed. While most seventh-century graves contain little or nothing, a few are richly furnished, pointing to a less equitable society. Likewise, some seventh-century buildings were both large and sophisticated; for example, Building C12 at Cowdery's Down had a floor area of 238 m^2 and employed an elaborate constructional technique of vertical, earth-set planks, probably with what has been interpreted as a suspended wooden floor.[31] More recently, a series of three 'halls', built on the spot of each other, have been excavated at Lyminge, Kent.[32] Some of these large halls were 'aisled', with rows of posts down their length taking the weight of the roof, as at Yeavering, Northumberland.[33] Halls had opposing doors on their long walls, as described in Bede's account of the sparrow's flight, supplemented, in some cases, by doors in their gable ends which may have played some role in ceremonial or ritual life. It has been estimated that the construction of hall C12 at Cowdery's Down would have involved 70 tonnes of raw materials, and was therefore no small undertaking.[34] The resource implications are alluded to in *Beowulf*: 'it came to his [King Hrothgar's] mind that he would command the construction of a huge mead-hall, a house greater than men on earth ever had heard of' and 'far and wide (as I heard) the work was given out in many a tribe over middle earth, the making of the mead-hall'. This hall (named Heorot), is described as 'this greatest of houses', and might be compared to the great hall at Yeavering. Here 'It was with pain that the powerful spirit dwelling in the darkness [Grendel] endured that time, hearing daily the hall filled with loud amusement; there was the music of the harp, the clear song of the poet', which led this monster to torment King Hrothgar's people.[35] Since great halls are the subject matter of such stories, it would seem likely that such epic poetry was read in them also.

In Icelandic sagas such halls (though invariably much smaller than those described in *Beowulf*) had an important political function, a place where guests to Iceland and Norway would be honoured and marriage alliances would be celebrated.

The middle Anglo-Saxon period (c.700–900) saw buildings becoming generally larger than those that preceded them, with a greater range in form, the 'two-square' plan no longer dominating. There does not seem to have been any tendency for large halls to be partitioned into smaller rooms: the annexes and compartments seen on some of the larger halls had largely gone out of use by the eighth century and may have been replaced by the small auxiliary buildings which appeared during the seventh century. These small buildings, with lengths of less than 6 m, may have provided private space separated from the communal life of the hall and are likely to represent what are described in the literature as 'bowers' (*bur, brydbur*). The *Anglo-Saxon Chronicle* (A, D and E)

records how in 755 King Cynewulf of Wessex was surprised and killed when staying with his mistress in a *bur* while his bodyguards were in another building.[36] In *Beowulf* some of those wishing to avoid becoming Grendel's victims were in 'sleeping-quarters quieter ... among the outer buildings'.[37] This is the sort of hall and bower layout seen at Cheddar, Somerset.[38]

The use of trenched foundations became more common – the technique being used on 75 per cent of buildings in the middle Anglo-Saxon period – although other methods of construction were employed. There does not appear to have been any correlation between building sizes and the type of foundation used: the situation was complex, with different types of foundations being employed within one settlement or, on occasion, on the same building, as at Catholme. It is possible that builders would, depending on circumstances and available materials, draw on different techniques in their repertoire. *Grubenhäuser*, including some large examples, are found on sites at this time, but they were less common and seem to have gone out of use during the ninth century.[39]

Drystone or gravel wall footings appear from the ninth century and seem to dominate in northern England, where the higher rainfall would cause the rapid decay of earth-fast posts. On the monastic site at Hartlepool, County Durham, stone foundations were found to have replaced earlier earth-fast structures.[40] In addition to prolonging the life of a building, stone foundations would have allowed the use of a framed structure. Gravel foundations set at ground level point to the use of framed buildings at Flixborough, Lincolnshire, although, in the absence of true mortise and tenon joints, it would not have been possible to use a prefabricated frame.[41] The high rate of finds recovery at Flixborough resulted in the discovery of nails, clench bolts and staples.[42] While the numbers involved appear high (1,463 nails, 27 clench bolts, 225 staples), there are too few of them to represent nailed construction. The surviving structure of the ninth-century water mill found at Tamworth, Staffordshire, demonstrates the use of simple but effective joinery with both mortise and tenon and half-lap joints being used and secured by pegs.[43] Finds of woodworking tools show what was available to Anglo-Saxons and necessary for house building: narrow-bladed felling axes, broad dressing axes and adzes, spoon bits for drilling holes and shaves for making the pegs to fix the structure together (Figure 3.5).[44]

Signs of repair are rare on the earliest known Anglo-Saxon buildings, suggesting that most were abandoned while still habitable: unusually, seventh-century buildings at Cowdery's Down and at Yeavering showed signs of rebuilding, but these sites represented the upper levels of society with a greater investment in large buildings. Evidence for rebuilding is

Fig. 3.4 Hall at Cowdery's Down, Hampshire (courtesy of Martin Millet, Simon James and the Royal Archaeological Institute; drawing by Simon James).

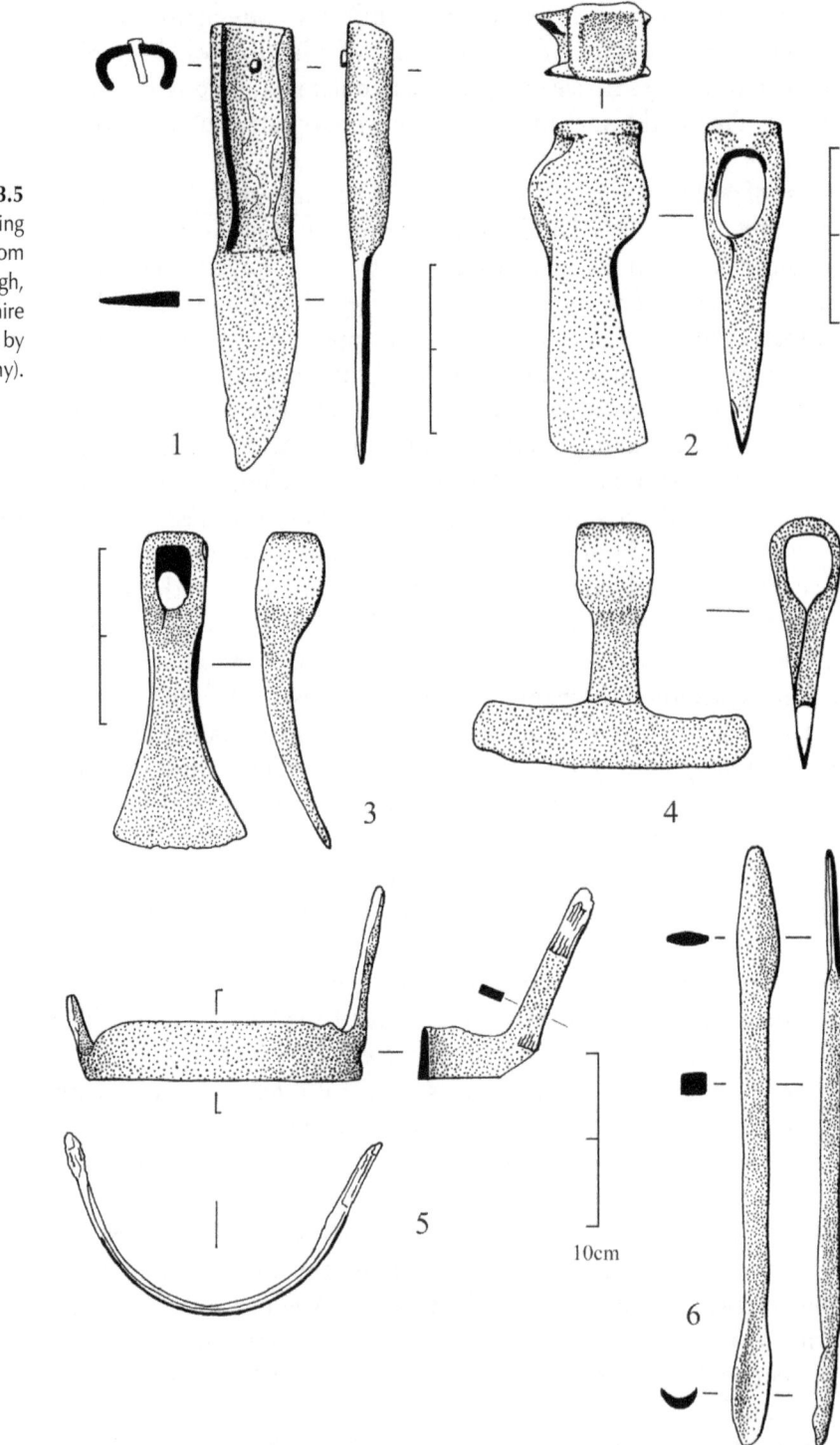

Fig. 3.5 Woodworking tools from Flixborough, Lincolnshire (drawing by Kevin Leahy).

Fig. 3.6 Reconstructed Anglo-Saxon buildings at West Stow, Suffolk (photograph: Kevin Leahy).

more common in the middle Anglo-Saxon period, when more settled conditions would have allowed feelings of permanence (Figure 3.6). At Flixborough, some structures were repeatedly rebuilt on the same footprint. Richard Darrah estimated that 0.2–0.25 metre diameter earth-set oak posts at Flixborough would have lasted around twenty years, with buildings needing major repairs after forty years.[45] At Catholme there was evidence for the replacement of some wall posts during the life of the buildings.

The later Anglo-Saxon period (*c.*900–*c.*1100) saw an increase both in the number of building forms and in the methods of construction employed. Buildings were less regular, with a more varied placement of doorways. At the beginning of the eleventh century, postholes again became common, but there is also evidence for the use of framed structures; it is thought that the mock framing represented on surviving stone church towers, such as Barton-upon-Humber, North Lincolnshire, and Earls Barton, Northamptonshire, mimic a framed wooden structure.[46] A surviving section of framed arcading from Bull Wharf, London, shows the elaborate nature of some of the timberwork.[47]

Excavations at Goltho, Lincolnshire, revealed evidence for partition walls and a raised 'high end' within a late Anglo-Saxon hall,[48] the opposed doorways being separated from an annex at one end and a larger room, containing a hearth, raised a half-metre above the rest of the building. Some intriguing new forms of structure also appear. Square buildings have been found at Springfield Lyons, Essex, and Bishopstone,

East Sussex. These are likely to have been towers, the latter set over a cellar.[49] In the tenth century aisled halls became more common, with the posts supporting the roof, running down the length of the building's interior.

Excavations at 16–22 Coppergate, York, revealed a wealth of archaeological evidence for Anglo-Scandinavian buildings (Figure 3.7).[50] Here, two main building types seem to have been used and a wide range of building techniques employed. The earliest buildings, dating to the mid-tenth century, were single-storey, with rectangular (8.2 m × 4.4 m) plans. They were constructed using vertical stakes set between timber uprights, around which were woven horizontal wattlework rods of oak, hazel and, most commonly, willow. There is no evidence that the buildings were wind-proofed using daub (though buildings elsewhere were), and wall-hangings or panelling may have been used instead.

The buildings at Coppergate were set at 90 degrees to the street, but it is not known how their frontages interacted with it as these parts were not within the excavated area. In London and Lincoln, the gable-ends of houses fronted the street. At Coppergate many buildings must have had a door at the rear, leading into a large yard. Fire (see below) provided the only source of heat and light, with ancillary lighting provided by cresset lamps (dishes containing animal fat and a floating wick) and candles, and most commonly rush-lights (the fat-soaked pith of reeds).[51] People would, of necessity, have gone to bed when darkness fell.

In the late Anglo-Saxon period buildings with sunken floors seem to be an urban phenomenon, although the possible tower at Bishopstone, had a basement.[52] The later Saxon subsurface structures at Brandon Road, Thetford, Norfolk, and at Coppergate are best interpreted as cellars. These structures differed from *Grubenhäuser* as they had vertical sides, often lined, gable posts were absent, floor surfaces were present and many had evidence for stairs space.[53] The need for cellars was a likely result of a pressure on space in an urban environment. At Lower Bridge Street, Chester, the floors were planked across at ground level, with access to the cellar down stairs from the outside.[54] From the late tenth century a new type of building was erected in York of which four were excavated at Coppergate. These buildings had sunken basements (with average cuts of 7.5 metres by 4 metres, and 1.6 metres deep) lined with horizontal oak planks held in place by a series of oak uprights; there was no evidence for the use of pegs, joints or nails in these structures. Buildings at this time were also constructed from vertically set planks, as in Goltho and London. The 'stave built' structures at Goltho used closely packed vertical timbers with complex joints between them, the making of which would have represented a substantial investment.

Fig. 3.7 Anglo-Scandinavian building remains at Coppergate, York (copyright York Archaeological Trust for Excavation and Research Ltd).

The foundations used to support late Anglo-Saxon buildings are of interest. Some were constructed of uprights forced into the ground like stakes, though it was more common for timbers to be placed in postholes and packed with stones. At Skeldergate, York, for example, rubble and cobbles were used.[55] Elsewhere, such as at Portchester, Hampshire,[56] and North Elmham, Norfolk,[57] a foundation trench was dug, in which uprights were placed. Another technique was to set uprights in a sill beam or to use rubble, upon which the uprights were placed, which would allow a framed structure to be aligned.

The layout of building plots at Coppergate is of note. Buildings here were close to one another, with little space between. Access was gained from the street (at the front) or via back doors. The back-yards of houses were long (being at least 43.5 metres in length), sloping down towards the River Foss, and were fenced for most of their length. Wattle-work paths were much in evidence, which, given the damp and muddy conditions close to the river, would have been necessary. There was evidence for wells and cesspits (see below), and some of the yards were subdivided by wattle-work fences so that livestock, especially pigs, could be kept.[58]

Although much of what survives archaeologically suggests that most Anglo-Saxon buildings were single storey, it is apparent some buildings were not. At Coppergate the late tenth-century buildings had sunken basements and a floor above, and are sometimes described as 'two-storey'. It is not entirely clear how the upper parts of the buildings were constructed, though it seems likely that the upright timbers retaining the basement walls also supported the upper storey. Even less certain is where a fire could have been safely positioned in such a building; presumably a stone or tile hearth would have been used on the upper floor. The existence of two-storey buildings is supported by documentary evidence; the *Anglo-Saxon Chronicle* (E) for AD 978 describes how 'all the foremost councillors of the English race fell down from an upper floor [*uno solario*] at Calne [Wiltshire], but the holy Archbishop Dunstan alone was left standing up on a beam'. Likewise, one of the scenes in the Bayeux Tapestry clearly shows feasting going on at first-floor level.[59]

There is little evidence for the roofs of buildings, though it seems most were thatched with straw. Shingles (wooden tiles) are suggested on some objects that imitate buildings (such as censer-covers and Viking hog-back 'tombstones') in the Bayeux Tapestry and (widely) in manuscript art, and therefore may have been used, though there is little archaeological evidence. The steep pitch of thatched roofs meant that Anglo-Saxon houses would have had large roof spaces, which would have been available for storage (see below), but it would have been surprising if the upper parts of the buildings were not used as accommodation. The use of open hearths and the absence of mural fireplaces would have posed problems, but these could have been overcome if the first floor extended over only part of the hall.

Substantial timber halls are also known through archaeology, such as at Cheddar, Goltho, Portchester and Waltham Abbey, Essex.[60] The buildings at Waltham Abbey are aisled, with internal posts that take the weight of the roof away from the side walls, which, it has been suggested, were constructed of turf,[61] but wooden planks or wattle construction seem just as likely. Some late halls such as Cheddar and Goltho appear bow-sided.

Building interiors

It is not known exactly how the interiors of Anglo-Saxon houses appeared and how they were decorated, but it is possible to build up a picture based on archaeology and other sources of evidence. Metalwork recorded by the Portable Antiquities Scheme shows that the Anglo-Saxons had a love of decoration, as almost all surfaces are ornamented. It is notable that much of the sculpture from Anglo-Saxon churches draws on profane, not religious, motifs, suggesting an active tradition of carved, wooden decoration in secular structures. The use of decorative soft furnishings is also well-attested in documentary sources.[62]

Most houses would have consisted of a single room with a central hearth at ground level. Floors were mostly bare earth, which, when compacted, can provide a good surface. It is possible that some were covered with organic materials, such as reeds, sedge or rush; straw would have broken down too quickly and hay was a valuable fodder. Some of the buildings in York had wooden flooring,[63] and tiles were also probably used at this time in some elite structures. At Goltho it was possible to trace a building which lacked any subsurface elements, as only its clay floor survived.[64] Excavations at Flixborough, a site undamaged by ploughing, revealed limestone gravel paths and yards between and around buildings.[65]

The hearth

The hearth was the most important feature of any Anglo-Saxon building; indeed, the word 'hearth' (OE: *heorth*) was used as a synonym for the house as a whole. The construction of hearths in houses varied little through the Anglo-Saxon period, but invariably they were placed on the central axis of the house. At Flixborough, the hearth was represented by a burnt area at floor level. In Viking Age York the rectangular hearth settings, typically measuring 1.8 metres by 1.2 metres, were normally clayed and demarcated by limestone rubble or reused Roman tiles.

Having an open fire within a domestic residence, though necessary, was risky, and the hearth was placed in a central part of a building where the fire was as far as possible from the walls and eaves. With the hearth at floor level it is fortunate that wool, used to make Anglo-Saxon women's skirts, is fire resistant. The potentially devastating impact of fire on domestic dwellings is apparent in the archaeological record. Some of the buildings excavated in York had evidence of fire damage, and Tamworth Mill had suffered a similar fate. The Bayeux Tapestry

Fig. 3.8 Building in the Bayeux Tapestry (by special permission of the City of Bayeux).

(Figure 3.8) shows a woman and child fleeing from their house, which had been set alight deliberately.[66]

Placing hearths centrally also ensured that the light of the fire filled as much of the building as possible, that its heat was evenly distributed and that as many people as possible could sit around when eating, drinking and relaxing. Sometimes the warmth of the fire was an unwelcome distraction in the eyes of parents expecting more from their idle sons. In the Icelandic saga, *The Saga of the People of Vatnsdal*, for example, Ketil 'the Large' complains that 'nowadays young men want to be stay-at-homes, and sit by the fire, and stuff their stomachs with mead and ale; and so it is that manliness and bravery are on the wane'.[67]

Hooked iron chains found at Sutton Hoo, Suffolk,[68] and Flixborough[69] show that metal cauldrons were suspended over the fire from the roof. Iron pieces from Lea Green, North Yorkshire, are likely to have come from a cauldron chain, suggesting that these items were present at what are now remote places.[70] Some Anglo-Saxon pottery vessels bear traces of sooting, demonstrating that they had been used on a fire; many have round bases which would allow them to stand safely among the embers in a hearth. Most Anglo-Saxon pots, however, had flat bases, so they must have stood on level surfaces. While bread, which formed the basis of the Anglo-Saxon diet, could be made without an oven (by baking on a slab over a fire), clay ovens are known, with a ninth- or tenth-century example from Flixborough, and possible finds from North Elmham;[71] there is also an oven depicted in the Bayeux Tapestry.[72] These ovens were heated by a fire set inside them, which was then raked out before the loaves were inserted. Deposits of burned stones found on Anglo-Saxon settlements may represent 'pot boilers', heated stones placed in a wooden vat to boil large quantities of water for cooking or industrial processes. Fire-cracked stones and charcoal have been found in pits at Catholme and Nettleton Top, Lincolnshire,[73] which suggests roasting took place in a fire-pit, although they could have also been used to raise steam in a sweat-house.

Entrances and windows
The tradition of having two opposed doorways in the long walls would have allowed a door to be opened on the side away from the wind, avoiding the danger of the sudden draft causing the fire to blaze up into the thatch. Doorways were often flanked by large posts, suggesting that they were an important element of a building which provided an opportunity for decoration and display, but also presenting a formal entrance that seems to have been respected in Anglo-Saxon society. Evidence at Chalton suggests that the doors swung into the buildings,[74] which would have allowed them to be firmly secured with wooden bars. The latch-lifters found in the graves of early Anglo-Saxon women seem too large to have been used on a chest and might point to door locks.

Late Anglo-Saxon illustrations do not show roof louvers, which would have allowed the escape of smoke from the open hearths. It is possible that the smoke was vented through openings in the gable ends, but it may have been left to find its own way out under the eaves. This would have given smoky, but snug, conditions, which would probably have been acceptable if the wood being burned was fully dried. The Anglo-Saxons would have mainly burned light wood rather than the logs we use now on open fires, which are extravagant and difficult to cut without a heavy saw. Coppicing will produce a continuous supply of wood suitable for burning, which, if carefully stacked for twelve months, will burn well and cleanly.[75]

The use and (even the) existence of windows is an open question; 'fresh air' was an anathema until recent times. Windows survive from churches, for example, the seventh-century examples at Jarrow, Tyne and Wear, and practicalities would suggest that there was some method of letting light into buildings. Glass and lead window canes, from sites like Flixborough, where they were found in mid-ninth-century dump deposits, suggest that some higher-status Anglo-Saxon houses had glazed windows, but it is always possible that the glass, particularly that which was deeply coloured, could have come from a church.[76] For most buildings, wooden window shutters would have sufficed; the church at Boxford, Berkshire, retains an Anglo-Saxon oak window board in which was fitted an internal shutter.[77] Some of the many iron fittings found on settlement sites like Flixborough are likely to have been fittings from doors and windows, as are the objects found in a deposit at Bishopstone. It is possible that some of the metal-detector finds of iron fittings recorded by the Portable Antiquities Scheme from sites like Lea Green or from Asby Winderwath, Cumbria, represent domestic fittings.[78]

Storage

Little is known of how the Anglo-Saxons stored organic produce. Settlements, especially those of the early Anglo-Saxon period, are interpreted as small communities, little more than extended families. However, the resources needed to store enough produce to enable even an enlarged family group, let alone a small community and its livestock, to survive a winter are considerable. Many foodstuffs were preserved using salt, an important commodity throughout the medieval period, and also by drying and smoking. The large spaces in the roofs of Anglo-Saxon buildings offered valuable storage space. Smoke and rising heat will preserve foodstuffs, particularly meat, and suppress insect pests, which could infest and destroy clothing and bedding. Storage in the roof would have also provided protection from damp. 'Cellars', such as those found in York and London, could have been used to store foodstuffs which needed to remain cool, such as meat and dairy products. A large jar covered with a wet cloth can also act as a cool box.

Grain was of vital importance to the Anglo-Saxons, which makes the lack of evidence for barns and granaries surprising. It seems unlikely that *Grubenhäuser* were used as granaries. They are unlike the grain storage pits of the Iron Age, which are dug into well-drained chalk and not the sand and gravel on which *Grubenhäuser* are usually found. If the pit was planked over, the grain would still be at great risk from the scourge of rats, which would have used the pit as a route into the grain. It is notable that post settings interpreted as granaries are found on continental sites, alongside *Grubenhäuser*, suggesting that the latter had a different role,[79] and that some other method of storage must have been used in those areas of England where *Grubenhäuser* are not found. Perhaps the most likely explanation is that the grain was kept on the straw in stacks and only threshed when needed, although it is clear from late Anglo-Saxon calendar illustrations that threshing was a seasonal occupation.[80]

Water and drainage

Access to water, particularly in the large amounts required by livestock, was as important a consideration as the need to provide drainage. Run-off from roofs could destroy a building's foundations, and waterlogging makes a site unpleasant. Two middle Saxon buildings at Flixborough had drainage ditches or soakaways along one of their end walls.[81] At Coppergate timber-lined drainage channels (and those reusing Roman tile) in the basement floors of some buildings demonstrate the practicalities of dealing with surplus water.[82] In tenth-century York much organic waste was dumped into backyards, and there is biological evidence that this had impact on local fish stocks.[83] Also found in these backyards were pits, some lined with interwoven wattle or barrels, which may have served as wells: two baskets were found used as well liners at Odell, Bedfordshire.[84] One was made from osier (willow) rods and gave a radiocarbon date of AD 520 ± 40. Timber-lined wells found at Portchester were 4.3 metres deep (14 ft) and dated to the ninth century.

Furnishings

There is some evidence for early Anglo-Saxon furnishings. Clothing and small, valuable items would have been kept in the iron-fitted chests which were sometimes used as their owner's final resting place, as at Flixborough; the presence of hinges and hasps in graves allows them to be recognised as chests. There are examples from the seventh century of women being buried on beds,[85] the iron fittings of which survive. There is also some evidence for chairs; the lid of an urn from Spong Hill, Norfolk, bears the figure of a seated man,[86] and a folding chair was found in the aristocratic grave at Prittlewell, Essex.[87] It is not clear if these finds represent high-class 'special' objects or if furniture was in general use. Many societies manage without chairs by squatting or sitting on the ground. It is possible that the objects found around the sides of the Prittlewell pit-grave reflect the practice of hanging things from walls. Barrels and baskets are known from Anglo-Saxon England and would have been familiar objects in houses.[88] A warp-weighted loom is a large object and, if kept set up in the house, would have had a dominating presence. It is, however, clear from Marta Hoffmann's study of warp-weighted looms in modern Norway that, when not in use, they were probably dismantled and stored.[89]

Late Anglo-Saxon wills record house furnishings that the dead left to loved-ones and the Church. These include 'hangings', 'seat-covers, table-covers, bedcovers, and bed-curtains', as well as 'tents'.[90] Such wills do not give descriptions of said items, though Elizabeth Coatsworth has reasonably suggested that some furnishings bequeathed by 'wealthy testators were richly decorated'.[91] Typical examples include the will of Wynflæd, an aristocrat, in which she gives to Eadgifu 'two chests, and in them her best bed-curtain and a linen covering and all the bed-clothing that goes with it', as well as 'a long hall-tapestry and a short one and three seat coverings'.[92] Also of note is the will of Æthelgifu, who gives to her 'kinswoman Wulfwynn ... a wall-hanging and a seat-cover' and to Leofsige 'three wall-hangings and two seat-covers'.[93] It is clear then that some Anglo-Saxon houses were richly and colourfully decorated, though one suspects most lived in less splendid surroundings.

The archaeological evidence for furnishings in the late Anglo-Saxon period is less forthcoming. At well-preserved later sites, such as Coppergate, there is little evidence, though a number of iron keys and brackets, as well as other fittings, were discovered, suggesting the use of chests. Used primarily for storage, it would be assumed, they may have also doubled as tables or benches. Here it is also possible that lines of stakes by walls in some buildings were the remains of wattle-reveted wall benches. In *The Saga of the People of Vatnsdal*, the house of Jokul, the wayward son of Ingimund, earl of Gotland, is described in some detail. Within the hall of the house were 'huge chests', 'sacks of wares and goods of every kind' and a 'large bed ... with splendid curtaining'.[94] Of note is the fact that Thorestein (who illegally enters Jokul's house and kills him in his bed) did not need to enter by force. Perhaps, then, with the comings and goings in most houses, as well as the number of people who lived in them, only chests that contained valuables were locked and not always the doors to rooms or the house itself. That said, some houses must have been secured. Keys are known (see above), and the girdle-hangers found in the graves of Anglo-Saxon women clearly represent keys also. Padlocks are also found in some early Anglo-Saxon graves. A mortise lock was found at Bishopstone, and slide keys were recovered at Flixborough.[95]

It has already been noted that the lack of evidence for daub at London and York suggests that some houses were furnished with wall-hangings to keep out drafts, and also presumably for decoration. In *Beowulf* the great-hall of Heorot had 'gold-embroidered tapestries' that 'glowed from the walls', embellished 'with wonderful sights for every creature that cared to look at them'.[96] Likewise, Goscelin the Fleming describes how his hosts transformed a dwelling described as a 'pigsty [rather] than a dwelling place for me', by decorating 'the walls and ceilings ... with curtains and hangings'.[97] The evidence from wills, highlighted above, also supports his description. The most famous of wall-hangings to survive, though crafted at the end of the Anglo-Saxon period and probably not typical, is the Bayeux Tapestry. Another, perhaps similar, was that commemorating the exploits of Earl Byrhtnoth (made famous in the poem *The Battle of Maldon*), which was presented by the earl's widow to Ely Cathedral.[98] It is likely that the exteriors of houses were also decorated. Depictions of buildings on the Bayeux Tapestry suggest the use of non-structural elements like arcading. Warwick Rodwell has argued that the stonework on some Anglo-Saxon churches only makes sense if it formed part of a coloured scheme of decoration.[99]

Work spaces

With the exception of milling, potting and iron smelting, few of the processes carried out by the Anglo-Saxons would have needed special structures. Metal casting was being carried out in a tenth-century timber building at Faccombe Netherton, Hampshire, but, without the hearths, the function of the building would have been unknown.[100] It is clear from the finds from Coppergate that a wide range of craft activities could be carried out that leave few recognisable traces in the buildings. The frequent discovery of clay loom weights, sometimes in rows, suggests that they were from buildings used as weaving sheds; but in some instances the weights are as likely to have been deposited after such structures were abandoned and therefore may not relate to the building's use. Some support for the interpretation of *Grubenhäuser* as weaving sheds comes from the excavation of Icelandic *jarðhús*.[101] These semi-subterranean buildings are of ninth- to eleventh-century date and usually lack axial postholes, though they have been shown not to have been planked over and to have contained hearths. Analysis of residues in the deposits on their floors showed them to have been used in the working of wool. At Goltho, tenth-century buildings were interpreted as weaving sheds, although the evidence, based on finds, is not conclusive. While excavations at Flixborough produced much evidence for textile working, most of the finds came from dump layers and the fill of a ditch, making it impossible to define any one structure as a workshop.[102]

Law codes of the tenth century indicate that activities like cooking, storage and stabling were, by then, supposed to be carried out in separate buildings, not in the houses, although this was not always the case, and may have only applied to the upper levels of society.[103] Indeed, there is literary evidence, albeit not readily supported archaeologically, that some buildings were reserved as 'fire-rooms', which may make sense in some contexts, particularly regarding workshops and the drying of some foodstuffs. In *Egil's Saga*, for example, Bard, seeing that Egil and his men were 'drenched' after a sea-voyage, 'let them into a fire-room', which the saga says 'stood away from the other buildings', where 'he had a large fire made up for them to dry their clothes'.[104] Incidentally, it was here that Egil and his men were also served food (but not ale) and were expected to sleep, demonstrating the multiple use of some rooms at least. A similar scene is described in *Beowulf* where 'they [Hrothgar's men] cleared away the benches, and covered the floor with beds and bolsters' so men could rest.[105]

Kitchens were recorded at Goltho, where they were marked by an area of burnt debris and fragments of daub, presumably from ovens.[106] Sites on which these ancillary buildings have been found are all late and appear to have been of higher status; evidence is, however, generally lacking for lower status settlements of this date. Buildings with associated cesspits or latrines have been found on later Anglo-Saxon sites, particularly in towns, such as London and York, where human waste presented problems. It is apparent that some of the cesspits had posts which supported a seat, but no clear evidence of screening for privacy. Cesspits are also known from rural sites such as Catholme and Goltho, where the aim was not hygiene but the collection of a valuable resource. Cesspits have been recorded on higher-status ninth- and tenth-century settlements at Cheddar and North Elmham.

Although there was thus a clear role for specialist ancillary buildings, the multifunctional role of most domestic houses, even in the late Anglo-Saxon period, is little doubted. At Coppergate, for example, evidence was discovered in homes for a vast array of crafts, including bone and antler working, the manufacture of wooden cups (from which Coppergate – street of the cup-makers – gets its name) and leather and metal working. These towns were economically advanced. Excavations suggest that these buildings were the heart of the Anglo-Scandinavian town, which benefited from extensive trading networks with the known Viking world.

Conclusion

The Anglo-Saxon period spanned more than 600 years during which many changes took place, and these are reflected in the design of buildings – Le Corbusier's 'machines for living in'. These changes were dictated by developments in society, economy, climate and environment, as well as the materials and resources available to their builders. Changes in building techniques were not particularly radical, and those used in one period remained in use or adapted in another. Houses were places where people could perform their everyday activities – sleeping, cooking, craft activities – in an environment protected from the natural elements, the rain and winter snow. In essence they were functional structures, though some were clearly designed to fulfil the special needs and requirements of their owner.

The fifth century had seen a move away from the buildings used in Roman Britain, as society fragmented and the economy was unable to support complex building techniques. Some features of Romano-British buildings might have continued to be employed – Anglo-Saxon houses cannot be wholly traced back to the Germanic homelands. The early buildings are small and remarkably uniform, perhaps catering for the needs of 'settlers' in a time of stress and environmental challenge. As the period progresses, the appearance of large halls implies more complex social roles for some structures, although there still seems to have been a place for 'bowers' – small, snug cottages, representing single rooms.

Workshops are sometimes difficult to recognise as many crafts must have been carried out in domestic buildings. The development of towns during the Anglo-Saxon period brought its own problems of high density occupation with the need to dispose of waste and make maximum use of space, perhaps using buildings with more than one level.[107] A notable feature of Anglo-Saxon houses is their multiple use and interfunctionality, and the extent to which they might have been utilised by many people, extended families, even communities, in a way not normally practised today. They were therefore a product of their time, and suited that time, the Anglo-Saxon period.

Many challenges remain for the future. The Portable Antiquities Scheme has shown just how much evidence for the Anglo-Saxons there is in the landscape, but there is a need to put these stray finds into an archaeological context. How were Anglo-Saxon houses used and how did they vary, geographically and temporally? There are also the ever present 'unknown unknowns' to trouble our sleepless nights. More data is needed, but perhaps improved surveying techniques, in particular advances such as 'LiDAR', which allows whole landscapes to be searched, and ground-penetrating radar, which has the potential to examine buried features without the need for a costly excavation, will increase our knowledge and understanding of this most important aspect of Anglo-Saxon daily living.

4

Place and Power: Meetings between Kings in Early Anglo-Saxon England

Damian Tyler

> *Nam Inhrypis basilicam polito lapide a fundamentis in terra usque ad summum aedificatam, variis columnis et porticibus suffultam, in altum erexit et consummavit. Iam postea, perfecta domu, ad diem dicationis eius, invitatis regibus christianissimis et piissimis Ecgfritho et Aelwino, duobus fratribus, cum abbatibus praefectisque et sub-regulis, totiusque dignitatis personae*
>
> For in Ripon he built and completed from the foundations in the earth up to the roof, a church of dressed stone, supported by various columns and side aisles. Afterwards, when the building had been finished, he invited to the day of its dedication the two most Christian kings and brothers, Ecgfrith and Aelfwini, together with the abbots, the reeves and the sub-kings; dignitaries of every kind[1]

Introduction

This chapter considers face-to-face meetings between kings in Anglo-Saxon England in the seventh and eighth centuries. It examines the kinds of places where these meetings took place (the built environments of kingly meetings), some of the reasons for kings coming together and some of the outcomes of these royal meetings.

Britain in the seventh and eighth centuries was a land of many small kingdoms. Thus there was inherently more likelihood here of kings interacting directly than there was in contemporary continental Europe, with its large polities, and kings did indeed regularly have personal, face-to-face meetings in early Anglo-Saxon England. Though not uncommon, however, such royal meetings were highly charged events, redolent with the rituals, ceremonial, symbolism and hierarchies of status and power. They required suitable venues – places that could provide accommodation suitable for kings, and that were also large enough, and well-provisioned enough, to accommodate and feed the royal retinues, which would typically include family, councillors, priests, household warriors and servants, together with their baggage and horses.

The number of Anglo-Saxon kingdoms declined significantly during the seventh and eighth centuries. In the first half of the seventh century a minimalist interpretation might argue for ten or a dozen, while a maximalist vision might see more than thirty. By the late eighth century there were five, and the independence of one of these, Kent, was soon to end. It will be suggested that some of the kingly meetings discussed here reinforced a system of multiple, interlinked and hierarchically organised kingdoms. Others, it will be argued, give glimpses of the centralising tendencies at work in Anglo-Saxon England during this period.

The meeting at Ripon

The quotation with which this chapter opens concerns an event which took place at some time in the 670s, when Bishop Wilfrid dedicated the new church that was to be the focal point of his monastic estate at Ripon, nowadays in North Yorkshire, then part of the kingdom of the Deiri.[2] This was a major event in the Northumbrian socio-political calendar and the northern elites were very well-represented. As we have seen, Wilfrid's biographer states that in addition to the two Northumbrian kings the attendees included 'the abbots, the reeves and the sub-kings; dignitaries of every kind'.[3] Not only was the ceremony well-attended, it was also calculated to impress. The building itself would have seemed remarkable to most of those present. To the modern eye, accustomed to the great cathedrals of the central Middle Ages, early Anglo-Saxon basilicas appear extremely small and rather plain structures. This would not have been the case in the seventh century. The church, built of dressed, mortared stone, was, for the time and place, a highly exotic addition to the landscape.[4] In addition to the architectural splendours of the building, high-status luxury goods were conspicuously displayed:

> *altare quoque cum bassibus suis Domino dedicantes purpuraque auro texta induentes populique communicantes, omnia canonice*

compleverunt ... Nam quattuor evangelia de auro purissimo in membranis depurpuratis, coloratis, pro animae suae remedio scribere iussit: necnon et bibliothecam librorum eorum, omnem de auro purissimo et gemmis pretiosissimis fabrefactam, compaginare inclusores gemmarum praecepit

The altar also with its bases they dedicated to the Lord and vested it in purple woven with gold; the people shared in the work, and thus all was completed in a canonical manner ... For he [Wilfrid] had ordered, for the good of his soul, the four gospels to be written out in letters of purest gold on purpled parchment, and illuminated. He also ordered jewellers to construct for the books a case made of the purest gold and set with most precious gems.[5]

Furthermore it was made abundantly clear whose generosity had made possible this splendid new edifice:

Stans itaque sanctus Wilfrithus episcopus ante altare conversus ad populum, coram regibus enumerans regiones, quas ante reges pro animabus suis, et tunc in illa die cum consensu et subscriptione episcoporum et omnium principum illi dederunt, lucide enuntiavit necnon et ea loca sancta in diversis regionibus quae clerus Bryttannus, aciem gladii hostilis manu gentis nostrae fugiens, deseruit.

Then St Wilfrid the Bishop stood in front of the altar, and, turning to the people, in the presence of the kings, read out clearly a list of the lands which the kings, for the good of their souls, had previously, and on that very day as well, presented to him, with the agreement and over the signatures of the bishops and all of the chief men, and also a list of the consecrated places in various parts which the British clergy had deserted when fleeing the hostile sword wielded by the warriors of our nation.[6]

Finally, we should note that there was ample time for the attendant elites to note and discuss all this pomp, ceremony and royal patronage:

Deinde, consummato sermone, magnum convivium trium dierum et noctium reges, cum omni populo laetificantes, magnanimes in hostes, humiles cum servis Dei inierunt.

Then, when the sermon was over, the kings started upon a great feast lasting for three days and three nights, rejoicing amid all their people, showing magnanimity towards their enemies and humility towards the servants of God.[7]

Though the church was the focal point of the occasion, there were clearly other buildings nearby. These must have included a hall for the feast, with attendant kitchens, latrines and stables. Many of the attendees doubtless slept in the hall, as was customary, but there was also presumably separate accommodation for the kings, the bishop and the more senior of the guests.

This chapter commences with Stephen's account of the dedication of Ripon because it provides more circumstantial detail for a meeting place and a meeting between kings in seventh- or eighth-century Britain than can be found in any other near contemporary English text. The other kingly meetings that will be discussed are preserved in rather more terse accounts. Thus Stephen's testimony is of prime importance, as it shows very clearly the kinds of ceremonial and audience these occasions might involve, and the kinds of places where they might take place.

Meetings on campaign

One type of occasion where kings met was on campaign. Powerful kings were sometimes supported in their military actions by less powerful rulers and their war bands. Early medieval kingship was inherently itinerant – the court was a mobile institution. Kings and their retinues moved around the kingdom from one royal estate to another. Warfare, a fundamental aspect of early medieval kingship, was an extension of this. A king's army was a stripped-down version of his court, and the army of an over-king, including as it did his subject kings and their followers, was his hegemony in microcosm. Thus, while meetings on campaign may have been in some ways rather more *ad hoc* than the other types of meeting we shall examine, there would certainly have been ritual, hierarchy, rivalry and displays of status, both while the armies were in transit and on the battlefield itself. A campaign such as this was as much about the relationships between allies as it was about their relationship with their enemy. One example of this is the ill-fated expedition of 655 of Penda, king of the Mercians, which culminated in the disastrous (from a Mercian perspective) battle of Winwæd. In his *Historia Ecclesiastica* Bede states that on this campaign Penda was accompanied by thirty *duces regii*.[8] There is some debate about the exact status of these individuals, and not everyone would see them all as kings. Kings were certainly among them, however. Bede tells us that Penda's entourage included King Æthelhere of the East Angles,[9] and the

Historia Brittonum shows us that Welsh kings were present,[10] though it only names Cadafael of Gwynedd.[11]

Penda's son Wulfhere also campaigned in the north at the head of an army that included other kings. Stephen of Ripon writes that:

> *Nam Wlfharius, rex Merciorum, superbo animo et insatiabili corde omnes australes populos adversus regnum nostrum concitans, non tam ad bellandum quam ad redigendum sub tributo servili animo, non regente Deo, proponebat.*

> Now Wulfhere, King of the Mercians, proud of heart and insatiable in spirit, roused all the southern nations against our kingdom, intent not merely on fighting but on compelling them to pay tribute in a slavish spirit. But he was not guided by God.[12]

It is less than clear how frequently, or for how long, an over-king could demand military assistance. It is likely that the determining factors would be practicalities such as the relative strengths of the parties, the concurrence or divergence of political aims and the frequency with which an over-king made war. A belligerent king such as Penda may have made frequent demands on the kings subject to his *imperium*. By contrast, Æthelberht of Kent, who as far as we know fought few if any battles,[13] may well have required much less service. Nevertheless, the ability to utilise the warlike potential of other kings was vital to the power of an over-king; this was an age in which political supremacy normally depended on success in battle, so even an unusually pacific over-king such as Æthelberht would have needed to demonstrate a potential military pre-eminence.[14] By adding the war bands of other kings to their own, powerful kings were able to build up armies of a size which otherwise would have been beyond their means. Thus allied kings were conduits through which the military resources of their kingdoms could be channelled into the warlike activities of the over-king. The personal nature of this bond was all-important: it was an alliance between individuals in which direct contact would be crucial. Military campaigns organised in this manner served to enhance the power and status of over-kings, but required the existence of other kings.

Unfortunately, our sources neglect to tell us much that we should wish to know about Anglo-Saxon warfare, and so we are forced to speculate about the built environment of the battlefield. A king on the defensive, fighting in his own territory, would have been able to draw on his own estates and those of his subjects to provision his army.[15] Before active hostilities commenced – and if victorious after them as well – he could probably expect to sleep under a roof. Those operating far from home may have carried some supplies with them, but must also have been heavily reliant on what could be seized on the spot. Nor do we know what an army camp was like. Houses, even whole villages, may have been commandeered for accommodation, and there may well have been tents, but it is likely that many warriors, and most servants, often found themselves sleeping under the sky.

While battles could of course be fought in a variety of settings, engagements at or near river crossings were not unusual. Æthelfrith of Bernicia defeated his Welsh opponents beside the Dee at Chester at some time before 616; Æthelfrith himself was defeated and killed by Rædwald, king of the East Angles, at the River Idle in Northamptonshire in 616, Penda met his end at the hands of Oswiu of Bernicia beside the flooding River Winwæd, somewhere in the vicinity of Leeds, and Ælfwine, king of the Deiri and one of Wilfrid's guests at Ripon, was killed by Penda's son Æthelræd at the Trent in 679.[16] This preponderance of battles at or near river crossings is probably partly due to the logistics of communications. Large rivers could generally only be crossed at certain places, so one could be reasonably confident of intercepting one's opponent at such a site. Partly also, however, it would have been a strategic move. Defending a river crossing against an attacker was sensible military strategy.

Royal visits

When two kings campaigned together neither was on his home ground. Kings did not, however, only meet in warlike contexts. They also visited each other's kingdoms. These 'royal visits' required suitably regal venues, and such meetings took place at royal estates. From both literary and archaeological sources we know that the focal point of any high-status estate was the main feasting hall. Constructed of timber and roofed with thatch, these were large, open spaces, able to accommodate many people. The largest hall at the royal palace site at Yeavering, Northumberland (Building A4), for example, was approximately 24 metres (80 ft) long and almost 12 metres (40 ft) wide (Figure 4.1).[17] The life of a royal court revolved around the hall. In the Old English poem *Beowulf* we see Heorot, hall of King Hrothgar of the Danes, used for feasting, entertaining, greeting guests, making speeches, discussing policy and as sleeping quarters for the king's followers.[18]

Though the hall was the main focus of a royal palace, however, there were of course other buildings – stables, storehouses, workshops, kitchens and latrines. There were also small chambers that could be

Fig. 4.1 Great Hall (A4), Yeavering, Northumberland (drawn by Maggie Kneen).

used for private meetings and as sleeping quarters for the king and his principal guests. Literary evidence suggests that such private chambers were generally separate buildings. The *Anglo-Saxon Chronicle, sub anno* 755, describes the slaying of King Cynewulf of the West Saxons by his rival Cyneheard while he was visiting a woman, possibly his mistress, at Merton. Cynewulf was attacked while he was in a private chamber with his hostess, separated from his men who were in the main hall.[19] Similarly, in *Beowulf*, Hrothgar, when retiring to bed with Wealhtheow, his queen, left the hall for a private chamber, and such outbuildings also provided safe sleeping places for his retainers when the attacks of Grendel made sleeping in the hall suicidally dangerous.[20] It is possible, however, that private chambers sometimes were attached to the main hall. The hall at Cowdery's Down, near Basingstoke in Hampshire, appears to have had chambers attached to the gable ends.[21]

In many 'royal visits' we see an unequal relationship in which the guest king was in some sense a client of his host. In the *Historia Ecclesiastica* there are several references to kings attending the courts of more powerful rulers. At some time between 597 and 616 King Rædwald of the East Angles received Christian baptism at the court of Æthelberht of Kent, at that time the dominant king in southern England.[22] We are told that Sigeberht king of the East Saxons often visited Oswiu in Northumbria and that on one of these occasions (c.653) he also was baptised.[23] The Middle Anglian king/princeps Peada, son of Penda, also visited the court of Oswiu, receiving there both baptism and Oswiu's daughter as wife.[24] Similarly, the South Saxon king Æthelwalh was baptised at the court of a more powerful king, in this case Wulfhere of the Mercians, probably in the early 670s.[25] Bede only refers to these meetings incidentally. Thus the examples he provides all involve a royal conversion, but it is clear that these were the exceptions; Sigeberht, for example, often visited the court of Oswiu, but was baptised only once.

In Ireland, another land of many small-scale kingdoms, minor rulers were obliged to make periodic attendance at the courts of their overlords.[26] We cannot be sure that in England such visits were a formal requirement and even in Ireland the reality was probably rather more *ad hoc* than the highly schematised picture presented by the law codes. Despite this it is probable that these visits served similar purposes in both areas. The symbolic act of submission would enhance the standing of the superior king, yet it also acknowledged the regal status of the inferior by publicising their unequal but mutual obligations. Because this interaction happened away from the less powerful king's own kingdom, his status there was not seriously undermined.

We shall now turn our attention to the possible agendas of these 'royal visits'. As with the royal councils recently discussed by Simon Keynes, we have precious little to go on.[27] There would certainly have been feasting and drinking, the conspicuous consumption typical of high-status social gatherings in most times and places. The hall would of course be the venue for this kind of conviviality. Presumably, issues of policy, such as future warfare, would be discussed. Such things might be debated in the hall, but might also be deliberated in a private chamber. The results of these discussions would be announced in public speeches. These again would generally take place in the hall, but, uniquely so far as we know, at Yeavering there was a purpose-built, wedge-shaped, tiered structure (Building E) (Figure 4.2) that appears to have been intended for public pronouncements.[28]

If both kings were of the same religious persuasion (by no means always the case in seventh-century Britain) we can guess that there might be cult activities – sometimes, as we have seen, there might be a kingly baptism. A marriage might be arranged or solemnised, as we saw with Peada's visit to Oswiu.[29] It can be suggested that other activities took place also. Gift giving and other forms of patronage played an important role in socio-political networks, and Anglo-Saxon literature makes it clear that this was an integral feature of the aristocratic vision

Fig. 4.2
The 'Theatre',
Yeavering
(building E)
(drawn by
Maggie Kneen).

of kingship: in *Beowulf* gifts are presented in full view of everyone at court, paraded across the open floor of the hall. King Hrothgar, as reward for his killing the monster Grendel, presents Beowulf with a standard, mail shirt, helmet, sword and eight horses. Beowulf's followers receive lesser but still rich gifts. All this is done publicly, ceremonially, in the hall and before the assembled court.[30] We see at least one instance in the *Historia Ecclesiastica* of a king receiving patronage from another. When Æthelwalh, the king of the South Saxons, accepted baptism at the Mercian court, we are told that *in cuius signum adoptionis, duas illi provincias donavit, Vectam videlicet insulam et Meanuarorum provinciam* 'As a token of his adoption Wulfhere gave him two provinces, namely the Isle of Wight and the province of the Meonware'.[31] Similarly, in *Beowulf*, Hygelac, king of the Geats, presents his nephew Beowulf with a hall and an estate of 7,000 hides, and this is bestowed publically, in the king's hall, before his court.[32] This kind of patronage was probably unusual at a royal meeting, the norm more likely being gifts of high-status luxury items such as weapons, horses and items of jewellery, or exotic, foreign luxuries like the *camisia cum ornatura in auro una et lena Anciriana una* 'robe embroidered with gold and a garment from Ancyra' sent by Pope Boniface V to King Edwin of Northumbria.[33]

Today it is axiomatic that there is no such thing as a free lunch. In the early Middle Ages there was no such thing as a free gift. Gifts carried obligations – the acceptance of gifts from another king represented a public acknowledgement of his superiority.[34] Given the limitations of our sources, we cannot be sure that ritual gift giving between kings generally took place during face-to-face interaction. A powerful king would, however, naturally seek to maximise the benefit to himself of his own liberality; despite the rhetoric of 'heroic' poetry, early medieval rulers were not so rich that they could afford to throw away precious resources to little purpose, and the effect would be much more powerful if both men were present in a royal venue when a gift was made. If so, a public presentation such as Hrothgar makes to Beowulf would enhance the prestige of both giver and recipient.

If patronage was the glue binding elites and kings together, the ability to take tribute provided powerful kings with valuable additional wealth, which might then be strategically redistributed. In seventh-century Britain we see clear evidence that tribute payments were a fundamental part of political structures. Oswiu made the Picts and Scots tributary, for example,[35] and his son Ecgfrith took tribute from the Mercians.[36] While the latter example shows a people paying tribute after defeat in battle, it is probable that tribute was routinely collected by English over-kings from subordinate rulers. The enigmatic text known as the *Tribal Hidage* lists thirty-five peoples. While there is much debate as to its date and context, it is generally taken to be a tribute list, originating in Mercia or Northumbria during the seventh or eighth centuries.[37] Not even the most belligerent Anglo-Saxon kings made war on such a scale that they were able forcibly to wrest tribute from thirty-five other rulers:[38] most payments must have been made with consent, if not with enthusiasm.

As with gift giving, there is no direct evidence that tribute payment was typically made in the presence of both kings, but, again, it is unlikely that powerful kings would neglect this opportunity to make a potent statement of dominance. Here also a comparison with early medieval Ireland can usefully be made. In Ireland the rendering of tribute was the personal responsibility of the inferior king.[39] It would have been impracticable, if not impossible, for a king personally to oversee the collection of tribute from many different peoples: the subordinate king was almost certainly a necessary link. Thus tribute payments enhanced the standing of powerful kings, but simultaneously safeguarded and entrenched the position of tributary rulers.

The subordinate king would require a collection point for the assembling of the tribute – material goods such as weapons, jewellery, ornamented vessels and also animals on the hoof – to be presented to his overlord. The most logical location for this would be one of his own royal estates. Similarly, the recipient king would need a place to receive them, and, once again, the best place to do this would be at one of his principal residences, where his court, the tributary king and his retainers and visitors from other kingdoms could all witness the act.[40] The built environments chosen for kingly meetings could thus communicate political and strategic messages beyond the simple act of giving and receiving tribute.

The types of royal meetings examined thus far equate with a hegemonal style of over-kingship that depended on personal relationships. These relationships were frequently expressed in face-to-face interaction in public, ceremonial contexts. Hegemonal over-kingship had many advantages. It provided an over-king with enhanced status and resources. It gave weaker kings protection and a greater degree of security than they could provide for themselves. It certainly made demands on them but, because the unpalatable aspects of over-kingship occurred externally to their kingdoms, these demands did not seriously compromise their regal status at home. It was also a system with benefits for local elites. Multiple kingships meant that kings were easily accessible, an important consideration when advancement and patronage depended on personal contact with the king.

Hegemonal over-kingship thus had some self-limiting features. The over-king made no direct demands on the inhabitants of subject kingdoms, everything was channelled through the local king. Because of this lack of integration, hegemonies collapsed as quickly as they were built up. In the first half of the seventh century dominance in southern Britain passed from Kent to East Anglia, then to Northumbria, and from thence to Mercia.[41]

Hierarchical meetings

We shall now turn our attention to other types of kingly meetings. Unlike those previously discussed, these involved powerful kings visiting the kingdoms of weaker rulers. It will be argued that these meetings tended to break down mutually beneficial hegemonal systems and helped to facilitate a more expansionist form of kingship.

In the year 664 various Northumbrian notables, and a number from other kingdoms, met at the monastery at *Streanæshealh*. This, of course, was the famous Synod of Whitby.[42] It was at Whitby that the ties linking the young Northumbrian Church to the Columban *familia* of monasteries were severed and Northumbria moved decisively, if not at first entirely wholeheartedly, into the orbit of Rome. Of particular importance for our purposes, the attendees included the two Northumbrian kings, Oswiu, the senior ruler, and his son Alhfrith, king of Deira. Also present were Agilbert, erstwhile Bishop of the West Saxons and Cedd, Bishop of the East Saxons.

Streanæshealh had been founded by Oswiu,[43] and was ruled by Hild, a princess of the Deiran royal house and Oswiu's cousin on the maternal side. This, then, was a royal monastery. As the chosen venue for such an important meeting, it must, like a secular royal estate, have been spacious, luxurious and well-provisioned. The discussions may have taken place in the church, or perhaps in a large room such as the refectory, but there must have been sufficient living and sleeping quarters, of sufficiently high standard, for all of Hild's high status guests and their retinues.

Bede tells us that this meeting at *Streanæshealh* was called in order to adjudicate between the two methods of calculating the date of Easter then current in Northumbria: that followed by the Columban Church and that of Rome. Oswiu the king followed the former, while his wife Eanflæd, the daughter of Edwin, educated since infancy under the protection of her maternal relatives in staunchly Roman Kent, adhered to the latter. This divergence, Bede tells us, caused confusion within the royal household each Easter.[44] Stephen of Ripon omits the enchanting (if implausible) description of domestic turmoil provided by Bede, but agrees that the reason for the meeting was disagreement over the dating of the Easter festival.[45] Certainly the Easter question and the subsidiary matter of the correct form of tonsure appear to have been the chief matters under open debate, but, as both Henry Mayr-Harting and Nicholas Higham have observed, Oswiu and Eanflæd seem to have managed to keep their respective Easter feasts without difficulty for many years. There is no apparent reason why this situation should have changed in 664, and we should, they argue, seek deeper causes.[46] Both scholars maintain that Whitby should be interpreted in the context of a growing rift between Oswiu and Alhfrith, caused by the latter's beginning to favour the Roman Church.[47] As Alhfrith disappears from our sources after Whitby, very possibly as a result of the attack that Bede tells us he made on his father, they may well be right.[48] Oswiu, by contrast, after holding onto his kingship – often against the odds[49] – for twenty-eight years in the violent world of seventh-century Anglo-Saxon politics, died in 670, as far as we know of natural causes, at the age of almost sixty.[50] When one reflects on the ends of the majority of Northumbrian kings, this perhaps says more for his political acumen than anything else.

The background to this conference has been discussed at some length because it gives some suggestion of the tensions that may have been present during meetings between kings. The place of Whitby in the development of the Church in England has been recognised (and written about) since the early eighth century. It can be suggested that it was also important in the protracted process of breaking down Deiran particularism. The meeting took place in Deira, Alhfrith's kingdom, yet it was with Oswiu that the powers of adjudication lay. Furthermore, a significant section of the northern elite was there to witness Oswiu's display of power. Stephen of Ripon informs us that those attending included *abbates et presbyteri omnesque ecclesiasticae disciplinae gradus*, 'the abbots and priests and men of all ranks in the orders of the Church'.[51] Bede also stresses the clerical presence,[52] but it is likely that there was also a large turnout of the lay elite. The retinues of both kings would be in attendance and important Church occasions in Northumbria typically had a large lay presence.[53] Thus there probably would have been many Deiran nobles present, and the lesson regarding the location of power would not have been lost on them. The fact that the meeting took place at *Streanæshealh*, founded by Oswiu and ruled by Hild, his elderly cousin and ally, rather than at Alhfrith's foundation of Ripon,[54] would have further underlined the message.

It is true that Whitby was very much of a 'one off', but it gives an indication of the kinds of ways in which powerful English kings were able to take advantage of the new religion and its built environment to extend their powers at the expense of other rulers. We shall now consider another type of kingly meeting, and this type of interaction was rather more common. We see in early Christian England a partnership between powerful kings and the Church. This partnership and the kinds of royal meetings and meeting places it facilitated are observable from the earliest days of English Christianity. The Augustinian mission was consciously targeted at Æthelberht of Kent. Bede tells us that because of his fear of magic King Æthelberht insisted that his first meeting with Augustine and his followers took place in the open air, on Thanet, but he soon brought them to his chief royal centre at Canterbury, where he gave them a residence, provisions and permission to preach their creed.[55] As their first church the missionary used the Roman-built church of St Martin, east of Canterbury. After the king had received baptism – the rite presumably performed in St Martin's – they were given permission to restore other derelict churches and to build new ones.[56]

It was not long before Æthelberht was using his new cult for the purposes of practical politics. In 604 he built a church, dedicated to St Paul, at London, and installed Mellitus as bishop there.[57] London was at that time part of the East Saxon kingdom ruled by Sæberht, Æthelberht's nephew and client,[58] and it is likely that both kings and their retinues were present at the dedication of Mellitus' church. Sæberht was already in a dependent relationship to his uncle, but this clear exercising of local patronage by the over-king would have undermined his position. When local elites came to depend on the patronage of an over-king, the positions of local kings were compromised.

We shall now return to Bishop Wilfrid and his new church at Ripon.[59] The dedication of this building was calculated to impress on the minds of the Northumbrian elite, Wilfrid included, the importance of gaining kingly favour. Royal powers of patronage were unambiguously stressed and this was done in a public, ceremonial, mystical context; we should not forget that Christianity in its Roman form was still a fairly new and exotic cult in the Northumbria of the 670s. The effect this of three-day-long gathering was to state that Ecgfrith and Ælfwine were kings worth following, but it is likely that the former king would have benefited more than the latter. Ripon was in Ælfwine's Deiran kingdom, yet the role of Ecgfrith as patron was clear for all to see. In Stephen's account Ecgfrith is named first, and if the charters[60] survived we should probably find his name before that of his brother. Thus the Deiran elites were being shown, as they had been at Whitby a decade or so earlier, that the over-king had direct powers of intervention which could impact on their lives, and needed to be courted. The standing of Ælfwine in his own kingdom was thus subtly undermined.

Having such a detailed description of the dedication of Ripon enables us to conceptualise the likely contexts of other donations to the Church. Stephen's account is unique in the detail of its content, but the events it describes were not uncommon, and records of hundreds of such grants survive in Anglo-Saxon charters. By examining these it is possible to see in action the strategies used by powerful kings to undermine the status of lesser rulers. One of these strategies was the insistence on the right to confirm, and by implication therefore to deny, the grants of less powerful kings. This process, as has long been recognised, is most clearly illustrated in the extant series of Hwiccan charters.[61] It has often been suggested that the Hwiccan dynasty were not indigenous to that province and had been imposed by Mercian rulers.[62] The same can be said of the ephemeral King Frithuwold of Surrey, whose grant of lands to Chertsey Abbey was confirmed by Wulfhere of Mercia.[63] It could be argued that kingdoms such as these were atypical, and that from the first Mercian kings exercised powers of patronage in these areas. Similar processes are observable, however, in kingdoms whose original independence is well-attested, and which retained indigenous kings well into the eighth century. Perhaps the best example of these latter is Kent.[64] In the seventh century kings of Kent issued charters without reference to anyone else.[65] By the middle decades of the eighth century Kent was well on the way to becoming a Mercian satellite. In 764 Offa, king of the Mercians, while in Canterbury, since time out of mind the chief seat of the kings of Kent, granted (for a sum of money) lands adjacent to the River Medway to Bishop Eardwulf of Rochester,[66] and the following year Eardwulf sought Offa's confirmation of a grant made by King Ecgberht II of Kent.[67] This is not to imply that when two kings were involved in a grant the donation was always made in the presence of both men. Demonstrably this sometimes was not the case. The witness list of Ecgberht's charter to Eardwulf makes it clear that Offa was at Peterborough when he gave his consent.[68] We know, however, that both Northumbrian kings were present at Ripon, and the diploma recording Offa's grant of 764 is witnessed by a Kentish king named Hæberht, and it seems probable that this individual was present in Canterbury when the grant was made.[69] Power to control the landscape thus communicated the status of kings, relative to one another.

Conclusion

In seventh- and eighth-century England kings frequently interacted in direct, face-to-face, public contexts. Though surviving records of these meetings are in the main extremely laconic we can with some confidence postulate that they were highly charged ceremonial occasions redolent with the symbolism of status, power and hierarchy, most of it evident in the built environment of such meetings. Some of these kingly meetings seem to have reinforced hierarchic yet mutually beneficial systems of over-kingship. Others tended to undermine these systems. These destabilising meetings frequently had an ecclesiastical aspect, and from the beginnings of English Christianity powerful kings were using the new religion and its spaces as tools of centralisation, often in the context of direct, personal interaction with other kings. In these meetings the dominant king intruded – physically, psychologically and symbolically – into the space of the less powerful ruler. The Church was in this context a subversive force. It is tempting, but probably unwise, to see these meetings as 'new', and the types discussed earlier in this chapter as 'traditional'. English kingship was, in the seventh century, a young and dynamic institution. It is likely that there had never been a stable situation.

This chapter closes with a brief look at a meeting between two seventh-century English kings that fits neither of the scenarios outlined above.[70] In the 630s or very early 640s the Northumbrian king Oswald was present at the court of King Cynegisl of the West Saxons. It is likely that Cyengisl's palace was near to Dorchester-on-Thames, the episcopal see of the missionary Birinus, a major actor in this royal performance. During Oswald's stay the missionary Birinus baptised Cynegisl. Oswald acted as his godfather, a position usually implying superiority. Oswald also, however, married Cynegisl's daughter.[71] Thus, symbolically, each became the father of the other in a carefully balanced expression of status. Such a religiously and politically charged meeting and its attendant ceremonies would have required a grand environment that reflected the royal and spiritual importance of the occasion, presumably one of Cynegisl's royal estates. As Birinus was given Dorchester-on-Thames as his seat, it is likely that Cyengisl's palace was near to this centre. The spaces in which such kingly meetings took place served to emphasise power structures and relationships – between king and king, and king and Church. Kingly power was thus negotiated with some finesse among the multiple kingdoms of the early period, in part through the manipulation of exchanges and the built environment of kingly meetings.

5

The Cuckoo and the Magpie: The Building Culture of the Anglo-Saxon Church

*Michael Shapland**

> I have decided after long deliberation about the English people ... that the idol temples of that race should by no means be destroyed, but only the idols in them. Take holy water and sprinkle it in these shrines, build altars and place relics in them. For if the shrines are well built, it is essential that they be changed from the worship of devils to the service of the true God.
>
> Pope Gregory to Mellitus, archbishop of Canterbury, AD 601[1]

Introduction

Christianity lacks architecture of its own. For its first three centuries of existence it had no dedicated buildings, as Christians met in private houses: the original meaning of *ecclesia* is simply 'congregation'. Under Constantine, the Church adopted the religious, civic and imperial architecture of the Roman Empire. As Christianity spread through Anglo-Saxon society this process of appropriation and adaptation continued, and was never far from the practice of secular life. Churches could be Roman basilicas of reused brick or Germanic halls of timber;

---

* The author would like to thank John Blair for this chapter's inception; Andrew Reynolds for his continued support; David Stocker, Meg Boulton and Duncan Wright for commenting on earlier drafts of this chapter; Richard Gem and Jill Atherton for the use of their drawing for Figure 5.1; Howard Williams for his kind permission to use the photograph in Figure 5.6; David Baker for his to use the photograph in Figure 5.7; and the editors of this volume for their invaluable guidance throughout.

they could be converted from pagan temples or laid out by kings in imitation of Charlemagne's imperial church in Aachen. Architectural elements such as naves,[2] towers and mausolea were constructed to different iconographic schemes or practical requirements, and could be sheathed in metal, plaster or carved stone. This chapter will draw upon archaeological, architectural and literary evidence to trace the influences and social practices underpinning the different forms of Anglo-Saxon church building – and the materials used in their construction – much of which would have been familiar to ordinary Anglo-Saxons as part of their experience of daily life.

There have been numerous attempts over the past century to identify standing structures from the Anglo-Saxon period.[3] Churches represent a unique and extremely valuable opportunity to experience standing Anglo-Saxon buildings, in contrast to many other secular types of buildings, for which we must rely on excavated plans and reconstructions. Several hundred Anglo-Saxon churches and fragments of churches survive above ground across England, ranging in date from the reputedly Roman chapel of St Martin in Canterbury, reused in the 590s by the Kentish royal house,[4] to the many 'overlap' churches from the decades either side of the Conquest which demonstrate the survival of Anglo-Saxon construction after 1066.[5] This material has been extensively catalogued and described over the past century,[6] and individual sites have benefited from detailed architectural and archaeological study;[7] Anglo-Saxon churches are also particularly well-represented in contemporary written sources, not least because of the ecclesiastical bias of surviving documents from the period.[8]

Given the unique opportunity presented by churches to our understanding of the Anglo-Saxon built environment the intention here is not to rehearse this considerable body of scholarship, which has been recently and ably synthesised elsewhere.[9] Instead, the aim is to explore the ways in which aspects of Anglo-Saxon church building articulated with the practice of daily living and the buildings of secular life. Churches were constructed from timber, stone, brick and metal, materials which embodied meanings far beyond their practical properties. We should also not think of a 'church' in this period as a coherent building class – as a variety of naves and chancels – but one encompassing crypts, towers, gatehouses, baptisteries and mausolea, all of which drew their form and symbolism from the buildings on which they were based, or from which they had been adapted. Christianity has no innate architecture except that which it has borrowed from pre-existing European practice, or has appropriated, cuckoo- or magpie-like, from a society's own buildings of power.

Appropriation and adaptation: the origins of Christian architecture

For its first three centuries of existence, Christian worship was practised in domestic contexts. The Church was simply its congregation, and its buildings were merely convenient spaces in which to meet.[10] Some of these 'house-churches' were adapted to their function; the dining room may have been enlarged as the formal meal developed into the Eucharist and a baptismal pool was sometimes provided, but a convenient tub or neighbouring bath-house were thought perfectly suitable.[11] A later development was the 'hall-church', built to house growing congregations for the Eucharist, which a mid-third-century source records as 'imitating the construction of temples'.[12] Nevertheless, there is no sense that buildings of Christian worship were holy, because that would be idolatrous.[13] This is an important point: as a codified, hierarchical religion, Christianity held obvious attractions for the Roman imperial system, and as a religion lacking dedicated building-forms and significant material culture, it provided a blank canvas upon which the emperor could impose his will.

Under the first Christian emperor Constantine I (306–337), the architecture, dress, imagery, ceremony and liturgy of the Church assumed imperial forms.[14] The Church associated Constantine with Christ himself, and blessed his empire as a reflection of heaven on earth, with Rome, at its centre, replicating the City of God.[15] The basilica was chosen to house the new religion, based on the standard public architecture of Roman civic halls and royal palaces. Any link with the existing house-churches and hall-churches was severed.[16] Every Roman town had a basilica, the building of popular assembly and the imperial cult, the shrine of which was usually contained within the basilica's apse.[17] This basilican model is evident in the spatial grammar of subsequent churches, where the nave hosts the public congregation and the eastern sanctuary is reserved as the focus of worship. Constantine and his successors also drew upon the architecture of centrally planned, often domed, imperial audience-chambers and tombs for great funerary and imperial churches such as the Holy Sepulchre in Jerusalem (mid-fourth century) and the Golden Octagon of Antioch (c.327).[18] Both the basilica and the centrally planned church form the basis of European Christian architecture and demonstrate the meaningful adoption of the existing architectural language by the *parvenu* religion. Christianity ceased copying temples and became fashioned after the Roman Imperial Cult.

The origins of Anglo-Saxon churches: British and Roman

There were two principal strands of Christian influence over the first centuries of Anglo-Saxon Christianity, the 'Roman' and the 'British', each of which had a different suite of ecclesiastical building techniques. The traditional place to begin is with the conversion of King Æthelberht of Kent (c.560–616) to Christianity in 597 as a result of St Augustine's mission from Pope Gregory the Great, which precipitated a century during which England's other kingdoms also became at least nominally Christian. These events are comparatively well-represented in surviving documentary sources, notably Bede's *Ecclesiastical History of the English People* (completed 731), but they obscure the fact that the 'native' Britons had already been converted to Christianity during the Roman occupation.

The earliest recorded Anglo-Saxon church is that of St Martin in Canterbury, which narrowly pre-dates the 'Roman' mission of 597. In the early 590s King Æthelberht married a Frankish Christian princess and repaired the reputedly Roman church of St Martin in the royal capital of Canterbury for her use.[19] Remarkably, parts of this church still stand: its chancel is built of Roman brick, and its later nave is of reused Roman stone and brick, laid in the Roman manner.[20] The dating of these phases is uncertain, but the use of Roman materials and construction methods on this ostensibly Roman building prefigures the profoundly Roman nature of the churches of the Augustinian mission and its aftermath.[21]

The churches from this 'Conversion Period' were essentially Mediterranean in form and construction, and many reused Roman sites and buildings as part of a deliberate policy of appropriating the Roman past (Figure 5.1).[22] They manifest the desire of successive Anglo-Saxon kings to associate their rule with the legitimacy and authority of the Roman Empire and its successor organisation, the Church.[23] Bede records that King Ecgfrith of Northumbria (670–685) brought masons and glaziers from Gaul to build churches literally 'in the manner of the Romans' (*more Romanum*):[24] the basilica at Lydd (Kent) so resembles the excavated third-century church in Silchester that it is uncertain whether it was constructed by the Anglo-Saxons or the Romans.[25]

There is substantially less information about British churches, and none now survives above ground.[26] Although they theoretically represent an unbroken link from the Romano-British churches of the fourth century, the available evidence suggests that by the Christian Anglo-Saxon period they resembled neither their third-century exemplars[27] nor the Roman churches of the Anglo-Saxon conversion.[28] This is well-illustrated by the complex sequence of churches at St Paul in the Bail, in the Roman forum

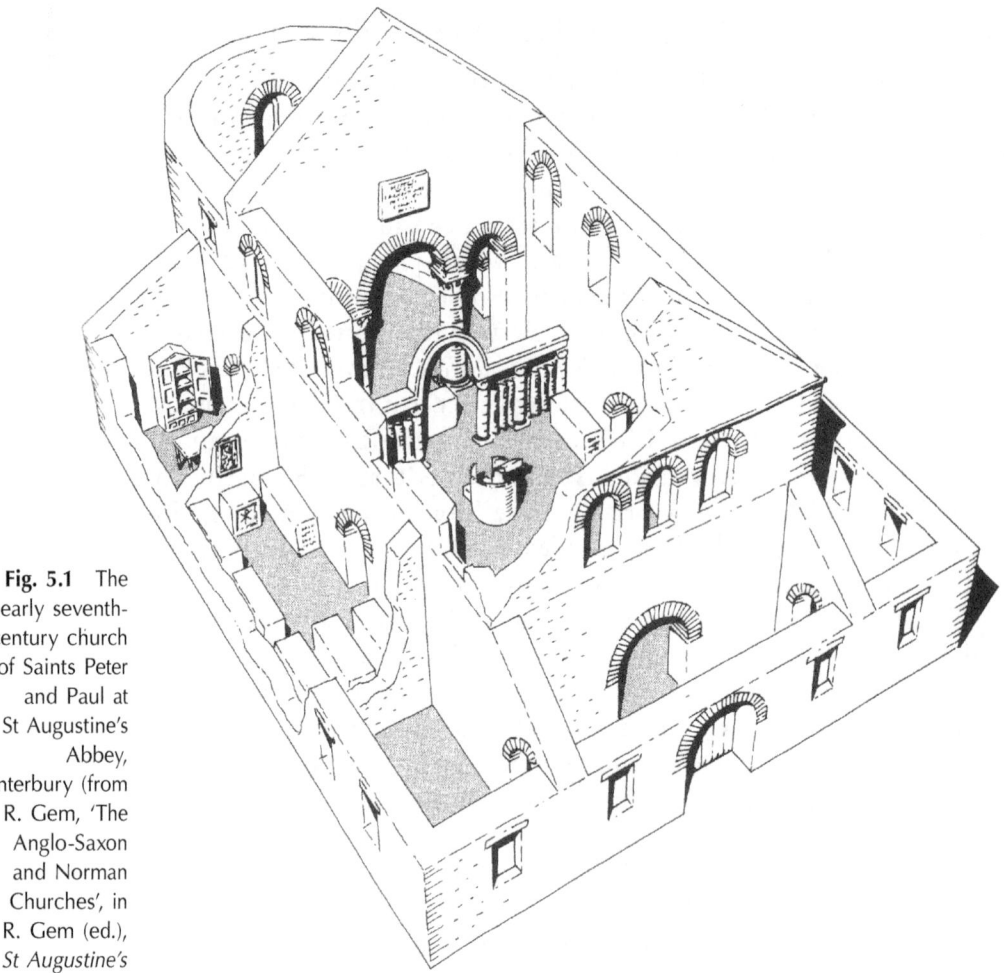

Fig. 5.1 The early seventh-century church of Saints Peter and Paul at St Augustine's Abbey, Canterbury (from R. Gem, 'The Anglo-Saxon and Norman Churches', in R. Gem (ed.), *St Augustine's Abbey, Canterbury* (London: B.T. Batsford, 1997), p. 99). Note its masonry construction, basilican form and the tomb chambers in the *porticus* either side of the central nave (reproduced with kind permission of Jill Atherton and Richard Gem).

at Lincoln, where the first church was a masonry structure of probable late fourth- or fifth-century date. It was replaced by a second, quite different, apsidal church of timber construction on the same site and orientation, radiocarbon dated to the fifth or earlier sixth centuries through burials associated with it.[29] The British community at Glastonbury was characterised by timber buildings from the fifth to the seventh centuries: in the late seventh century, the West Saxon King Ine (688–726) incorporated the timber-built *vetusta ecclesia* ('Old Church') of St Mary into his refounded abbey.[30] To these few examples can be added churches in the former British kingdoms of Bernicia, which had its cult centre on the Holy Isle of Lindisfarne, and Deira, which was centred on York. Although Bernicia and Deira were ruled by Anglo-Saxon kings from the later sixth century, they retained a considerable degree of their British identity,[31]

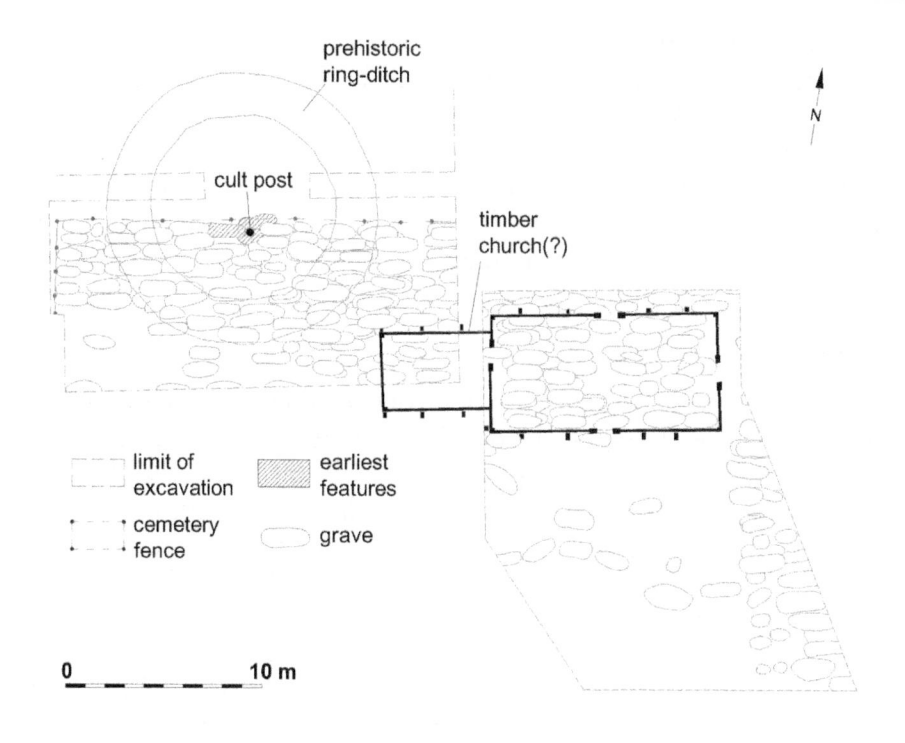

Fig. 5.2 The excavated putative seventh-century timber church and cemetery on an existing cult focus at the royal Bernician site at Yeavering (drawn by author) (from B. Hope-Taylor, *Yeavering: An Anglo-British Centre of Early Northumbria* (London: HMSO, 1977)).

and their conversion too was strongly influenced by existing strands of Christianity in Britain and Ireland. There is a persistent tradition that Edwin, the first Christian king of Northumbria (d. 633), was baptised not by Paulinus of the Roman mission but Rhunn, son of King Urien of the British kingdom of Rheged.[32] Ireland had been converted by the Romano-British missionary Patrick in the fifth century, and early saints such as Ninian personify the powerful links between Ireland and the post-Roman kingdoms of Britain. Edwin's successors Oswald of Bernicia (634–642) and his brother Oswiu (642–670) were converted to Christianity during their exile among the Irish following the battle of the Idle in 616. On their return c.634 they reintroduced Christianity to Northumbria, accompanied by the Irish bishop Aidan, who established his see at Lindisfarne and built there a timber church. His companion and successor Finan rebuilt it 'after the Irish method, not of stone but of hewn oak, thatching it with reeds'.[33] Aidan also constructed a timber church adjacent to the Bernician royal centre of Bamburgh,[34] and his monastery at Melrose established a daughter-house at Ripon (Deira) with a timber church soon after.[35] The first church of the important Deiran royal house at Whitby (founded c.657) may also have been of timber.[36] Finally, a suggested timber church attributed to King Oswald has been excavated at the Bernician royal centre of Yeavering (Figure 5.2).[37]

The striking thing about these churches is their timber construction, in contrast to the brick and stone which characterised the Roman churches of the Augustinian mission and its aftermath. Bede described St Ninian's stone church at Whithorn as 'a method unusual among the Britons', explaining that Ninian had been instructed in Rome.[38] In this way, the founding strands of Christianity in England were intimately related to the materials used in their construction.

Timber

Although timber churches were not uncommon on the Continent during the early medieval period, the decision to build in timber in seventh-century England was a deeply political act involving the decision whether to align the English church with the Roman mission or with existing British, Welsh and Irish traditions.[39] This conflict culminated in the victory of the Roman faction at the Synod of Whitby in 664. Such fierce controversy over the correct shape of the tonsure and the date of Easter seems petty to the modern mind, but these are merely the visible tip of profound and deeply rooted questions of identity and religious appropriation. The Irish tonsure is thought to originate with the pagan cult leaders – 'druids' – of the pre-Roman Iron Age,[40] and the Christian festival of Christ's passion and resurrection was named after the pagan goddess *Eostre* whose cult centred on the rebirth of life heralded by the Spring equinox.[41] The question of whether to sever conceptually these ancient British and Irish links in favour of direction from Rome was a heavy one; Bede and other early ecclesiastics characterised the construction of timber churches as *morem Scottorum*, 'after the Irish method',[42] in contrast to churches built of stone 'in the Roman manner'.[43] Finan's church of hewn oak, Aidan's timber chapel at Bamburgh and the timber church which apparently succeeded the putative pagan temple at the Northumbrian palace at Yeavering (Figure 5.2) can be seen as statements of insular identity which drew upon the British tradition of timber church construction, for which only the most meagre evidence survives.

Brick and stone

The Anglo-Saxon Church was established following the Roman mission of 597, and this Roman affiliation was decisively reaffirmed at Whitby in 664. On both occasions religion was expressed through architecture. Although churches would continue to be constructed of timber in the later seventh and eighth centuries, the overwhelming direction would be towards churches of brick and stone executed in the Roman fashion. Existing timber churches were prominently rebuilt in stone, such as at Ripon in the year after the synod, where the church was also rededicated by Bishop Wilfrid – the leader of the Roman cause – according to Roman liturgy and practice.[44] The same year, Wilfred had the cathedral in York rebuilt in stone.[45] At Hartlepool, founded by Aidan of Lindisfarne in 640, five timber buildings in the abbey complex were partially rebuilt in stone during the eighth century, and there is evidence that the church was plastered and painted to resemble masonry. This has been interpreted as an attempt by the increasingly impoverished house to conform to the new Roman consensus.[46] The transition from timber to stone after the Synod of Whitby is also visible in newly built churches. At Escomb (County Durham) (Figure 5.3), the late seventh-century church was constructed of reused Roman stone, but its proportions are that of the putative timber church at Yeavering (Figure 5.2). It was therefore 'a bridge between two very different traditions'.[47]

Stone churches built in the Roman manner characterised the remaining three centuries of Anglo-Saxon architecture, but the construction of timber churches continued at the local level. From the tenth century onwards the great estates of mid-Saxon monasteries were fragmented into

Fig. 5.3 The late seventh-century church at Escomb (County Durham), viewed from the south-east (from G. Baldwin Brown, *The Arts in Early England: Anglo-Saxon Architecture*, 2nd edn (London: John Murray, 1925), p. 111).

what would become local parishes, largely as a result of lordly agency. This was due to the growth in ownership of private estates, and the construction of private churches to minister to them.[48] Excavation and limited documentary evidence have revealed modest timber predecessors beneath many of these churches, indicating that they have been rebuilt in stone.[49] Around the year 1000 alternative provisions were made in the dedication liturgy for anointing of the exterior of timber and stone churches,[50] and a 'great rebuilding' of these churches in stone has been argued for the eleventh century.[51] This was enabled – or instigated – by the development of freestone quarrying in England for the first time since the Roman period.[52]

It is difficult to imagine the impact that these modest stone churches must have had as they spread across the English landscape. Until the tenth century almost the only stone buildings in existence would have been the still-prominent remains of the Roman occupation and a relatively modest number of cathedrals and monasteries: the Anglo-Saxons had no tradition of stone construction outside of these limited contexts, despite their mastery of the art. Recent research has emphasised quite how rigid this distinction was between building in timber, which encompassed nearly all known secular buildings, and building in stone, which was almost exclusively confined to ecclesiastical structures.[53] There is persuasive literary and archaeological evidence that the Anglo-Saxons perceived stone as the material not just of Rome and the Roman Church but as the material of permanence, as opposed to timber, which was the perishable material of the cyclical natural world and transient human life. The only proper context for stone was in God's house, and it would have been impertinent to imply earthly permanence in one's secular buildings, since only the human soul was eternal.[54]

The attraction of stone buildings for Anglo-Saxon lords was nevertheless considerable. The tenth and eleventh centuries were characterised by the rise of the local aristocracy and the division of the landscape into private estates, and given the comparatively fluid nature of aristocratic status at this time families may only have held their position for a generation.[55] The construction of prominent stone churches would have lent them legitimacy by implying, or manufacturing, the permanence of their position and land tenure.[56]

The curation of church fabric

The Anglo-Saxons used architecture to give material expression to the power of the past not only through the construction of new stone churches, but also by curating old churches of both stone and timber.

One of the dramatic differences between Anglo-Saxon and Norman church-building lies in the attitude towards old buildings. The Normans constructed vast and architecturally coherent cathedrals and great monastic churches in England during the eleventh and twelfth centuries, arguably beginning with Westminster Abbey in the reign of Edward the Confessor (1042–66). The Norman desire was for order and clarity:

> He destroys well who builds something better ... I would not allow buildings however much esteemed to stand unless they were, according to my idea, glorious, magnificent, lofty and spacious, filled with light and altogether beautiful. (Goscelin of St Bertin, writing in Canterbury, c.1090)[57]

For this reason, no pre-Conquest cathedral or greater monastic church now survives above ground.[58] The Anglo-Saxons, on the other hand, valued old buildings as embodiments of the past made potent by the accumulated lives of those who had worshipped and been buried within, and by the authority and history of the English Church.[59] Writing in the early twelfth century, William of Malmesbury recorded the rebuilding of Worcester Cathedral in the 1090s at the end of the tenure of Wulfstan, England's last remaining Anglo-Saxon bishop:

> The word was given for the old church, the work of St Oswald, to be stripped of its roof and demolished. Wulfstan stood there in the open air to watch, and could not keep back his tears. His friends mildly reproved him ... He replied: My view is quite different. We unfortunates are destroying the works of saints in order to win praise for ourselves.[60]

At St Augustine's Abbey in Canterbury, Abbot Wulfric (1047–59) demolished part of the early seventh-century churches of Saints Peter and Paul and St Mary to make way for a rotunda, which was abandoned uncompleted in 1061. Writing in 1097, a monk staying at the abbey attributed its failure to the anger of the Virgin Mary at the partial destruction of her church.[61]

Anglo-Saxon monastic sites were rarely replanned or rebuilt, but expanded organically through time.[62] This preference for incremental expansion can be related to Gregory the Great's original exhortation to retain rather than demolish the cult buildings of the early Anglo-Saxons.[63] The great monastic sites of Canterbury, Winchester and Glastonbury are excellent examples of the aggregation of several early churches into a coherent cult centre. At Canterbury, the early to mid-seventh-century

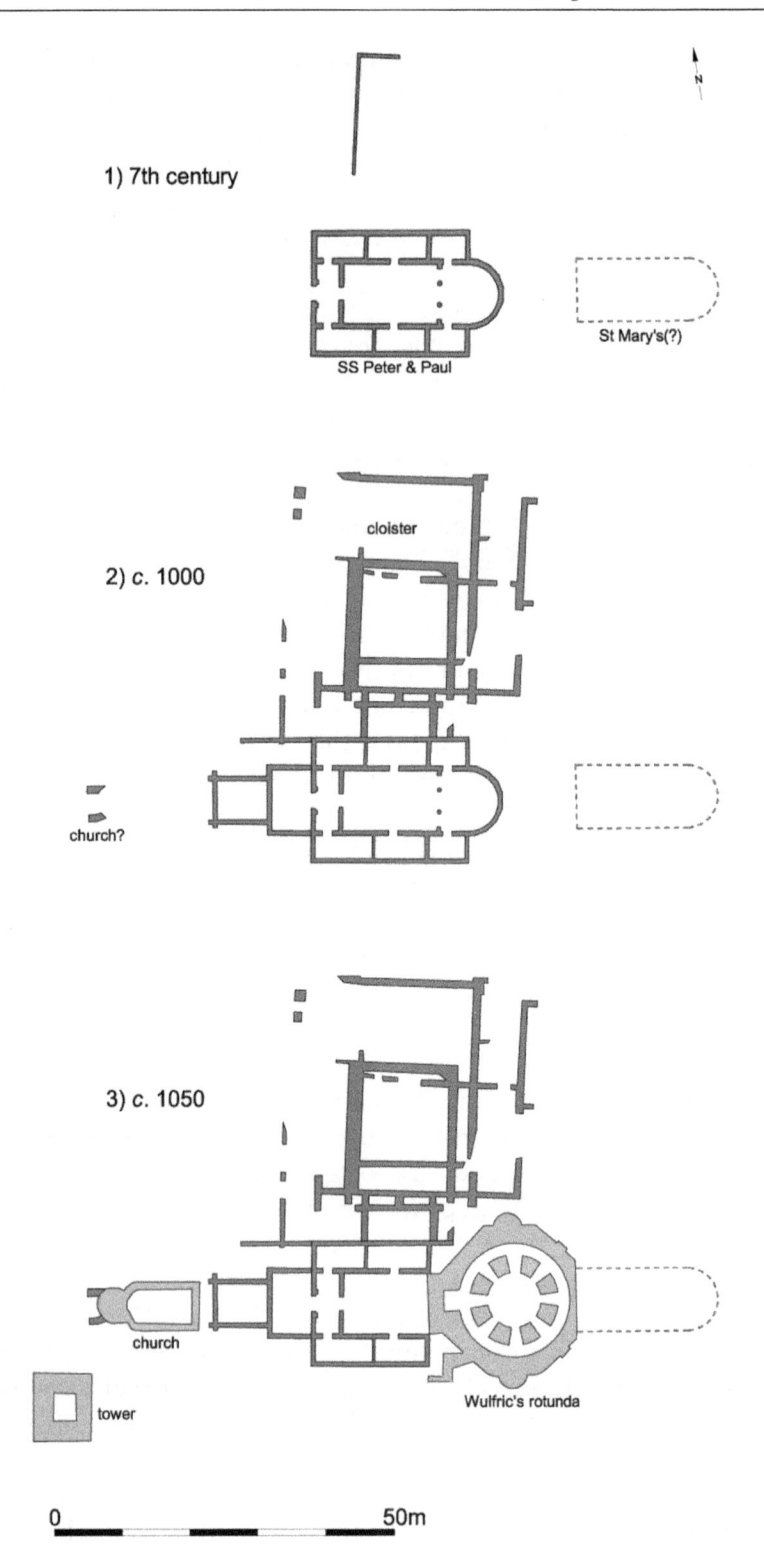

Fig. 5.4 The slow development of two great Anglo-Saxon monastic churches.

5.4a St Augustine's Abbey, Canterbury (drawn by author, simplified from R. Gem, 'The Anglo-Saxon and Norman Churches', in R. Gem (ed.), *St Augustine's Abbey, Canterbury* (London: B.T. Batsford, 1997), 90–122).

1) 7th century

SS Peter & Paul

St Mary's(?)

2) c. 1000

cloister

church?

3) c. 1050

church

tower

Wulfric's rotunda

0   50m

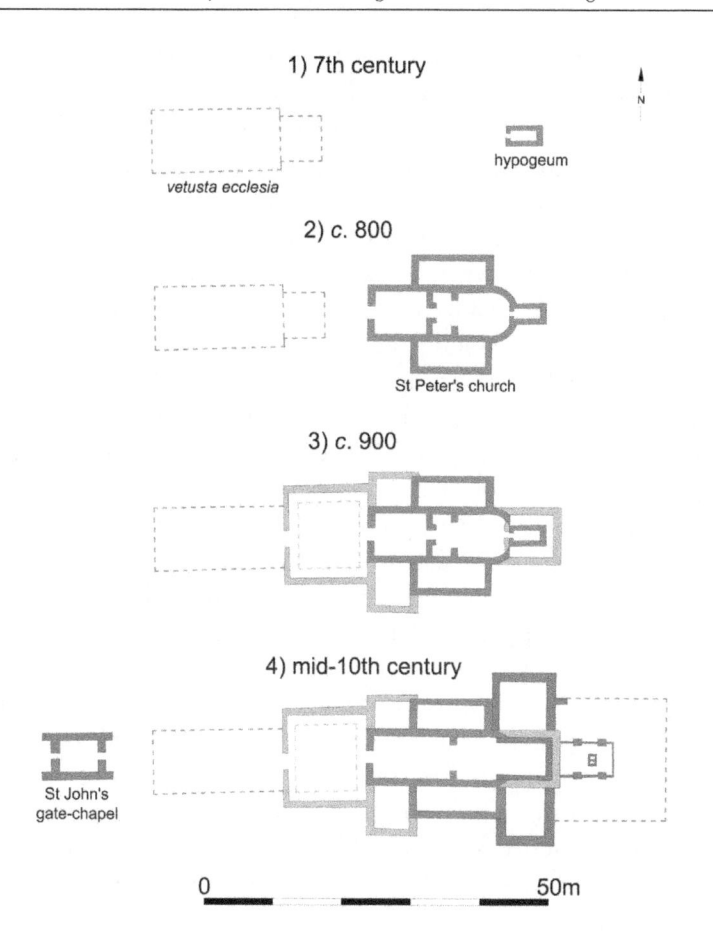

5.4b
Glastonbury, which incorporated an early hypogeum and timber church, or *vetusta ecclesia* (drawn by author, based on P. Rahtz, *The English Heritage Book of Glastonbury* (London: B. T. Batsford, 1993), p. 81).

churches associated with the period of St Augustine's mission were remodelled in the late tenth and eleventh centuries with the addition of a cloister, a mortuary chapel and a free-standing tower,[64] culminating in Abbot Wulfric's efforts to connect two of the original churches with a great rotunda (mentioned above). At Glastonbury, the old timber church of St Mary was joined by the church of St Peter, built by King Ine (688–726), which incorporated an early stone hypogeum on the site. In the tenth century, St Peter's church was expanded to the east with several *porticus* and a tower, and connected to St Mary's church with an atrium; a chapel-cum-gatehouse dedicated to St John was also built to the west, and an early form of cloister to the south (Figure 5.4).[65] At Winchester's Old Minster, King Cenwalh's church of c.648 was joined by a tower dedicated to St Martin before the mid-tenth century. The tomb of St Swithun lay between the two structures. Construction started on a great imperial *westwerk* in 971, which grew over succeeding decades to incorporate both churches and St Swithun's tomb; Cenwalh's church was also dramatically expanded at this time with *porticus*, a crossing-tower and an enlarged east end.[66]

In each of these three cases, the Anglo-Saxon builders had the ability, resources and imagination to sweep away the existing structures in favour of a new scheme, but this option was chosen neither at these sites nor at any other site known from the period. This is in stark contrast to the end of the eleventh century, when the wholesale replacement of each site with a single great Norman church was under way. Canterbury, Winchester and Glastonbury rank among the most prominent and wealthy ecclesiastical sites in Anglo-Saxon England, and many of the significant works undertaken came under the auspices of the tenth-century Benedictine Reform movement, which was closely associated with architectural developments on the Continent and enjoyed the political and financial backing of the king, so other options would clearly have been available.[67]

The reverence for the past extended beyond the curation of entire churches to encompass fragments of buildings and other sacred material. Fonts were commonly buried beneath their replacements rather than being discarded, and whole floors were translated into new churches and rededicated.[68] A significant amount of the sculpture known from Anglo-Saxon England, including architectural fragments, is preserved reused in churches of pre-Conquest date; while its presence may in some cases be casual, in others it would have been no less meaningful than reused Roman stonework.[69] This phenomenon applies to timber as well as masonry, as indicated by Bede's account of a seventh-century church near Bamburgh:

> Penda, king of Mercia, came with a hostile army to these parts destroying everything he could with fire and sword; and the village in which the bishop had died, together with the church ... was burned down. But it was astonishing that the buttress alone, against which the bishop had been leaning when he died, could not be devoured by the flames though they destroyed everything around it ... Shortly afterwards it happened that the same village and church were again burned down ... on this occasion too the flames could not touch the buttress ... So when the church was rebuilt for the third time, they put the buttress, not outside as before to support the structure, but inside the church itself as a memorial of the miracle, so that people entering the church could kneel there and ask for God's mercy.[70]

This beam was preserved *in memoriam miraculi* and was exploited for its miraculous curative properties, in which sense it appears to have been treated in no lesser fashion than the relics of a saint. Similar regard is visible in Archbishop Theodore's seventh-century *Penitential*, which states that wood from Anglo-Saxon churches should not be used for any other purpose than to repair another church, or to fuel fire to bake bread for a monastery.[71]

Entire churches of timber are also known to have been preserved and revered almost as relics. Bishop Finan's church at Lindisfarne was encased in lead by a subsequent bishop, Eadberht (688–698),[72] as were both Glastonbury's *vetusta ecclesia* and the earliest church at York (albeit according to later sources).[73] Also at York, the minster's early, free-standing timber bell-tower, which incorporated a chapel, was similarly treated.[74] In 801, Alcuin gifted Archbishop Eanbald:

> A hundred pounds of tin for carrying out the necessary works, and four lattice-work screens. It seems right that the bell-house (*domuncula cloccarum*) be covered in tin, *as a fitting adornment in view of the reputation of the place.*[75]

This has been convincingly interpreted as the 'enshrinement' of church buildings,[76] the life-size version of the building-shaped reliquaries of precious metal known from the period. The enduring reverence in which Bishop Finan's church at Lindisfarne was held is indicated by the fact that St Cuthbert's community dismantled it when they fled the sacking of Holy Island and carried it with them on their peregrinations, re-erecting it at first at Norham, then Chester-le-Street.[77] In this way, the building materials of Anglo-Saxon churches transcend modern categories of brick, timber and stone to encompass age and contemporary meaning which, like saints' relics, gave the Church authenticity.

The origins and meanings of Anglo-Saxon church buildings

As we have seen, the materials from which the Anglo-Saxons constructed their churches were chosen for reasons beyond the immediately practicable, according to meanings rooted in the history of the English Church. The same thing can be said of the forms these churches took. It was stated at the beginning of this chapter that the Christian Church lacks an innate architecture: its earliest buildings were simply adapted from the dwellings of the faithful, which were replaced by forms appropriated from the Roman state. There is not space here to trace the origins and meanings of every aspect of Anglo-Saxon church building, so three principal forms have been chosen to illustrate the extent to which Anglo-Saxon church-building practice articulated with secular and pre-Christian life: naves, mausolea and towers.

Nave and chancel

The basilican plan of late antique church naves was modelled on the assembly hall of the Roman state. The churches built in England after the Roman mission of St Augustine (597), particularly in southern England, were directly copied from these Gallic and Mediterranean basilicas, such as Saints Peter and Paul in Canterbury (Figure 5.1) and Reculver (Kent). The Kentish churches of this early period in particular comprise a reasonably coherent group characterised by their use of apsidal east ends, triple arcades and Roman masonry techniques, all of which are thought to have originated in Italy and North Africa.[78] There appears to have been a close association between church nave and secular hall in Anglo-Saxon England, which may in some cases have its origins not in Roman assembly halls but in domestic timber halls of insular practice.[79]

The timber churches which characterise post-Roman Britain and seventh-century Northumbria appear to have been based on pagan halls. They were both of timber construction, quite unlike the churches of the Roman mission: no known domestic halls of this period were stone.[80] The squared chancel of many early Anglo-Saxon churches, particularly in the north of England, such as Escomb (County Durham) (Figure 5.3), is almost unknown on the Continent. They may preserve the squared annexes of the halls at Yeavering and Cowdery's Down,[81] one of the few aspects of early Anglo-Saxon hall construction distinctively insular in form, which does not resemble anything seen on the European mainland at this time (Figure 5.5).[82] In England, generally, the axial (end-on-end) alignment of many early monastery churches, from Jarrow in Northumbria to Canterbury in Kent, is very unusual in continental Europe, but is shared by Anglo-Saxon secular complexes at Yeavering and Chalton.[83] Aspects of social behaviour and spatial organisation of pagan halls have also been related to ecclesiastical practice: the lord's feast becomes communion, the fire and the dais at the 'high' end become the altar and conventions of those who speak from the high end of the hall – such as narrative poets – and those who must listen is analogous to the delivery of a sermon.[84]

This speculative argument becomes more compelling if one accepts that the halls of pre-Christian kings were focal points for religious practice and manifested royal cults.[85] High-status pagan Anglo-Saxon tomb-chambers such as Sutton Hoo and Prittlewell were versions of halls appropriately furnished with the deceased's grave goods, providing a natural continuity with burial in God's hall: the church.[86] The scant

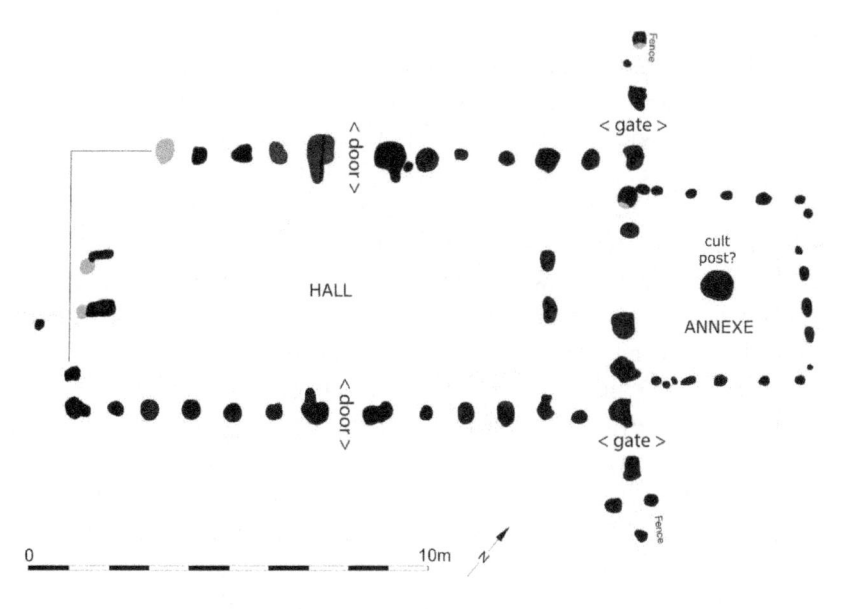

Fig. 5.5 Cowdery's Down, Hampshire, plan of the seventh-century hall (building A1). Note the square eastern annexe containing a prominent post, suggested as the cult focus of the building (drawing by M.G. Shapland, from M. Millet, 'Excavations at Cowdery's Down, Basingstoke, Hants: 1978–1981', *Archaeological Journal* 140 (1983), pp. 151–279).

archaeological evidence for pagan Anglo-Saxon 'temples', such as Building D2 at Yeavering, show them to have been timber halls little different from the others on the site.[87] The square-ended annexes of certain early Anglo-Saxon halls – which arguably became the distinctive square chancels of many Anglo-Saxon churches – may have been the cult focus of these halls.[88] They resemble a class of square pagan 'shrines',[89] and the central posts of several examples may be related to pagan cult posts of a type known from various early English and north-west European written and pictorial sources (Figure 5.5).[90] These posts are thought to have been incorporated into Christian belief as analogues of the cross, so it is appropriate that they occupied the same part of the hall as the altars in the chancels of the later churches.[91] The acceptability of modelling churches on pagan halls can again be traced to Pope Gregory's letter concerning the expediency of transforming temples into churches.[92]

From the mid-tenth century onwards, as earlier stated, lords constructed churches on their estates, commonly in association with their residences.[93] The great majority of these aristocratic churches would have been too small to house a public congregation[94] – even assuming popular church attendance was widespread in this period – and yet they took the form of small chapels with a nave and chancel when other building forms such as the tower-nave church and the household chapel were potentially available.[95] Perhaps the nave-and-chancel was particularly acceptable to the late Anglo-Saxon aristocracy because it was an essay in stone of the familiar aristocratic hall, with the additional connotations of piety and permanence that their masonry construction afforded.[96]

Mausolea

The early Christian Church was rarely concerned with disposal of the dead, and churches did not become focal points for burial in England until the late Anglo-Saxon period.[97] Early attitudes discouraging church burial began to change across Europe with the growth of the cult of saints' relics, so by the seventh century exceptions were increasingly being made for the worthy dead such as kings and high-ranking ecclesiastics.[98] Nevertheless, burial *ad sanctos* was commonly confined to peripheral structures distinct from the main body of the church, principally utilising either *porticus* or detached mausolea.

The earliest evidence for these structures in England is at St Augustine's Abbey in Canterbury, where Bede records the burial of early Kentish kings and ecclesiasts, including St Augustine and King Æthelberht, within the north and south *porticus* of the church of Saints Peter and Paul (Figure 5.1). This church, rather than the nearby cathedral, subsequently became the mortuary church for the royal dynasty of Kent. Bede also records an early royal burial *porticus* in York, where the head of King Edwin of Northumbria was interred by his successor Oswald in the porch of the newly completed cathedral.[99] Seventh-century burial *porticus* have also been identified at the important Northumbrian monasteries of Wearmouth, Ripon and Hexham.[100]

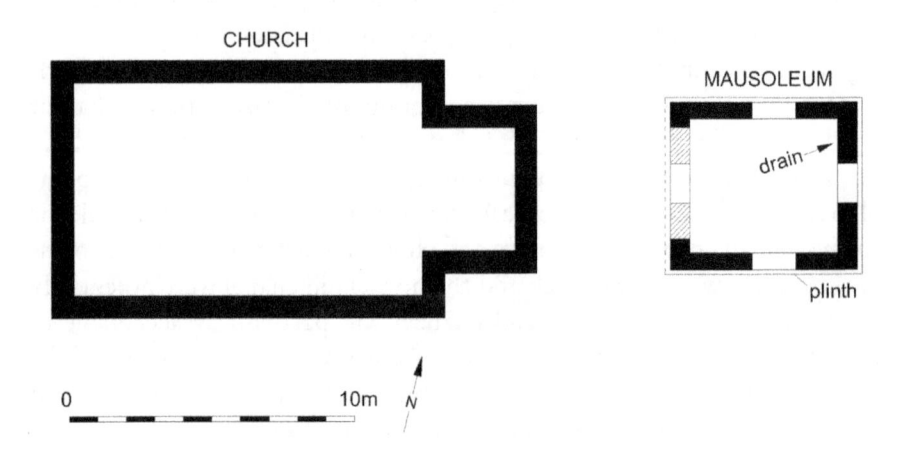

There is considerable evidence for mortuary chapels in this early period, although it is often unclear whether a particular church was constructed for this purpose.[101] The earliest may be the curious stone *hypogeum*, or subsurface tomb, at Glastonbury which was incorporated into the east end of the later church of St Peter in the early eighth century (Figure 5.3). An eighth-century mausoleum was excavated east of a church in the Anglian phases of the monastery at Whithorn.[102] The tiny excavated mausoleum of St Andrew at Hexham also lay immediately to the east of its abbey church; it has been tentatively associated with King Ælfwold of Northumbria (d. 786).[103] A sunken Roman mausoleum was reused east of Wells Minster (Somerset) from the seventh to the tenth centuries, after which it was replaced by a second detached mausoleum, square in plan.[104] A free-standing tomb was constructed at the east end of the cathedral at Worcester for the eighth-century nobleman Wiferd and his wife Alta.[105] The consistent location of these small, detached structures to the east of their parent churches further indicates that they were part of an established building practice.

Many of the best examples of free-standing Anglo-Saxon mausolea are associated with royal burials. The church of St Pancras at Winchcombe originated as a mausoleum (*monumentum*) with a crypt for King Coenwulf of Mercia (ruled 796–821), his heir Cynhelm and his father Cuthberht.[106] It may have resembled the near-contemporary, free-standing mausoleum of King Wiglaf of Mercia (827–839) and his successor St Wystan (d. 849), which also had a crypt, at the important royal centre of Repton.[107] The remains of King Æthelbald of Mercia (716–757) are also thought to have been translated into what became an important burial place for the Mercian royal house. Its crypt partially survives incorporated into the adjacent church, its four spiral columns possibly evoking the baldachin, or canopy, marking the tomb of St Peter in Rome (Figure 5.6).[108] A second burial

Fig. 5.6 Eighth-century royal mausoleum at St Wystan's church, Repton.

5.6a Plan redrawn by M.G. Shapland, from H.M. Taylor, 'St Wystan's Church, Repton, Derbyshire: A Reconstruction Essay', *Archaeological Journal* 144 (1987), 205–45; M. Biddle and B. Kjølbye-Biddle, 'Repton and the Vikings', *Antiquity* 66 (1992), 36–51.

5.6b Photograph by kind permission of Howard Williams.

structure, suggested as a mortuary chapel, lay sixty metres to the west, consisting of a two-celled sunken structure converted in the 870s into the chamber of a burial mound housing a princely burial and ossuary associated with the Viking Great Army.[109]

A free-standing mausoleum with a crypt was constructed immediately east of St Oswald's Priory adjacent to the royal palace of Kingsholm in Gloucester, which was founded at the beginning of the ninth century by the Mercian rulers Æthelred and Æthelflæd to house the relics of the Northumbrian king Oswald.[110] It is likely that all three royal figures were buried in the mausoleum, which was square in plan with a crypt supported by four central piers, and is therefore closely comparable to the examples at Repton and Winchcombe. A century later, in 1001, King Æthelred II (978–1016) granted a royal manor at Bradford on Avon (Wiltshire) and its monastery to Shaftesbury Abbey, and constructed there a mortuary chapel to house the relics of his half-brother King Edward the Martyr (975–978).[111] This church, which survives in remarkably complete state, takes the form of a modest rectangular nave and chancel with two large *porticus*. The southern of these is thought to have had a modest crypt,[112] potentially combining the idea of the burial *porticus* discussed above with the crypts of the detached mausolea considered here. Finally, King Cnut (1016–35) constructed a centrally planned mausoleum at Bury St Edmunds, to the east of the abbey church, to house the relics of King Edmund of East Anglia (855–869). Cnut may also have intended it as his own mausoleum.[113]

The common thread running between these structures is the desire to be buried outside the main body of a church. In the early period this was due to the widespread prohibition of burial *ad sanctos*, and by the later Anglo-Saxon period to the status that such distinguished treatment would have conferred. The clearest origin for these structures lies in pre-Christian Roman imperial tombs, which were centrally planned structures that developed from the circular reveted mound of the first emperor, Augustus (d. AD 14), to two-storey circular or octagonal domed mausolea from the mid-third century onwards.[114] The mausoleum-chapel of the first Christian emperor Constantine in Constantinople was also of this distinctive centrally planned form, which was considered sacred throughout the early medieval period.[115] The emperor Charlemagne's imperial chapel at Aachen (modern Germany; late eighth-century), which was also his mortuary chapel, was copied from these Roman imperial tombs and became an influential model for early medieval, high-status mausolea in England and Europe:[116] Cnut's mausoleum at Bury St Edmunds, which shares Aachen's dedication to St Mary, is one example.[117]

A second suggested influence for high-status burial in conceptually separate structures lies in pre-Christian burial mounds, which royal churches and mausolea have long been argued to have supplanted as dynastic monuments.[118] More recently, studies across Western Europe, including England, have traced an upsurge in the construction of monumental mounds in tandem with the rise of Christianity. Both barrows and churches were monumental statements of ancestry and cult which differed in their mode of expression, but which were qualitatively similar.[119] Indeed, Roman imperial mausolea were themselves derived from pagan burial-mounds of much earlier practice, of which the reveted mound of the Emperor Augustus is but a late, transitional example.[120] In this respect it is tempting to relate the distinctive subterranean crypts of several Anglo-Saxon royal mausolea to the tomb-chambers of dynastic burial mounds.

Towers

Towers are a liturgically unnecessary adjunct to the main body of medieval churches, only becoming common in England in the tenth or eleventh centuries.[121] Despite their relative ubiquity by the late medieval period, their origins are obscure, and since they are a startlingly elaborate means of simply ringing bells their original purpose is contested.[122]

There is no firm evidence for church towers in England until the early tenth century, and none before *c*.800.[123] Nevertheless, even then the landscape of England was dotted with towers to an extent that is rarely appreciated. The Romans had constructed many: several lighthouses and signal-towers appear to have remained in operation until at least the time of Bede.[124] A line describing 'towers in ruins' (*hreorge torras*) occurs in the Old English poem *The Ruin*,[125] and a watchtower apparently existed on Lindisfarne in the late seventh century.[126] In 1066 William the Conqueror stayed in an unidentified 'broken tower' (*fractam turrim*) on his march from Dover to Sandwich,[127] before laying siege to a 'proud tower' (*elatam turrem*) at the gates of London.[128] Certain of these early towers were valued by the Anglo-Saxon Church, such as the Roman *pharos* at Dover, which still survives as the western tower of the late tenth-/early eleventh-century church of St Mary-in-Castro (Figure 5.7).[129] The clearest evidence for the influence of secular towers on those built by the Anglo-Saxon Church lies in the status-affording towers of the local aristocracy.

Anglo-Saxon lords constructed free-standing church towers – termed 'tower-nave' churches – at their residences, of which twenty-one are known to have existed between the late tenth and the end of the eleventh

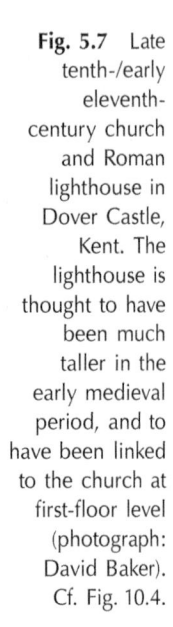

Fig. 5.7 Late tenth-/early eleventh-century church and Roman lighthouse in Dover Castle, Kent. The lighthouse is thought to have been much taller in the early medieval period, and to have been linked to the church at first-floor level (photograph: David Baker). Cf. Fig. 10.4.

centuries: most survive, albeit in much-altered form.[130] While many had small chancels and *porticus*, they lacked naves, meaning that their principal space for worship was contained within the base or upper rooms of the tower (Figure 5.8). Their limited capacity combined with their elaborate form indicates an elite function, which is borne out by the location of twenty of these towers within or adjacent to the manorial *curiae* – enclosures – of their lords, many of which were fortified. One tower-nave was built at Bury St Edmunds Abbey shortly before 1044 by Earl Ælfric, a powerful regional magnate, whose family used it as a dwelling.[131] Many of these lordly tower-naves articulated with focal places of secular power in the landscape such as fortifications, hundred meeting-places and beacon-systems, and they are argued to have profoundly influenced the form of early post-Conquest castles, into which several of them were incorporated. Anglo-Saxon lords had constructed non-ecclesiastical towers at their residences from at least the later ninth century onwards (see below), so the question remains how much influence these secular towers had on the form of lordly tower-nave churches.

A growing number of these secular towers, all of which are of timber construction, are known from the lordly residences of late Anglo-Saxon England.[132] Of these, the earliest and best-understood is Bishopstone (Sussex), a substantial cellared timber tower of which the destruction by burning is dated to the late ninth or early tenth centuries. It lay at an enclosed estate centre and minster complex, and is interpreted as an architectural manifestation of lordship.[133] Documentary evidence may associate towers of this type with the accomplishment of aristocratic status: the early eleventh-century *Geþyncðo* ('Promotion Law'), compiled in the *Textus Roffensis* (c.1125), lists various buildings as prerequisite for a lord, including a *bellhus*, 'bell-house'.[134] This is supported by place names such as Belstead Hall (*Belestedam* 1086) in Broomfield (Essex), which derives from *belhus-stede*, 'the site of the *belhus*'.[135] More certain is the use of the iconography of towers by the Anglo-Saxon royalty to convey their authority. A series of coins were minted in Chester in the name of Edward the Elder (899–924), during the West Saxon domination of Mercian territory, which bear the image of a tower on their reverse.[136]

These lordly timber towers were not tower-nave churches, and appear a few centuries earlier than the manorial tower-naves of late tenth- and eleventh-century England. Nevertheless, the influence of lordly timber towers upon manorial tower-naves is in some cases pronounced. Although, as discussed, the majority of known tower-naves were stone, the greater survivability of stone compared to timber may obscure a parallel tradition of timber tower-nave churches, of which only one possible example is known from a manorial context: the lordly residence at Springfield Lyons (Essex).[137] Here, a small square structure with substantial foundations of probable tenth-century date, interpreted as a timber tower, had a smaller eastern annexe containing a grave. It was the only building on the site containing a burial, suggesting that it functioned as an aristocratic tower-nave church.

The suggested timber origins of lordly tower-naves churches is most evident in the prominent use of pilaster strip work – lengths of freestone thought to be a skeuomorph of timber framing – at two of the most famous examples, Earls Barton (Northamptonshire) and Barton-upon-Humber (Lincolnshire) (Figure 5.8).[138] It has been argued that pilaster strip work echoed timber building practice due to a desire for visible continuity with the traditional timber construction that underlies so much of Anglo-Saxon architecture.[139] As discussed above, the Anglo-Saxons maintained a rigid distinction between building in timber, which encompassed nearly all known secular buildings, and building in stone, which was almost exclusively confined to ecclesiastical structures.[140] If lordly tower-naves were essays in stone of existing secular timber towers, early examples may have used pilaster strip work to emphasise these origins, and to underline that these ecclesiastical towers retained their established secular dimension.

An existing tradition of lordly timber towers may also inform the more general question of the origins of the western towers of local churches,[141] which have long been suggested as lordly status symbols.[142] Thirty-seven Anglo-Saxon western towers are listed in Taylor's 1978 gazetteer,[143] of which (where known) around 80 per cent either lie adjacent to or are incorporated into manorial *curiae*, or enclosures.[144] Far greater study is needed into the dating of these towers and any adjacent manorial residence, but, crude as this picture is, it is indicative of a close relationship between the aristocracy and the construction of western towers in the late Anglo-Saxon period. It is therefore striking that one of the earliest and best-preserved examples of an Anglo-Saxon western tower – the early tenth-century example in Barnack (Northamptonshire)[145] – displays prominent pilaster strip work and is located within an early

Fig. 5.8 Two Anglo-Saxon lordly tower-nave churches, both with prominent pilaster strip work, both of probable early eleventh-century date.

5.8a Earl's Barton, Northamptonshire.

5.8b Barton-upon-Humber, Lincolnshire (photographs: M.G. Shapland).

manorial *curia*.[146] Anglo-Saxon church towers undoubtedly have their origins in the mainstream of European ecclesiastical architecture, but they may also have carried something of the form and associations of an existing tradition of lordly timber tower construction.

Conclusion

From its beginnings, Christianity has always borrowed existing building forms for its churches and appropriated these structures for worship. In common with the majority of early Christian architecture, the Anglo-Saxons based the forms of their churches on Roman practice, which harnessed St Augustine's mission to the authority of the pope and manifested this allegiance in brick and stone. Existing British and Irish strands of Christianity had a parallel tradition of church building characterised by timber construction, which was particularly influential in the Anglo-Saxon kingdom of Northumbria. Anglo-Saxon church naves could therefore evoke the brick basilicas of Rome or secular halls of timber, and their mausolea the tombs of the emperors or the burial mounds of their ancestors and kings. In the later Anglo-Saxon period, the forms of aristocratic church towers may have owed much to secular towers of lordship, and their stone construction evoked traditional timber-framing techniques.

Anglo-Saxon church-builders used brick, timber and stone to build their churches, often reusing these things from existing structures for reasons of belief, practicality or social meaning, as befits the magpie nature of the early Christian church. Metal was also used in church building to cover ancient structures in order to make them both relic and reliquary from which the English Church could draw upon the authority of the past. Old churches were suffered to endure despite their often inadequate size or awkward location: expansion and renewal resulted in distinctive accumulations of structures of various dates at the greater Anglo-Saxon monasteries, until they were swept away by the Normans. In these ways the materials from which the Anglo-Saxons made their churches, as well as the forms they took, made them as much eloquent statements of belief and political allegiance as they were practical spaces for worship.

6

Landmarks of Faith: Crosses and other Free-standing Stones

Elizabeth Coatsworth

Nu ic þe hate,   hæleð min se leofa
þæt ðu þas gesyhðe   secge mannum,
onwreoh wordum   þæt hit is wuldres beam,
se ðe ælmihtig god   on þrowode
for mancynnes   manegum synnum
and Adomes   ealdgewyrhtum.

Now I command you, beloved man, that you tell people about this sight, reveal in words that it is the tree of glory on which Almighty God suffered for the many sins of mankind and Adam's ancient deeds.[1]

Introduction

Free-standing sculptures are, apart from buildings and the rather surprising case of the Bayeux Tapestry,[2] the largest artefacts to have come down to us from the pre-Conquest period in England. They range in size from (for example) the Ruthwell cross at more than 518 centimetres (17 ft) in height, to small grave markers complete at less than 30.5 centimetres (1 ft). They come also in a variety of forms, some recognisable as cross shafts and heads, occasionally as steles,[3] as bases of other monuments or as grave markers of a considerable variety of forms, and with a range of decoration both figural and aniconic, with or without inscriptions, which can be dated by comparison with decoration in other media, or, in the case of inscriptions, with changing styles of lettering or linguistic forms. With the doubtful exception of some of the smallest grave slabs, which may have been buried below the surface in the grave,[4] all these monuments were meant to be seen, whether placed inside churches, in the precincts around a church or an ecclesiastical community or in the wider landscape. What these sculptures meant to those who commissioned and made them, or to the contemporary viewer, has been a preoccupation of serious scholars of this material since the nineteenth century.[5] Indeed, W.O. Stevens, in 1904, though now out-of-date in many ways, listed most of the categories of possible function still of interest today – titling them memorial, mortuary, boundary, sanctuary, standard and oratory crosses – and many of the relevant contemporary sources.[6] Nevertheless, this interest has increased and become more speculative since the 1990s: Rosemary Cramp has summed up both past concerns and more recent trends in a historiographical analysis which also provides a useful, though still only partial, bibliography to the topic.[7] *Inter alia*, she notes different approaches to the analysis of the religious meaning of various major monuments, possible ecclesiastical and/or secular implications in relation to position on boundaries or borders or in relation to specific centres and regional differences in style, while also opening up the discussion to other ways of interpreting ornament: to express conversion messages, for example, or to show lay patronage or involvement. Her study affirms that interpretation of sculpture is 'not helpful [when it considers] there is only a single solution to a monument's significance'[8] and that there is danger in taking monuments out of their local, regional and period contexts. Bearing these considerations in mind, I want to enter this debate with a study based on the surviving monuments in a landscape centred on the ecclesiastical parish of Dewsbury, which was also in some way related to a royal estate focused on Wakefield, for both of which entities the documentary evidence is all post-Conquest: the contemporary evidence rests solely on the sculpture itself. Is it possible to show when and to whom these monuments might have been familiar, and what purposes they fulfilled in the daily life of a monastic or aristocratic community, or the wider population? The parish and estate to be defined are both from a region which I know well, the West Riding of Yorkshire.[9]

The regional context

The West Riding

The West Riding (Figure 6.1) was much larger than the modern county of West Yorkshire, stretching further to the north-west and also to the south: in fact, it touched on five other counties apart from the old North and East Ridings of Yorkshire: Westmorland, Lancashire, Cheshire, Derbyshire, Lincolnshire and Nottinghamshire, an indication that large

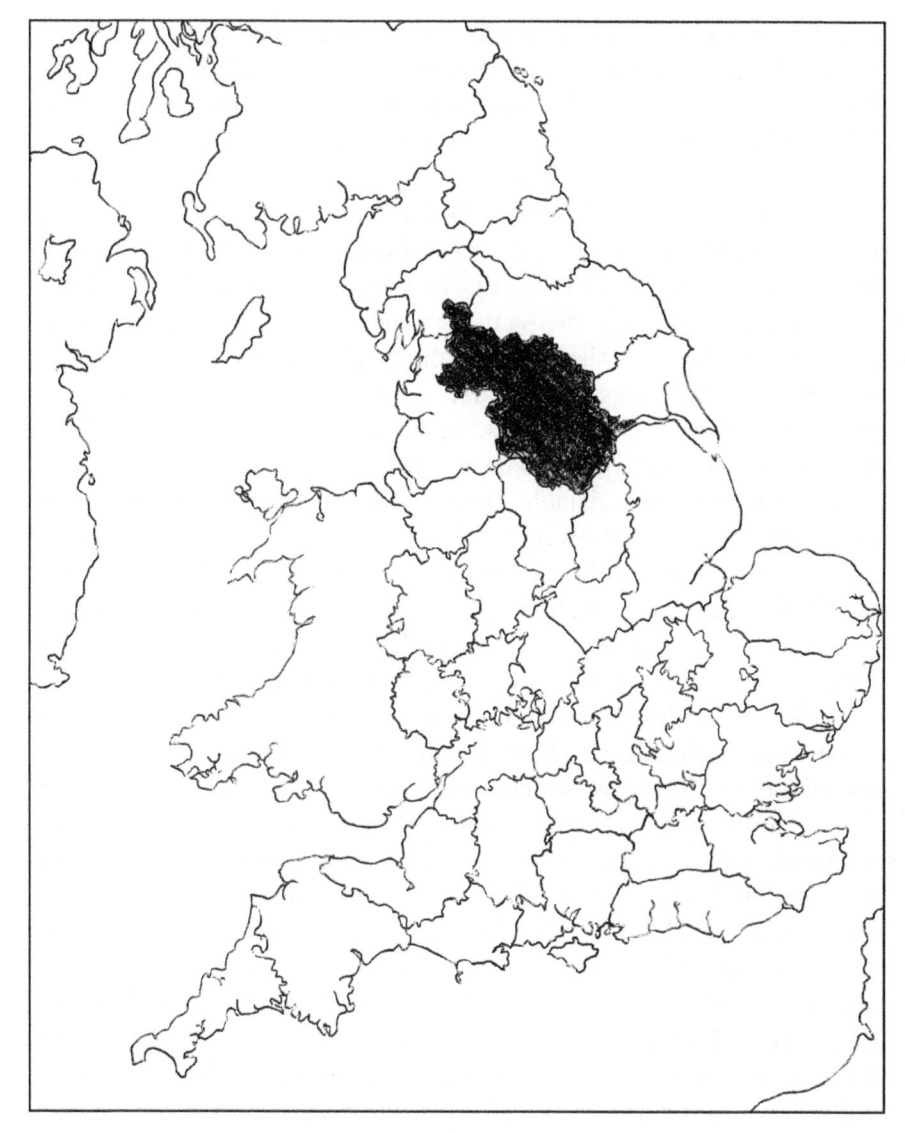

Fig. 6.1 Map showing pre-1974 boundaries of counties in England, the West Riding in solid black (copyright Alexandra Lester-Makin).

parts of it bordered on much earlier divisions, including, for example, within the pre-Conquest period, other kingdoms. Although its early medieval borders are to some extent speculative, there are some natural boundaries in its varied terrain, and its early history also suggests some divisions.

For example, it certainly extended from the flat lands south and west of York gradually rising to the west through relatively gentle hills (the band in which the major ecclesiastical centres of Ripon and Dewsbury both lie), then through bare fells and moors to the eastern slopes of the Pennines, cut by the southern Yorkshire dales, with two of these,

Fig. 6.2 The Parish of Dewsbury. The shaded area indicates roughly the area defined as the parish in M.L. Faull and S.A. Moorhouse (eds), *West Yorkshire: An Archaeological Survey to AD 1500*, 4 vols (Wakefield: West Yorkshire Metropolitan County Council, 1974), vol. 4, map 15. Solid symbols represent sculptures in the parish or on its boundaries; open symbols are for centres outside the parish, for location purposes. Some pre-1974 county names no longer exist: e.g. some of the West Riding is now West Yorkshire; Westmorland has been subsumed into Cumbria.

Airedale and Calderdale, in the area of concern. The whole lay within the pre-Roman territory of the Brigantes, while east Yorkshire was the land of the Parisi, with Roman York on the frontier between the two tribes. The Roman roads to the west largely follow the river valleys, and so for obvious reasons do later settlements. The east–west division continued into the post-Roman period into the seventh century, through the continuance of post-Roman British kingdoms or enclaves (Craven in the north-west and Elmet to the east and south, including the Dewsbury/ Wakefield area), though their actual extent is problematic because of the paucity of evidence on the ground. Topography and the high proportion of marginal land suggest a sparse population, but Christian burial practices without grave goods also account for the relative invisibility of these people. Certainly there are no fifth- to seventh-century Anglian cemeteries with their datable grave goods in the area, unlike in the east.[10] Anglo-Saxon burials in west Yorkshire date only from the seventh century, after the last British king of Elmet was expelled by Edwin of Northumbria in 617: all these are on the eastern border of Elmet, indicated by place names such as Sherburn in Elmet, and Barwick in Elmet.[11] The earliest evidence for Anglo-Saxon occupation in the whole of western Yorkshire is north of Elmet in the Ripon area (and there is some linguistic evidence that the name Ripon implies a people living on a border).[12] There is evidence, documentary and other, to confirm that the borders between the two kingdoms of Northumbria/Deira to the north and east, and Mercia, south and west, were hard fought over a long period, and that south-west Yorkshire may always have been a border area. Thus the Sheffield Cross is located in Yorkshire and has some Yorkshire traits, but also has features in common with its Mercian neighbours at Eyam, Bradbourne and Bakewell in Derbyshire.[13] Large areas of west Yorkshire seem to have been in royal hands, some subsequently donated to the church. For example, Tanshelf was a royal vill in 1066, according to the Domesday record;[14] land around Ripon, and probably also around Otley and associated sites in Wharfedale, was donated to St Wilfrid through the patronage of Ahlfrith, sub-king of Deira: these became estates of the Archbishop of York to the end of the Anglo-Saxon period and beyond.[15]

The Dewsbury/Wakefield area

The area around Dewsbury and Wakefield is less well-documented, and seems oddly empty of all save place name evidence on maps representing the pre-Conquest period,[16] but there is some evidence that it followed a similar pattern to the rest of the West Riding. Margaret Faull and Stephen Moorhouse suggested that Dewsbury was a pre-Conquest

mother-church, but their only evidence is from later medieval records of tithes paid to Dewsbury by dependent churches carved out of the original area to serve growing local needs.[17] This process went on post-Conquest, but they accepted as pre-Conquest dependent-only parishes with 'old, established churches of parochial status' for which the only evidence is, in fact, the presence of pre-Conquest sculpture. Thus parishes, chapelries or townships which paid tithes to Dewsbury and which had pre-Conquest sculpture of varying dates – Bradford, Hartshead, Kirkburton, Kirkheaton, Thornhill, Rastrick and Wakefield – were therefore accepted as representing parts of the parish in the pre-Conquest period (and all save Hartshead and Rastrick are indeed later parish centres). This evidence therefore seems to show the (probably slow) spread of church buildings across the landscape. The parish of Dewsbury identified by these means extends from Wakefield in the east, along the Calder valley, widening west of Dewsbury to encompass tributaries of the Calder to the south, and almost the width of the south side of the Aire valley to the north (with Bradford and Stanbury its most northerly sites with surviving sculpture), and at its westward edge encompassing the eastern slopes of the Pennines (with Todmorden and Stansfield, its sites with sculptures, furthest to the west (Figure 6.2)).[18] However, the included areas ascribed to Huddersfield and Almondbury parishes have no sculpture at all, while Halifax has none at its parish centre: ecclesiastical centres for these parishes cannot be shown for the period pre-1086. Dewsbury and Thornhill are both said to have a priest and a church in 1086; Wakefield is said to have two churches and three priests, but it is not clear as to where exactly these were situated, apart from Wakefield itself.[19]

There is, however, Domesday Book evidence for both Wakefield and Dewsbury as royal vills, interesting in view of Dewsbury's minster status. The entry for Wakefield, for example, reads: 'this manor was in King Edward's lordship. Now in the king's hands'.[20] Stansfield is named as one of the outliers of the Wakefield estate, so the western edge seems coterminous with that posited for Dewsbury parish. The Domesday entry for Dewsbury itself reads: 'The land belonged to Wakefield. However King Edward had a manor in it. Now it is in the king's hands'.[21] Dewsbury and Wakefield remained in the post-Conquest manor of Wakefield, which keeps to the eastern and western edges as proposed for the parish, though with some additions north and south of its eastern arm, but cut in two by holdings granted to Ilbert de Laci.[22] Faull and Moorhouse also suggest that Wakefield's name implies it was an important gathering place before the Conquest (from *wacu*, 'watch, wake' and *feld*, 'tract of open country'), which could be an indication of a politically important centre. There is also evidence from an unpublished excavation within Wakefield Cathedral of a skeleton probably associated with the pre-Conquest church, which was found beneath a wall of Norman date, wearing a ring decorated in the Trewhiddle style, thus attesting to the site's social importance in the late ninth to tenth centuries.[23] The name Dewsbury (Dewi's *burh*) also implies a pre-Conquest fortification. In the later period, while West Yorkshire has overall fewer Scandinavian place names than the rest of Yorkshire, there are in the area between the rivers Calder and Aire 'virtually no Scandinavian names at all', which suggests a continuance of Anglian domination of this area in the late pre-Conquest period.[24]

Faull and Moorhouse, on the evidence of its status outlined above, believed Dewsbury, with its major sculpture collection, was not only a mother-church, but a 'minster', defining such establishments as monastic in origin, often centres for missionary work over a large area, and often established on the initiative of kings or others of very high rank since they required considerable endowment of land to make them viable. Current thinking on minsters suggests that the terms *monasterium* (Latin) and *mynster* (Old English) were used by contemporaries interchangeably for any type of religious community, whether monastic, clerical or lay, or a mixture, and that such groups might have various roles which might or might not include a pastoral mission to the surrounding area.[25] The importance of royal endowment in the pre-Viking period, however, seems to hold good, and such original foundations, if holding sway over a large enough area, could indeed become mother-churches. Over how wide an area, if any, a pastoral role would have been exercised is debatable, especially in the earlier part of the period. Bede offered two models for a religious community: in his praise of Lindisfarne, he tells of people flocking to the church or the monastery to hear and learn from a visiting preacher; but he also says: 'If by chance a priest came to a village, the villagers crowded together to hear the word of life; for the priests and the clerics visited the villages for no other reason than to preach, to baptise, and to visit the sick, in brief to care for their souls' with a follow-up implication that they were not interested in taking on new land (and therefore increased wealth) to build monasteries 'unless compelled to by the secular authorities', because they were 'free from the taint of avarice'.[26] It is impossible to know whether this represented a general rather than an ideal model, but is something to be borne in mind in view of the width of the area proposed for the parish of Dewsbury. There is also evidence for groups of linked religious communities, like Monkwearmouth-Jarrow, or Whitby with a daughter foundation at Hackness.[27] This could be interesting in the light of the cluster of sites with sculpture in close proximity to Dewsbury. Recently, the choice of certain types of location as appropriate for a sacred space has been explored, with Dewsbury as an example of those sited by a river.[28]

Sites with sculpture in the area of Dewsbury Parish/Manor of Wakefield

Table 6.1 shows sites with sculpture in the area defined by Faull and Moorhouse, with two additions. Birstall is not mentioned by name in Domesday Book, though it is in the area of Gomersal, which is included there. It was possibly the site of a Roman villa, and its first element (*burh-*) suggests a fortified site, but not necessarily a pre-Conquest one since the name is first recorded only in the twelfth century.[29] Woodkirk lies between Dewsbury and Leeds: this area is part of West Ardsley, said in Domesday Book to be under the jurisdiction of Wakefield, and

Table 6.1 Sites with sculpture in the area of Dewbury Parish/Manor of Wakefield

	Dewsbury Parish	Manor of Wakefield	Parish centre	Church 1086	Priest 1086	Number of sculptures	Inscriptions	Figural sculpture	Aniconic	Sculpture before 950	Sculpture post 950
Birstall						1			X	X	
Bradford	X					2			2		X
Dewsbury	X	X		X	X	15	4	8/9	6/7	X	X
Hartshead	X	X?				1			1	X	
Kirkburton	X	X				1		1			X
Kirkheaton	X					5	1	1	4	X	X
Mirfield	X					1		1			X
Rastrick	X	X				1			1	X	
Stanbury	X	X?				2			2	X	
Stansfield	X	X				1			1		X
Thornhill	X			X	X	10	4		10	X	
Todmorden	X	X				1			1		X
Wakefield	X	X		X2	X3	1			1	X	
Woodkirk		X		X	X	1			1	X?	

therefore probably part of the royal vill pre-Conquest. It also had a pre-Conquest church.[30] Only four sites have clear evidence of priests and churches, but Stansfield is named in the section which defines the manor of Wakefield and its outliers: as mentioned above, however, it is impossible to know where any of its two churches and three priests actually were, though Wakefield most likely had at least one of each.[31]

Dewsbury is clearly an important site. It has a large collection of sculpture, most of exceptionally fine quality, and is one of the relatively few sites (in the whole of northern England) with a number of inscriptions. It is within walking distance of Thornhill, another site with a considerable surviving collection of sculpture, also with a number of inscriptions. Kirkheaton, with five surviving pieces including one inscription, is as unknown from contemporary records as all the other sites in the area. Wakefield itself, important as a royal estate centre, has only one cross, but its position and ornament give it considerable interest.

There are various ways in which this group can be interrogated, with a view to assessing their visibility in the immediate area for which they were made, and their likely meaning in the lives of contemporary viewers (though as stone monuments have a long life, we must be aware that their original intended meaning – if we can even grasp that fully – will not have lasted even to the end of the pre-Conquest period). Some points we can make relate to the physical position in the landscape or within the confines of a settlement, some to the iconography of physical scenes and/or the content of inscriptions, in which it seems the original patrons and makers speak to us directly. Not all sculptures fit into categories provided by old or recent research: in what follows I will consider first the apparently overt messages of iconography and inscriptions, then the significance of distribution and finally possible ways of interpreting aniconic monuments.

Sculpture with a faith-proclaiming message

Sculptures with a liturgical and/or specifically community-oriented meaning

A group of six sculpture fragments from Dewsbury (numbers 1–3, 4–5 and 9) have long been recognised as important for their iconography. W.G. Collingwood believed these fragments represented one single cross.[32] It seems more likely that they represent parts of two major crosses at this site, based on a close reading of the edge mouldings.[33]

The two crosses are of exceptional interest, both for the quality of carving and their subject matter. The cross represented by fragments 4, 5 and 9 is different from the other in having surviving non-figural decoration, an interlaced medallion scroll which shares characteristics with other major Deiran sculptures of the late eighth to ninth centuries with links to Otley and therefore is an indication that this site was in close touch with contemporary centres in Yorkshire in the late eighth to early ninth centuries.[34] The remaining figural ornament consists of four scenes. The first is of a Virgin and Child, possibly originally accompanied by the three Magi (it is incomplete on the left). The Virgin and Child face each other, and the Christ child is represented blessing (showing his divinity) and holding a scroll (representing his role as the divine *Logos*). The image has a long ancestry,[35] but the type represented here was widely known in England and Ireland, as shown by three examples from the seventh to the eighth centuries – on the coffin of St Cuthbert, in the Irish Book of Kells, and on the front of the Franks Casket (with Magi)[36] – and in eighth- to ninth-century Northumbrian sculpture at Sandbach, Cheshire, elevated to the top of the figured broad face of the cross-shaft from Eyam, Derbyshire, its arched frame missing,[37] and within West Yorkshire on Collingham 1.[38]

Two further scenes depict miracles of Christ, both identified by inscriptions in Roman script. The upper shows the wedding at Cana, in which Jesus turned water into wine (John 2: 1–11), with Christ standing behind a row of four water jars, accompanied by the Virgin and by St John as the witnessing apostle. Below is the miracle of the loaves and fishes, sometimes called the Feeding of the Five Thousand. This scene, attested in all four gospels, is given a particularly Eucharistic emphasis in St John's Gospel (John 6:1–14, as well as verses 23, 35 and 51). Both scenes were viewed as prefiguring the Last Supper, and the last also the institution of the Eucharist. The conjunction of all the three scenes on the shaft is particularly interesting, in that all, especially if the Virgin and Child scene included the Adoration of the Magi, are epiphanies: occasions on which the Godhead of Christ was revealed. In the Visigothic and Gallican liturgies (though not in the Roman liturgy which Bede followed), the Adoration of the Magi and the Wedding at Cana, along with Christ's baptism, were commemorated on the Feast of the Epiphany; this practice was known at Lindisfarne in the seventh century, as attested in all manuscripts of the *Anonymous Life of St Cuthbert*, and in one version the Feeding of the Five Thousand also appears.[39]

The fourth scene, on Dewsbury 9, most likely the lower arm of the head of this cross, has an angel, with a tonsured figure below and in front of him holding a scroll and kneeling or crouching at his feet. The obvious and most likely explanation is that it is a representation of St Matthew accompanied by his man/angel symbol, as on the lower arm of the head of the Ruthwell cross.[40] In its indication of the evangelist as a monkish scribe, it is more like the mid-eighth-century Stockholm Codex Aureus,[41] while the position, with the symbol directly behind the apostle, is like that in the Lindisfarne Gospels.[42] Michelle Brown surmised that 'accompanied' evangelist portraits in the Lindisfarne Gospels and the Book of Cerne 'simultaneously symbolise Christ, the Gospel writers, the scribe who faithfully transmits the scriptures and the aspirations of the faithful'.[43] The identification of a monk/scribe takes on further layers of meaning if we consider a related sculptural image emphasising Pope Gregory the Great as a scribe, for example,[44] or another similar image attached to a scriptural verse praising those who study and meditate on the law and found in a historiated initial beginning verse 1 of Psalm 1, in a Psalter of *c*.800 from Corbie in northern France (Amiens, Bibliothèque Municipale, MS 18).[45] The similarity of an evangelist/monk/ecclesiastic kneeling before an angel on Otley 1, another shaft in the West Riding notable for its association of apostles and angels, strengthens this association with Psalm 1, with the study of and faithful adherence to the Law and its transmission as the intended message.[46] The overall theme of this Dewsbury cross could therefore be the revelation of Christ's Godhead, and the mission of a specifically monastic community to meditate on and transmit the truths revealed through instances of epiphany. It is not too much of a stretch to say that this cross could have been used as a backdrop to the particular liturgical occasion of the Feast of the Epiphany, but it would also have been appropriate to the celebration of the Mass at any time; it could also have been used a teaching tool, and/or as an aid to devotion.

The other, round-shafted cross represented by the fragments Dewsbury 1–3 shows a seated figure of Christ, identified by an inscription, and with standing robed figures all turned to face him. The programme and layout of the upper tier is the same, or very similar to that at the top of the round shaft at Masham, North Yorkshire, with apostles standing on arcades, suggesting that the complete upper register would have had Christ and all twelve apostles.[47] This is possibly an extended version of the *Traditio Legis* in which Christ gives the law to the apostles, or more likely the Mission to the Apostles, whereby Christ sends out the apostles to spread the Word to all nations.[48] The late seventh-century coffin-reliquary of St Cuthbert is decorated on one of its sides with the twelve apostles led by Peter and Paul: these could be interpreted as observers bearing witness both to the Incarnation represented by the Virgin Mary on one end of the coffin and to the figure of Christ, who is shown blessing and holding a book amidst the symbols of the four evangelists on the top of the coffin, making this last an apostolic mission scene.[49] In sculpture, one of the best known examples of the same theme is the Hedda Stone from Peterborough.[50] A variant of the *Traditio Legis*, which includes the investment of St Peter with the keys, was represented on one of the Sandbach crosses, of similar date. The date of all these sculptures presupposes a revival of interest in the late Antique, early Christian imagery, already noted as a feature of Carolingian art of the late eighth and early ninth centuries.[51]

It is very difficult to think the message of these two crosses is not pertinent to the work of the community at Dewsbury: they seem to prove it at least was a fully monastic community which conceived of itself, indeed proclaimed itself, as having a teaching and missionary role. Either or both of these crosses could have stood outside the church but within the bounds of the monastic precinct. They would have been part of the backdrop of the lives of those in the monastic community, and as I have suggested could have been used for teaching and preaching at specific times of the year, or as daily meditation on the meaning of the monastic life. How often they were seen by the laity (with the broad exception of the lay people who provided the day-to-day work on the monastic estate, perhaps) when they were first set up is debatable: visitors to the monastery would have seen them, and these would have included the wider community within walking distance along the lines suggested by Bede, as previously discussed. Dewsbury clearly remained an important centre as it became the mother-church for a wide area – so that in time the monuments as well as the church building would have become significant elements in the local landscape – but some of their early, monastic meaning may well have been lost as styles changed, and as the church integrated into the developing parish structure.

A message we can take from them, however, is how closely connected with other major early monastic centres, including apparently the community at Lindisfarne, was this unrecorded community of Dewsbury. There is another small fragment, Dewsbury 8, which is as deeply and finely modelled as any pre-Viking Northumbrian sculpture: it may have been another cross like the two just discussed – and of the same date, though possibly by a different hand.[52]

Foci of devotion: the crucifixes at Dewsbury and Kirkburton

The cross shaft and head in four pieces, now reconstructed with missing areas replaced by modern stone in All Hallows Church, Kirkburton, has a figure of the crucified Christ which fills the head and extends at least halfway down the shaft: it stands out against the cross as if applied in a manner reminiscent of an ivory or metal figure attached to the front of a wooden or metal cross.[53] Crossheads treated like crucifixes had appeared in Northumbrian sculpture by the first half of the ninth century (see Rothbury, Northumberland),[54] and one designed like a metalwork cross even earlier (Hoddom, Dumfriesshire).[55] However, metal and ivory crucifixes with the hands and head overlying the edge mouldings are a ninth- to eleventh-century feature, while the very long loincloth worn by Christ also occurs on late work, such as a miniature in a psalter from St-Germain-des-Près, c.1030–60 (Paris, Bibliothèque Nationale, MS Lat. 11550, fol. 6).[56] The interlace terminates at the top with a twisted loop which would be at home in Viking Age sculptures with an Anglian heritage, as on the great cross from Leeds.[57] There is evidence from the tenth and eleventh centuries for the placing of processional staff crucifixes behind altars, a practice which could have led to the evolution of the sculptured staff crucifix for this position – thus some evidence for the Kirkburton cross as a focus of devotion, likely to have stood behind a principal altar of the church.[58] The plainness of its back and sides, which have edge mouldings but no other decoration, supports this view. It is an exceptionally fine piece, suggesting a church and indeed a patron of some importance. The proximity of the church to Dewsbury, and its inclusion in the Manor of Wakefield, the pre-Conquest royal estate, must be significant.

Dewsbury has a fragment which can be reconstructed only as a staff crucifix with the loincloth-clad body of Christ in the shaft, his upper body, head and arms in the cross head (Dewsbury 6).[59] Although less modelled in style than Kirkburton it has similarly slender proportions and stands within Anglian traditions of sculpture in its overall layout and programme. Some features relate it to the earlier sculptures from the same site. It is therefore probably somewhat earlier than the Kirkburton example – early to mid-tenth-century rather than tenth- to eleventh-century – and it indicates the continuing importance of Anglian Dewsbury into the Viking Age. Its unweathered condition suggests it never stood outside, but ornaments on all four faces suggest it was not intended to be viewed from only one side. This begs the question of where it stood within the church, perhaps at a major altar at a crossing, which visitors and worshippers might have been able to walk around.

Commemorative sculptures

Crosses with commemorative inscriptions

These are confined to the two ecclesiastical sites of Dewsbury and Thornhill. Dewsbury, which, as we have seen, has three inscriptions on cross fragments in Latin and in Roman script identifying figural sculpture, and also has one unusually small and delicately carved cross head (Dewsbury 10), with an incomplete memorial inscription in the vernacular which, in a carefully considered discussion, John Higgitt concluded was set up by someone in memory of his unnamed son. I suggested the small scale of the monument was appropriate for a child.[60] This provides evidence of use of the church by the laity even in the pre-Viking period – though the evidence only tells us about the rich, royal or aristocratic (and literate, presumably), who could afford such monuments.

There are no fewer than four memorial inscriptions at Thornhill, all on cross shafts, one (Thornhill 1) in Roman script, and three in runic (Thornhill 2–4).[61] Numbers 1, 3 and 4 were set up by men in memory of other males: number 2 is unusual in being set up by a woman in memory of another female, possibly a relative, as both names end in -*swiþ*. Thornhill might have been a daughter church of Dewsbury – perhaps originally a double house (of both male and female religious) – a tempting view as it is within walking distance of Dewsbury – or it might have been a church set up slightly later to serve the needs of a site with a wealthy and literate lay population, such as was suggested by the small cross head from Dewsbury. With no documentation and no archaeology, it is difficult to know, but this group of memorials was clearly important to its community at the time.

Grave covers and shrines[62]

Grave markers without inscription are also memorial sculptures. The area has two, at Dewsbury and Mirfield. The Dewsbury example (No. 15)[63] is clearly a recumbent monument, with connections to pre-Viking, house-shaped tomb- or shrine-covers. Its house shape and pentagonal section link it with the Hedda stone from Peterborough of the late eighth or early ninth centuries, another example from a period interested in reviving late antique and early Christian forms as well as iconography,[64] while its scroll links it with a fragment of a possible cross-base (Dewsbury 14) of ninth-century date.[65] I do not believe this piece is any later, even though the carving of the scroll is somewhat more clumsily carved, often seen as a feature indicating later copying of the motif. One feature alone, however, its tegulated (tiled) roof, led J.T. Lang to include it in his classification of hogback-shaped monuments, as an example of his group X.[66] It seems to me more interesting if one views this as a possible forerunner of the Viking Age monument type, which Lang showed was not an import but actually developed first in Yorkshire, in an area of Viking settlement.[67] It marks Dewsbury again as an influential centre of innovation in the late pre-Viking period, with continuing wide contacts in the Northumbrian monastic sphere.

The Mirfield grave marker is similarly interesting, since it has two animal heads on the top, reminiscent of the hogback form, even though here they face outward and the piece is also much smaller. Parallels may be found in the grave markers thought to have come from the foot of graves, found under York Minster, some of which have facing or addorsed beasts.[68] The rest of its decoration (a twist on one side and a simplified animal on the other; on one face, a pseudo-basket plait, on the other, a figure carrying a cross in an arched panel) makes it look like a late and very simplified version of an Anglian cross shaft – tenth to eleventh century. The apparently saintly or Christ-like figure does not suggest a secular monument, but Mirfield seems not to have become independent of Dewsbury until the thirteenth century, which raises the possibility that in the pre-Conquest period it was a subsidiary house of a still functioning ecclesiastical centre.[69] Certainly this piece suggests a patron with some sense of sculptural types from elsewhere in the immediate area, including the major ecclesiastical sites across Yorkshire in the late pre-Conquest period.

All these grave markers are in different ways fine pieces of sculpture, and as such they would at this period have been very much the prerogative of the wealthy and well-connected, both ecclesiastical and lay. They might originally have stood inside churches or in graveyards – in which there is some evidence for the interment of royal or aristocratic lay patrons.[70] Gradually these graveyards would have had a more general use, but markers such as those above all imply wealthy and in some cases literate patrons. Again, they would have become more generally and regularly visible as churches came over time to operate more as we would expect of modern parish churches.[71]

Statements of territorial power or possession?
Wakefield
The presumed centre of a pre-Conquest royal vill, and of the post-Conquest Manor of Wakefield, has only one surviving pre-Conquest sculpture, albeit a rather fine one.[72] It is a rectangular cross shaft patterned solely with interlace, with connections with late pre-Viking sculpture in Cumbria (Addingham 2 and Waberthwaite 2),[73] and elsewhere in Yorkshire (Hauxwell 1, N. Yorkshire; Kirkdale 8 and Hackness 1 in east Yorkshire).[74] It also has strong links with Thornhill 2, strong enough to suggest it is part of the same group. Whether it stood in the church or outside, it has to be seen as a statement of the royal and ecclesiastical connections of the estate.

Boundary markers?
Some crosses seem to have functioned in the landscape as boundary markers for territories or estates within them. There are no fewer than five cross bases grouped around Dewsbury, although two (Birstall and Woodkirk) are outside the areas defined by Faull and Moorhouse as the Parish of Dewsbury.[75] Woodkirk has nothing but its form and angle mouldings to show it was related to the others, as it has no other decoration by which to date it.[76] Bases, of course, would have been needed for most cross-shafts; indeed one (Dewsbury 14) is from Dewsbury itself.[77] The other four are placed at a distance, in an arc from the west of Dewsbury to its north-east, and apparently in relation to an important Roman road in the area, Margary 712, which runs from York via Tadcaster and Leeds to Chester, via Manchester.[78] Rastrick stands at a junction between 712 and 720aa; Birstall and Woodkirk, though on opposite sides of 712, are both close to the junction with 721 (see Figure 2.1 in this volume).[79] All those with decoration have a complex of features which relate them with each other and with sculpture

at Thornhill or Wakefield, as well as with other major pre-Viking monuments in Northumbria.[80] They seem to represent the northern and western edges of the spread of sites with sculpture related to Dewsbury in the pre-Viking period. It is not hard to see the four (Rastrick, Hartshead, Birstall and Woodkirk) as defining the heart of the ecclesiastical estate of Dewsbury rather than the larger area ascribed to the Parish. None is more than eight kilometres from the centre, which calls to mind Blair's surmise that 'by 800, most people outside the highland zone were within what they would have considered a reasonable walking distance from a minster' (i.e., within a radius of 5 to 8 kilometres – 3 to 5 miles),[81] although how quickly the area outside this would have been populated by churches is harder to see. Dewsbury itself, of course, and Thornhill, Wakefield, Kirkburton, Kirkheaton and Mirfeld are all to the south and east of the arc suggested by the cross bases: they imply a well-populated and prosperous area, with a number of churches (or centres of some kind with crosses), in a landscape also relatively well supplied with sculptures and buildings of religious significance. The wider area ascribed to the parish and to the royal vill, mainly further into the Pennine uplands, would have been more sparsely populated, and sculptured landmarks are also rarer.

There are sculptures on the western edge of the greater Parish of Dewsbury which are also on the western edge of the western half of the Manor of Wakefield as defined by Faull and Moorhouse. In these cases all are cross shaft or head fragments. The most notable feature of all these fragments, however, is that none of them looks to Dewsbury for inspiration. The furthest north, the two fragments from Stanbury, have a tenth- to eleventh-century simplification of the earlier interlace and scroll patterns. Their immediate connections are not with Dewsbury or indeed any Yorkshire sites, but with a fragment from Colne in Lancashire, and more widely with Cumbria.[82] The complete shaft and head from Todmorden, just on the Yorkshire side of the present county border, relates to similar sculptures in Burnley and Whalley in Lancashire, all difficult to date but probably tenth- to eleventh-century crosses on an old route, therefore possibly way- rather than boundary-markers.[83] But if these two were boundary markers, they are as likely to be defining the eastern edge of estates or territory to the west, rather than the western edge of Dewsbury/Wakefield areas. Stansfield is the only one of these extreme western edge sites clearly named as part of the Wakefield state in Domesday Book (see above, pp. 120–23). Its shaft fragment has animal ornament with some relations in western Yorkshire, for example, with Ilkley 3 and Otley 3, which were also influenced, as this piece clearly was, by Mercian work, as well as some examples with isolated empanelled animals from north Yorkshire (Brompton 3 and Kirklevington 3).[84] While it is notable that the sculptures which show the strongest relationship with Dewsbury seem to lie within the area defined by the cross bases discussed above, crosses at Mirfield, Kirkheaton, Kirkburton and Thornhill, Stansfield, like the shaft at Wakefield, seem to show the intellectual connections and reach, as well as the extent, of the royal estate.

Literacy as an indicator of major ecclesiastical and royal/aristocratic connections

A number of inscriptions have already been noted at two sites.[85] Dewsbury has three inscriptions, in Latin and in Roman script, which identify the content of three of the figural scenes – one on Dewsbury 1 and two on 5, and therefore on both of the two major shafts with figural ornament. The closest Anglo-Saxon parallels to these are the inscriptions on the crosses from Bewcastle and especially Ruthwell and are 'a further reminder of the invisible threads which connect literate stone-carvers across the length and breadth of pre-Viking Northumbria'.[86] In addition, Dewsbury has one, and Thornhill has four, of the eighteen surviving vernacular memorial inscriptions in sculpture from the north of England, so almost a quarter of the total. There is no indication that any of the figures named, whether donors or those they commemorated, were ecclesiasts, so possibly these represent secular, royal or aristocratic practice in setting up such memorials. There is a further interesting example from this area, on a ninth- to tenth-century sculpture from Kirkheaton, with a runic inscription with a rare vernacular carver's signature: *Eoh worohtæ*.[87] Together, these provide extraordinary evidence of a literate and well-connected community in the Dewsbury area.

The significance of aniconic sculptures

Most discussion of pre-Conquest sculpture concentrates on those with figural ornament, and/or inscriptions, simply because these make the search for the contemporary significance and use of such monuments at least appear more possible to the modern mind – although several writers have shown how potentially delusional such an appearance of understanding can be, when pieces are rarely complete, and have lost colour and other means by which meaning could have been clarified.[88] However, the majority of pre-Conquest free-standing sculptures, whether from monastic or other sites, have neither figures nor inscriptions: only various forms of plant ornament, some with birds or animals in their branches or scrolls; animal ornament; abstract patterns (such as interlace or other forms of geometric decoration) or a mixture of these. Table 6.1 shows the distribution between these two broad types, figural and aniconic. From this it is clear that only two sites – Dewsbury and Kirkheaton – appear to have a mixture of aniconic and figural sculptures, but, as always, caution is needed as most are fragments, and we have no means of knowing how many are lost.

Rosemary Cramp recently raised the possibility that some aniconic monuments could have represented influence from the iconoclastic controversies which racked the church in the Byzantine empire, only to suggest that this is probably unprovable, while stressing that crosses ornamented with the vine scroll, 'with its Christological and Eucharistic symbolism [could] be as potent a source of devotion as a figure'.[89] An example which must certainly have been seen in this way is the so-called Acca's cross from Wilfrid's monastery of Hexham, Northumberland.[90] There have been other attempts to ascribe contemporary meaning to such monuments, such as Carol Neuman de Vegvar's speculation as to what they might have meant in popular belief to non-ecclesiastical audiences, but for which documentary evidence is completely lacking.[91] None of the cross bases discussed above has any figural ornament, but again we cannot know how the crosses which stood in these bases were decorated. Although admittedly incomplete, none of the pieces on the edge of the area – Stanbury, Bradford, Todmorden, Stansfield or Wakefield – has any hint of figural ornament. One suggestion (by Neuman de Vegvar and others), that Rogation-tide processions were a very likely occasional use for such crosses, is particularly interesting, Rogations being specific days set aside to ask for God's mercy and associated from an early period with processions around an area such as a parish or estate.[92] Such crosses could have interacted at some level with popular religion, but the only evidence for their use belongs to the educated ecclesiastical world, and this gives little clue to as to what popular religion might have made of them.

This does not mean that secular interests played no role in the design of crosses. Such decoration throughout the period emulated the changing styles of metalwork both in pattern types, and in the painting and addition of actual metal pieces. Thus the designers of the sculpture used a contemporary secular understanding of splendour and value, which as part of that society they would have shared, in a way which would have been widely recognised and understood by a range of contemporary audiences, as a means of emphasising the central importance of the symbol of the cross itself. The Thornhill memorial inscriptions, all on aniconic monuments, perform the same function for literate observers when they refer to the monument, presumably a cross when complete, as a *becun*, a sign.

In addition, Cramp has speculated recently that a group of West Saxon crosses with interlaced reptiles suggested lay affiliation, influenced by Viking Age contacts with Scandinavian art.[93] Her original study also looked at the difference between types of interlace on crosses with vine scrolls, with its easily recognised Christological meaning, against those with more formal plants and animal ornament. These suggestions could be of particular interest when we look at sites with aniconic sculpture which seem particularly related to Wakefield, including Wakefield itself, Thornhill and Stansfield. In particular I would point to the vernacular memorial inscriptions from Thornhill and Dewsbury, including the only certain example in sculpture commissioned by a woman. Nevertheless, the parallels with pieces at all three sites are with other important ecclesiastical centres, such as York, Otley, Ilkley, Hackness and Kirkdale, all major centres of sculptural activity, several with royal or aristocratic connections, showing the high social level of even secular sculptures in the pre-Viking period.

Conclusion

All the sculptures in the area seem to be designed for visibility. There is evidence for major crosses both inside and outside churches, with memorial crosses outside churches probably a slightly later development.[94] Of the two great Dewsbury crosses, one seems to have a clear liturgical programme and to refer to the contemplative life of the monk and the importance to transmission of the monk/scribe; the other seems to be concerned with proclaiming the role of the church in the world: maybe these interpretations give some insight into their relative positions. The use of crosses as teaching crosses seems well-attested even quite late in the period.[95] The staff crucifixes at Dewsbury and Kirkburton seem to be a later development, but to be clearly *foci* for devotion, best placed inside their respective churches.

The presence of vine scroll ornament at Dewsbury supports it as a monastic establishment. Kirkheaton, which has only interlace and a little scroll decoration, but which has indications of a nimbed figure on one piece, and one inscription, is most likely also a religious community of some kind. There is nothing as early as the earliest and best work at Dewsbury, but the appeal to Anglian tradition is strong and its closeness to Dewsbury suggests the church could be a later offshoot. Thornhill is more interesting: the quality of the sculpture, an example of vine scroll and the high level of literacy manifested by its inscriptions could suggest a religious community, perhaps a daughter house of Dewsbury (its geographical proximity and the early date of the sculptures would suggest that): but, equally (and in this I have changed from the more tentative view in my earlier study),[96] the aniconic ornament and the nature of the inscriptions could imply a high-level, at least aristocratic community, able as wealthy patrons to call on the best sculptors, whether themselves monastic or at least working in that *milieu*.

These memorials were certainly meant to be seen: they are statements of social importance and connections as well as of personal loss. Many students of crosses have noted texts which indicate that aristocratic families had crosses on their estates, even in front of their houses: for example, in the Life of St Willibald, it is recorded that, as a sick child, the saint was offered by his parents before a cross because, as was the custom, many estates had not a church but a cross.[97] The crosses at Wakefield and Stansfield could fall into this category. The Thornhill group suggests an early manifestation of the inscribed grave marker moving into the estate church yard, at this stage confined to the highest social levels.

Blair thought the evidence for crosses as estate boundary markers slender,[98] but the cross bases on the roads which partly circle Dewsbury certainly have the appearance of defining the heart of the ecclesiastical estate, while the vaguer or absent links in date, style and ornament with the more peripheral pieces suggests a much more distant relationship over a wider but more sparsely populated area, with closer ties only a gradual development. Oddly, the ideal relationships of a centre to which people were able to come and a more distant pastoral relationship with outlying areas, which Bede posited for Lindisfarne and its surrounding communities, seems to fit the physical remains in the landscape around Dewsbury rather well.

7

Landmarks of the Dead: Exploring Anglo-Saxon Mortuary Geographies

Sarah Semple and Howard Williams

> *Him ða gegiredan   Geata leode*
> *ad on eorðan   unwaclicne,*
> *helmum behongen,   hildebordum,*
> *beorhtum byrnum,   swa he bena wæs;*
> *alegdon ða tomiddes   mærne þeoden*
> *hæleð hiofende,   hlaford leofne.*
> *Ongunnon þa on beorge   bælfyra mæst*
> *wigend weccan;   wud[u]rec astah,*
> *sweart ofer swioðole,   swogende leg*
> *wope bewunden   (windblond gelæg),*
> *oðþæt he ða banhus   gebrocen hæfde,*
> *hat on hreðre.*

The Geat race then reared up for him / a funeral pyre. It was not a petty mound, but shining mail coats and shields of war / and helmets hung upon it, as he had desired. / Then the heroes, lamenting, laid out in the middle / their great chief, their cherished lord. / On top of the mound the men then kindled / the biggest of funeral-fires. Black wood-smoke / arose from the blaze, and the roaring of flames / mingled with weeping. The winds lay still / as the heart at the fire's heart consumed / the house of bone.[1]

Introduction

Landscape perspectives have transformed our understanding of the early medieval world, but their emphasis is often upon the world of the living: settlements, farms, field systems, roads and estates.[2] In many accounts, burial places are absent or play only a supplementary role in shedding light on inhabited space. Conversely, early medieval graves, well-recognised since the eighteenth century, have tended to be intensively studied through the artefacts and bodies they contain rather than in terms of their spatial dynamics.

This gap has been filled in different ways over the last fifty years. Some studies have explored the shifting landscape locations of 'pagan' and 'conversion period' cemeteries.[3] The origins of minster churches and their burial grounds, and the subsequent development of the parochial system, have also been linked to the origins of 'Christian' burial in different guises, although it is now recognised that 'field cemeteries' were the norm for the rural population until the Viking Age.[4] These publications and others have made major contributions to understanding early medieval mortuary geography, yet just as many landscape studies have ignored burials; recent papers, even when taking a 'landscape' perspective, have tended to regard burial sites as undifferentiated dots on a distribution map and as little more than bi-functional places of corpse-disposal and commemorative landmarks.[5]

Despite a growth of evidence advanced through new research and discoveries, narratives of mortuary geography can remain simplistic, even though a rapid and linear progression from pagan grave-field to Christian churchyard is in general now recognised as inaccurate and simplistic. The idea of shifting mortuary terrains, resonant to the living on many levels, has been overlooked, as has the complex spatial organisation of particular burial sites and the evidence for multiple localities within any particular area where the dead might be interred contemporaneously.

To move forward with a robust framework for understanding early medieval mortuary geographies, scholars must escape the romantic dichotomy of regarding the early medieval dead as either confined to the dead pagan 'communities' situated on the periphery and borders of the living world, or safely bounded within churchyards under Christian pastoral care. While there is widespread recognition of the variability in early medieval burial sites and their spatial components, only a handful of studies have considered them as places of memory within complex and evolving historic landscapes, despite evidence for rich overlapping and changing burial terrains across the period.

This chapter offers a new introduction and framework for just such an approach to early medieval mortuary geography. Here we regard burial places as active locales, laden with meaning and potentially serving many functions and roles across space and time. Burial grounds are argued as fluid phenomena in terms of their form and significance, attracting changing and complex biographies from inception to abandonment. For instance, some burial sites might have very short histories of use – whether by design or by chance – restricted to a single burial or a small group of graves in rapid succession before falling into disuse.[6] Archaeological research can also reveal burial grounds that have multiple phases of use, evolving over decades and centuries and receiving hundreds, sometimes thousands, of burials in the process. In such instances, burial places not only retained, but accrued and transformed as locales where memories and identities were invested in the landscape.

In many cases, burial location is influenced by some form of preceding architecture – whether natural or human-made: a spur, a river bend, a house, a boundary, a route, an ancient monument, a church, a chapel or other locus. These features, if they remained visible, could become enduring landmarks, attracting successive interments and forging relationships between graves and the locale through repeated 'reuse'.[7] Yet this approach must also contend with the 'afterlives' of burial grounds: many endured as landmarks themselves for decades and centuries after abandonment whereas others reveal evidence that they were rapidly discarded, forgotten or overlain by settlement or other activities.[8] Hence, throughout the Anglo-Saxon period, burial grounds were complex, varied and shifting spaces of mourning, and of remembering and forgetting.[9]

This chapter deliberately avoids any attempt at a single, monolithic narrative aimed at replacing the traditional viewpoint of pagan grave-field to Christian churchyard. Instead, we explore a series of themes in early medieval mortuary geography, taking examples from either side of, and from within, the conversion period. We hope that by doing so we prompt new ways of writing about early medieval burial that are less restricted by historical event-horizons, emphasising how burial places might have operated as 'time marks' in a varied and changing environment of southern and eastern Britain from the fifth to the eleventh centuries. We hope to show how, as locales operating on different scales and significances, burial places were mnemonic and social agents: places where burial took place and other gatherings occurred and where the dead – individually and collectively – were constituted as inhabitants and actors within Anglo-Saxon social and religious life. Our examples reveal the range of ways that early medieval people engaged with such places as they inhabited and moved through their daily world.

Previous and current research

Since the earliest antiquarian discoveries, the locations of Anglo-Saxon graves have been considered as indicators of the socio-political, economic and religious life of early medieval people. Early reports focused near-exclusively on artefacts and burial customs, yet occasionally they ventured inferences about landscape. For example, John Yonge Akerman,[10] writing about his excavations at Long Wittenham, now in Oxfordshire, noted that the area's place names and graves revealed that the earliest Saxon settlements were drawn to the 'natural attractions' of the Thames valley. Others regarded location in terms of heathendom: graves at Broughton Poggs, Oxfordshire, for example, were connected by Akerman to springs: the natural places of veneration by 'our heathen forefathers'.[11] John Kemble saw burials as indicators of settlement, but influentially suggested that pagan graves might be located on boundaries, away from the landscapes and habitations of the living.[12] Vistas were taken into account in these romanticised visions of the heathen past: both Akerman and Richard Cornwallis Neville emphasised views and panoramas, the latter underlining the 'commanding position' of the Little Wilbraham cemetery in Cambridgeshire.[13]

A more systematic approach to burial location became a key component of the nineteenth- and twentieth-century culture-history quest to use early Anglo-Saxon grave-finds and cemeteries to chart the English conquest.[14] Burial location was explored via the distribution map of cemeteries, burials and find-spots in relation to Roman roads, towns and villas, topography and (in particular) river systems.[15] For individual cemeteries, historical narratives of settlement were generated in relation to their location: cemeteries next to Roman towns became evidence of settled *foederati* to protect extant sub-Roman populations (see, for example, Caistor St Edmund, Norfolk)[16] and burials along water courses reified historical accounts of Germanic invasion.[17]

By the 1970s serious attempts were being made to consider, both quantitatively and contextually, burial location from socio-political and territorial perspectives. Desmond Bonney's investigation of the relationship between burial and boundaries was key to this development,[18] followed by a systematic study by Ann Goodier.[19] Since then, burials and boundaries have continued to receive attention in studies that integrate burial and topographical analysis with historical and place name evidence.[20] A range of other interleaving factors are now considered relevant to cemetery placement, such as topography, fields, routeways, water courses, viewsheds and proximities with ancient monuments;[21] analyses using Geographic Information Systems of the locations of known settlements and cemeteries and metal-detector finds recorded by the Portable Antiquities Scheme[22] have considerably enriched our understanding, as well.[23] Research has also revealed how, in middle and late Anglo-Saxon England, a pattern of fixed churches with churchyards slowly developed.[24] The Christian landscape was punctuated with landmarks to the dead, not only churches, but chapels and community and household burial grounds.

Two further categories of archaeological site, long recognised, but only recently integrated into discussions of mortuary geography, also featured in the mid- to late Anglo-Saxon landscape. Burial places of social outcasts, revealed through the reinterpretation of well-known sites and new discoveries, have seen appraisal as visible markers of power and authority as well as religious exclusion,[25] while standing stone crosses with memorial functions (among other roles), projected the identities of secular and ecclesiastical elites out across the landscape.[26] These later enduring markers may have continued a pattern of display established prior to Christian conversion in the location of prominent burial mounds.[27] Some are demonstrably located on boundaries by important routes;[28] others are likely to have been situated in relation to churches or sites of assembly.[29]

The Christianised landscape was also a terrain in which ancient monuments and places, including burial mounds, accrued associations that lingered on in memory and folklore.[30] Place names and charter bound terms provide an insight into a landscape populated with imagined ancestors and heroes: natural features such as hills, pools and stones, as well as ancient monuments and places of burial, materialised the real, imagined and mythical dead in the world of the living.

While not denying important shifts in the organisation and meaning of mortuary practice and its material traces during the period, we hope here to emphasise persistence of practice despite shifts in burial locations. In other words, we identify a varied but enduring significance in the role of the graves, cemeteries and other monuments as landmarks through which memories of the dead, individually and collectively, were facilitated and negotiated. From this basis, we begin by arguing that the dead were powerful and empowering elements within the world of the living, occupying a central rather than peripheral place: the dead (often but not always ancestors of those who disposed of, mourned and remembered them), in different ways and through varying strategies, are argued here as active forces in the Anglo-Saxon landscape.

Burial sites as places

Burials as mnemonic citations

The dead cannot bury themselves, and we can assume that every funeral attested within our record – cremation or inhumation – was managed by one or more individuals and involved many participants and audiences. Complex and elite burials such as the wealthy, early seventh-century ship-burial beneath Mound 1 at Sutton Hoo, Suffolk, or the rich 'princely' chamber-grave from Prittlewell, Essex, are easily distinguished as the results of highly complicated and dramaturgical performances involving time, labour and the staged display and consignment of cadavers and material culture into a prominent, monumental burial facility.[31] Performance and procession are likely to have been significant to the early medieval cemetery as a place of power.[32] For Anglo-Saxon England, we lack the detail offered by the frequently quoted tenth-century account of Ibn Fadlan describing the burial of a *Rus* chief on the Volga.[33] Archaeological evidence does, however, attest to comparably elaborate, high-status funerals in early England, and these were probably attended by large crowds, lasted several days and involved a host of performers, from the grieving relatives to ritual specialists, and even sacrificial victims (animals and just maybe humans) (Figure 7.1).

Fig. 7.1 A visual reconstruction of an Anglo-Saxon funeral capturing how such events may have involved the gathering of family and mourners (artist's impression by Aaron Watson inspired by the location of the seventh-century bed-burial on Swallowcliffe Down. Reproduced with kind permission of Aaron Watson).

Every funeral at every site will have been different in terms of how many attended and how much investment was placed in the event, but the act of transporting a corpse to a cemetery and its burial at the very least necessitated the presence of one or two others. Individual, elite funerals were made memorable through their performance, but their role in cumulative commemoration came by the fact that the same *place* was selected and new graves were placed in relation to still-visible existing monuments: mnemonic citations.[34] In this way the buried dead became participants in each new funeral, creating an ancestral palimpsest: these cumulative assemblages of graves and mounds created real and constructed lineages of the communities from those interred. To retain efficacy, these cemeteries needed to be maintained and augmented. We generally accept that cemeteries expanded over time, but we rarely consider how such processes were managed, how burial was organised and arranged, how ongoing burial practices were encouraged and how graves were protected from grave-robbing and more casual environmental and animal disturbance.

The challenge of the archaeological evidence is that above-ground surface traces often elude us. It is recognised that prehistoric and Roman monuments, perhaps augmented and elaborated with shrines and posts, could have constituted collective foci for some cemeteries in the fifth and sixth centuries and more commonly in the seventh century, perhaps continuing through the eighth and ninth centuries.[35] At sites like Apple Down in Sussex[36] or Broadstairs in Kent,[37] a variety of traces indicate above-ground structures – from standing posts to small and large square and rectangular structures – built, we assume, from wood, wattle and other organic materials. These cemeteries we might envisage as monumentalised terrains, visually evident within the landscape. Such locations accrued monumentality through a process of successive acts of building, maintenance and decay rather than single episodes of building large mounds.[38] Collectively rather than individually, these markers would have had a powerful visual impact on those active within, and in the vicinity of, the cemetery, even if individual memorials lasted in good condition for less than a generation.

We do not know if such structures were regularly maintained by the living. The occasional example at Apple Down implies some four- and five-post/structure settings associated with cremation burials were altered over time with the replacement of corner posts and the insertion of further cremation burials.[39] At the same site, inhumation graves were

Fig. 7.2 The surviving burial mound at Taplow, Buckinghamshire: a seventh-century princely grave (photograph: Howard Williams).

sometimes deliberately inserted into structures previously occupied by cremation burials,[40] suggesting these seemingly ephemeral structures may have had complex life-histories of their own. The maintenance and abandonment of standing structures is often a feature in discussions of the lifespans of settlements,[41] but such processes may have played an important role within the cemetery, too. Whether or not these were literally 'houses for the dead', such grave markers could have served as semi-permanent and collective repositories for the dead, sometimes maintained or reused, others, left to decay.

Before, during and after conversion, more enduring structures – burial mounds in earth or cairns in stone, and later stone tombs – were constructed over and for graves. Barrow cemeteries are arguably more common in the period of conversion than they were in 'pagan' cemeteries,[42] although the survival of surface traces is most likely the result of taphonomic chance rather than the hard-and-fast contrast often supposed between 'flat' and 'barrow' cemeteries.

It is all too easy to visualise barrow cemeteries such as Greenwich, Greater London, just as they survive today, as places defined by a spread of apparently contemporary grassy mounds.[43] However, cemeteries were developed over time, and to a visitor in the late sixth century some barrows would have appeared old and covered with vegetation, and others newly built would have perhaps retained a more regular, turf-built shape or stood out as chalk or clay mounds, distinguished by the colour of the local natural soils.

Though details of the precise appearance of cemeteries are not preserved in written or illustrative sources, archaeological evidence does underline how repeated acts of augmentation – involving successive burials, new markers and monuments, as well as the reuse of burial places and older monuments – may have made cemeteries meaningful places of memory. Cemeteries, with barrows in different states of vegetative regeneration or new, repaired, reused or decaying markers, may have visually mapped out genealogies in death – a narrative spectacle that told the viewer of the life and death of a family, a community or even a dynastic line.[44] At Uncleby, in East Yorkshire, an old prehistoric mound was enlarged and augmented with each additional early medieval burial, the grave mound growing in diameter and height as one or more communities used it as a place to bury their dead.[45] In this way whole cemeteries can be reconceptualised as places of *cumulative memory*, landmarks to the 'communal dead', places where the entire cemetery offered a 'history' about that community. At some sites individual and group stories might have been visually picked out through the palimpsest of markers, just the way today a group of gravestones in a churchyard can attest to power of a single family across several generations or to a tragic loss of life for a small community.

Burials and structured activities in cemeteries

The 'shape' of cemeteries provides an important, tantalising insight into the power of the dead as structuring agents for the activities of the living. The most obvious structuring principle is the founder grave, where one or more burials of early date, usually well furnished and often monumentalised, were situated as the first burials on a site. This is not as discernible a feature in England as it is on the Continent, but is well-illustrated, for example, at Finglesham, Kent, a well-known site with a fully published catalogue,[46] recently analysed by Duncan Sayer.[47] The wealth of the cemetery is concentrated in a small number of graves. Sayer identifies three burial plots in concurrent use, but plots A and C were the wealthier ones.[48] The founder graves within plot A may have been two early sixth-century wealthy graves – H2 and 204 – perhaps the 'ancestors' for an extended household who continued to bury their dead around these graves for several generations.[49]

Such relationships imply early burials may have had a performative role, their spatial relationship forming a key part of the decision-making and ritual around the subsequent funerary events. They also imply that memory or myths surrounding the 'founder' graves may have been active in shaping later funerary events on the site. However, at many sites, like those explored by Sayer,[50] not all subsequent graves are 'satellites' to ancestral burial mounds; instead, there is a more complex process of location and relocation of burial plots, some contemporaneous, others successive, in which graves 'cite' each other over generations.

One way of approaching these relationships is to consider burial topography through precise chronological phases, as explored recently in the work of Duncan Sayer, who used a generational approach to the cemeteries of Berinsfield, Oxfordshire; Apple Down, West Sussex; and Mill Hill, Deal, Kent.[51] In these instances, as at Finglesham in Kent, we can chart in broad terms the evolution of polycentric cemeteries and identify clusters of graves as particular 'generations' in their development. The terrain of the cemetery takes on a new dimension as an active and changing space with multiple, co-occurring burial plots in use over multiple generations. This is evident also at Buckland, Dover, in Kent, where excavations of the larger cemetery revealed a complex, evolving patchwork of more than twenty-three foci or plots: seven established in the fifth century, with more beginning during the sixth and seventh centuries as the earlier ones were abandoned. Within these foci, clusters and rows of graves mark out affinities and distinctions within the clusters, although 'founder graves' were elusive.[52] Some of the plots endured through many phases of the site, and some might represent 'reuse' at an intra-site level, with burials reactivating long-abandoned burial plots. The changing use of the terrain will never be elucidated with certainty, but Buckland does show how spacing could be fluid and used as an ordering and differentiating principle, separating out activity at different periods and between different burial groups: families, households or other social collectives.

Street House, Loftus, in North Yorkshire, offers, by contrast, evidence of a strictly defined and 'planned' early Christian cemetery arena.[53] Here, in the seventh century, a remarkable and apparently single-phase cemetery of 109 inhumation graves was laid out in reference to an earlier and larger Iron Age/Romano-British enclosure. West–east aligned graves were used at Street House to create the cemetery space. A double row of end-on-end burials marked out the cemetery's northern edge, and two corners of the southern edge of a rectangular space. A single continuous row, partly in-filled with a second row, marked out the western edge, and a similar but incomplete arrangement can be seen to the east. Only two graves intercut at Street House. This implies that the site was laid out with markers we can no longer pick out and/or that it was created quickly, with the dug graves visible as reference points for the positioning of each new interment. An entrance or opening was left clear on the southern side and a second possible entrance on the eastern side. Internally there were further graves, including a spatially discrete bed-burial, a circular mound, a sunken-featured building (interpreted as a 'mortuary house') and a large setting of posts, perhaps a large timber structure. Together, this evidence suggests that the space inside this mortuary enclosure was an active place and the bed-burial was of special status. In fact the 'architecture' of the entire cemetery conveys a sense of theatre. The novelty and unusual nature of the layout is theatrical in its own right, but the creation of an internal, bounded space hints at ongoing rituals with the dead as 'overseers' or even participants in the activities. The layout intimates too that, at certain sites, individuals or groups of people – whether families, monks or clerics – might act as 'cemetery designers'. The inclusion of the dead themselves as key props within such 'designs' points to an intentional selection; not all the dead were invited to be part of such arrangements. Some individuals, it seems, were more powerful in these designs. The 'boundedness' and entry point also hint at restrictions on the movement and access of living participants as well. The Street House cemetery, created at a time when Christianity was becoming established in England, although quite differently constituted, echoes the later structuring principles and organisation of burial within and outside a church: important graves acted as foci within the enclosed sacred space, and graves around the outside clustered around and defined the sacred ground around the church.[54]

Beyond burial: assembly and cult

The large cremation cemeteries of the fifth and early sixth centuries in eastern England attest to 'communal' or group activity as well, but of a distinctive nature not found in later centuries. First, the multiple burial of urns in apparently individual pits implies that the dead were collected, gathered together by the living until ready to be deposited as a group, or else the grave was kept accessible and open to further insertions before finally being covered by a mound or marker. Second, the extent of these burial places could be considerable, with Spong Hill, Norfolk, and Loveden Hill, Lincolnshire, containing well over 2,000 cinerary urns each. Both appear to have served communities.[55] Furthermore, it is possible that burial was simply the most visible aspect of a wide range of socioeconomic and cultic activities taking place at prominent locations, places connected to a local sense of identity and origin. Loveden Hill, for example, is well-known as a site where a small, natural, barrow-shaped knoll provided a main focus for the funerary activity in the fifth century and may have persisted as a zone of assembly into the Christian era.[56]

What is equally revealing is that these 'cemeteries as central places' ceased as large-scale mortuary locales prior to the advent of

Christianity.[57] Instead, smaller inhumation cemeteries dominated, and mixed-rite cemeteries, where both cremation and inhumation operated in tandem, endured beyond the lifespans of the large central cemeteries. These smaller burial places may have maintained similar roles, however, as places for gathering and focal activity such as visits, veneration and assemblies. Attention was recently drawn to the small yet compelling body of evidence for eating and drinking activities at early Anglo-Saxon cemeteries, evidence all too easily overlooked because of its ephemeral nature.[58]

A handful of sites provide additional evidence for the later importance of cemeteries as places for activity other than burial. Saltwood, Kent, is an important new discovery for a range of reasons. Over 200 burials were located here, distributed across four discernible clusters or foci, three focused on Bronze Age barrows. Saltwood has provided clear evidence for activity on the site after inhumation burial had ceased. A middle and late Anglo-Saxon phase of activity comprises clusters of pits to the west and east ends of the excavated area and includes stray finds from the topsoil. The site is likely to be the meeting place of the Domesday hundred of Heane, suggesting a long biography of use and reuse for this locale following the end of its use for burial.[59]

Not every hundred meeting place can be connected to an ancient site or feature, let alone an early Anglo-Saxon cemetery, but additional instances are known. Stuart Brookes has identified a number of meeting-places that have an association with early Anglo-Saxon burial sites.[60] An informative example can be found on the Isle of Wight. There are several possible assembly sites attested by place names, but one of these is Bowcombe Down, the site of an early Anglo-Saxon barrow cemetery, broadly dated between the fifth and sixth centuries.[61] The cemetery occupies a prominent location, a high ridge or connecting spur with extensive views to the north and south. Several Bronze Age barrows provided a focus for early Anglo-Saxon activity which included cremation as well as inhumation burials. These types of site, though rare, suggest that early Anglo-Saxon cemeteries and places of burial could continue to exert a profound influence in later centuries in the shape of local administrative practices.

The use of early cemeteries as later places for assembly is attested in the south and east of England. Examples are sporadic but intriguing, such as Greenwich Park and Mill Hill at Deal.[62] There is insufficient evidence to claim any kind of model, but we can at least suggest that for some populations, cemeteries were important central places, intrinsic to local and regional identity, visited for funerary activity, perhaps feasting, decision-making or rituals connected to ancestry; some clearly continued to exert a strong influence, surviving as meeting places within late administrative arrangements.[63]

Landscapes of the dead
Burials, cemeteries and settlements

Anglo-Saxon cemeteries were long thought to exist separate from settlements, perhaps on the edge of the cultivated world of the living. Increasing evidence points, however, to the integration of the dead within the settlement itself and for close spatial relationships between cemeteries and settlements. The excavations at Yeavering in Northumberland revealed a site with remarkable integration between the developing settlement activity and the positioning of burials.[64] To the west of the complex, burials were initially situated with reference to a standing post and square enclosure focused on what the excavator termed the Western Ring Ditch. Through the developed phases of the palace complex at Yeavering, burial remained a key active practice. Burial AX situated at the threshold to the Great Hall, for example, must have been made with reference to this monumental building, with the funerary ceremonies and the interment taking place not far from the eastern entrance area of the structure. Even within the latest phases of the site, which may have remained active into the eighth century, burial was still present, with a great density of burials situated to the east of the complex around structure B – thought to represent a timber church.[65] Although Yeavering stands out as a particularly remarkable example, settlement sites in the Till and Tweed valleys are often paired with cemeteries. The palace complex at Sprouston in Roxburghshire, for example, can be seen in aerial photographs to be accompanied by an enclosed cemetery.[66] This may be a regionally distinctive trait, generated out of the long-term 'frontier' status of this northern border landscape. At Yeavering, however, burials are intimate to the design and architecture of the site over time, implying burial ritual was bound to the activities of the living on the site. The alignments of buildings, standing posts and burial *loci* imply an intrinsic connection between the interred dead and the activities of the living.

Far less structured, but no less interesting, are the appearances in the eighth century of human bodies and body parts in settlement contexts. At Yarnton, Oxfordshire, human burial seems to have taken place at the immediate edge of the settlement.[67] Infant burial too is claimed as a phenomenon on settlement sites in this post-conversion era.[68] Such disposals might present evidence of experimentation, prompted by pressure to abandon existing traditions, combined with the influence of incoming practices and ideas. These practices are certainly short-lived, but do intimate that at times individuals and communities carried out funerary activity within the domestic sphere.

Wics and later towns offer evidence for the most complex mortuary geographies. At *Hamwic*, Southampton, Hampshire, at least two seventh-century burial sites existed, but as the settlement expanded and consolidated a series of further burial sites was established, some associated with churches, and others not.[69] The mortuary geographies of late Saxon and Anglo-Scandinavian urban centres such as Norwich, Lincoln and York remain under-researched, but the assemblages of stone sculpture from different church sites across York make it possible to identify contrasting commemorative environments chosen by ecclesiastical, lordly and mercantile elites within the evolving urban topography.[70] For example, at St Mark's, Wigford, Lincoln, stone sculpture and extensive excavation revealed burials from the mid-tenth century onwards associated with a wooden church, and reorganisation in the eleventh century with the building of a new stone church. Originally explored by Brian Gilmour and David Stocker[71] and recently reviewed by Zöe Devlin,[72] St Mark's shows how individual cemeteries might accrue specific topographic 'funerary narratives', with stone grave-markers commemorating the identities and affinities of specific elite families.[73] St Mark's also reveals how this mortuary geography was integral to the rebuilding of the church, showing the punctuated equilibrium of acts of rebuilding by which social remembering and forgetting could be orchestrated and earlier burial plots adapted and destroyed.

Travelling with the dead

The best-known example of a cemetery or burials located with reference to water courses is the dynastic burial ground of Sutton Hoo, where large, primary barrow burials were constructed to be visible to those traversing and travelling inland from the coast into the early political territory of East Anglia, or indeed leaving to travel across or along the coasts of the North Sea.[74] Rather than just landmarks, we might think of these burial sites as active mnemonic agents within the Anglo-Saxon landscape. Elizabeth O'Brien,[75] inspired by the analogy of early medieval Irish literature, has argued for prominent (if not necessarily isolated) high-status barrow burials acting as 'sentinels' in the early historic landscape. Taplow, Buckinghamshire, is another example, the large burial mound located in relation to two bends of the River Thames (Figure 7.2). This mound, possibly part of a now-destroyed larger barrow cemetery, was constructed within a prehistoric hill fort with commanding views to the west, south-west, south and south-east.[76] In this instance, as Leslie Webster argues, the Taplow grave would have dominated those traversing along the Thames valley from the heartland of the *Gewissae* down through smaller territories towards the western edges of Kentish hegemony around London. This fluid and contested landscape might explain the significance of such furnished graves.[77] Burial grounds may well have taken on a role as more than territorial markers, acting as protective forces situated to keep coastal entry points and inland river routes secure, under the watch of the ancestral dead. The eighth-century account of Wilfrid's running aground on the South Saxon coast describes how a '*magus*' raised himself on a large *tumulus* or grave mound to perform a visible act of aggression directed at Wilfrid and his companions. This account may hint at a wider recognition of mounds as guardians and sources of ancestral or protective power.[78]

Terrestrial topographies

Stuart Brookes has made convincing arguments for the important role of Roman roads as structuring forces in the placement of cemeteries and thus the shaping of territory in the early kingdom of Kent.[79] Recent research on the cluster of cemetery activity at Eastry and Woodnesborough in Kent takes such ideas a step further.[80] The positioning of a number of burials and cemeteries in immediate visual and proximate relationships to a stretch of Roman road connecting a pair of early royal/cultic locations, hints at travel and movement being key factors in the conception of an early micro-territory or royal and cultic heartland.

The funerary record in East Yorkshire provides an interesting northern analogy. During the fifth to eighth centuries, the chalk Wolds, a wooded upland environment delimiting the Vale of York and the Driffield basin, was used for a number of individual inhumations and cemeteries. The Wolds was not a special zone, but the changing nature of the practices employed suggests an increasing need in the seventh century for burials to be experienced and seen as prominent visual features by those travelling between the core zones of power and settlement. The Vale of York and the Driffield basin are both argued to be important early heartlands.[81] The kings of Deira are recorded in action (or in death) at the royal vill at York, at another vill elsewhere on the River Derwent, at a cult-complex at Goodmanham and later at Driffield too, suggesting a further royal vill near Driffield.[82] Movement between these royal centres, dictated by the need for kings to travel to maintain authority, suggests the Wolds represented a kind of buffer zone, seasonally exploited and settled and traversed by elites who needed to manage core zones in an expanding kingdom.[83] Routes across this wooded upland landscape include prehistoric tracks and Roman roads, and the early medieval cemeteries and burials across the Wolds are all located within visual and physical reach of these known land routes, for example, at Painsthorpe Wold, where four cemeteries sit in close proximity, reusing prehistoric monuments situated closest to the Roman road (Figure 7.3). Considering all the information together asks us to view funerary evidence of different dates and to think about how such events might be used cumulatively to signal territory, authority and legitimate control. It requires us to envisage Anglo-Saxon communities and populations as conscious in their choice and design of funerary landscapes, working with an awareness of different scales of signalling in order to convey messages and narratives to a range of audiences.

Burial may indeed have been used in the same period at an even more ambitious scale. Many pre-Christian and conversion-period burial sites in prominent locations, such as the seventh-century male buried at Ford, Laverstock, Wiltshire, with weapons, a hanging bowl with crab apples, show signs of heavy investment, such as a large chamber and a raised mound.[84] Swallowcliffe Down, also in Wiltshire, represents a similar phenomenon, a female bed-burial of the seventh century, centrally placed into a large prehistoric barrow.[85] Both examples were on historic routes and hence not as remote and isolated as they might first appear. Furthermore, these burials were prominent and visible along these routes.[86] These burials were meant to be seen, encountered as enduring markers and some perhaps even inter-visible network of ancestral graves.[87]

A cluster of early medieval burials at Roundway Down, Wiltshire, encapsulates the enigma of these types of mortuary acts. The routes from most directions up onto this upland are steep, and yet at least four locations were used for sixth-/seventh-century burials.[88] New barrows may have been built as well as old barrows reused. At least two burials were well-furnished – a female-gendered assemblage with a box or bed and a typical suite of Byzantine-style jewels, and a possible male with a gaming board.[89] Similar to sites such as Cuddesdon in Oxfordshire[90] or Lowbury, now in Oxfordshire,[91] these were not principally sited to be visible places from the valley floor. If visibility was important, then it appears to have been in relation to extensive vistas – from one hilltop and horizon to another – as much as a signal meant for the immediate locality and lowland settlement below. In other words, these burials may not have been conceived as isolated statements. At the grandest of scales we could envisage them as intentionally created, a visually interlinked network of ancestral watchers situated across the borderlands and contested zones that lay between territories and kingdoms, created cumulatively, perhaps, with each burial reinforcing the network, and, in turn, inspiring another – an elite colonisation of, and competition for, territory.[92]

Fig. 7.3 View of a reused prehistoric barrow on Painsthorpe Wold, East Yorkshire: the early Anglo-Saxon burials and cemeteries reusing these large mounds flanked an early route across this landscape (photograph: Sarah Semple).

Taking a multi-scalar approach to the Anglo-Saxon funerary record is profitable; it reveals just how important the dead may have been in terms of structuring activities and signalling conceptions of space and territory. By collapsing chronologies and seeing proximate and remote burials, often treated in isolation, as potentially connected events, we can reconceive how early medieval people experienced and lived with the dead, and actively used and drew on them in their own multi-scalar reworkings of the landscape.

Sacral terrains

Monasteries established in the second half of the seventh and early eighth centuries provided a new kind of mortuary geography.[93] At Ripon, for example, multiple churches and sacred markers and several Christian burial grounds marked out a monastic landscape. There are intimations at Ripon that this developing sacralised terrain in part reflected or echoed a pre-Christian mortuary geography.[94] It is well-recognised that there is little evidence for pre-Conquest churches and monastic complexes situated *directly* over early Anglo-Saxon, pre-Christian burial grounds – later ideological appropriations such as Repton also remain

Fig. 7.4 Ripon Cathedral in its landscape setting: Ailcy Hill hidden in the clump of trees to the right of the cathedral. Early Christian monuments and activities may have been used to convert this wider landscape (photograph: Axel Steenberg and Sophie Steenberg).

rare examples of site-specific acts.[95] The issue may be, however, the scale at which we have approached the issue of 'cult continuity'. At Ripon, multiple Christian foci, including the minster, chapels and crosses were established across a terrain also marked by several cemeteries, some certainly Christian, some undated and one (Ailcy Hill) with a definite pre-Christian, sixth-century beginning (Figure 7.4).[96] In this instance a place of pre-Christian significance may have been 'dealt with' as a landscape, rather than as an individual place or feature. Sam Turner has argued for such Christianising processes over wide areas of landscape in southwest England.[97]

The ways in which we think about cemeteries and landscapes as places serving a local or regional hinterland may also be a limiting factor in the interpretation of burial practice. Ann Coles has recently used English place names to suggest the existence of macro-level conceptions of space and travel and the usual small limits that we might assume applied to a rural community's sense of space and place.[98] Rather than serving an immediate locality or region, we should perhaps consider that some cemeteries may have served as repositories for the dead from far more dispersed populations. The development of scientific investigation using strontium oxygen isotope variations drawn from surviving skeletal data is providing new information on the composition of burial populations.[99] At West Heslerton in North Yorkshire, lead strontium isotope analysis revealed that the early medieval population buried at the site was a mix of local and non-local groups.[100] At the fifth-century cemetery at Ringlemere, Kent, similar analyses suggest a proportion of the population had spent part of their lives in another region, perhaps the west of Britain.[101] At a superficial level, such information provides an insight into the profile of a living population, supporting the idea of communities with mixed geographic origins or descent. There is room, however, to think about such results in terms of funerary activity and ritual. Do such cemeteries represent nothing more than the local place of disposal for the local resident community, or might such places serve a much wider population that perceived themselves as linked to a certain place by political or familial ties? Perhaps we have underestimated how far early medieval populations might travel with the dead to ensure their burial in a family plot or a site closely allied to a sense of origin, lineage or identity.

In rare instances, we do have evidence for early medieval funerary activity and ritual that was geographically ambitious in scope. For example, the journey made by the monks of Lindisfarne with the remains of Cuthbert is an iconic tale, caused, according to the sources, by the Viking raiding and destruction of the monasteries in the north-east of

England. The resting places of the saint have been marked out for a millennium by holy foundations connected to the cult of Cuthbert.[102] The monks were exiles, travelling from place to place with the body before arriving at Chester-le-Street and, eventually, Durham. By the eleventh century, the various stopping places and resting places of the saint served to structure a spiritual landscape connected by a network of potent places of sanctity.[103] The remains of St Cuthbert emerge from these stories as an active agent in the structuring of ecclesiastical power in the north-east. Even earlier in time, Bede describes how the Northumbrian Christian King Oswald was slain in battle by Penda at *Maserfeld*, thought to be Oswestry.[104] Not only were body parts collected and revered as relics (the head travelling with remains of Cuthbert and the community), Bede describes how the place became a site of pilgrimage, with a great pit excavated by people who took 'away the very dust from the place where his body fell'.[105]

The Anglo-Saxon dead (at least the Christian ones) emerge from these accounts as powerful agents, mapping out and driving cult activity and pilgrimage. Such sources also hint at people engaging in travel to iconic and sacred locations associated with the dead some time before medieval pilgrimage emerged as a formal and structured experience with royal and ecclesiastical sanction. A question for the future is whether this is confined to Christian tradition or whether these aspects – the use of places of burial by dispersed communities, long journeys to burial sites, the commemoration of special places connected to the funerary ritual and visits to places of the dead to gather mementoes – could reflect aspects of ritual present in a pre-Christian era, as well.

Landmarks for the dead: cenotaphs and commemoration

In the Christian era, the sources reveal an immense emphasis was placed on the act of dying.[106] The deathbed scenes of Cuthbert and Bede describe the gathered audience, drawn to the powerful moment during which the individual was conceived as being between two worlds, that of the living and of the dead. Christianity demanded that the living were proactively involved in interceding for the dead through prayer. New forms of commemoration emerged, executed in stone and probably in wood, as well.

The establishment of cenotaphic commemoration finds a clear footing in the early medieval landscape through the evidence of the *Corpus of Anglo-Saxon Stone Sculpture*.[107] Some of the carved stones have been identified as commemorative monuments for the dead, as, for example, among the collections of stones surviving from Lindisfarne and Hartlepool.[108] Alongside the investment in such enduring and at times elaborate grave markers, other forms of display involving the dead also developed, and these can also be connected to elite signalling and displays of power.

Power and display: structured experiential landscapes

Execution cemeteries, places for the killing and disposal of individuals who had transgressed secular law and religious norms, can be recognised as early as the seventh century.[109] It is not until the tenth century, however, that a highly organised system, including places of judgment and places of execution and burial for felons, is unequivocally apparent in archaeological and written sources.[110] Careful mapping suggests execution sites were nearly always situated on local administrative or hundred boundaries, always in visible positions, frequently next to or overlooking major thoroughfares or routes (land and water)[111] and usually placed in association with earlier (prehistoric and sometimes early Anglo-Saxon) monuments and burials.[112] Such choices were, it seems, driven by a need to signal and reinforce the idea that these unfortunates were being consigned to heathen places, liminal sites outside Christian sanctity, suitable only for the torture, killing and disposal of the damned.[113]

The tenth-century pattern is sufficient to demonstrate a vision of power in which the visible display of executed felons was an important element in a planned network of royal authority, which adopted theatrical display as a way of signalling and maintaining authority. Those holding elite positions of authority were not just signalling their power over people, but over the supernatural as well. By using places associated with

Fig. 7.5 Reconstruction of a late Anglo-Saxon gallows site, positioned on an old earthwork on the chalk down land (reproduced with kind permission of Andrew Reynolds; copyright Sarah Semple).

the heathen dead, they conveyed the message that even in a Christian era they still had power over such places, able to consign unfortunates at will to hellish damnation in ancient heathen places.[114] A vivid illustration of the true vision and reach of late Anglo-Saxon royal power is the landscape connecting Winchester to Old Sarum. As a traveller exited north from Winchester, Old Dairy Cottage, situated immediately north of the settlement, would come into sight. Situated on downland overlooking the Winchester to Silchester Roman road, this execution site was active in the ninth and tenth centuries, with archaeological and written evidence for the display of decapitated heads, no doubt intended to inspire visual horror.[115] Turning and travelling west along the Roman road linking Winchester to Old Sarum, a traveller would next have encountered Stockbridge Down. Positioned in an impressively visible position marked by a non-sepulchral barrow, this quite large execution cemetery site was active in the tenth century. Decapitates were present, and two large postholes have been interpreted as the setting for a gallows (Figure 7.5).[116] Some 4 kilometres (2.5 miles) further on, past Stockbridge, is Meon Hill, a rise of downland that lies south of the Roman road. Execution burials were located here in the ditch of the rampart of an Iron Age hill fort, and finds indicate activity in the tenth century, with evidence for decapitations and possibly hangings for our traveller to witness.[117] Finally, on arriving at Old Sarum, to the south of the Roman road, a traveller might have found an execution site situated in relation to an old but undated barrow on a natural elevation. The site is undated, but at least fourteen burials were recovered, all with tied hands, suggesting perhaps the use of hanging rather than decapitation.[118]

The rule of the house of Wessex in the tenth century was dynamic and expansive, with the Vikings representing a constant military and political threat, and for at least a time the achievement of a 'unified' Anglo-Saxon England occurred under the rule of Athelstan.[119] Power in the old heart of Wessex was sustained through a number of important and long-lived royal residences and estates. The regular system of hundred units and estates extant in Hampshire and Wiltshire in this era, tied to such a rigorously organised judicial system, with its own distinct 'visual' geography, implies a far-reaching vision of power in the traditional heart of the ancient kingdom that used killing, burials, ancient burial places and landscape as a means of establishing and signalling royal power for all to see. The ways that the bodies of felons were treated in life and in death are further evidence of the assertion of power that such sites could represent. Mutilation and injury, as well as display of bodies and heads, demonstrate that crimes against the powerful could result in the forfeiture of an individual's bodily integrity and bodily privacy, as well as his or her life.

Handling the dead

Sequences at funerals

The elaborate dress fittings found in some early Anglo-Saxon inhumation graves, including brooches, clasps, buckles and straps, reveal that a corpse might be interred in costume and wrapped in layers of clothing or cloth.[120] The dressing of a corpse is a considerable undertaking, requiring close work with a cadaver, and needs to be done after *rigor mortis* has dissipated. It is likely, as some evidence suggests, that bodies were left a number of days before interment. The dressing of the body was only one element, however, of potentially elaborate post-mortem rituals. The miniature tools found in cremation burials include items that may have been connected to personal grooming: tweezers, miniature shears and ear scoops.[121] We cannot be certain, but it seems likely that such instruments would have been used, along with cloths for washing and combs for arranging head and facial hair, in the preparation of the body for cremation or indeed for inhumation.

Later written sources, from a Christian milieu, provide textual insight into death rites. The eighth-century *Life of St Guthlac* by Felix describes how Abbess Ecgburh presented Guthlac with a lead coffin and winding sheet in advance of his death.[122] After his death, Guthlac's sister

Pega buried him with these items in his church – a timber structure built on the island of Crowland next to the ancient barrow in which the Saint had dwelt. A year later the body was disinterred. The account implies an inspection of the corruption of the garments and body by Pega before she wound the corpse again in a new sheet and had it placed in the coffin, but the coffin was not again interred in the earth.[123] As Victoria Thompson has carefully revealed through her exploration of documentary sources, these kinds of familiar practice – the washing and wrapping of the corpse – are also incidentally mentioned by writers like Werferth.[124] Death was not just intimate for families; it could involve many others. In an account of late Anglo-Saxon gild activity, members were responsible for brethren who fell ill or died up to 100 kilometres (60 miles) from home, with a company of fifteen to thirty men obliged to ride with the dying or dead man carried in a cart.[125] Thus, evidence exists across the period to suggest that relatives and associates could expect to be in extremely close contact with the human corpse.

Bodies and body parts

How normal it was, across the Anglo-Saxon era, to exhume and handle human remains, fleshy or de-fleshed, remains difficult to ascertain. Grave robbing, an activity that necessitated the broaching of the grave and disturbance of the corpse, has recently been explored in detail by Alison Klevnäs, who suggests that excavated evidence attests to an intense outbreak of grave disturbance in Kent in the seventh century, paralleled in Merovingia, signalling a change in approach to the place of burial.[126]

In late Anglo-Saxon England, the increasing interest in relics – the body and body parts of Anglo-Saxon saints – resulted in some unusual activity by members of Christian monastic communities. Two accounts survive that describe monks knowingly or unknowingly digging in ancient barrows, on the hunt for human remains.[127] Although body fragments were kept and circulated as Christian relics, including heads, limbs, digits and even hair,[128] it is worth remembering that some eighty whole body shrines are documented in late Anglo-Saxon England,[129] underlining a distinct late Anglo-Saxon interest in intact human remains.

The disturbance and dismemberment of corpses thus did occasionally take place, but for a wide variety of reasons. In 1040 King Harthacnut ordered the exhumation of Harold I from Westminster, the beheading of the corpse and its disposal in a river or fen.[130] Unusual accounts, like that of the *Life and Miracles of St Modwenna*, recount the disinterment of individuals believed to be troubling the living, and their post-mortem mutilation: in this instance, decapitation and the placement of heads by legs and the removal of hearts, which were carried across running water to a junction of parish boundaries, where the hearts were burned on a pyre.[131]

These late Anglo-Saxon events seem extreme, rather than a norm, perhaps pointing to a disinclination to disturb and disperse human remains after burial. It is certainly the case that evidence for popular rites involving the handling or circulation of human body parts remains extremely rare. A group of seven human teeth was located at the shoulder of a male interred in the seventh-century cemetery at Marina Drive, Dunstable, Bedfordshire. They did not belong to the individual and seemed to have been held in a small bag and might have had an amuletic function.[132] A century or so later, Alcuin wrote condemning the popular practice of the carrying of 'bones in little bags',[133] but the contrastingly frequent mention of animal bone amulets may well explain his words.[134] The late Anglo-Saxon magical charms do record practices such as visiting a cemetery to step over a dead man's grave (*Lacnunga* 169) and the taking of 'a piece' of a child's grave (we might assume earth or soil) to ward off miscarriage and infant death (*Lacnunga* 170), but no mention is made of the use of human body parts in these popular magical/medicinal rituals and recipes.[135] A unique and obscure find, dating between the ninth to twelfth centuries from Baston, Lincolnshire, appears to be a 'mask' manufactured from the facial part of a human cranium. This was recovered alongside a second partial human skull from a ditch on an iron-working site at Baston, Lincolnshire – attesting to what seems to be an exceptionally rare example of popular activity involving the handling of disinterred or curated de-fleshed human remains.[136]

Conclusion

Even by the late Anglo-Saxon era, when archaeologists have traditionally considered death as being regulated, bounded and confined geographically to minsters, churches and consecrated cemeteries, evidence points instead to death and the dead being agents in the world of the living through their remains, graves and monuments. To travel through the late Anglo-Saxon landscape was to experience a terrain marked by the ancient burial places of the heathen past, old folk cemeteries and barrows associated with long dead princes and kings, active places of judicial killing and execution burial where bodies and body parts were displayed and where stone markers and structures housed the Christian dead and commemorated them. Body parts and bodies were displayed in monasteries and churches, and the tombs of saints were venerated.

We have argued here that by taking a non-linear approach, collapsing chronologies and adopting a multi-scalar perspective, we can begin to show the ways in which the dead were agent and powerful in the world of the living before, during and after the conversion.

In the pre-Christian and conversion periods, populations used burials proactively to shape territory, define lands and create a sense of belonging. The experimentation with elite graves in the seventh century begins to take on more ambitious connotations if we re-envisage such acts as connected rather than isolated. Indeed, by seeing burials in cemeteries and isolated or dispersed graves and burials as a series of 'cumulative' acts, we can begin to reconceptualise the multilayered meanings that were being invested in the landscape through the handling, treatment and interment of the dead. We have also argued that places of burial were not wholly 'liminal' or inactive, but that evidence instead points to some cemeteries and graves being the focus of activities which might sometimes have included re-accessing and circulating human remains and mortuary material cultures. Funerals were a form of theatre: repeated visits to cemeteries allowed mourners to enact rituals and performances, and the spaces and monuments within those cemeteries provided a context and stage for such acts. Monuments, whether reused ancient features, new mounds, timber structures or later Christian commemorative markers and crosses, visually marked out places of the dead, but also commemorated them, making the dead relevant to the living population. The connections with later assembly sites, and hints in the archaeological record of temporary gatherings and eating or feasting at some sites, also serve as a clear indicator that we should begin to reconceive cemeteries and burials as visited places that were not on the periphery of the world of the living, but powerful in the daily lives of Anglo-Saxons, before and after the changes wrought by Christian traditions.

8

Boundaries and Walls

Margaret Worthington Hill and Erik Grigg

> ... *bronda lafe*
> *wealle beworhton,   swa hyt weorðlicost*
> *foresnotre men   findan mihton.*
>
> They constructed a wall round the remains of the flames [of Beowulf's pyre] in a way very wise men could most splendidly contrive it.[1]

Introduction

Since prehistoric times, banks and ditches have been built to divide land, defend settlements or surround sacred sites, so we know that the Anglo-Saxons did not enter or leave a wild and empty landscape. Indeed, England in 1066 was a well-ordered kingdom with boundaries dividing fields from each other, towns from the countryside, religious sites from the profane world outside and one man's estate from another's. What percentage of these boundaries the Anglo-Saxons made themselves and which were older units of land is a matter of speculation. Unfortunately, dry stone walls are hard to date and wooden fences leave only the most ephemeral of traces. Luckily, the Anglo-Saxons also dug earthworks that include huge monumental dykes that still run for many kilometres across the landscape, small ditches designed to delimit estates, large banks that surrounded towns and religious enclosures and agricultural and woodland boundaries. This chapter will look at these various types of boundaries and their impact on the Anglo-Saxon landscape.

Dykes

The early medieval period witnessed the building of some of the most famous earthworks in England, including Offa's Dyke, Wat's Dyke, the

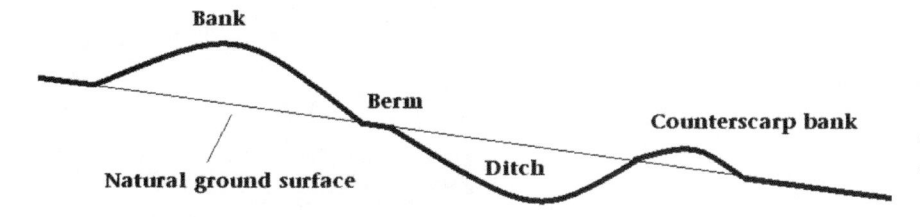

Fig. 8.1 Features found on Anglo-Saxon dykes.

Cambridgeshire Dykes (Devil's Ditch, Bran Ditch and Fleam Dyke), Bokerley Dyke and Wansdyke. The terms 'dykes' and 'ditches' seem to have been used interchangeably for banks and ditches of different sizes and lengths, ranging from those many kilometres long with ditches two metres deep and banks up to four metres high, to short earthworks that have a shallow ditch and low bank. The dykes of the Anglo-Saxon period are quite distinct from prehistoric and later medieval earthworks. Prehistoric examples often have multiple banks and ditches while Anglo-Saxon dykes generally have a single bank and ditch, sometimes with a small counterscarp bank beyond the ditch. They invariably 'face' downhill (that is the ditch is lower than the bank), a deliberate design feature possibly indicating the direction from which attack was expected (Figure 8.1). One of the authors (Erik Grigg) has recently completed a doctoral thesis on early medieval dykes that identified 118 potentially early medieval dykes in Britain. If we eliminate the examples from Cornwall and those sufficiently far into Wales not to be Mercian that leaves 100 potential Anglo-Saxon dykes.

Unfortunately, few of these earthworks are securely dated, partly because dykes of all periods are hard to date as there are rarely any associated finds buried with them as there are at a cemetery or the rubbish pits of a settlement. For a few dykes, however, analysis of the lower levels of the ditch fill using radiocarbon dating or optical stimulated luminescence has provided a firm, early medieval date.[2] We can also assume a dyke is probably early medieval if an Anglo-Saxon charter records it, if it has an Old English name or if it either cuts Roman features or the soil sealed underneath contains Roman pottery sherds.

Offa's Dyke, which runs north–south near the Anglo-Welsh border, is by far the largest early medieval earthwork. It consists of a bank with a ditch on the western side (Figure 8.2). Although the modern, long-distance footpath that bears its name runs from Prestatyn on the North Wales coast south to the Severn Estuary, the built earthwork does not. Extensive excavation and survey have shown that the earthwork ran largely continuously from Treuddyn near Mold southwards to

Rushock Hill north of Hereford, a distance of some 103 kilometres.³ The earthwork is assumed to have been built by King Offa of Mercia (757–796) as that is what we are told by Asser, writing in the late ninth century. Asser claimed that it ran 'from sea to sea', but the earthwork does not appear to reach the sea at either end.⁴ It is unlikely that he would have known exactly where this earthwork began and finished, but Asser was probably familiar with the work of Bede, who wrote of the Roman emperor Severus (193–211) having separated the conquered from the unconquered people with an earthwork built from 'sea to sea'.⁵ The same expression had been used by Gildas in the sixth century to describe either the Antonine Wall or Hadrian's Wall as 'the British were told to construct across the island a wall linking the two seas'.⁶ Perhaps Asser was mistaken when he used the same Latin phrase for Offa's Dyke. A recent radiocarbon date suggests parts may be older (430–652) and that Offa could have utilised some pre-existing earthworks to save on labour.⁷

We can never be sure what purpose (or purposes) these enigmatic dykes fulfilled. In recent years, scholars have increasingly argued that such earthworks had a symbolic or political rather than a practical purpose and were built by rulers to unify their kingdom in opposition to the 'foreigners' on the other side of the earthwork.⁸ The very act of gathering people together to build earthworks would galvanise and bond those people; their construction was an exercise in nation building.

While defining a kingdom may have been one purpose of the larger earthworks, it is harder to make that case with the smaller dykes. They were more likely attempts to stop raids, especially as they cut routeways with no sign of an original gateway appearing in any of the excavations of any early medieval dyke. Even the case for the larger dykes being expressions of royal power is based on supposition rather than positive evidence. If we found evidence of kings boasting about their earthworks in chronicles, on coinage or through inscriptions, the theory would have firmer foundations. There seems to be no evidence of such boasting, unless Asser's erroneous claim that Offa's Dyke ran from sea to sea is an echo of Mercian propaganda, and dykes rarely seem to be contiguous with borders. The structure known as Wansdyke probably consists of two unrelated earthworks with a massive space between them rather than the remains of an attempt to delimit the entire northern border of Wessex.

Fig. 8.2 The southern end of Offa's Dyke on Rushock Hill, Herefordshire (photograph: © Clwyd-Powys Archaeological Trust. CPAT photograph CS00-057-0001).

Charter evidence suggests that Anglo-Saxon estate boundaries bisect Wansdyke without deflecting off course, as is also the case with later parochial boundaries.[9] Offa's Dyke is not generally contiguous with the modern Anglo-Welsh border (with only 10 per cent of the central section from Treuddyn to Rushock Hill matching national borders and 22 per cent matching parish boundaries)[10] though the Anglo-Welsh boundary has changed in a number of places at various times since the ninth century. For Wat's Dyke the correspondence is even lower, with only 4 per cent of the dyke now contiguous with parish boundaries. However, the correspondence between Wat's Dyke and hidated, administratively divided lands at Domesday is considerably greater, suggesting that this boundary continued to be recognised for some years after it was built.[11]

The correspondence of the Cambridgeshire Dykes with administrative boundaries is much higher, between 90 per cent and 100 per cent for Devil's Ditch, Bran Ditch and Fleam Dyke, possibly because they form distinct features in an otherwise flat landscape (Figure 8.3). It seems strange if East Anglian rulers were building dykes just to mark their western border: they would twice have had to dig new ones when this border fluctuated, and they apparently felt no need to mark any of their other frontiers. It is more likely, especially during the early Anglo-Saxon period, that the borders between kingdoms were zones rather than lines on the ground that could be marked by an earthwork. Instead of unifying a kingdom, perhaps most dykes were designed to

Fig. 8.3 Devil's Ditch near Newmarket (photograph: Erik Grigg).

keep people out; it has even been suggested that the mighty Offa's Dyke was itself a stop line against raiders.[12] Rather than being border markers, dykes were probably unmanned earthworks where locals could gather to repulse raiders, and were set back from the frontier to avoid having inhabitants overrun by a sudden attack. Estate, parochial, episcopal and national boundaries largely ignore most early medieval dykes; this is exactly what we would expect if their function was to defend rather than define. As many are grouped in parallel lines, a raider circumventing one would then face another.

Estate boundary markers

Estate boundary marker earthworks are less well known than those like Offa's Dyke and are smaller in length and scale, often having a shallow ditch to each side of a low bank. Their function, however, is more self-evident as they mark the limit of all or part of Anglo-Saxon estates.

Two examples from Oxfordshire illustrate this type: Ælfrith's Ditch or Dyke, located between the parishes of Kingston Bagpuize and Fyfield, and Bica's Dyke near Compton Beauchamp.[13] Ælfrith's Dyke and an associated earthwork called Short Dyke run from the Thames to the River Ock along the same alignment as the present boundary between the two parishes. The earthwork is comparable to a hedge, with two parallel ditches half a metre deep and about two metres wide. Two Anglo-Saxon charters of 956 (S828) and 965 (S829) record the earthworks as *ælfredes beorh* and *scortandic* in the bounds of an estate, although the authenticity of these charters has been questioned.[14] A third charter, dated 971 (S1216), mentions the estate, but not the earthworks; this charter is probably genuine.[15]

The second example is Bica's Dyke near Compton Beauchamp, Oxfordshire. This is also relatively small in scale as the ditch is less than a metre deep and approximately two metres wide. It is contiguous with a parish boundary and is recorded in a charter of 955 (S564) as *Bican dic* in an Anglo-Saxon charter that also mentions another earthwork called Readan Dyke.[16] While these earthworks suggest that occasionally the Anglo-Saxons dug earthworks to mark the bounds of their estates, such features are not widespread along most estate boundaries. Perhaps the examples that do exist were places where there was some conflict about the location of an estate boundary, while in most areas Anglo-Saxon land owners considered a written description of their estate sufficient.

Settlement boundaries

It was once thought that the Anglo-Saxons who first arrived in Britain were afraid of the Roman remains they found there. However, it is now clear that some of the abandoned Roman settlements, fortifications and boundaries were occupied in the early period. For example, evidence from the Roman fort at Birdoswald on Hadrian's Wall in the north-west has revealed that far from being abandoned, a large timber building was erected on the site of the Roman granary.[17] Life at Wroxeter lingered on into the post-Roman period,[18] but it could hardly still be called an urban centre, while other cities like Silchester and Caistor-by-Norwich were abandoned. Even walled Roman towns like Lincoln, London and Canterbury that later re-emerged as urban settlements may have been partly or totally abandoned for periods in the immediate aftermath of the end of Roman rule. Where not abandoned, such sites would have provided ready-made boundaries for their inhabitants.[19]

In contrast, many (though not all) Anglo-Saxon settlements in the fifth and sixth centuries can be shown to be unenclosed, with the dwellings dispersed about the agricultural land, such as at Wharram Percy, North Yorkshire, and at West Stow, Suffolk.[20] They seem to have been abandoned at some time in the eighth century when there was a general change to a smaller number of nucleated but still unenclosed settlements.[21]

The arrival of the Vikings created the necessity for defences around at least some settlements. Initially these were in King Alfred's Wessex, where a network of banks and ditches with a wall or palisade were created around some existing settlements, and others defended sites which were constructed at strategic points where no settlement had previously existed. These fortified settlements are recorded in the Burghal Hidage; although the earliest version dates to the eleventh century, it probably copies a West Saxon document from about AD 910–920.[22] Interestingly, the document gives a calculation of how many men were needed for a given length of a fortification, which equates to one every 1.25 metres. These *burhs* seem to have been centres to facilitate military operations where local men called on to fight in the army, known as the *fyrd*, could gather. They also served as a protection for the general population of the neighbourhood and a safer and controlled place to mint money and to trade goods. While some *burhs* like Winchester and Chester were based on Roman sites, others were new foundations such as Watchet in Somerset, Lydford in Devon and Wallingford in Oxfordshire.[23] At the former, existing walls need only be refurbished, but at the latter new earthworks were constructed.[24]

Cemeteries and religious enclosures[25]

When the Anglo-Saxons arrived in Britain the natives were defining their burial grounds with boundary ditches like the late-Roman cemetery at Poundbury in Dorset that continued in use after the end of Roman rule.[26] The pagan Anglo-Saxons in contrast seem to have had no need to enclose either their cemeteries or their religious sites, the wall around Beowulf's pyre notwithstanding. Even where linear features appear on excavation reports of Anglo-Saxon cemeteries, they usually seem to pre-date or post-date the cemetery.[27] It is possible that archaeologists have focused their efforts on the actual burials and therefore missed evidence of enclosures around the site, but it seems unlikely that this would be the case with all excavations if such features were commonplace. As many Anglo-Saxon cemeteries are on the fringes of modern parishes and as the climax of the poem *Beowulf* suggests that mighty warriors may have been buried at the edge of a kingdom to guard over it, some scholars have suggested that Anglo-Saxon burials mark territorial borders.[28] However, Anglo-Saxon burials in the Avebury region suggest they are more likely to be placed on prominent positions near routeways than on the edge of territories.[29]

After the conversion to Christianity, churches, many of which served monastic orders, appeared on the landscape. Sometimes they were enclosed; perhaps, where these boundaries existed, they were seen as a way of separating the sacred from the profane secular settlements that frequently grew up outside their gates. Modern evidence for these boundaries comes mostly from monastic sites as, since their dissolution, some sites have become available for excavation. A late Saxon ditch excavated at Glastonbury Abbey, for example, was two metres deep and two metres wide.[30] Some Anglo-Saxon religious communities used pre-existing enclosures such as Roman forts to delimit their monastic enclosure.[31] The construction of hedges or walls round parochial churchyards probably started in the late Anglo-Saxon period, but as many remain in use today for burials the evidence for their extent and dating is harder to establish. The redundant church of Barton-upon-Humber has been extensively investigated, and the earliest burials there appear to date from the ninth century.[32] The boundaries we see around many of our present-day Anglican churches may indeed date back to Anglo-Saxon times.

Agricultural boundaries

The question of whether the land was divided up into the types of fields we see today with hedges and fences is one that has exercised the minds of landscape archaeologists and historians for some time. Whether the fields were small or large, it would have been essential to keep animals and crops separate and permanent boundaries would seem most appropriate.

A number of different types of boundaries can be used to define a field: walls, fences, banks, ditches or hedges, and these are often used in combination (a hedge on a bank, for example). Of the 14,342 landmarks cited in the boundary clauses of Anglo-Saxon charters, 378 are hedges (usually referred to as a *haga*) and 32 walls, though it should be noted that the paucity of charter evidence from the north where dry stone walls are more common may have skewed these proportions.[33] This data obviously represents a tiny proportion of all the field boundaries in Anglo-Saxon England. Fences leave little trace, and if they were more prevalent than hedges in the Anglo-Saxon period it would be hard to detect. Surveys on the Peak District have tentatively identified features that can help date stone walls, but an 'Anglo-Saxon' style has not been differentiated from a general medieval pattern of walling.[34] Max Hooper suggested that we could date hedgerows by the number of species of shrub in a measured length of hedge; however, once a hedge is over 1,000 years old, this method ceases to be accurate, and as we cannot date hedges accurately by other methods it is hard to test this thesis.[35]

The laws of Ine of Wessex (688–726), however, provide definite textual evidence suggestive of the importance of agricultural boundaries in Anglo-Saxon England. One law states that:

> A commoner's premises shall be fenced (*betyned*) both winter and summer. If they are not enclosed (*untyned*) and a beast belonging to a neighbour strays in through the opening he himself has left, he shall have no claim in the beast [but] he shall drive it out and suffer the damage.[36]

The law also states that common land and meadows or other partible land should be fenced; for those who have not completed their fencing whose cattle eat the common crops or grass, compensation is required for those who have completed theirs. A subparagraph goes on to state that if an animal breaks down a hedge and wanders into a cornfield the owner(s) of the corn can kill it. The owner of the beast is then entitled to its hide and flesh, but is not entitled to compensation for the loss of the beast.

The document known as *Rectitudines singularum personarum*,[37] dated to the tenth or eleventh centuries, gives the duties of people of various status and some of these also mention boundaries. The *thegn*, for example, must service the king's deer fence if the king so requires. At the next level down, the duties of a *geneat* or high status tenant include cutting the deer fence and building and fencing fortifications. The list continues down through the various ranks of free and unfree men. *Rectitudines* also informs us that a shepherd has twelve nights' worth of dung at Christmas. This makes it likely that the sheep were kept in a fold in winter, at least at night, perhaps for their protection from predators such as wolves. Whether the fold was a temporary hurdle enclosure or something more substantial is not clear.

One of the most crucial questions about Anglo-Saxon field boundaries is how much the pre-existing landscape pattern influenced it. Scholars often assume the Anglo-Saxons reused older field boundaries; as people had been exploiting and partitioning the British landscape for millennia they certainly did not enter an uninhabited wilderness.[38] William Hoskins postulated that a parish boundary marked by a road running between two large hedgerows near Cheriton Bishop in Devon which is cited as an 'old dyke' in an Anglo-Saxon charter (S830, dated 976) was a prehistoric boundary.[39] While he may have been correct in his surmise that this marked the continuity of one prehistoric boundary reused by the Anglo-Saxons, it is perhaps significant he cited no other similar examples. So-called 'Celtic' fields are presumed to pre-date the arrival of the English and are often seen in relief when the sun is low in the sky on the downs of England; that these are areas now given over to pasture suggests the Anglo-Saxons actually largely ignored the existing field patterns.[40]

In pockets of the country, however, there is convincing evidence that the Anglo-Saxons took over a pre-existing system of fields. An argument has been made for a pre-Roman, loosely rectilinear field pattern and trackway system that can be identified where a Roman road has cut across this pre-existing system,[41] and, using fieldwork and early map evidence, this pattern has been observed, for example, in areas of Mercia around settlements such as Wroxeter and Lichfield and to the south in the Avon valley around Alcester, Stratford-upon-Avon and Droitwich.

In some parts of the country, there are groups of parishes, each of which contains the remains of a Roman villa; this pattern suggests it is not just the fields, but Roman estates may have evolved intact into modern parishes.[42] Where parishes contain the remains of a Roman villa (for example, around Cheddar in Somerset and in parts of Dorset) and hedgerows that mark the parish boundary are contiguous with estates cited in Anglo-Saxon charters, it is tempting to speculate that the subdivisions of the landscape we see today pre-date the Anglo-Saxon conquest. For example, hedges mark the majority of the borders of the parish of Withington in Gloucestershire, two early Anglo-Saxon charters (S1429, dated 736–737 and S1255, dated 774) cite it as an estate and the parish contains the remains of a Roman villa.[43] However, the phenomenon of a parish containing a single villa may be coincidental as it only occurs in a handful of locations. In the West Midlands, the extreme south-west (Devon and Cornwall), the north-west and the Fens, there are very few known sites of Roman villas. In those parts of the country where there is a villa in each parish, moreover, these villas often lie at the edge of the parish, suggesting that even if there is continuity the focus of the estate and the area of land attached to it must have changed. Even in areas where villas are common there is often rarely one villa per parish, and a handful of parishes (Wollaston and Yarwell in Northamptonshire, Feltwell in Norfolk and Farningham in Kent) actually contain two or more villas, suggesting it is unlikely many villa estates formed the basis for Saxon ones. Hoskins claimed he identified Roman estates boundaries at Holme-next-the-Sea in Norfolk and at the Roman villa at Ditchley in Oxfordshire which influenced modern field boundaries, but even if we accept the circumstantial evidence he cited they may be the exceptions rather than the rule.[44]

A more systematic survey has been undertaken that could give us a comprehensive insight on the amount of continuity in field boundaries. The study was called 'Fields of Britannia' and was led by Stephen Rippon at the University of Exeter; it ran for three years (2010–13) and examined hundreds of excavation reports to see if there was some continuity between the layout of Roman rural settlements (field boundaries, for example) and the Saxon landscape. Unfortunately, at the time of writing only the provisional interim reports were available.[45] In some areas, like the Vales of Gloucester, the project concluded that there was continuity at 79 per cent of the sites studied, but in most areas it averaged out at 60 per cent. This result appears to confirm that in many areas the Anglo-Saxon invasion meant very little disruption for the local population who carried on farming the same fields as their ancestors had in Roman times. These figures, however, probably overestimate the amount of continuity, as the study only included sites where there was good archaeological evidence of both Roman and post-Roman settlement; abandoned Roman sites or an Anglo-Saxon site established at virgin locations were not included. Moreover, even for the delimited range of sites studied, the results suggest that, while 60 per cent of field boundaries in areas of settlement continuity were largely unaffected by the end of Roman rule and the Anglo-Saxon invasion, at 40 per cent of sites the landscape was reorganised (possibly in the early medieval period) along very different lines. The preliminary data from this study is fascinating and significant, although it does not include the entire story.

We know the Anglo-Saxons founded some settlements on virgin sites that cannot have been Roman estate centres, like West Stow, while some others, like Mucking, were at locations the Britons had long abandoned; early sites in general seem to have avoided Roman roads.[46] The issue is complicated in that settlements also shifted in the middle Saxon period, meaning that even where the Anglo-Saxons did inherit an older pattern they may have completely reorganised that landscape over time.[47] Where we can demonstrate that the Anglo-Saxons continued to use the same field boundaries in some parishes, without other evidence (either soil analysis or pollen evidence) we cannot be certain those fields did not change in use from, say, arable land to pasture.[48] Neither can we be certain the fields were exploited from the same farm or by descendants of the same farmers, as models of overall continuity might suggest. If a farm is abandoned, any new farmer would find it easier to clear the scrub from the fields than the mature trees that establish themselves on hedgerows, so the same field system might be used, but in different ways, and by different settlers.

At virgin sites where the Anglo-Saxons do not appear to have followed earlier settlers, Roman or Briton, direct archaeological evidence of Anglo-Saxon field boundaries is often scant. An examination of dig reports from a number of early Anglo-Saxon sites like West Stow, Mucking and even the extensive excavations at West Heslerton reveals little archaeological evidence of field boundaries. The Anglo-Saxon features found during an excavation at Riby in Lincolnshire are typical of such sites. Ditches marked the line of stock compounds or enclosed domestic dwellings and these enclosures were later reorganised, but they were too small to be fields and did not follow the alignment of previous features.[49] Perhaps the early Anglo-Saxons preferred to enclose small areas near their dwellings to control animals, leaving their fields largely open.

The question remains: if the Anglo-Saxons reused some existing agricultural boundaries, transformed others and at times utilised their own unique methods of organising agricultural land across England, how might we assess their impact on the landscape? In the Peak District, as across much of the Midlands, the smaller farmsteads that slowly drifted across the landscape as the wooden buildings were gradually replaced over time were reorganised into nucleated stable settlements, a move probably associated with the creation of the open field system.[50] We cannot know whether the Anglo-Saxons across the period laid down open fields on completely new lines (perhaps in areas of open pasture), made the large fields by simply merging older fields, or both. Either of the latter two possibilities would mean that the outer hedgerows were of some antiquity.

Research for this study found that, when drawn on an Ordnance Survey map, Saxon estate boundaries are often coterminous with modern parish bounds, which in turn are usually marked with hedgerows, making for tempting speculation that these hedges date back at least as far as the Anglo-Saxon period.[51] For example, Anglo-Saxon charters describe an estate covering the northern third of the parish of Piddletrenthide in Dorset (in particular S744, dated 966); the parochial boundaries and (where they are not the same) estate bounds are marked by large hedgerows.[52] It is thus likely that some of today's parish boundaries, as well as the hedgerows and ditches that often mark them, could date back to Anglo-Saxon times, if not further.

Nonetheless, while some modern boundaries may follow the same lines as Anglo-Saxon estate boundaries and some even older Roman or prehistoric boundaries, it is improbable that all do. Those who believe there are large parts of England where the pattern of the landscape dates back millennia are probably underestimating the ability of people in the past to reorganise fields and estates completely. The emergence of the manorial and parochial systems in particular suggests that the Anglo-Saxons were quite capable of reordering the landscape, and some of their efforts may still be visible. We know the Normans established numerous new towns (usually with markets, a church and a castle) across large parts of England and Wales and that during the enclosures the pattern of landholding across large swathes of the countryside was utterly transformed; it is entirely possible the early medieval period saw similar widespread changes.

Woodland

Woodland was a valuable resource and needed to be managed if sufficient and suitable timber was to be available. Mature trees for use as main supports in buildings were often oaks that would regrow after pollarding or coppicing, the former occurring as the tree is cut above head height to stimulate the growth of thin young branches or wands, and the latter as the tree is cut much lower down to form a stump or stool. Hazel, willow or similar species would be cut down and the wands used for the wattle and daub infill of walls. While some of the timber could be grown without protection from animals, regeneration of young trees after felling of mature timber, or after harvesting an area of hazel stools, would require that animals be prevented from grazing the new shoots. Posts and rails for fencing, hurdles for temporary enclosures or protecting cottage plots with vegetables and poultry, staves for barrels, spokes and felloes for wheels, wood for turning on a lathe to make bowls and wood suitable for making charcoal were needed. Christopher Grocock found that an area of good coppice produces about 84m^3 of harvestable wood per hectare every sixteen years,[53] although wands suitable for interweaving can be cut from hazel stools approximately every seven years.[54] Harvesting in autumn would need to be done in rotation to produce a regular supply, with wands used shortly after harvesting while still supple.

Such an important resource was clearly valued and rights to its use were guarded by those in authority. Damage to woodland is dealt with by Ine's eighth-century laws, which state that if a person destroys a tree by fire without permission he must pay 60 shillings, since his fire is a thief.[55] The next clause states that someone cutting down trees in a wood must pay 30 shilling for each of three trees, but no more, as the axe is an informer, not a thief. A tree's size also appears to have mattered in calculations: the subsequent clause requires 60 shillings for cutting down a tree that can shelter thirty swine. The sums involved may sound modest by modern standards, but would have been enormous in the seventh and eighth centuries, an indication of how valuable trees and the woodland were considered to be. A charter of 866 (S212) by King Burgred of Mercia gives a sense of how royal grants to woodland might have been used: he grants the right to pasture pigs in a wooded common and to harvest five wagons of good rods and one oak for building every year, with wood for fires as necessary.[56]

Given the importance and tightly guarded status of woodland among the Anglo-Saxons, it is possible that woodlands had clearly delineated boundaries. In the later medieval period, people defined the boundaries for woodlands by fences and banks; however, without documentary evidence, it is difficult to date many of these park pales and woodbanks. Scholars have sometimes assumed some woodland boundaries were Anglo-Saxon or even older in date, as Hugh Braun did when discussing the parks of Middlesex.[57] Three earthworks which scholars have postulated are early medieval could also have acted as woodbanks: Minchinhampton Bulwarks in Gloucestershire, Bunns Bank in Norfolk and Park Pale near Topcliffe in Yorkshire, but all are hard to date.[58] With all three, it is possible that they were originally Anglo-Saxon structures that were later reused as woodbanks or park pales. Bunns Banks was certainly part of Buckenham Park, which was established in the twelfth century, but, as it only formed one side, it was probably an unrelated older structure reused for convenience.[59]

There is good evidence from Essex and some from Warwickshire of banks in woods of an Anglo-Saxon date that owners of different patches of woodland dug to delimit their property, but the boundaries, banks and ditches that ran around whole forests are probably a post-1066 phenomenon.[60] Perhaps the boundary lines for woodland were products of the trees themselves; the boundaries to keep animals from unlawful entry could have been the animals' own enclosures.

Conclusion

The Anglo-Saxons did not enter an empty landscape; they appear to have reused as well as shaped their environment in unique ways. They reused many older boundaries, some of which still influence the course of modern hedges or roads. At virgin sites in the pagan period, they probably lived in an open landscape with small enclosures around their homes. As Anglo-Saxon England developed, however, they radically altered the landscape, partitioning one estate from another, towns from countryside, religious sites from the outside world and fields from other fields, woods or pasture. Remarkably, at least some of those boundaries may have survived, despite the ravages of the Enclosures, the Agricultural Revolution, the Industrial Revolution and modern planners. Some Anglo-Saxon earthworks were more short-lived (especially the dykes discussed in detail below), and, though they survive, they no longer form administrative or political boundaries.

Appendix. Dykes

Offa's Dyke

Cyril Fox studied Offa's Dyke during a number of three-week-long summer expeditions from Cardiff in the 1920s and early 1930s. He reported his findings in *Archaeologia Cambrensis* in each volume between 1925 and 1931 for Offa's Dyke and 1934 for Wat's Dyke. These were brought together in one substantial volume in 1955.[61] He explained areas where no earthwork was to be found as having been too densely wooded to make an earthwork necessary. This was current thinking in the early twentieth century, but a better understanding of the sequence of vegetation in the landscape renders this view untenable.

In 1971, the Offa's Dyke Project, directed by David Hill and later co-directed by one of the present authors (Margaret Worthington Hill), carried out excavation and survey on the earthworks examined by Fox in the Welsh Marches.[62] The Offa's Dyke Project provided training for numerous University of Manchester extra-mural archaeology students. They excavated and made detailed topographical surveys of the earthwork to record the scale and form of the dyke and its siting in the landscape. However, no artefacts or other dating material were found, which is not unusual along the western border of Mercia where a lack of pottery or coins made dating difficult before new methods were developed. The survey showed that the earthwork had a uniform width with a horizontal distance of some seven metres from the centre of the bank to the centre of the ditch on moderate slopes. Excavation showed that the distance from the bottom of the ditch to the top of the bank was at least four metres.

Wat's Dyke

Wat's Dyke was also part of the Manchester project and follows a similar line to the northern end of Offa's Dyke. It is further east and shorter and runs from Basingwerk on the Dee estuary in the north to a marshy area near the confluence of the rivers Vyrnwy and Severn near Maesbury in Shropshire, a distance of approximately 63 kilometres (40 miles). Wat's Dyke also marks the western limit of land recorded as hidated in the 1086 Domesday surveys for Shropshire and Cheshire.[63] It consists of a bank on the eastern side and a ditch to the west of a similar size to those on Offa's Dyke. The Offa's Dyke Project applied the same excavation and survey strategy to Wat's Dyke as they had to Offa's Dyke. Both earthworks are similar in form and scale and are situated in the landscape to maintain good views to the west.

This earthwork was also undated, and past opinions varied as to whether it pre-dated or post-dated Offa's Dyke. In 1998, a radiocarbon date was obtained from the remains of a fire below the bank of Wat's Dyke at Maesbury Road, Oswestry by Shropshire County Council. This gave a radiocarbon date within the late-Roman/early post-Roman period and is sometimes quoted as dating Wat's Dyke.[64] However the excavator, after careful consideration, has withdrawn this date, as no turf line was found, and it has been shown on other excavations on Wat's Dyke that the area of the bank was first de-turfed and the turves used in the make-up of the bank.[65] However, in recent excavations by Tim Malim and Laurence Hayes,[66] in advance of development in Gobowen, Shropshire, optically stimulated luminescence dates from the base of the ditch were produced that give a 'most probable' date of between 792 and 852, suggesting that it was possibly built when Cenwulf (796–821) reigned over Mercia. He died at Basingwerk in 821, where he is thought to have been campaigning against the Welsh of that area, but one might perhaps imagine that he was also inspecting one end of the new earthwork.

An interesting observation noted in the Malim and Hayes report might suggest how the manpower was raised to build the earthwork. Marker stones were found below the bank on its eastern (Mercian) side at intervals of approximately 1.6 metres. Malim and Hayes note the similarity between this length and the calculation attached to the Burghal Hidage document that says this is the optimum length of defensive *burh* wall per defender.[67]

Cambridgeshire dykes

These are usually taken to include, from north to south: Devil's Dyke, Fleam Dyke (possibly including High Ditch) and Bran Ditch. They are substantial earthen banks with ditches to their south-west, similar in scale to those of Offa's Dyke, but much shorter in length. The dykes would have been flanked by wetlands to the west and woodland to the east in the early medieval period. They seem to bar access along a strip of open land along which the prehistoric Icknield Way ran. Early medieval radiocarbon dates have been obtained for Fleam Dyke, while Anglo-Saxon weapons have been found in the bank of Devil's Dyke.[68]

As early as 1921, Cyril Fox was publishing his excavations and observations on these earthworks, particularly the Fleam Dyke.[69] He continued reporting, with William Palmer, in the same journal during the following three years. Excavations in the Fens continued, and at Bran Ditch the remains of two individuals were found buried in the ditch that Fox thought to be those of sheep stealers.[70] Later, the remains of approximately sixty individuals were found. These were mostly mature males, juveniles up to twelve years old, possibly two females and a still or newborn child. They all seem to have met a violent death with most displaying trauma suggesting decapitation. Skulls were separate from the body in many cases and it would seem that the bodies were already corrupt when buried. The few finds associated with the burials were early Saxon. The lack of grave goods made the original excavators believe that they were Christian and that a massacre had taken place of the people defending the ditch.[71] In 1976, it was argued that this had been a place of execution known in Anglo-Saxon as a *cwealmstow*, though the inclusion of a newborn baby seems rather unusual for such sites.[72]

Wansdyke

Once considered a single earthwork, Wansdyke is now usually split into West Wansdyke and East Wansdyke, as there is a significant gap of over 25 kilometres between them. The western earthwork runs from Maesknoll in the west to Horsecombe Brook, while to the north is the River Avon and Bath. The eastern earthwork runs from north of Devizes in the west and almost to Savernake Forest in the east.

Fig. 8.4 West Wansdyke (photograph: Erik Grigg).

West Wansdyke

This earthwork runs for about 14 kilometres and seems to have been faced with a revetment.[73] The bank is up to 1.7 metres high and the ditch up to 2.8 metres deep (Figure 8.4).

East Wansdyke

This earthwork runs for approximately 20 kilometres eastward from Morgan's Hill to the edge of Savernake Forest. It is larger in scale than West Wansdyke, with a bank up to 3 metres high and a ditch nearly 4 metres deep in parts, but has no revetment. It appears in a series of Anglo-Saxon charters, though we should always be cautious of assuming the dates that appear on such documents are accurate as they could be later forgeries, or a scribe could have used bounds taken from much older documents. The earliest surviving written reference to East Wansdyke is in an Anglo-Saxon charter (S272) dated 825, though it only survives in a much later copy and the bounds look copied from a later document (S1513) dated 900.[74] These first charters call it *ealdandic* or 'old dyke'. The next charter gives the name of Woden (or rather *Wodnes dic*) to East Wansdyke (S368), though it says the grant was first made by Æthelwulf (839–856) though the charter is dated 903; it is followed by a series of tenth-century charters (S424, S449, S647 and S685) that also use the name.[75] Material dumped in the ditch of East Wansdyke shortly after it was abandoned produced a radiocarbon date of 890–1160.[76]

The Bedwyn Dyke
This is a dyke east of Savernake Forest some 2.4 kilometres long which runs between Great Bedwyn and Little Bedwyn. The bank is up to 2 metres high and the ditch up to 1 metre deep. A charter for Little Bedwyn dated 778 (S264) mentions *quoddam vallum in haran dene*, but does not mention the name of the dyke.[77] It has been suggested that Bedwyn Dyke is a part of East Wansdyke, but it seems to be complete as it stands, and it is perhaps significant that the name Woden is not attached to this earthwork in an early source. In 1892, skeletons 'slain in battle' were found nearby.[78]

The Rowe Ditch
This dyke near Pembridge in Herefordshire bisects the valley of the River Arrow and is one of the short dykes examined by the Offa's Dyke Project as it was thought that it might be a continuation of Offa's Dyke southwards from Rushock Hill and across the Herefordshire Plain. Nine excavations across the earthwork showed that it consisted of a bank and ditch of a similar scale to Offa's Dyke.[79] It runs from north to south with the ditch on the west and is v-shaped and some 1.8 metres deep. In the north, the bell-end of the ditch was found on rising ground at Vallet Covert. To the south, excavation showed it to be present on rising ground up to the buildings at Pitfield Farm. It would seem that the southern end is under the farmyard, as no evidence for a bank and ditch was found beyond. The earthwork blocks the valley of the River Arrow to those approaching from the west. Although no longer visible on the floodplain adjacent to the river, excavation showed the full depth of ditch to be present and aligned with the upstanding earthwork to north and south. The earthwork in the northern part of the valley bottom had been altered in modern times when a water meadow system was developed. A series of stone leats (or artificial watercourses) to carry water from

the western side were inserted through the bank so that the eastern field could be flooded in the winter to encourage early spring growth. The bank had also been widened and flattened in some lengths to allow access along its top when the fields were flooded.

The earthwork has long been known to overlie Roman remains, and sherds of Roman pottery were found below the bank during excavation at Heathy Fields. The earthwork is mentioned in charter bounds for Staunton on Arrow in 958 (S677) when Edgar, king of Mercia, granted land at Staunton on Arrow and a *haga* in Hereford to Ealhstan, his faithful minister.[80] Thus, we have a post-Roman earthwork built before the mid-tenth century. Among the boundary markers in the charter the following are mentioned: a dyke; a boundary fence; Æthelwold's hedge; the swing gate (*hlidgeat*); the [Rowe] dyke gate (*dicesgeat*); a third gate (*thridde geat*); and a paved road (*straet*). The bounds can be followed on a detailed map, but, more importantly, the boundary and most markers can be identified on the ground today.

Wantyn Dyke

Eleven excavations of this earthwork showed it to be a continuous earthwork running east to west, starting and ending on the rising valley sides and blocking the valley route. The scale of these banks and ditches is similar to that of the Rowe Ditch, and all have a single ditch.[81]

Other dykes

There are numerous other possible Anglo-Saxon earthworks in England, and only a selection of those dykes that can possibly be dated to the Anglo-Saxon period is considered here. Others include the Swaledale Dykes, the Aberford Dykes and the East Hampshire Dykes.[82] Some of these lie in close proximity to the Welsh border, probably designed to control routeways. In one small area close to the modern boundary between Powys and Shropshire there are two earthworks, the Upper and Lower Short Ditches that straddle the upland trackway known as the Kerry Ridgeway. A radiocarbon date from the Upper Short Ditch of 540–660 suggests it was early medieval in date.[83] Both ends of each earthwork rest on steep-sided valleys, and they seem to face west as their banks are to the east while the ditches are over a metre deep to the west, creating a barrier to movement.

9

The Landscape of Late Saxon *Burhs* and the Politics of Urban Foundation

Jeremy Haslam

> Those who were severely afflicted ... [now] loudly applaud the king's foresight and promise to make every effort to do what they had previously refused – that is, with respect to constructing fortresses and to the other things of general advantage to the whole kingdom.[1]

Introduction

In his discussion of Norman planned towns of the late eleventh and twelfth centuries, Keith Lilley has made the important general observation that town plans can be used as 'texts to provide historical narratives which may be compared with the discourses of history offered by other sources and approaches', and has explored ways in which the analysis of urban form gives a 'wider understanding of the intimate dialectic between urban space and medieval society'.[2] As such, it is seen as one of the keys to understanding political processes 'which involved the conquest, consolidation and colonization of territories within frontier contexts'.[3] While the expansion of Norman hegemony in England was facilitated by the creation of urban places largely through the agency of aristocratic elites, it is generally recognised that the creation of fortified *burhs* by the king in late Anglo-Saxon England was an important agent in the processes of political expansion and the consolidation and control of territory. Richard Abels has said of King Edward's general strategy in eastern Mercia in the early tenth century, that it 'took the form of imposing the king's personal lordship upon the Danish landholders ... who chose him as their lord and protector', and he sees the *burhs* as prime agents in this process.[4] David Griffiths has also commented on the role of *burhs* as agents in the consolidation of royal authority in northern Mercia.[5]

For Lilley, new Norman towns also 'reflect deliberate attempts at consolidating political control by encouraging local integration, partly through facilitating commercial expansion and population influx'.[6] I have argued elsewhere that the same *rationale* can be applied to the function of late Saxon *burhs* as agents of the coercion and control of populations, to the end of putting in place strategic defensive measures against the Viking presence.[7] This process, however, was not determined by strategic considerations alone.[8] As with the new Norman towns discussed by Lilley, this political control was arguably facilitated by a new sense that commercial activity would be focused on these new *burhs*, which is directly evidenced by the reform of the coinage and the development of new minting places in the 870s.[9] This process would have found direct expression in the movement of people into these new centres in a way which must have had considerable impact on the general population, through changes in the distribution of people between 'town' and 'countryside' that would inevitably have had dynamic (and perhaps dramatic) effects on social mobility and social stratification and the way that people would have access to more opportunities to learn new skills.

It is the purpose here to bring together a body of evidence which will demonstrate that one of the principal ways in which this control on the part of the king was exercised was through the creation of fortified settlements which were socially and economically sustainable – that these were in essence new planned towns. This view, put forward as an evidence-based model more than forty years ago, in particular by Martin Biddle,[10] is contrary to that of a number of commentators in recent years who have denied that the new *burhs* of the late ninth and early tenth centuries in both Wessex and Mercia had developed urban functions, or were anything more than campaign forts or places of refuge which performed localised defensive functions. These views will be discussed below. It will be argued, furthermore, that this process of the creation of the *burhs* in both Wessex and Mercia in the late ninth and early tenth centuries was a major force in the transformation of the landscape of the time, which also involved fundamental and far-reaching episodes of territorial or local government reorganisation on a kingdom-wide scale.

The plan-form of burhs

It is the plan-forms of these new *burhs* of the period, which, taken as a group, can provide material for an alternative historical narrative. Biddle's classification of the *burhs* of Wessex that are listed in the Burghal Hidage characterises them in terms of their situation and site type (former Roman towns, new rectilinear *burhs*, new *burhs* on promontory sites with irregular perimeter and burghal forts).[11] An alternative classification – and in the context of this paper, one which is more meaningful – would be by plan-form. While the plan-forms of these places are determined by their site and situation as well as by the intention and aspirations of the original planners, these are not the only factors. The outcome of the planning process – the plan-form – would have been determined by decisions about the appropriateness of particular sites within the strategic context that the *burh*-builders had to address, the sizes and population levels of the territories given to support them, as well as the particularities of the geographies of their site and situation. The analysis of plan-forms allows the identification of themes and variations in all these aspects, and therefore gives a window into the broader intentions which lay behind the formation of these *burhs*. That similar plan-forms are found in contrasting sites and situations shows that plan-forms with common characteristics are indicative of similar functions. They can therefore give a new and unique perspective on issues relating both to the development of urbanism and to the strategic intentions of their originators in the ninth and tenth centuries.

Apart from those *burhs* of the Burghal Hidage and of others in Mercia mentioned in the *Anglo-Saxon Chronicle* which show no internal organisation (mainly the reused hill forts – concerning which nothing can be meaningfully said about whether they were or were not set out as permanent settlements), the plan-forms of the remainder comprise two main groups: rectilinear and linear. Biddle's analysis of the archaeological evidence relating to urban form in these *burhs* concentrated on the evidence from the larger rectilinear *burhs*, in particular Winchester. Apart from isolated examples of other *burhs* with different plan-forms such as Lydford, his discussion did not extend to the remainder, which he characterised as 'promontory *burhs*' – although he emphasised the common elements in the plan-forms of all the *burhs*.[12] His approach, however, was that if other *burhs* shared characteristics with those with more specific archaeological or other evidence of early features, then these could be reasonably inferred to have had common origins. He was, in effect, implicitly treating these as members of a single polythetic group (of which more below).

Fig. 9.1 The two *burhs* of Maldon (shaded half tones) in their immediate landscape setting. The first *burh* of 912 lies to the west of the second *burh* of 916. The scale is the same as that in Figs. 9.4–9.11. North to top.

It is with the group of *burhs* with essentially linear plan-forms that this analysis is concerned. This group, and that with more rectilinear plan-forms, share some members (e.g. Winchester, Bath and Cricklade), but are characterised by generally contrasting site types and situations. This group with essentially linear plan-forms may be described as the 'High Street' type, in which the main topographical features are arranged around a long High Street which runs between and connects two gates at opposite ends of a circuit of defences, along which burgages, or individual land-holdings within the town, are arranged at more or less right angles to its length. These *burhs* generally occupy distinct and distinctive topographical situations on spurs or promontories, generally placed at, and by inference guarding, river crossings and/or causeways. This landscape context of the *burhs* is brought out in many of the plans illustrated in Figure 9.1 and Figures 9.4 to 9.11. There may also be some side streets or lanes arranged at right angles to the High Street. This particular plan-form is also found in some of the *burhs* of the early tenth century in Mercia which were brought into being in the phase of conquest of Danish-held territory by both King Edward the Elder in central and eastern Mercia (as well as East Anglia) and by his sister Æthelflæd as ruler of western Mercia. Although it would be both timely and desirable, the limitations of space here mean that it is not possible either to present a full gazetteer of these *burhs* or systematically to update the gazetteer of the *burhs* of the Burghal Hidage in Wessex published nearly twenty years ago by David Hill.[13]

The two *burhs* of Maldon

Of particular importance in the development of this discussion is the example of the two *burhs* at Maldon, Essex, considered as new additions to the built environment of the late Saxon landscape, which are mentioned in some detail in the *Anglo-Saxon Chronicle* in 912, 916 and again in 917.[14] The first was clearly a campaign fort, built to provide a defence of the Blackwater estuary from possible attacks by Vikings from the sea for King Edward's forces while they built the *burh* at Witham. The *burh* of 916 would, however, have been, from the evidence discussed below, established as a more permanent settlement. A close examination of the archaeological and topographical evidence for their layout will be published elsewhere; the results of this analysis are, however, shown in Figures 9.1 and 9.2. The *burh* of 916 provides a model for the development of *burhs* of the High Street type, and the two *burhs* taken together provide evidence which casts new light on the differences between campaign forts and more permanent fortified *burhs*,

Maldon – two burhs

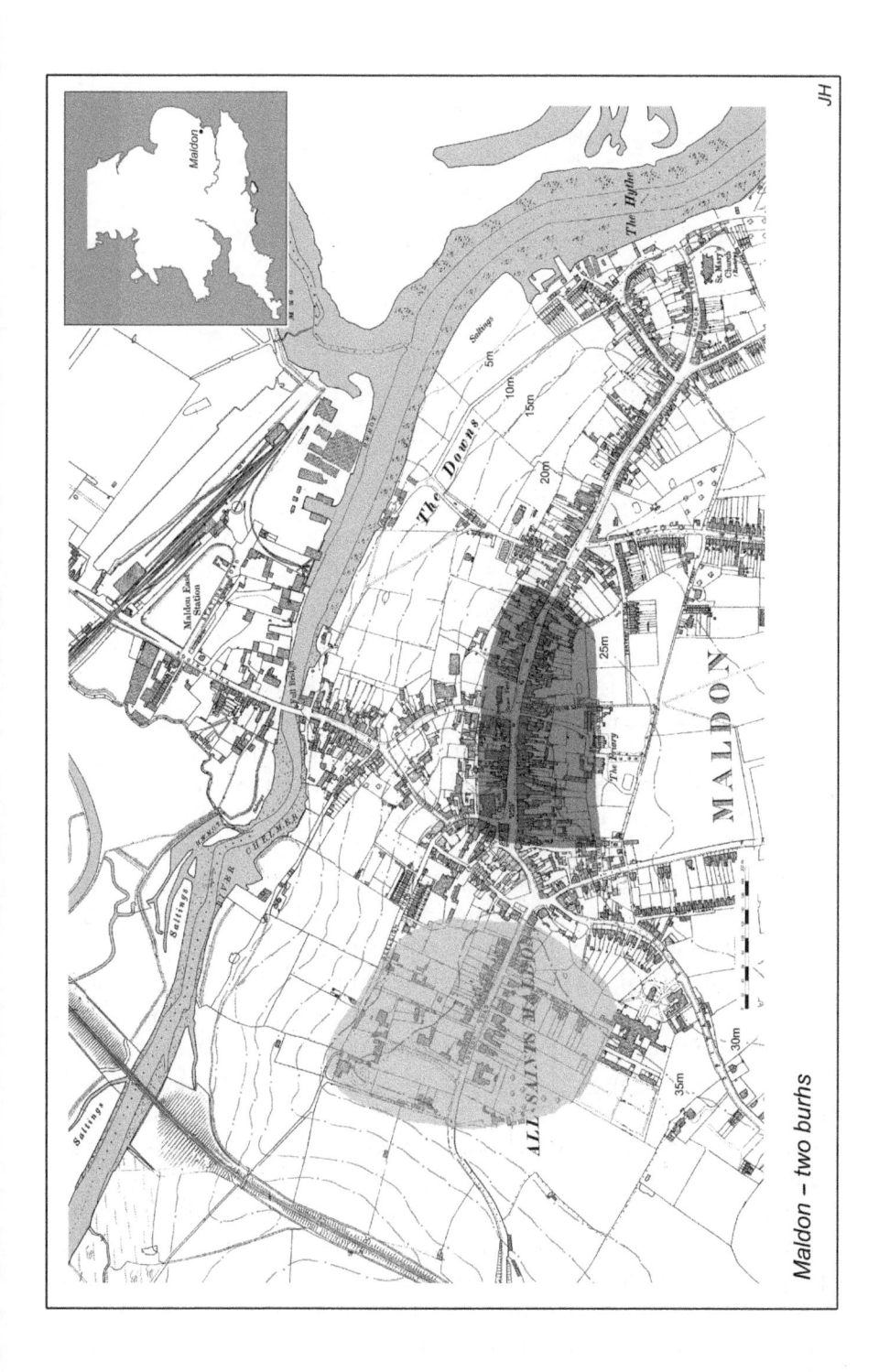

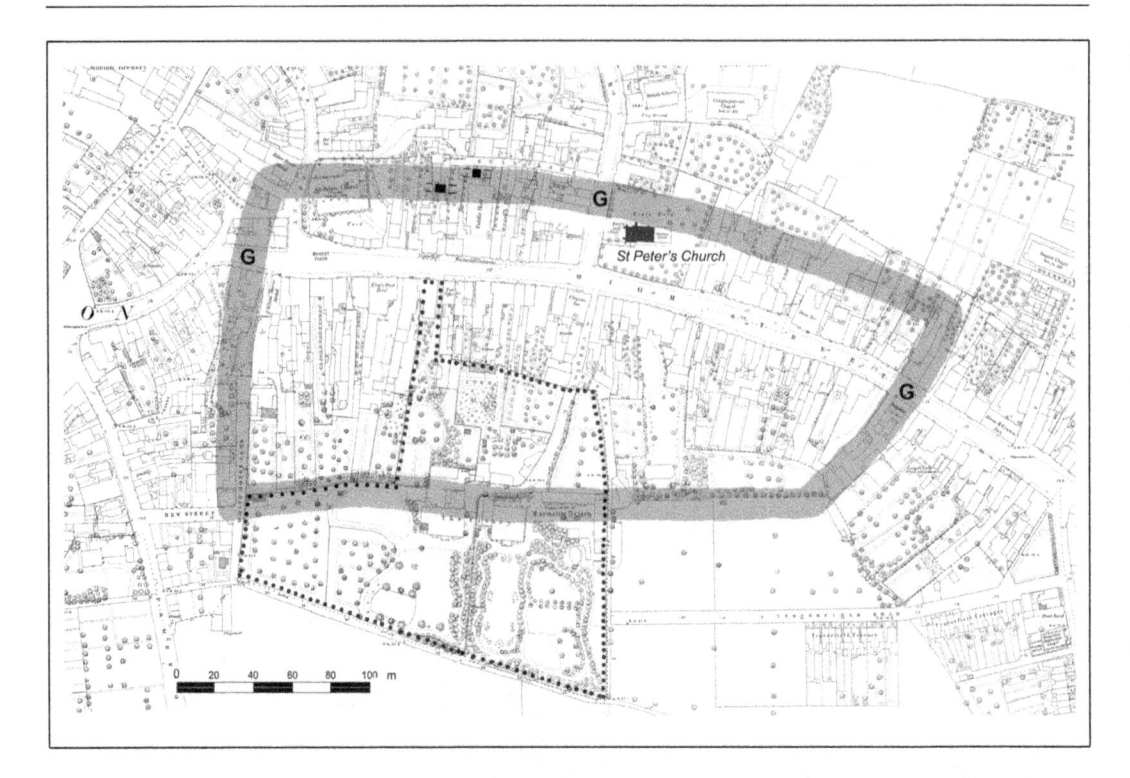

as well as the development of the latter type as new planned towns in Mercia and East Anglia in the early tenth century and by extension in Wessex in the late ninth. An important aspect of the evidence relating to the *burh* of 916 is that it is also shown in the annal of 917 in the *Anglo-Saxon Chronicle* as being an effective military installation which was clearly at 'battle-readiness' at the time, when the inhabitants, aided by contingents from 'outside', countered an attack by Viking forces from East Anglia who clearly felt threatened (with good reason) by Edward's previous successful capture of Colchester a month or two beforehand. In summary, it will be argued that an analysis of both the archaeological evidence and the evidence of the town plan (as shown in particular in the Ordnance Survey 1:500 map of 1875) combine to show that the location of the *burh* of 916 can be placed along the High Street to the east of the *burh* of 912, which was located on top of the hill to the west (Figures 9.1 and 9.2).

First, the course of the western line of the defences of this suggested *burh* is indicated by a zone characterised by an irregular arrangement of property boundaries (as shown on the 1:500 Ordnance Survey map of 1873–75) between a 'plan unit' of long regular burgages fronting the High Street to its east and the rear of another group of burgages on a different alignment to its west. The south-western line of the defences is indicated by the common rear (southern) boundary of these long burgages fronting the High Street. The northern line is deduced from the existence of what can be interpreted as two parallel ditches to the north of the High Street, shown to be late Saxon in excavations (shown in Figure 9.2). The eastern line of the defences is, like the western line, indicated by a zone marked by an irregular layout of property boundaries. It is significant that the church of St Peter, with its large parish surrounding Maldon, is centrally located within this defended *enceinte*, and that this point is also marked by a road leading into the defended enclosure of the *burh* from the bridge and causeway to its north. This clearly forms a diversion from an earlier routeway leading from the bridge in a south-westerly direction, which can be traced in the built landscape. It can be concluded that the spatial relationship of all these features is best interpreted as comprising the landscape footprint of a defended enclosure with a characteristically 'urban' layout – i.e., an urban *burh* – and that this can most naturally be identified as the *burh* of King Edward the Elder built in 916 as a replacement for the more temporary campaign fort of 912 on the hill to its west (as shown in Figure 9.1).

An important corollary of this analysis is that the regularity of the group of burgages in the south-west quarter of the *burh* in particular can be seen as having resulted from their formation at the same time as the defences as part of the process of the layout of the *burh*. This contention is supported by other archaeological evidence. Archaeological work at 62–64 High Street, excavated in 1971–72 by Stephen Bassett, showed, in the words of the excavator, that 'a continuous succession of fully urban structures fronting the present line of High Street' within the width of the single burgage could be taken back to the early tenth century, with Stamford Ware found associated with the earliest of these. These (and other) observations form the basis for the deduction that all the burgages within the defended *enceinte* at the same time as the defences. The *enceinte* of the *burh* would have been sited adjacent to an extra-mural market area to its west, which by 916 was probably already established and approached by routeways from all directions, and to an existing, probably mercantile settlement around the minster of St Mary's and the *hythe* or waterside trading area to its east.[15]

On the basic premise that this ensemble of features formed an inter-functional unity, the burgages within the *burh*, the church and the approach road from the north were laid out by a process of controlled land allocation at the same time as the construction of the defences as part of a single planned development. The evidence of the *Chronicle* demonstrates that by the autumn of 917 – less than eighteen months after the initial construction of the second *burh* – there was a resident

Fig. 9.2 Maldon – reconstruction of the extent of the *burh* of 916 on a background of the Ordnance Survey 1:500 map of 1873–75. The defences are shown as a notional line about 18 m to 20 m in width, to include bank and external ditches. The dotted line shows the extent of the precinct of the medieval Carmelite Friary. North to top.

population within the *burh* who were ready and able to act in its defence. These men are specifically mentioned in contradistinction to those who came to the defence of the *burh* 'from outside'.[16] I have elsewhere argued at length that one of the fundamentally important mechanisms by which late Saxon *burhs* were constructed and manned from their inception was through the attachment of a tenement in the *burh* to the estate of a thegn or other landholder by the king, to the end of coercing these thegns and their men to provide services to enable the construction, maintenance and proper functioning of the *burh*. This result was achieved through the principal of reciprocity, by which the gift of the tenement set up obligations on the part of the thegn to the king to perform services at the central *burh*. In this way *burhs* were characterised by heterogeneous tenure from the start.[17] This mechanism provides a direct causal and functional web of connections between the evidence of a resident force or garrison within the defences of Maldon shown in the events of 917 in the *Chronicle*, the means whereby this resident population was established by the king and the evidence from the spatial relationship of the line of defences to the burgages – in which, it must be presumed, the garrison who fought the Vikings from East Anglia in 917 were accommodated.

The spatial relationships of all these features imply that they were laid out to operate together as an integrated 'ensemble', the constituent features of which were designed to function together as a system. Similar inferences can be made in regard to the evidence from a number of other places.[18] The importance of the example of the *burh* at Maldon is that the documentary evidence recorded in the *Chronicle*, combined with the topographical and archaeological evidence for the primacy of the burgages in the town plan and their relationship to the defences, demonstrate that it was planned, laid out and settled within a short time from its inception. There seems little doubt that this new settlement would, by the standards of the time, have been considered urban. It fulfils Biddle's definition of a planned town as a 'place which has been laid out in a regular pattern at one moment in time with the purpose of dividing and apportioning the ground for permanent settlement'.[19] This new model gives some supporting evidence for the way in which new urban *burhs* of the early tenth century were laid out, how they were able to act so effectively as strategic instruments which defended vulnerable areas against Viking incursions, and how they enabled the king to exert a new level of control over populations to the end of enforcing their services towards achieving these strategic and other goals.

The *burhs* of Wessex and Mercia

This conclusion has wide implications for considering the status and the function of places in both Wessex and Mercia which can be included in the class of burghal plan-forms which I have characterised above as comprising the High Street type. Of the thirty-one *burhs* listed in the Burghal Hidage in Wessex there are perhaps seventeen places which exhibit this plan type. Also included are Barnstaple, Guildford, Marlborough, Kingsbridge and Totnes, which were arguably replacements at an early stage in the development of the system for the hill fort *burhs* of Pilton, Eashing, Chisbury and Halwell, respectively.[20] These are listed below, with their plans included in Figure 9.1 and Figures 9.4 to 9.11.

One important aspect of the classification of these places is that the *burhs* of the Burghal Hidage arguably formed a unitary *system* which was instigated and set out by King Alfred during a brief period in the later 870s which can be identified as a unique window of political opportunity. In this period Alfred was able to regain lands to the north of the river Thames which he had lost for a short while as a result of the 'Partition' of Mercia recorded in the *Chronicle* under the year 877, a situation which was made possible by his victory over the Danes at Edington in the spring of 878. This period was brought to a close with the absorption of greater Mercia under the control of Alfred to form a new polity in late 879 or early 880, which contemporaries called the 'Kingdom of the Anglo-Saxons'.[21] After this time the area defined by the territories owing allegiance and services to the *burhs* listed in the Burghal Hidage (including Oxford and Buckingham) would not have existed as a unified and separate geopolitical entity. It is necessary to stress this in view of the development of a contrasting viewpoint by John Baker and Stuart Brookes, who see the *burhs* of the Burghal Hidage as being the result of a piecemeal, progressive and long-drawn-out process of strategic response to Viking incursions at different times as the ninth century rolled into the tenth.[22]

One of the principal reasons for seeing these *burhs* as a unified system is that the burghal territories of all the *burhs* listed in the Burghal Hidage in the central Wessex shires can be shown not only to interlock spatially but also to straddle the river Thames in a way which shows that the river did not form a major boundary at the time of the formation of the burghal system (Figure 9.3).[23] The spatial interconnection of these territories, which applies *a fortiori* to those in the rest of Wessex to the west and east of this group, shows that these *burhs* and their territories (including, emphatically, Buckingham and Oxford

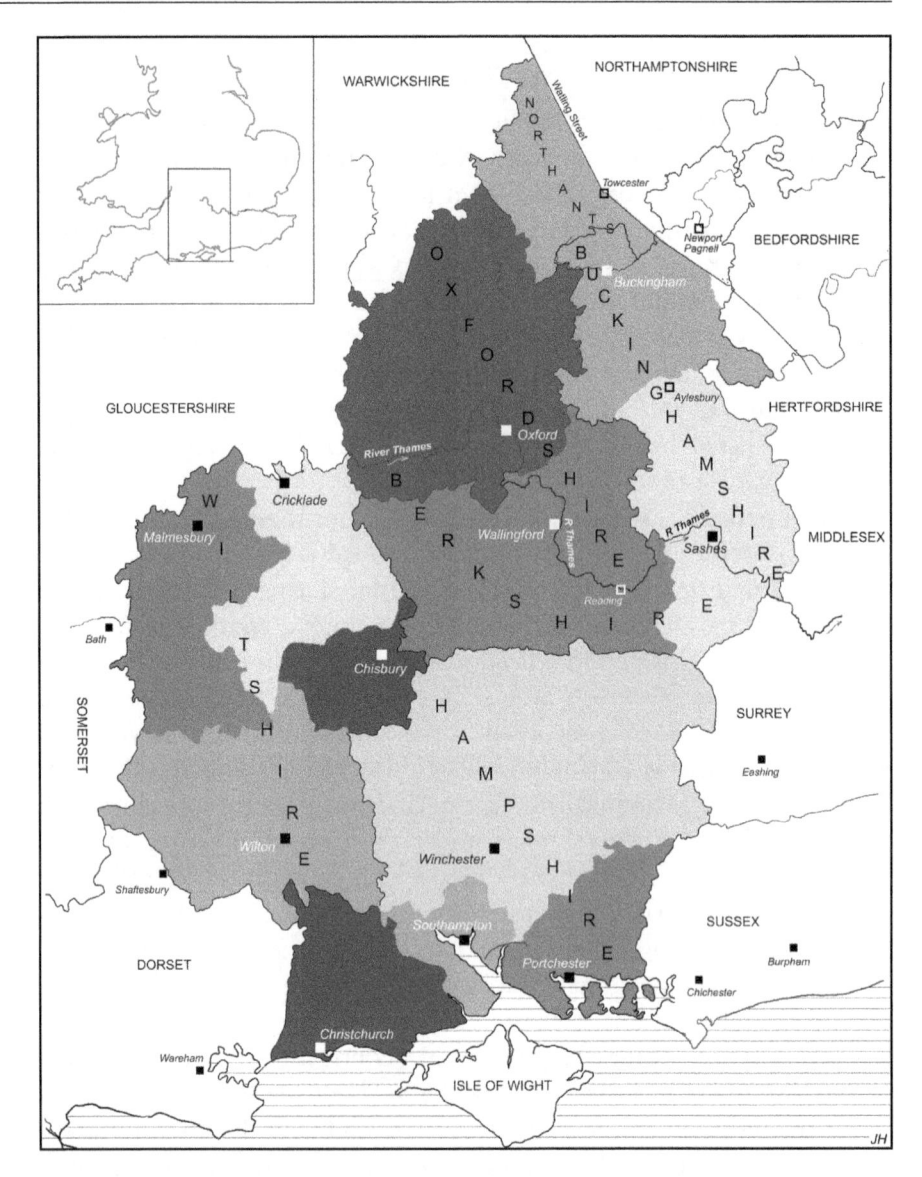

Fig. 9.3 A reconstruction of the interlocking burghal territories of three areas in central Wessex (a) Oxfordshire, Berkshire and Buckinghamshire (and part of Northamptonshire); (b) Hampshire; (c) Wiltshire. Reconstructions are based on detailed analyses in Haslam, *Urban–Rural Connections in Domesday Book and Late Anglo-Saxon Royal Administration*, 19–27, 33–37, 96–116. The shires of Oxfordshire, Berkshire, Buckinghamshire and Northamptonshire were later developments, and were formed by fusion and fission of the earlier burghal territories; this is discussed ibid., 127–31.

Solid square symbols represent *burhs* included in the Burghal Hidage; open square symbols represent later *burhs*. North to top.

to the north of the river Thames) must have been formed by the same act of state as essential and complementary elements of a contemporary system. The existence of any one of these territories necessarily implies the existence of all its neighbours, and therefore, by extension, the existence of all the *burhs* in the system as a single entity brought into being at one moment in time.[24] These *burhs*, including Buckingham, must be regarded therefore as contemporary foundations, created within a coherent geopolitical unit that represented the full extent of the 'Kingdom of the West Saxons', prior to the political changes implied in the formation of the 'Kingdom of the Anglo-Saxons', which was consequent on the extension of King Alfred's hegemony over western Mercia from *c*.880. The fact that, as demonstrated in this chapter, the *burhs* in Wessex of the High Street type exhibit such a remarkable degree of uniformity in their plan-form lends further support to the idea that they were conceived and laid out within a single and unified political as well as strategic context. In this way the built environments of the *burhs* can be seen as being the instruments by means of which a new political order was put in place and upheld.

As well as those in Wessex, there are a number of *burhs* in Mercia which exhibit the plan-form characterised here as the High Street type. These include examples in western Mercia, which originated in the reigns of Æthelflæd and Æthelred in the later ninth and early tenth centuries, and by Edward the Elder in both eastern and western Mercia in the period 911–920. The plan-forms of this group as a whole are more varied than those in Wessex, and as well as those of the High Street type include other types with rectilinear, radial-concentric, oval, near-circular and half-circular plans. It is not possible even to begin to analyse the variety of plan-forms here. Those of the High Street type are listed below.

For the purpose of this analysis it is appropriate therefore to regard all the *burhs* of the High Street type as a single group, based on common characteristics of their plan-form, notwithstanding that these comprise subgroups which can be distinguished by their differing historical origins in Wessex and Mercia. However, the basic continuity between the political and strategic policies of the West Saxons under King Alfred, and those developed by his son Edward the Elder in eastern Mercia and East Anglia and by his daughter Æthelflæd and son-in-law Æthelred in western Mercia, has been emphasised by Simon Keynes.[25] Instances of this continuity are likely, therefore, to include strategic planning, and the fundamental rationale of *burh*-building in all aspects of function and layout, and, in particular, the ways in which *burhs* were used as instruments of both strategic and political control, as mentioned above.

In this political context, it would be expected that the *burhs* of Mercia in the early tenth century would have shown the application of practices learned in the Wessex phase of *burh*-building of a previous generation.

This extended system can therefore be meaningfully considered as comprising a true polythetic group. The significance in considering this group as such is, first, that a number of characteristics or attributes of the group as a whole are demonstrable by evidence in most, but not all, members of the group, and, second, that attributes shown by some members of the group but not by others can be reasonably inferred in those which do not exhibit those particular attributes.[26] The composition of the group is here a key factor. In this case the group as a whole is composed of all the *burhs* of the Burghal Hidage which show evidence in later sources of a regular layout of the particular plan-form under discussion. This grouping explicitly excludes those *burhs* for which there is no evidence of such features. Also excluded – at least for the immediate purposes here – are those *burhs* in both Wessex and Mercia which show rectilinear planning. This is, admittedly, a somewhat artificial grouping, in that these latter are demonstrably part of the same contemporary system and formed in the same political, social and strategic milieu to those forming the former group.[27]

Burhs of the High Street type in Wessex listed in the Burghal Hidage include the following:

Axbridge
Bridport
Buckingham
Christchurch
Langport
Lewes
Lydford
Lyng
Malmesbury
Shaftesbury
Southampton
Watchet
Wilton

To this list may be added *burhs* which replaced hill forts:

Barnstaple
Guildford
Kingsbridge

Marlborough
Totnes

These total eighteen and are contrasted with *burhs* with rectilinear layouts:

Bath
Chichester
Cricklade
Exeter
Oxford (primary *burh*)
Wallingford
Wareham
Winchester

These total eight. The remaining ten (out of a total of thirty-one listed in the Burghal Hidage), which are not discussed here, do not exhibit any evidence of a surviving internal plan-form.

Burhs of the High Street type in Mercia and East Anglia include the following:

Worcester (Worcestershire)
Oxford (second *burh* of c.911) (Oxfordshire)
Stamford (two *burhs*, to the north and south of the river) (Lincolnshire)
Maldon (second *burh* of 916) (Essex)
Newport Pagnell (Buckinghamshire)
Woodbridge (Suffolk)
Beccles (Suffolk)

Woodbridge and Beccles arguably formed elements of a systematic coverage of *burhs* and their territories in East Anglia which were put in place in or soon after the submission of East Anglia and Essex to King Edward in 917,[28] as an essential means of establishing his political control of the area. It is hoped to explore this theme in a later publication. These *burhs* are shown on Ordnance Survey maps at a common scale in Figure 9.1 and Figures 9.4 to 9.11.[29]

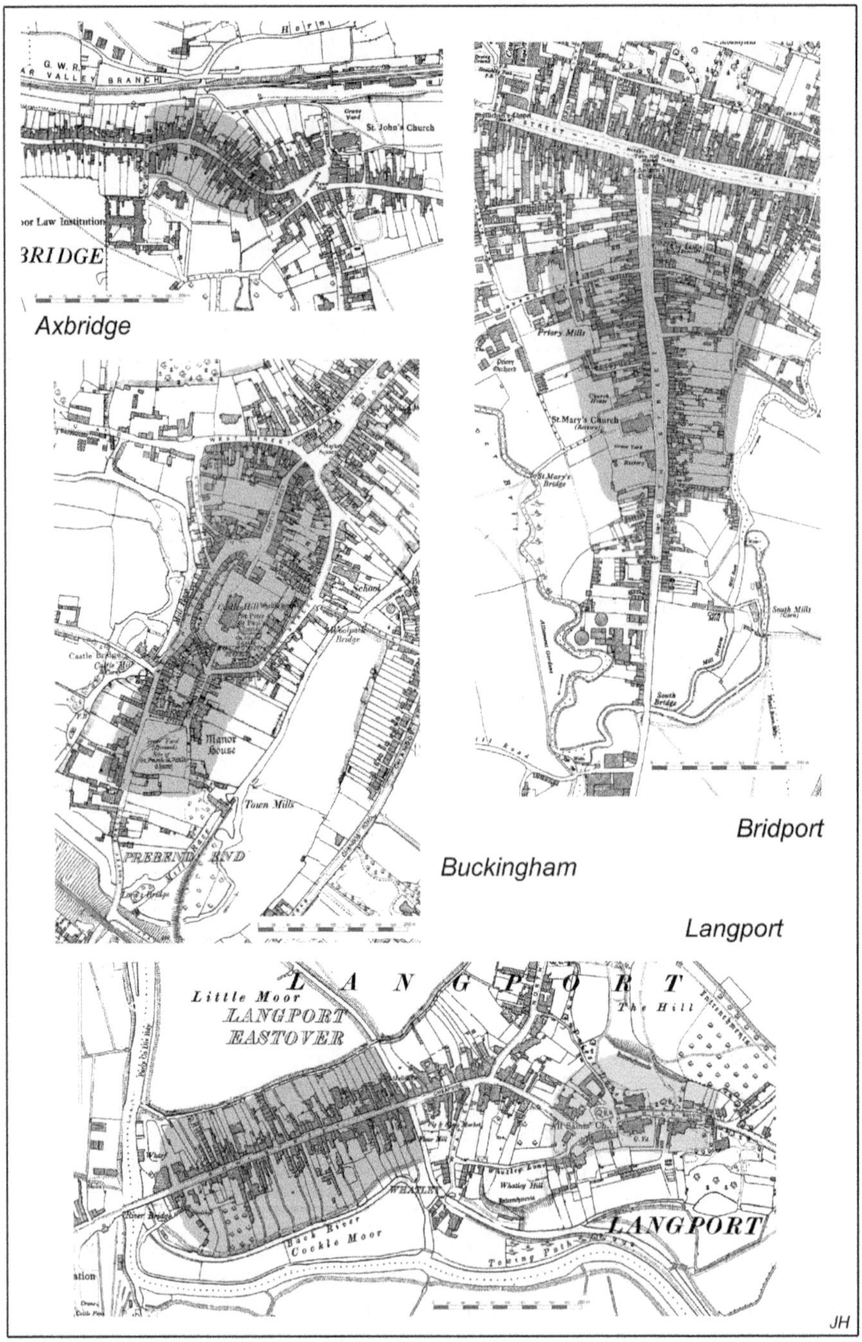

Fig. 9.4 The extent of the *burhs* (shaded) at Axbridge, Bridport, Buckingham and Langport. North to top.

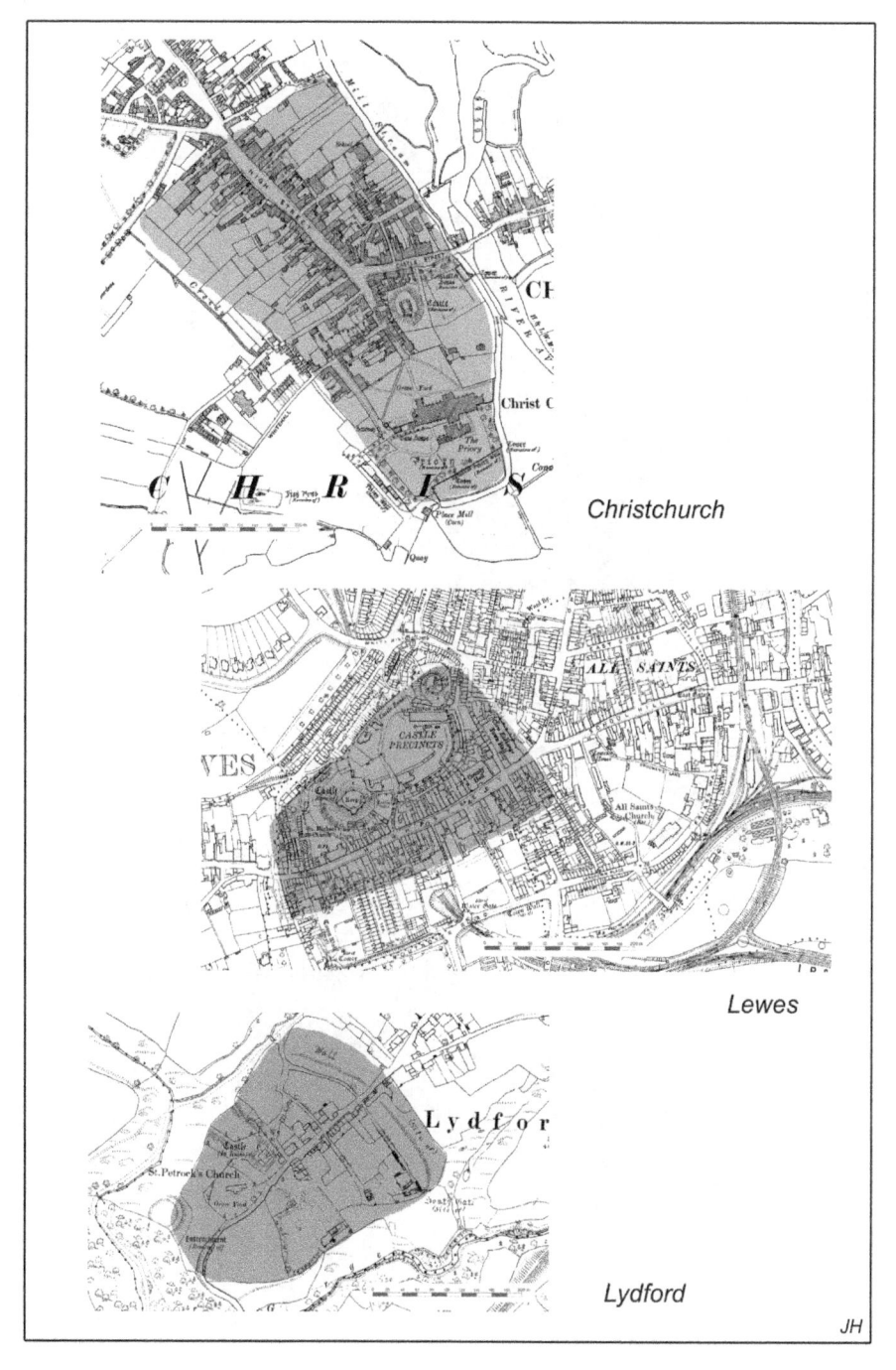

Fig. 9.5 The extent of the *burhs* (shaded) at Christchurch, Lewes and Lydford. North to top.

Christchurch

Lewes

Lydford

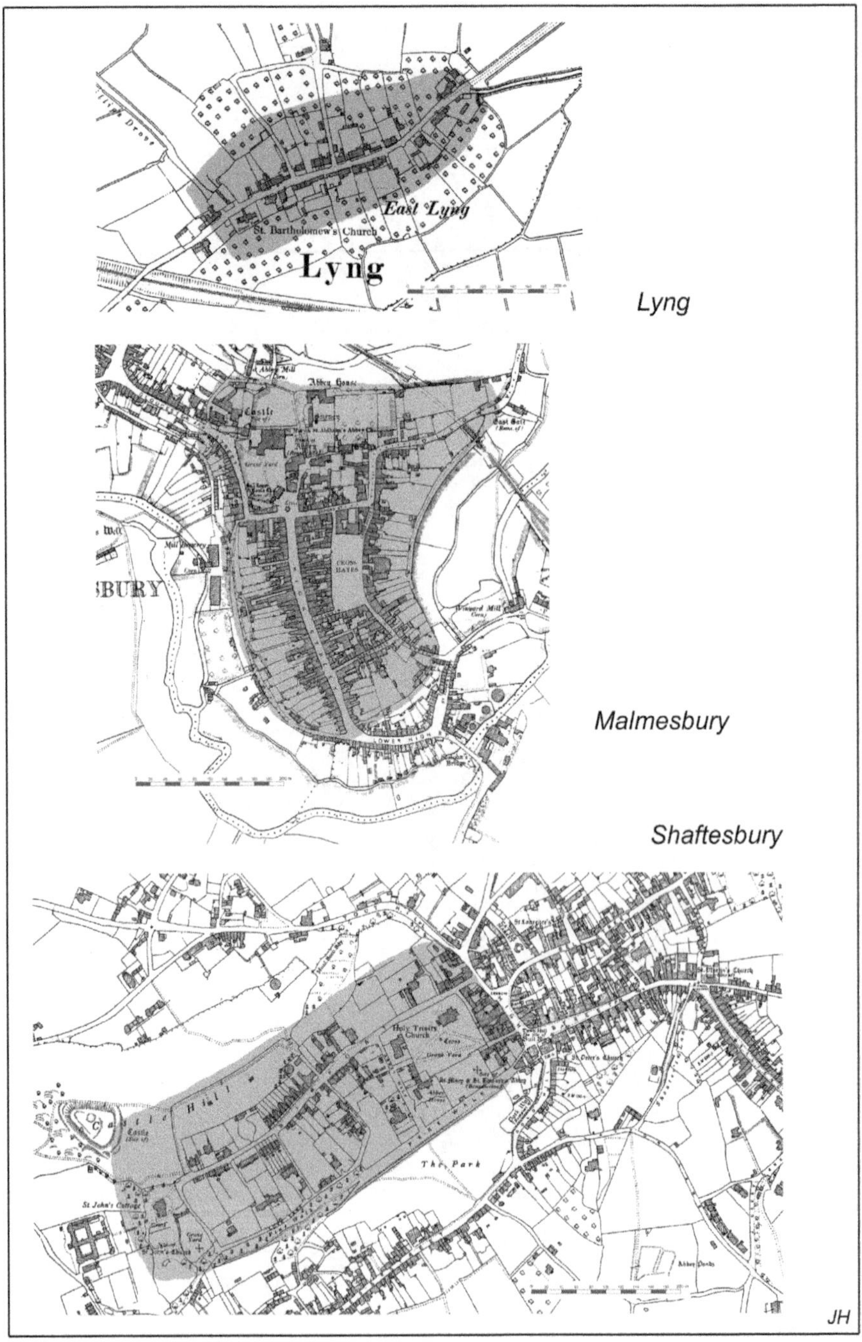

Fig. 9.6 The extent of the *burhs* (shaded) at Lyng, Malmesbury and Shaftesbury. North to top.

Lyng

Malmesbury

Shaftesbury

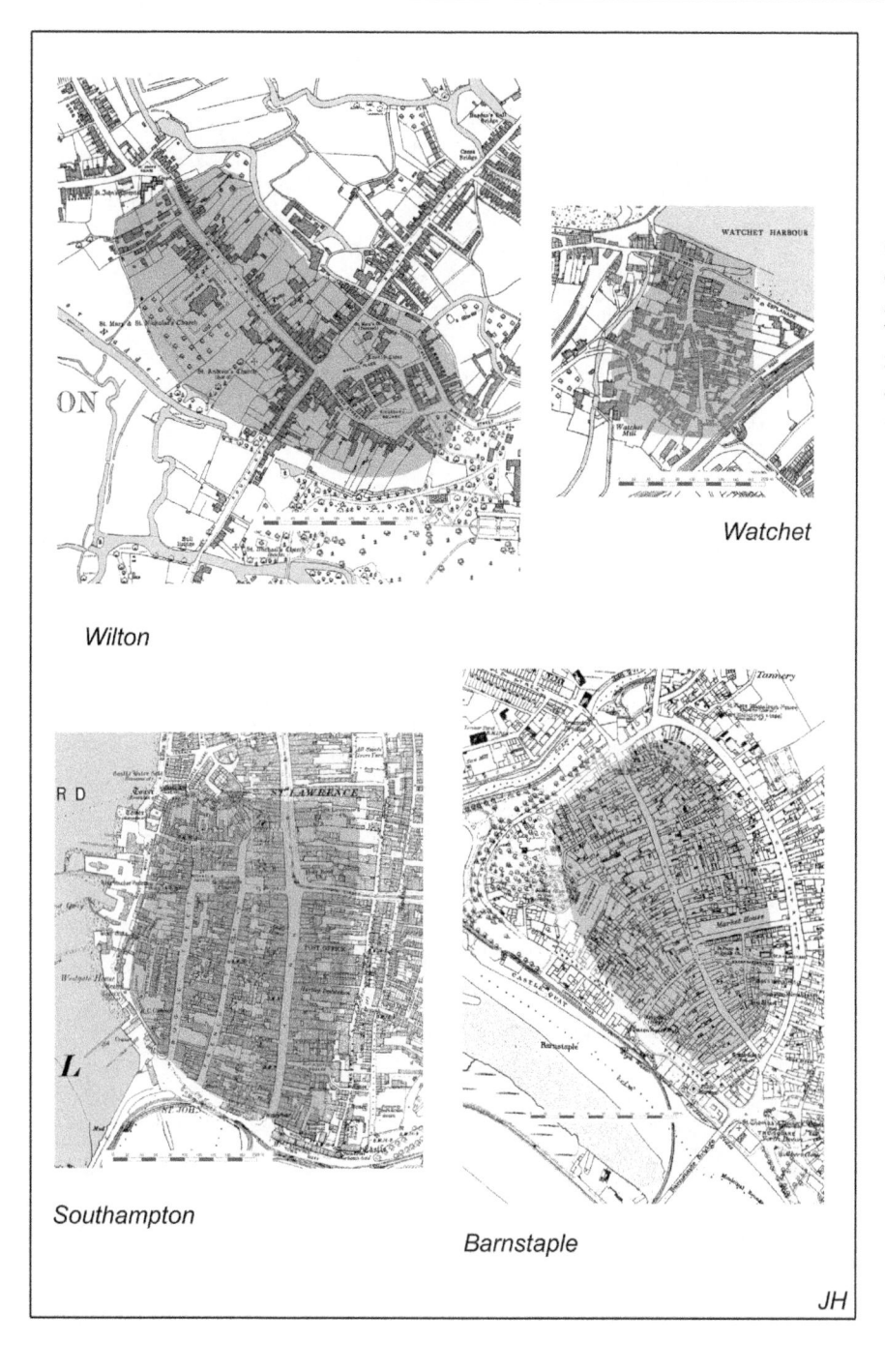

Jeremy Haslam Landscape of Late Saxon *Burhs* 197

Fig. 9.7 The extent of the *burhs* (shaded) at Wilton, Watchet, Southampton and Barnstaple. North to top.

Fig. 9.8 The extent of the *burhs* (shaded) at Guildford, Kingsbridge and Marlborough. North to top.

Oxford (secondary burh)

Stamford (N & S burhs)

Worcester

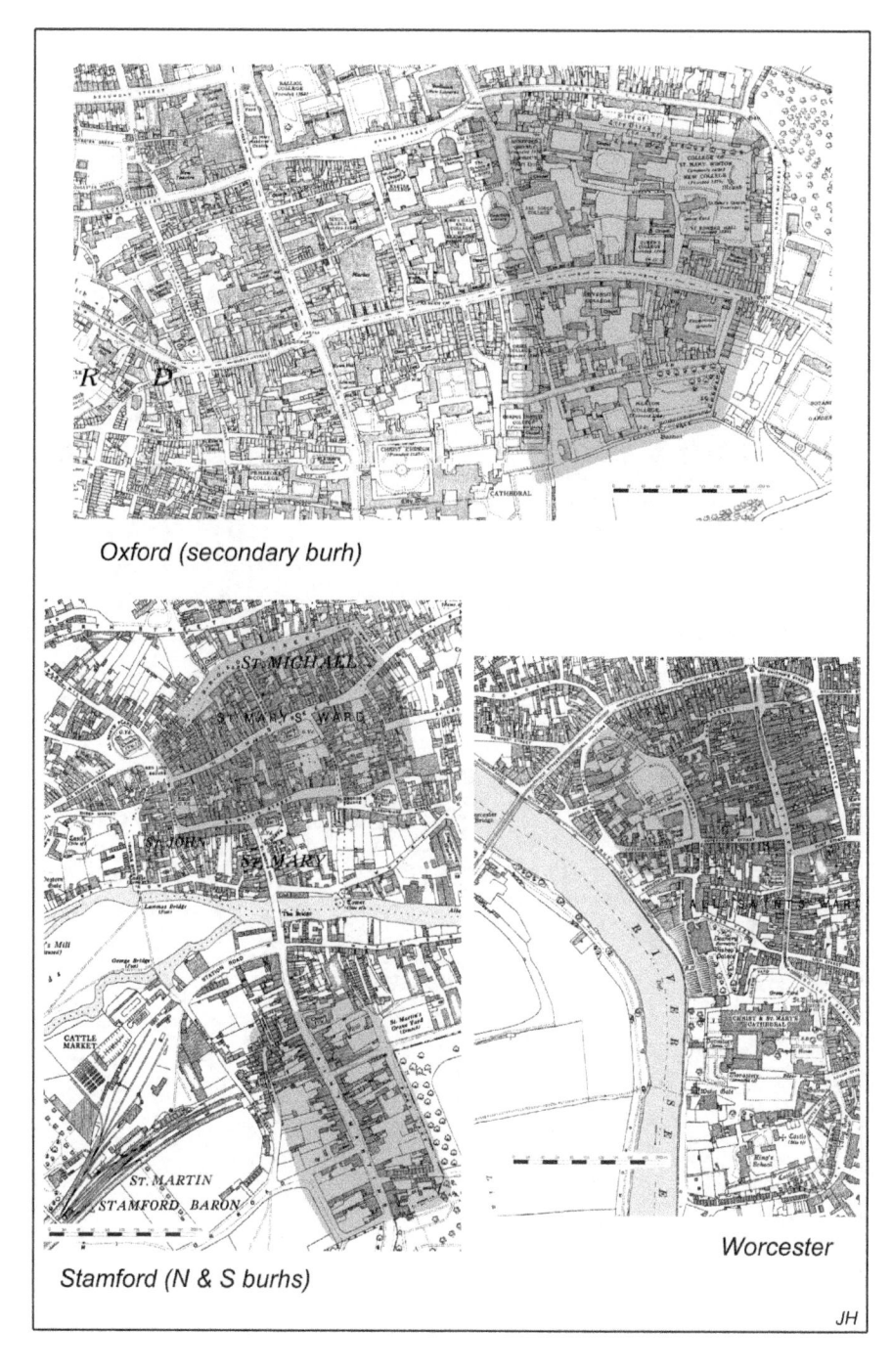

Fig. 9.9 The extent of the *burhs* (shaded) at Oxford (second *burh* of *c*.911), Stamford (two *burhs* on each side of the river) and Worcester. North to top.

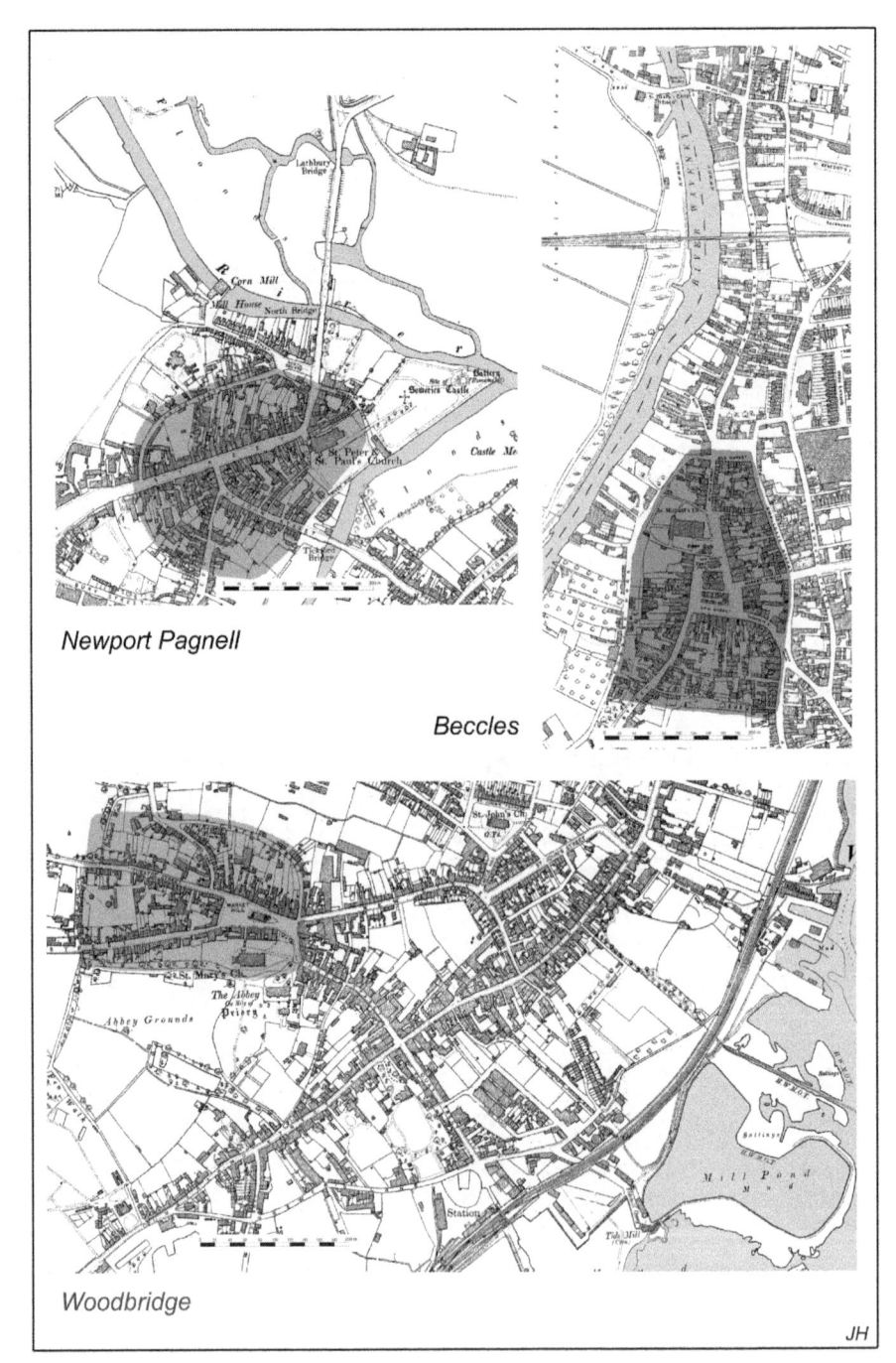

Fig. 9.10 The extent of the *burhs* (shaded) at Newport Pagnell, Beccles and Woodbridge. North to top.

Newport Pagnell

Beccles

Woodbridge

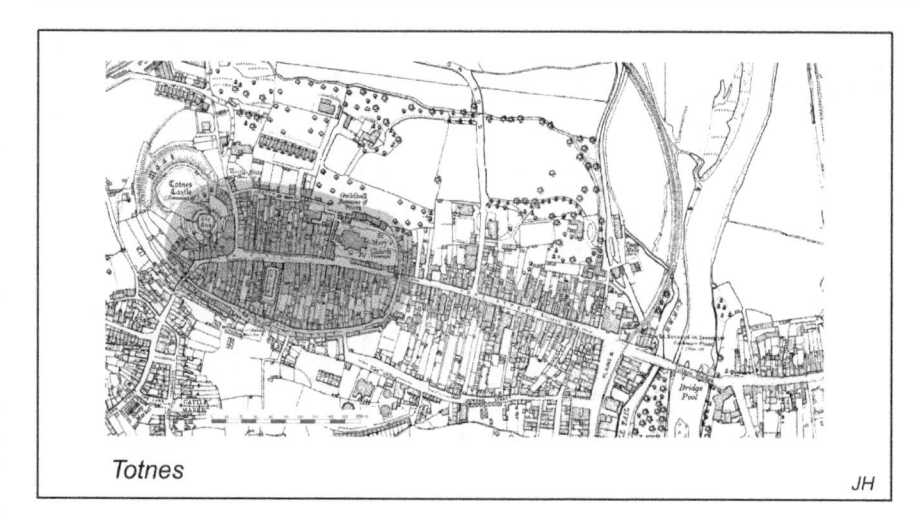

Fig. 9.11 The extent of the *burh* (shaded) at Totnes. North to top.

Discussion

The evidence from Maldon, discussed above, arguably demonstrates that the various topographical elements which comprised the *burh* – defences, the single spinal High Street, the centrally placed church (St Peter's), regularly laid-out burgages and the approach road from the north leading from a bridge – should be considered as being an ensemble of features which operated together as a spatially coherent entity. These features therefore constituted a built environment designed with a specific purpose (see Table 9.1)

From this coherence, it can be inferred that all these features were designed from the start to work together as a whole with an integrated and mutually supporting set of functions, and that they were therefore contemporaneous in origin.[30] That these must have been established as a single act of planning and land allocation is confirmed by the evidence from the *Chronicle* that the place contained a resident population which functioned as a garrison only a few months after its initial setup. The position of this *burh* between a probable market area adjacent to the gate of the earlier campaign fort to the west (itself on the site of an important memorial cross), a middle Saxon *hythe* or waterside trading area (possibly a minor *wic*) and the minster church (St Mary's) to the east, shows that it would have been well placed to act as a newly planted town whose inhabitants would have been urban traders.

The fact that most of these characteristics are shown by other *burhs* of the same plan-form, which form the single polythetic group discussed here, allows the deduction that all these *burhs* were also laid out to perform the same functions – essentially, newly built towns with resident

Burh	Ai	Aii	B	C	Di	Dii	E	F	Gi	Gii	H	J	K
Burhs listed in the Burghal Hidage (late 870s)													
Axbridge	+			+	+		+	+?	+				+
Bridport		+	+		+			+	+				+
Buckingham		+	+	+		+	+	+	+		+		+
Christchurch	+		+	+		+	+	+	+		+		
Langport		+	+	+	+		+	+	+		+		+
Lewes		+	+	+	+				+		+		
Lydford	+		+	+	+			+	+				
Lyng	+		+	+	+				+				
Malmesbury	+		+	+		+		+	+		+		
Shaftesbury		+	+		+								+
Southampton	+		+		+				+		+	+	
Watchet		+	+			+		+	+				+
Wilton	+		+	+		+		+	+		+		
Replacement burhs (late 9th century)													
Barnstaple	+			+	+			+	+			+	+
Guildford		+		+	+			+	+				
Kingsbridge			+	+	+			+	+				
Marlborough	+		+	+	+		+	+	+				+
Totnes	+		+	+	+			+	+				+
Burhs of the 'High Street' type in Mercia and East Anglia (late 9th and early 10th centuries)													
Worcester	+		+	+				+			+	+	+
Oxford *(second burh of 913)*	+			+	+			+	+			+	
Stamford *(southern burh)*		+	+	+	+				+				
Stamford *(northern burh)*		+		+	+		+	+	+		+	+	+
Maldon *(second burh of 916)*	+			+	+	+		+	+	+	+?	+	+
Newport Pagnell	+	+	+	+	+		+	+	+				+
Woodbridge		+	+	+	+			+	+				+
Beccles		+	+	+	+				+				+

populations who were engaged in trade as well as defence. As I have argued elsewhere, the presence of heterogeneous tenure in most of them at the time of Domesday (and in many cases at earlier dates) also implies that these arrangements were set up by royal fiat at the time of the initial formation of each of the *burhs*, by a combination of inducement and coercion of the populations of their dependent territories. The thegns and other landholders who acquired these properties in the *burhs* were in consequence constrained by a web of obligations, ultimately to the king,

Characteristics:
Ai archaeological evidence of defences, and/or a ditch or ditches
Aii topographical or documentary evidence only of defences, and/or a ditch or ditches
B sited on a topographically distinct spur of land
C close topographical association with a causeway and/or a bridge
Di presence of a church topographically associated with the *enceinte* of the *burh*
Dii or presence of an earlier minster church within or near the defended *enceinte*
E place name evidence of nearby Portfield (or similar) (this is not a comprehensive list)
F close spatial association with the site of a mill (often called Port Mill, King's Mill or Town Mill)
Gi topographical evidence of regularly arranged burgages fitting part or all of the intra-mural space
Gii archaeological evidence of contemporaneity of one or more burgages within the system with the layout of the defences
H heterogeneous tenure in pre-Conquest charters and/or Domesday Book
J archaeological evidence of early tenth-century occupation within the defended *enceinte*
K close spatial association of a market area with the defended *enceinte*, usually extra-mural to one of the gates

Table 9.1
Characteristics of *burhs*

to perform duties which were geared to the physical construction and maintenance of the built environment of the *burhs* and to the defence of the *burh* and its territory. This process must have represented one of the most important ways by which the king would have been able to create and sustain the newly planted settlements in these *burhs* as a group.[31] The development of a network of mints within some of the regionally important *burhs* as part of this process demonstrates that this coercion and control of the populations was to have a commercial or trading dimension.[32] This process may be seen as another way in which the king would have been able to maintain and develop control of the populations of the *burhs* and their territories, as well as to facilitate commercial interactions which were designed to contribute to the ways in which these new towns could become sustainable or self-supporting environments.

This conclusion puts a rather different perspective on recent attempts to play down, or even to deny, the significance of these *burhs* as places which were founded as new towns. Andrew Reynolds has made the bold statement that 'one of the most significant realizations in Anglo-Saxon archaeology [is] that ninth-century burghal foundations were largely devoid of settlement activity up to perhaps two or three generations, or up to one hundred years, after their initial construction'.[33] This conclusion appears to be predicated on Grenville Astill's view that the *burhs* 'had an important military and political role that was retained for perhaps as much as a century, and only after that did the settlements acquire further urban attributes'.[34] This argument seems to assume that these *burhs* initially had few or no urban characteristics, with little evidence of 'settlement activity' before the later tenth century, a conclusion based generally on the paucity or sometimes the absence of archaeological evidence demonstrating industrial and craft production in the Wessex *burhs* until then. The argument begs the question as to whether the garrisons installed in these *burhs* did or did not represent 'settlers', and makes the implicit assumption that the *burhs* should more appropriately be perceived as barracks. It also raises the issue as to whether these *burhs* were operating within the context of a 'command economy'. Thus, Astill characterises the tenth century as the 'lost century for the *burhs* of Wessex'.[35] This situation may be seen as standing in marked contrast to the development of places with 'true' urban attributes in the northern and eastern Danelaw at the same time.[36]

It is the survival of topographical or spatial attributes of these *burhs*, which were arguably formed as an expression of the full functionality of the *burhs* as new towns that were newly laid out as sustainable settlements, which provides a counterbalance to this series of conclusions. This body of evidence, furthermore, is reinforced by a number of aspects of the built environment of the wider landscape in which they are set. The minimising view of Astill, Reynolds and Holt (below) ignores, for instance, the urban aspirations embodied in the creation and laying out of new *burhs* of the High Street type at Barnstaple, Guildford, Marlborough, Kingsbridge and Totnes as probable replacements to small non-urban fortresses on less accessible sites, arguably in the 890s,[37] as well as the ubiquitous creation of large urban *burhs* in Mercia in the early decades of the tenth century in Mercia and East Anglia, noted above.[38] These views also run counter to the evidence from the urban–rural connections recorded in later sources, which arguably show that the *burhs* were laid out from the start with heterogeneous tenure – i.e., they accommodated both customary burgesses owing dues to the king, as well as non-customary burgesses whose tenements were appurtenant to the rural estates of the thegns of the particular burghal territories – and that this pattern is one of the more important strands of evidence which demonstrates that the *burhs* were set out as planned settlements from the start. This conclusion appears to be demonstrated unequivocally by the spatial intermingling of these two types of tenements in Winchester which can be reconstructed from later sources, which can only have arisen by a simultaneous process of land allocation of these two types of tenements within the *burh*. The logic of these observations implies, as Biddle has pointed out, that this arrangement originated in the 'apportionment of land in the city at the time of the reorganisation under Alfred'.[39] Similar patterns which can be observed in, for instance, Oxford, Wallingford and Gloucester demonstrate the formation of what must be seen as a characteristically urban layout in the same political and developmental context.[40]

Furthermore, the evidence from Maldon indicates that the internal space of the new *burh* of 916 would have been laid out from the beginning with regular burgages with little internal open space. The same inference can be drawn from the patterns of burgages in several other places. Those in Axbridge, Langport, Newport Pagnell, Kingsbridge and Totnes, in particular, show clearly how the burgages were laid out in a manner which was constrained by, and formed within, the envelope formed by the line of the defences of the *burh*, a relationship also shown, for instance, in Christchurch, Wilton, Bridport and Guildford. The more complex pattern of burgages, for instance in Barnstaple, also shows how those fronting some of the side streets interlock in a step-like fashion with those fronting the main street, indicating contemporaneity. Since the same pattern, with variations, can be recognised in almost all the examples discussed here – even allowing for the processes of fusion and fission of individual plots, and of the partial loss of these patterns through, for instance, the imposition of Norman castles on the townscape – it seems a reasonable inference that this way of organising space within the *burhs* was the norm.

This conclusion is in contrast to the view of Robert Higham, among others, who has suggested that 'it is now generally argued that townscapes of multiple, long, narrow tenements, characteristic of medieval towns, were not primary features of the burghal period. They probably developed, under pressure of population growth and economic activity, from the late tenth century onwards'.[41] This view, of course, begs the question as to how the internal spaces of the *burhs* of the High Street type were organised before this process took place, and at what time and by what means these regular patterns were brought into being. It also fails to account for the arrangements which must have accompanied the formation of both the ubiquitous customary tenements of the king shown in particular in Domesday Book (tenements which must necessarily have been contemporary with the foundation of all *burhs*), as well as the non-customary tenements attached to rural estates which were intermingled with them, as discussed above. This pattern can be contrasted with the arrangement in which relatively large enclosures were held by thegns and others in the larger rectilinear *burhs*, subsequently to become subdivided into smaller tenements and perhaps a church.[42] This minimising view also overlooks the long history of the organisation of urban spaces into discrete tenements or burgages arranged in relation to streets in orthogonal patterns, as one aspect of land allocation within the urban landscape of middle Saxon *wics* (or urban trading places) at London, *Hamwic* and elsewhere.[43] It would seem improbable that the new burghal spaces of the *burhs* of the 870s would not have been the direct heirs to this culture of spatial organisation within urban places.

The *burhs* in a wider landscape

There are also a number of features of the landscape of the *burhs* and their hinterlands which formed an essential infrastructure to their existence, and which therefore provide evidence of the underlying intentions which brought them into being as essentially sustainable settlements. Amongst these features would have been mills, which in most of the places considered are sited in close spatial association with original features of their layout (and often called Town mill, Port mill or King's mill in later sources). These appear to have been newly built as part of the infrastructure of the new *burhs*. Since the mills themselves together with their leats or supply channels would have represented considerable feats of both landscape engineering and construction, and therefore of investment in labour, it must be inferred that these *burhs* would have been intended to function from the start as socially and economically viable units. An example of the significant role of a mill in the economy of a new *burh* is the King's Mill at Cambridge. Its close spatial relationship to both the King's Ditch (which formed the outer defences of the *burh*) and the upstream point of the canalisation of the river demonstrates its contemporaneity with the foundation of the *burh*. An analogous situation can be shown at Langport, where the mill and its leat (extending more than 6 kilometres upriver), the east gate of the *burh* and the extra-mural market place are contiguous.[44] The same set of spatial and functional relationships can be inferred from other examples, such as the Port Mill at Christchurch.[45] The significance of the mill in the urban economy would be that it would have acted as a royal manorial perquisite, providing flour for the new population of the *burh* in return for payment to the king. Of equal significance in this regard are the areas of land adjacent to a number of *burhs*, the Portfields, which were perhaps the fields set aside for use by the inhabitants of the new *burh*.[46] The existence of both mills and Portfields as features which were arguably provided for the inhabitants of these *burhs ab initio* supports the idea that the *burhs* were founded to function as new settlements which were viable and sustainable as both social and economic units on a number of different levels. However, through this process both mills and fields would, in different ways, have served to build yet another layer of royal control into the social structure of the *burhs*, binding the new populations ever more tightly into their web of obligations to the king through the design and organisation of the built environment itself.

Another significant way in which the development of this system of *burhs* impacted the late ninth-century landscape was the development of communications. As well as requiring defences, streets and other features of the wholly new land allotment involved, the *burhs* were in general sited to command routeways, both by water and land.[47] The topographical situations of most of these *burhs*, as shown in the maps in Figure 9.1 and Figures 9.4 to 9.11, show that most of them were associated with bridges and causeways, in such a way as to demonstrate that in many cases these structures may have been newly built at the same time as the *burhs*. Axbridge, for instance, was associated with a long causeway over the then-marshy Somerset Levels, as well as a bridge over the tidal river Axe (not shown in Figure 9.4), though this may well have preceded the formation of the *burh* itself. The siting of other *burhs* such as Maldon, Langport, Totnes, Newport Pagnell and Lewes, and the two *burhs* at Stamford, to name but a few shown in the maps (Figure 9.1 and Figures 9.4 to 9.11), would not have made sense in the context of the time if their associated bridges and causeways had not been a part of their overall design and function within the landscape from the start.[48] The development of these in association with the *burhs*, and the development of certain routeways which utilised these, have clearly had an effect on the landscape, which has, in many cases, lasted until modern times.

As already pointed out above, one of the most important ways which the development of the systems of *burhs* brought into being in Wessex, Mercia and East Anglia in the late ninth and earlier tenth centuries impacted the contemporary administrative landscapes lay in the imposition of fundamental, far-reaching and kingdom-wide episodes of local government reorganisation, which involved the creation of systems of interlocking burghal territories. In Wessex, this new way of organising the landscape was the subject of the arguably contemporary Burghal Hidage document, which records the hides by which these territories were assessed. Each of these territories would have defined an area of land in which the holders or occupiers of estates owed services or obligations to the central *burh* which it surrounded. I have argued elsewhere that in Wessex these territories would have been formed within the envelopes represented by the earlier shires, while those of the *burhs* of Wallingford, Oxford, Sashes and Buckingham, in the later shires of Berkshire, Oxfordshire and Buckinghamshire, formed contiguous territories which pre-dated the formation of the shires and which straddled the river Thames. The Mercian shires, however, were formed by a subsequent complex process of amalgamation and fission of these burghal territories. The creation of these burghal territories was perhaps the principal way in which the king could exercise control over populations to the end of providing an effective strategic response to Viking incursions. The lives and the allegiances of all landholders and their dependents within these territories were from this time inextricably linked to the particular *burh* in whose territory it lay. This arrangement was to last until the time of another major cadastral reorganisation of the burghal territories in Mercia to form larger shires, arguably in the mid-tenth century.[49]

As suggested at the beginning of this chapter, the physical and spatial evidence of the built environment as a whole, relating both to the *burhs* themselves as well as to their situations within a wider landscape, generates a new 'historical narrative' which provides a corrective to the minimising tendencies which follow from the assumption that the absence of artefactual evidence from excavations necessarily indicates the absence of specifically 'urban' characteristics or functions of *burhs* in general. A similar critical reappraisal of the evidence from Worcester supports this analysis. Nigel Baker and Richard Holt have discussed evidence which is taken as demonstrating that the planning of the internal space of Worcester, and therefore of all *burhs* (in particular the rectilinear *burhs* such as Winchester), was not a feature relating to the processes involved in their foundation.[50] Baker and Holt draw this conclusion from their consideration of evidence relating to various features of the topography of Worcester, combined with the documentary evidence of the well-known charter of the late ninth century. Holt concludes that 'The Worcester borough [*burh*] of the 890s had indeed the military purpose that the foundation charter names – it was built for the protection of the people, as a fortress and a refuge for use in emergencies. There was no intention of founding a town (with all that that might entail)'.[51] I have reconsidered this evidence and these arguments elsewhere, and as an anti-thesis to Holt's have given reasons for concluding that a new *burh* at Worcester was founded in *c.*880 as one element of a system of such *burhs* (which included London) which was created within the context of the new polity known as the 'Kingdom of the Anglo-Saxons'; that it was essentially a newly planted and planned town with a new population engaged in trade; that it was laid out to a pattern common to the other *burhs* of the High Street type discussed in this chapter; and that it would have been characterised by heterogeneous tenure from the time of its foundation as a *burh*.[52]

These issues raise the question of how far these *burhs* functioned as 'emergency' refuges, or communal defended fortresses. The observation that these *burhs* of the Burghal Hidage were located no more than 35 kilometres (20 miles) or so from any place in Wessex has generated the ubiquitous assumption these were supposedly accessible to the general population fleeing Viking raids.[53] However, as already argued, the plan-form of the *burhs* under discussion, which was the norm in Wessex and common in Mercia, shows that from the start their internal spaces were largely filled with burgages or tenements occupied by the inhabitants of the *burh*. There would have been little room within their defences to house large populations seeking shelter. A consideration of the circumstances of the time, as well as of the logistics entailed in this *burh*-as-refuge set of assumptions, would suggest that rather than abandoning their estates and villages for flight to the nearest *burh* at the first sign of trouble the general 'rural' population would have had little choice in the matter of fleeing or not fleeing. The very notion of the *burhs* as refuges or places of safety for the general population, other than perhaps for some of the elites or thegns on horseback who had a personal stake in the organisation of their construction, needs to be seriously questioned. Even then, the thegns would have been required to act as the fighting contingent. The even spacing of *burhs* in the landscape, as recorded in the Burghal Hidage, must be a product, rather, of the need to place them in such a way that the labour and services of the populations of their assigned territories could most easily be directed towards upholding the central *burh*. As both Gareth Williams and Richard Abels have pointed out, the open spaces not occupied by burgages or tenements in the larger rectilinear *burhs* are more likely to have been used as fortified supply dumps (which would have included livestock) to reinforce the functionality of the new mobile army (the *fyrd*), whose job it was to protect the workers in the field, as well.[54] These functions could be accommodated to some extent, though less satisfactorily, within *burhs* of the High Street type discussed here.

Holt does, however, pose an important issue – which is essentially that addressed in this chapter. He asks: 'how well founded is the perception that a layout of streets and presumably an apportionment of property was part of the original borough [*burh*] design? To answer that, we need to re-examine the chronology and the circumstances of the acquisition by the boroughs [*burhs*] of a form associated with subsequent urban development'.[55] As pointed out above, this enquiry must take into account the significant class of evidence represented by the development of associated infrastructures such as mills, fields and bridges, which are a sign of the complexity of the social and economic development of these *burhs* that is hidden by the paucity of the archaeological and documentary evidence. It is concluded from the evidence discussed in this chapter that the *burhs* of the High Street type were indeed *initially laid out* with an overall plan-form which was ubiquitous, complex, structured and capable of flexible adaptation to different sites and situations. Furthermore, it is clear that their internal organisation was designed to accommodate a permanent population, and that these characteristics cannot have been acquired at an indeterminate period after the foundation of these *burhs* as 'refuges' and fortresses or 'strongholds'. These places must be seen, therefore, as being – certainly by the standards of the time – characteristically urban.

It must be concluded that this process of urban formation was therefore part of the intention of the royal founders from the start.[56] That the same plan-form used so widely in Wessex in the first phase of burghal formation was utilised repeatedly (though with many variations) both in the design of the 'replacement' *burhs* in Wessex in the late ninth century as well as in Mercia in the early tenth shows that this solution was successful and effective in achieving its multifaceted ends. The same conclusion must also apply to the rectilinear *burhs*, which are not discussed here in detail. Whether or not these places fulfilled the aspirations of their originators in their subsequent development, this evidence does indeed show (as Biddle argued nearly forty years ago) that these *burhs* represent the outcome of a wholly new urbanising initiative – 'a watershed in European urban evolution'.[57] This was, furthermore, associated with a kingdom-wide local government reorganisation involving the creation of a system of interlocking burghal territories.

In conclusion, it can be argued that underpinning the setting out of these planned and defended settlements and their territories as integrated systems within the various kingdoms in the late ninth and early tenth centuries was the rationale that they formed the principal means whereby the king was able to assert the degree of political and social control of the population of his kingdom that he needed to prosecute his strategic, political and social agendas. The most pressing of these was the need to create a stable bulwark against future Viking depredation and domination. But, as is shown by the evidence presented in this chapter, this could only have been achieved by the creation of settlements which were not only strongholds or fortresses, which were new additions to the built environment, but which were also sustainable elements on different levels – social, economic and legal – and which were able to draw on the obligations of all the people. That this system was remarkably successful in doing just that – at least until overtaken by events in the middle and later tenth century – is in itself evidence for this thesis.

Appendix. Notes on the *burhs*

Burhs listed in the Burghal Hidage

AXBRIDGE
A detailed analysis of the evidence relating to the plan-form is given elsewhere.[58] The suggested defended area of the *burh* forms an ensemble with an extra-mural market area and a church outside the east gate, and a long causeway and bridge over the Somerset Levels and the river Axe to the south.[59]

BRIDPORT
The layout of the *burh* is discussed by Laurence Keen.[60]

BUCKINGHAM
The length of the single spinal street has been interrupted by the imposition of the Norman castle. On the analogy with Christchurch, the area of the *burh* is taken here as extending to the south of the old church in Prebend End (probably an earlier minster), which was demolished in the 1770s, and replaced by a new church on the castle site. Given the constraints of the physical topography of the site, this would, however, have involved the laying out of a length of defences out of all proportion to the area enclosed. It is perhaps more probable therefore that the burghal defences only reached as far south as the southern edge of the castle, leaving the old minster church as extra-mural. The persistent (but mistaken) idea that a second *burh* was built at Buckingham in 914 to form a double *burh* is perpetuated in the discussion in the Extensive Urban Survey (EUS) for Buckingham, which still holds to the view that this was sited to the south of the river.[61] There is, however, no evidence for the footprint of a *burh* in the landscape here, as pointed out nearly a century ago by the writer of the *Victoria County History*.[62]

CHRISTCHURCH
A recent analysis of the archaeological and topographical evidence has been put forward elsewhere.[63]

LANGPORT
From the evidence of the town plan and other evidence it seems most likely that the *burh* lay along the causeway to the east of the bridge – a classic example of a *burh* of the 'High Street' type.[64] A probable hill fort on top of the hill to the east may, however, have been utilised in earlier and later times as a local defence and lookout post, its church

and east gateway possibly originating in a phase of (re)fortification in the late tenth century.[65]

Lewes
Landscape and archaeological evidence are discussed by Roland Harris in the Lewes EUS.[66]

Lydford
This is described elsewhere.[67]

Lyng
The landscape context and topography are discussed in a recent study elsewhere.[68]

Malmesbury
This is described elsewhere.[69] See also the EUS, where an unnecessarily complex (and unevidenced) 'evolution' of the plan-form is proposed.[70] Recent excavations on the defences have also been published.[71]

Shaftesbury
This is discussed by Laurence Keen, and further by John Chandler, and Simon Keynes.[72]

Southampton
Numerous excavations in the town have identified the majority of the course of the late Saxon defences. The oft-repeated hypothesis that the Burghal Hidage reference to *hamtune* refers to a *burh* at the Roman site at Clausentum on the east bank of the river[73] is based solely on the correspondence of the length of the defences of Clausentum to the supposed length calculated from the hidage given to Southampton by means of the formula in the calculation appended to version A of the Burghal Hidage. As shown elsewhere, this is illogical (because the range of variation in the degree of correspondence renders any such predictions meaningless and of no value as evidence)[74] and anachronistic (since the calculation from which these calculations are derived probably originated in the late tenth century, and had nothing to do with the origination of the system).[75] This hypothesis should therefore be given no countenance. There is no other evidence which points to the use of Clausentum as a late Saxon *burh*, but there is extensive archaeological and other evidence that the Saxon *burh* and its defences lay on the site of the medieval town.

Watchet

The exact extent of the *burh* is not at all clear, either from indications in the built topography or the lie of the land; there has been significant coastal erosion at several times throughout the last millennium.[76]

Wilton

The topography has been discussed elsewhere.[77] Recent excavations of the western defences of the *burh* are also published.[78] The evidence of heterogeneous tenure in Domesday Book and earlier gives some indication of its early importance.[79] The eastern half of the *burh* as shown was at least partly occupied by the royal 'palace' site and its associated minster church, probably from the early eighth century if not earlier. As with Christchurch, it would appear probable that the late ninth-century defences enclosed this area as well.

Replacement burhs in Wessex

These five *burhs* have been regarded by many commentators as being 'urban' replacements for so-called 'emergency' *burhs* in hill forts which were constructed in the initial phase of the setting up of the system described in the Burghal Hidage. I have argued elsewhere that these were built in the context of the second wave of Viking incursions in the early 890s.[80]

Barnstaple

The topography and historical context are discussed elsewhere.[81]

Guildford

The topography and historical context are discussed elsewhere.[82]

Kingsbridge

I have made a case for the development of Kingsbridge as a *burh* at the head of the Kingsbridge estuary in south Devon, as a replacement (with Totnes) for a hill fort *burh* at Halwell. The area of the *burh* suggested in Figure 9.8 is a modification of that originally proposed.[83]

Marlborough

The topography and historical context are discussed elsewhere. The area of the *burh* in Figure 9.8 (which includes a probable zone of ditches) is a modification of that originally proposed.[84] The existence of this *burh* is not recognised in the EUS covering Marlborough (a conclusion based entirely on the absence of evidence), but forms an important element in the discussions of Baker and Brookes.[85]

TOTNES
The topography and historical context of Totnes, as well as archaeological work on the defences, are discussed elsewhere.[86] The strategic context is also discussed further by Terry Slater and Paul Luscombe, and the general context of all the *burhs* in Devon by Robert Higham.[87]

Burhs in Mercia
WORCESTER (WORCESTERSHIRE)
The origins and extent of the primary *burh* at Worcester are discussed elsewhere. The *burh* was added on to the north side of the former Roman enclosure in which the cathedral was placed. There is some uncertainty concerning the question as to whether the line of the defences on the river or western side lay near or on the crest of the hill slope, or whether they encompassed an early *haga* which lay nearer the bank of the river.[88]

OXFORD (SECOND BURH OF 913) (OXFORDSHIRE)
The hypothesis of the origins of the secondary *burh* as a creation of King Edward as a new *burh* in 913, and its layout and early development, are discussed elsewhere.[89]

STAMFORD (TWO BURHS, TO THE NORTH AND SOUTH OF THE RIVER) (LINCOLNSHIRE)
The northern *burh* of the pair at Stamford has been assumed in all past discussions to have been of Viking (Danish) origin.[90] The archaeological evidence, however, shows that the Danish fortified stronghold in the later ninth century was on the site of the later Norman castle to its west. The northern *burh* is suggested as having been founded subsequently to the southern *burh*, which is mentioned in the *Chronicle* under 918, and built to reinforce the submission of the 'people who belonged to the northern borough [i.e., the Danish army]'. The plan-form of the northern *burh* is strongly indicative of the layout of a *burh* which was formed with the same urbanising intentions as can be recognised in most of the other examples discussed in this chapter, rather than of any known Danish town or fortification.[91] From a spatial or topographical point of view, both *burhs* are very much of a piece, built as a strategic unit.

MALDON (SECOND BURH OF 916) (ESSEX)
This is discussed in detail above.

NEWPORT PAGNELL (BUCKINGHAMSHIRE)
I have discussed the reasons for suggesting that a *burh* at Newport Pagnell was the second *burh* built by King Edward's forces when he

stayed at Buckingham in 914, and that this cannot therefore have been sited at Buckingham.[92] Its plan-form could be considered a modified version of the simple High Street type, with a secondary street leading from the High Street to a crossing of the river to the south-east. The EUS summarises more archaeological evidence which supports the hypothesis of the existence of a fortified *burh* here.[93]

WOODBRIDGE (SUFFOLK)

The existence of the *burh* at Woodbridge is inferred from topographical evidence. The extent of the *burh* is well-defined by the topography of the area on the end of a pronounced spur of land around the church. This appears to have been connected to the putative bridge across the river (indicated by the place name) by the present New Street and Brook Street, in apparent close physical association with the arguably contemporary tide mill.

BECCLES (SUFFOLK)

A *burh* at Beccles is also indicated clearly in the topography. This lay on the hilltop above the river Waveney, and was, as with Woodbridge, connected with a bridge to the north by a long street (Ravensgate) which leads from the north gate of the putative *burh*.

10

Signalling Intent: Beacons, Lookouts and Military Communications

John Baker and Stuart Brookes

And then towards midwinter they took themselves to their prepared depots, out through Hampshire into Berkshire at Reading; and they did, in their custom, ignite their beacons as they travelled; and travelled then to Wallingford and scorched it all up, and then turned along Ashdown to Cwichelm's Barrow, and there awaited the boasted threats, because it had often been said that if they sought out Cwichelm's Barrow they would never get to the sea.[1]

Introduction

Beacons and lookouts played a key role in the networks of local and regional communications of Anglo-Saxon England during the Viking Age (ninth to eleventh centuries). While the large fortified centres of the period are well-known, the nature of interconnections between them and smaller-scale local arrangements has only recently received attention. Written evidence, place names and landscape archaeology together allow for the reconstruction of elements of signalling and sighting systems. This contribution presents the historical evidence for beacons, discusses the context within which beacons and lookouts developed and draws upon a series of case studies to reveal local systems of communication in the landscape of Anglo-Saxon England.

Beacons and lookouts in written sources

On the face of it, evidence for the use of beacons in Anglo-Saxon England may appear meagre, but David Hill and Sheila Sharp have argued convincingly that it reflects a much wider employment of this type of signalling.[2] Their seminal article on the topic drew together the various strands of documentary evidence in order to provide a firm basis for what they described as a 'commonplace' assumption that a beacon system was used by the West Saxons in their wars against the Vikings. As they showed, direct documentary evidence for the maintenance of lookout posts in Anglo-Saxon England is limited to the early eleventh-century *Rectitudines singularum personarum*, which lists *sæweard* or 'sea watch' as a duty both of thegns and of cottars,[3] and a Cornish charter of the late tenth century that includes *uigiliis marinis* as one of the obligations from which the land was not exempt.[4] Indirectly, however, the famous description of the watchman of the *Scyldingas* in *Beowulf* may reflect early medieval practice in England; the description of his approach to the new arrivals on the coast seems to echo the *Anglo-Saxon Chronicle*'s account of the first Viking marauders in Wessex, whom the local ealdorman confronted (fatally as it turns out) and directed to the nearest royal vill.[5]

These allusions are complemented by occasional reference to beacon fires and beacon systems in Anglo-Saxon England. The most explicit of these is a late tenth-century French account by Richer of Reims, of King Athelstan's signalling across the English Channel,[6] but Hill and Sharp draw attention to two other sources that may point to the existence of beacon systems in Anglo-Saxon England: the setting up of a system of fire signals in Norway by King Hakon the Good, who had been fostered at the English court by King Athelstan, from whom he may well have inherited his military strategies; and a possible allusion to the construction of 'piles of wood' or 'beacons' (*rogi*, oblique form of Medieval Latin *rogus*) in a suspect, late tenth-century charter relating to Sherborne Abbey in Dorset.[7] Direct, vernacular reference to beacons is, however, harder to discern. Although Modern English *beacon* descends from Old English *bēacen* (Anglian *bēcun*), the generalisation of the meaning 'a signal-fire' seems to be a late, perhaps Middle English development.[8] In Old English contexts it has the more general senses 'sign, portent', and can denote a physical symbol, such as a banner, standard or monument; it can also denote a signal, but reference to audible signals is more clearly attested than to visible ones.[9] The assertion that the imagery of beacons (or at any rate beacon-fires) is a significant feature of Old English poetry should therefore be treated with caution;[10] but the Anglo-Saxons were familiar with the concept of lighthouses, and in the compound *bēacenstān* – which glosses Latin *farus*[11] – Old English *bēacen* must be a reference to a signal-fire.

One rather oblique use of the term is potentially significant. Under the year 1006, the *Anglo-Saxon Chronicle*, in describing the advance of the Vikings through Hampshire and Berkshire, claims that they kindled (*atendon*) their *here beacen* as they went.[12] Formally, *herebēacen* could be singular or plural, and it would be possible to interpret it as 'standard';[13] that is, destructive fires were, metaphorically, the military standard that announced the presence of Vikings. However, Old English *herebēacen* also glosses Medieval Latin *farus* 'lighthouse' (i.e., light-signal for mariners), and it seems likely that this is an early instance of (*here*)*bēacen* in reference to signal-fires.[14] Thus the Vikings are said to have kindled their beacons as they progressed across the country. These Anglo-Saxon references may be few, but can be placed within much wider contemporary and diachronic contexts. Beacons – individually or as elements of a system – are attested across Europe from ancient times and throughout the medieval period, and fire signals seem to have been used in Britain during the Roman and late medieval periods.[15] That beacons were not a part of Anglo-Saxon life would be more surprising than that they were.

Further evidence of Anglo-Saxon beacons may be provided by onomastic sources. The element *bēacen*, *bēcun* is indeed evidenced in place names, but pre-Conquest examples are rare and subject to the semantic uncertainties discussed above.[16] A second element that might relate to beacons is Old English *ād*, which is used of a 'funeral pyre', but may in some place names denote 'a beacon'.[17] Even so, another meaning, 'a limekiln', can be involved, and the number of secure instances of Old English *ād* in place names is small. Much more widespread are place names with elements such as Old English *weard* and **tōt(e)*, denoting watchmen or lookout places. These are especially widespread in southern England, but can be identified across the country (Figure 10.1).[18] The presence of a beacon is not a prerequisite of lookout sites, since communication of messages can be carried out by other means; but since fire signals are attested in medieval England, it seems likely that maintenance of lookout posts and of beacons often went hand in hand.

Hill and Sharp used evidence of this kind – specifically the occurrence in charter bounds of the compound *weardsetl* 'watch-house' – to show that some beacons recorded in sixteenth-century sources were on sites used for keeping watch in much earlier times.[19] On that basis, they conjectured the existence of an Anglo-Saxon warning system, stretching

Fig. 10.1 Distribution of Old English *weard* and **tōt(e)* place names in England, along with other places mentioned in the text. Elevation data source: SRTM.

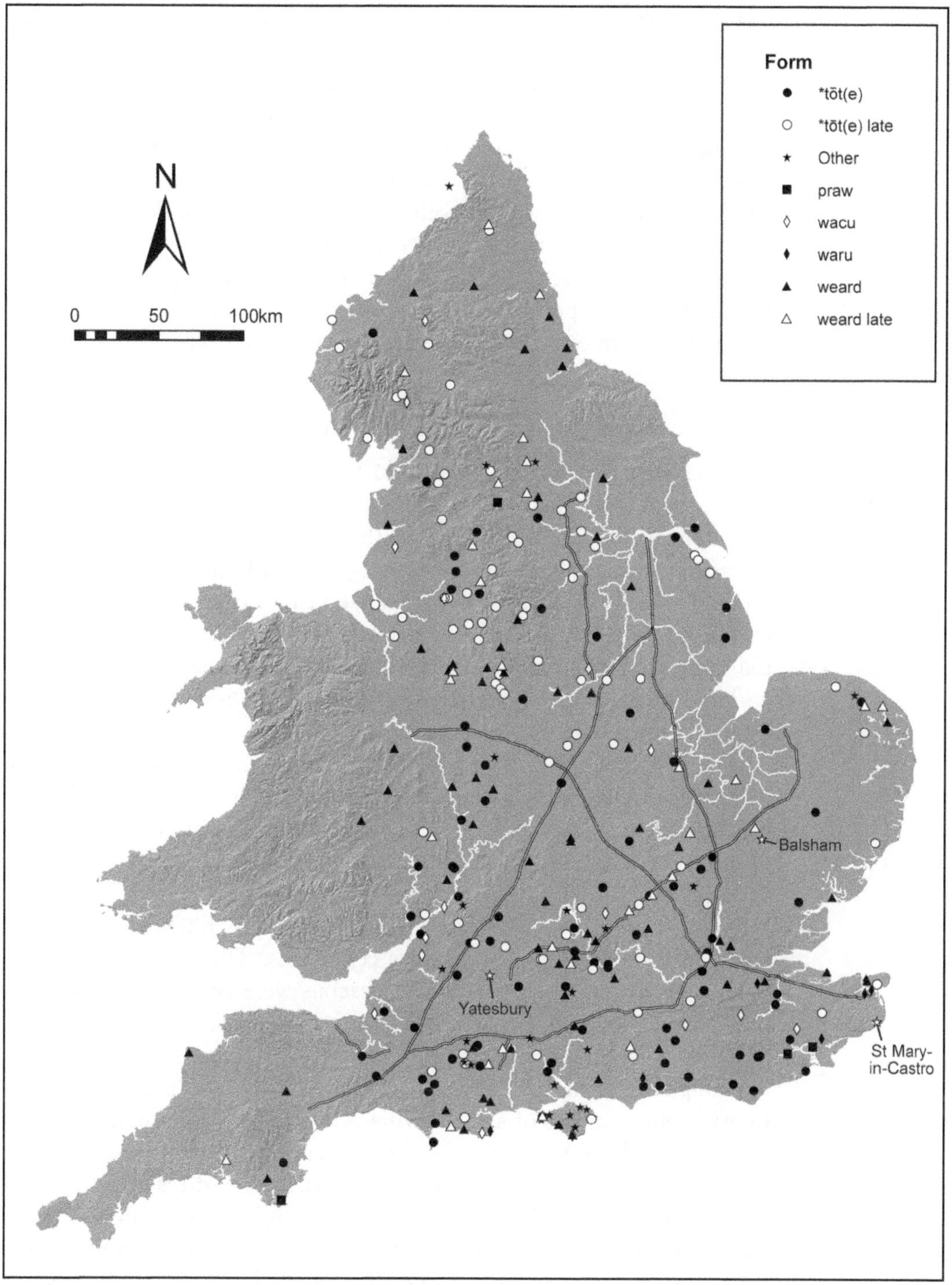
Form
*tōt(e)
*tōt(e) late
Other
praw
wacu
waru
weard
weard late
N
0 50 100km
Balsham
Yatesbury
St Mary-in-Castro

from the Solent to the Berkshire border. They argued, convincingly, that networks of this kind are so tightly interconnected that the removal of one beacon might cause the whole thing to become redundant; thus, the documented sixteenth-century networks might already have been quite ancient. Jake Shemming and Keith Briggs have posited an extension to this Anglo-Saxon system by exploring further place name evidence,[20] and other links, as well as other possible chains of lookouts, have been identified.[21] If signal-fires were associated with these observation points, as seems highly likely, and if the networks existed as early as the Anglo-Saxon period, then beacons must indeed have been a very common feature of the early medieval English landscape.

Physical characteristics of Anglo-Saxon beacons

If the existence of beacons in Anglo-Saxon England is beyond serious doubt, the written sources provide very little insight into their physical appearance. That they necessitated the existence of heaps of firewood seems obvious; both Medieval Latin *rogus* and Old English *ād* (which are paired in an OE gloss) have a range of meanings that encompasses this sense. Old English *ād* also had the sense 'funeral pyre', as indeed did classical Latin *rogus*.[22] Rune Forsberg also noted the compound *ādfīnig* in a Hampshire charter, which he took to refer to a place where firewood for a beacon was stored.[23]

The apparent use of bonfires for signalling in early sources should make us mindful to the types of messages being conveyed.[24] Bonfire beacons were a relatively simple signalling medium, relying on the visibility of smoke during daylight and of firelight during the darkness of night to convey pre-determined messages. Their effectiveness was very much dependent on clear visibility, and it is likely that they fell out of use in poor winter weather conditions. This was certainly the case in the sixteenth century when beacons were continuously manned only from March to October.[25] There was also little flexibility in the message to be transmitted, and the adequate response needed to be unambiguous, with the likely rejoinder to an early warning being simply to bring out numbers of armed civilians or troops, while simultaneously readying civilians for flight. In the sixteenth century, sources suggest that individual beacons may have comprised triple fires at key points on the coastline, double fires at points just inland, and single fires at points further inland.[26] No such evidence is so far forthcoming for the early Middle Ages, and it may be that signals had to be reinforced by messengers.[27] Bonfires may also have served a further role in controlling the movement of unauthorised persons or those with a nefarious intent abroad at night.[28] Beacon use of this kind is a way of policing a territory, perhaps controlling routes and the populations moving along them. In both instances the siting of the beacon has to relate to routeways in order to see and be seen.

One theme recurrent in the sources is the notion that beacon signals were transmitted by setting fire to buildings. This is a feature of the Athelstan episode recounted by Richer (*tuguriorum incendio presentiam suam iis qui in altero litore erant ostendebant*, 'they made their presence known to those who were on the other shore by burning huts', and *domus aliquot succensae*, 'some houses were set on fire'),[29] and is an implicit aspect of the imagery of the *Chronicle* entry for 1006. Galbert of Bruges's account of Robert the Frisian's arrival in Flanders in 1071 has him announcing his presence by setting fire to a house in Kapelle (*domum incenderent*, 'they set fire to a house').[30] Hill and Sharp explain Richer's account of the burning of hovels as a mistaken reference to the remains of Charlemagne's wooden lighthouse at Boulogne.[31] The use of *herebēacen* to gloss *farus* may lend weight to this, in the light of the *Chronicle* entry for 1006, but Richer's is clearly not an isolated example. Either former lighthouses, in such disrepair that they resembled houses or hovels, dotted the English and Frankish coasts, or these accounts reflect some other reality or perception of beacons. It is worth noting a scene in the Bayeux Tapestry, after William's arrival in England but before the battle of Hastings, which shows the burning of a house, under the caption *hic domus incenditur*, 'here a house is set on fire'.[32] Gale R. Owen-Crocker argues persuasively that this is one of several scenes influenced directly or indirectly by Roman sculpture.[33] Nevertheless, it is worth considering what action the scene is intended to convey in the light of the examples discussed above. The image depicts a woman and child fleeing from the flaming building, and an obvious interpretation is that this represents the ravaging of Sussex by Norman troops, except for two curious features. First, according to the Latin explanation, only a single house was set on fire – this seems a rather lacklustre ravaging. Second, those responsible are apparently unarmed. An alternative explanation, that the house was somehow obstructing the progress of the Norman army, seems unsustainable – it is hard to see how a single house could be so problematic and noteworthy, and its charred remains might anyway present a continuing obstacle. The position of this episode within the tapestry is also noteworthy. In the previous scene, William receives intelligence relating to Harold's movements; in the following one the Normans start to march towards battle. What the scene might depict, then, is the use of a beacon signal to rally forces ready for the advance.

Of course, reference to the burning of houses might be no more than a trope, but it is worth considering the practical merits of such a method of signalling. On top of the obvious display of authority tied up in the burning of a house, there could have been more than one reason why domestic dwellings were expressly set alight to send signals. First, at times when the obligation to maintain a beacon system had ceased to be enforced, it may be that potentates did indeed make use of existing buildings when the situation was urgent enough. In other words, even though systems of watch and signalling have existed at times of intense military threat, they perhaps fell out of use during prolonged periods of relative peace. Alternatively, it is possible that setting fire to houses was a way of using a predetermined system to challenge the English to battle. A similar tactic seems to have been employed by the Viking *here* 'army' of 1006 on its way through Berkshire, as earlier noted. The effectiveness of the tactic depends to some extent on the degree to which watchmen could pinpoint the location of established beacons. An experienced watchman might have been able to tell the difference between a genuine beacon and a burning house, since the two would be in different places on the horizon. In that case, *ad hoc* signalling of the kind described by Richer and by Galbert of Bruges might have been better served by *ad hoc* beacons; use of a more established beacon site might, after all, have risked setting off a national alarm. A third possibility, related to the second, also presents itself: attackers could have used fires as a way of throwing English defensive measures into confusion. Accounts of beacon use in 1545 suggest that many false alarms, raised by wrongly identifying ships in the Channel, by stubble burning, or by malicious hoaxers, often kept bands of men out all night, causing considerable irritation.[34] Duke William may have preferred to fight tired rather than well-rested militia.

Archaeological evidence for beacons and lookouts

Few beacons have been positively identified through excavation, but, given the ephemeral archaeological trace a bonfire might leave, this is perhaps unsurprising. One particularly important example was discovered at Yatesbury in Wiltshire in 1994.[35] Yatesbury village sits partially within an enclosure which originated in the late Roman period and which was apparently maintained at intervals until the mid-eighteenth century. Andrew Reynolds equates this enclosure with the Old English *burh-geat* – a structure of particular significance, as it is mentioned as one of the thegnly attributes in the eleventh-century compilation known as the *Geþyncðo*.[36] Of particular interest was a mound situated on the western side of the enclosure circuit which was shown through excavation to be originally a turf-built barrow of early Bronze-Age date, subsequently remodelled (Figure 10.2). The summit of the mound had been flattened and then subjected to intense burning, the evidence for which was a fire-reddened soil which extended to a depth of up to 0.3 metres. A ditch had also been cut into the lower part of the mound, the basal fill of which contained a large, unabraded sherd of late Anglo-Saxon oxidised, stamped pottery. The ditch was then filled with two distinct layers of charcoal-rich and burnt soils separated by a layer of cleaner soil, indicating that two major episodes of burning, or at least clearance of burnt debris from the mound, had taken place.

The Yatesbury beacon mound is an important find for several reasons. It demonstrates that almost any place imbued with a viewshed (the area visible from a fixed vantage point) over the surrounding landscape could serve as a beacon. There was very little evidence for the physical construction of the monument, as its principal built character was in origin a prehistoric mound. Whilst this may appear a somewhat makeshift arrangement, it does nevertheless tally well with the similar *ad hoc* beacon lighting encountered in the written sources.

This is not to say that *some* beacons, particularly those which, unlike Yatesbury, passed into local toponomy, were not maintained, or periodically reused, over a longer time-scale. This continuation of use is one

Fig. 10.2 Excavations under way on the Yatesbury beacon platform in 1994 (photograph: Andrew Reynolds).

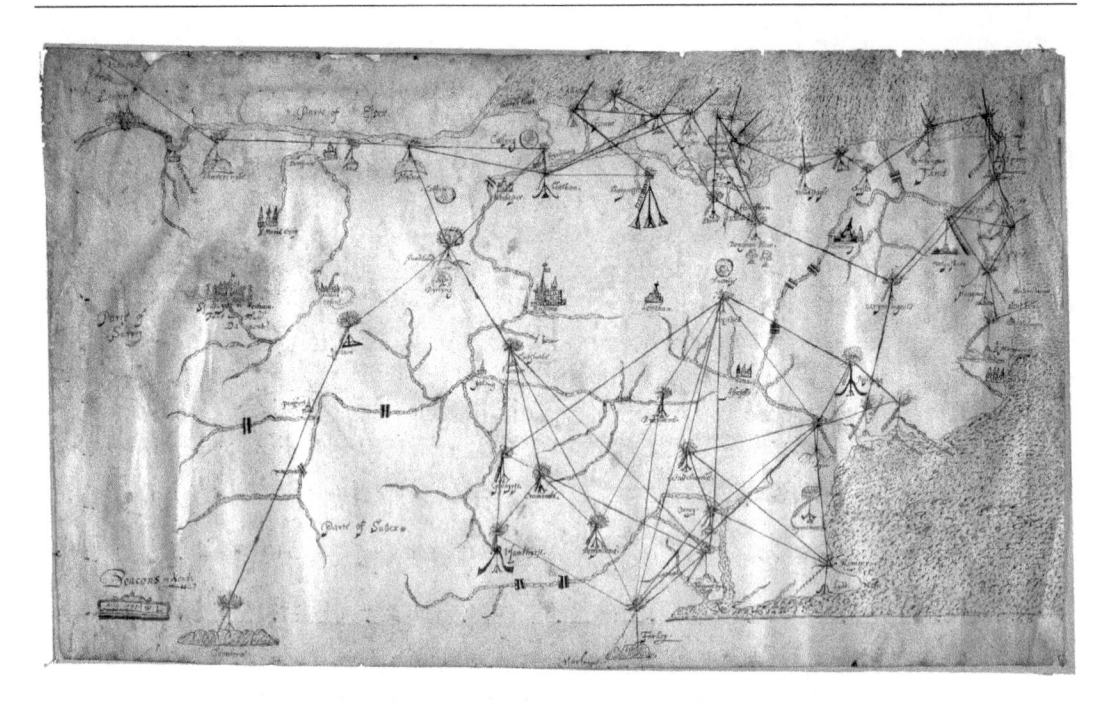

of the implications of Hill and Sharp's observation that the *weard setl*, 'watch house', of the Highclere and Burghclere Anglo-Saxon charters, which must have been used as a lookout in the tenth century or earlier, also served as an Armada beacon in the sixteenth century, and indeed later came to be called Beacon Hill.[37] Similar instances are relatively easy to identify. Tothill Terrace, by Minster-in-Thanet in Kent,[38] which contains Old English **tōt(e)* or Middle English *tot(e)* 'lookout', is believed to have been part of a late fourteenth-century beacon system overlooking the Wantsum Channel – an important waterway leading into the Thames estuary – built by Edward II and Edward III for the protection of the south coast.[39] It also appears as the beacon of *Mynster* on William Lambarde's map of the beacons of Kent, dating to 1585 (Figure 10.3).

Archaeological evidence for this process of continual reuse may be provided by a beacon at Wardhill, the highest point of Shapinsay in the Orkney Islands. Excavated in 1999, the beacon first took the form of a low earthen platform, possibly of Viking origin.[40] This mound was superseded by a horseshoe-shaped stone structure of indeterminate date which perhaps served as a wind screen and allowed for better control of the fire, evidence for which was provided by layers of intense burning within the structure.[41]

Given that the essential qualities of signalling systems – visibility and elevation – remain the same throughout time, it is probable that many beacons first recorded in the medieval period have more ancient origins. These same qualities must, however, not lead to unqualified assumptions. For example, for reasons outlined by John Baker,[42] it is likely that the Bronze-Age univallate (single rampart) fort of Ivinghoe Beacon in Buckinghamshire was a pre-Conquest lookout commanding the high ground over an intersection of the Icknield Way and Watling Street.[43] By contrast, there are no real grounds for believing that similar reuse of a Neolithic and Bronze Age barrow at Beacon Hill in Grimsby, north-east Lincolnshire, indicates the same kind of time-depth. The mound certainly seems to have been used as a beacon from 1377, but partial excavation of the barrow in 1935 appears to indicate its use in the Anglo-Saxon period only as a site of secondary burial.[44] By a similar token, Glastonbury Tor in Somerset has topographical characteristics well-suited to use as a beacon site; but the structural evidence from the excavated summit is probably too inconclusive for assumptions of that kind.[45] It is important, therefore, not to prejudge the archaeological evidence on topographical grounds.

In some respects the archaeological evidence for Anglo-Saxon sighting systems is even more meagre than that for signalling, although these do leave a greater imprint on the built environment. One of the more remarkable architectural survivals in Kent is the lower 12.5 metres of a Roman lighthouse, or *pharos*, which stands at the highest point within what is now Dover Castle (Figure 10.4). It originally stood twice as high, and together with a second lighthouse on the western heights of Dover served to guide ships into port.[46] Immediately to the east the *pharos* adjoins a large cruciform church of St Mary-in-Castro, built c.1000. The *pharos* was not quarried to build the church, and their proximity cannot have been accidental. There is antiquarian evidence for an internal balcony and above-ground doorway at the west end of the church,[47] which aligned with a post-Roman doorway cut into the east wall of the *pharos*, suggesting the two were linked by an above-ground walkway.[48] Since the church already had a substantial tower, the *pharos* must have been curated for reasons beyond those of practicality.

One explanation for this building is the strategic location of the church and *pharos* within the probable site of an Anglo-Saxon fortified *burh*.[49] However, it seems never to have played a part in the system of coastal defences as portrayed in William Lambarde's sixteenth-century map. Despite its superb view over the Channel, the *pharos* was intervisible neither with known Anglo-Saxon beacon sites nor with those known from sixteenth-century maps.[50] Possibly, it served as a western tower or 'westwork' for St Mary-in-Castro.[51] Alternatively, the *pharos* may have continued its original function in signalling to sea traffic. It may even be possible that the *pharos* was used to communicate with the Tour d'Odre

Fig. 10.3 Map of beacons in Kent, by William Lambarde, 'commissioned by Lord Cobham in order to have multiple copies made, as a guide to the effective use of beacons. The positions of about fifty beacons are marked, with lines indicating the direction of the signals given off by them'. Originally published/produced in 1585. Many of these beacons have been shown to be located at the same positions as their Anglo-Saxon predecessors. British Library MS Add. 62935, 9 (© The British Library Board).

Fig. 10.4 Photograph showing the relationship between St Mary-in-Castro church (left) and the Roman *pharos* (right), as well as the substantial earthwork in which they are sited (courtesy of Detraymond, Wikimedia Commons). Cf. Fig. 5.7.

north-west of Boulogne – another Roman *pharos*, rebuilt on the orders of Charlemagne in 810.[52]

Whilst St Mary-in-Castro is a unique survival of the Anglo-Saxon built environment, the inclusion in later beacon systems of sites likely – on documentary, onomastic or architectural grounds – to have had pre-Conquest churches highlights the possibility that many ecclesiastical structures had a similar signalling function.[53] Certainly, the construction of beacons was one of the specified military responsibilities of Sherborne Abbey in 998, but it is uncertain whether these structures can be linked to actual ecclesiastical buildings.[54] The late tenth-/early eleventh-century tower-form church of Wickham (Berkshire) does, however, provide a potential example (Figure 10.5). Before its rebuilding in 1845, the tower of St Swithun's is described as having had a flat roof with a coping forming a parapet.[55] As soot was also found on its internal walls at this level, the roof structure was interpreted as the base for a beacon. Topographical considerations strengthen this interpretation. Wickham is located at the highest point of Welford parish, adjacent to the intersection of Ermine Way and Margary 53, only 13 kilometres south of Icknield Way. It was intervisible with Inkpen Beacon to the south, as well as three further

Fig. 10.5 Photograph of Wickham tower-nave (photograph: M.G. Shapland).

beacon place names less than 10 kilometres away to the north, the closest of which – Warrendown Row (*weardan dune*) in Leckhampstead parish – is named in a charter of 943.[56] The evidence therefore raises questions about the potential role of ecclesiastical and secular towers in civil defence. Certainly both were situated physically at the heart of local communities, and in the case of secular towers are likely to have been linked also to systems of military mobilisation.

At Yatesbury, the association of the beacon mound with a putative thegnly enclosure makes the link between systems of civil defence and lordly power explicit. Henry of Huntingdon's account of an attack on Balsham (Cambridgeshire) in 1010, which is discussed in more detail below, gives the church tower a central place in the narrative, and has been interpreted by Michael Shapland as a reference to part of a beacon system.[57] Finally, Lambarde's map includes four beacons at places with names specifically indicating the presence of a church in Anglo-Saxon times.[58]

In the evidence set out here, then, we can perceive a practical use of natural and built environment. The common thread is the use of elevated positions and especially structures, whether prehistoric artificial mounds or secular and ecclesiastical towers. Significantly, it is the relationship between these structures from which greater insights can be drawn.

The communications environment

Understanding how beacons operated depends largely on our ability to establish the systems to which they belonged. All beacons must belong to a system of some kind – even activation of a single beacon links signalling personnel with both a source of information (intelligence obtained in person or through surveillance) and the recipient of the signal (such as a military post or the general population). In the absence of detailed accounts of working beacon systems from the early medieval period, it is principally through careful analysis of the landscape that the extent and nature of signalling systems can be suggested. The evidence for systems is largely circumstantial, but nonetheless compelling, and can derive from an analysis of the relationship of one beacon or lookout to another, using, for instance, lines of intervisibility to assess their potential connectedness; an examination of the specific relationship between individual lookouts and local infrastructure, where viewsheds can facilitate an assessment of the viability of a signalling system and consideration of the socio-political context – or how beacon sites relate to territorial boundaries, defensive structures and thoroughfares.

This approach was applied by Barrie Cox, who noted the potentially telling arrangement of place names indicative of lookouts and strongholds around the boundaries of Lindsey and Rutland,[59] while Graham Gower noted the proximity of lookout place names to an important routeway from London to Chichester.[60] Following these leads, analyses of lookout intervisibility, location relative to frontiers and sites of strategic value and proximity to routeways have suggested the existence of a number of beacon systems relating to defensive strategies of the late Anglo-Saxon period.[61] These can apparently be of vastly different scales, from the possible pairing of a single observation point with a known stronghold, through chains of lookouts along important roads, to national early warning systems.[62] One example of a sighting system can similarly be linked to a wider defensive landscape. Several possible beacon sites have been recognised lying in close association with Offa's Dyke – the great linear earthwork, probably built in the late eighth century, separating Mercia from Wales.[63] Lookout place names such as The Tutt in Hewelsfield parish, Gloucestershire,[64] and perhaps Totnor, near Brockhampton in Herefordshire,[65] lie directly behind Offa's Dyke (from the English perspective), and acted presumably for the benefit of settlements lying immediately along the frontier. Just 2.5 kilometres to the west of a significant kink of Offa's Dyke lies Worsell Wood in Radnorshire. Though the absence of early forms makes any firm interpretation impossible,[66] the name might conceivably derive from the Old English *weard-setl* 'watch-house' – an apt description of the prominent knoll on which Worsell Wood lies, which overlooks both the ridge-top approach to England along Hergest Ridge, and the gap between there and Bradnor Hill, through which a tributary of the river Arrow flows and an important routeway passes. Worsell Wood would be the only clear case of a forward-facing beacon associated with Offa's Dyke, that is to say one whose likely function was to forewarn of an approaching threat from Wales.

Potentially the most instructive analysis (in terms of Anglo-Saxon England) is provided by Michael Shapland,[67] who suggests that an episode in Henry of Huntingdon's *Chronicle* may effectively describe use of a church tower as part of a signalling system. The *Chronicle* recounts for the year 1010 that the Danes attacked Balsham in Cambridgeshire, where: 'one man, worthy of widespread renown, climbed the steps of the church tower which still stands there, and strengthened both by the place and by his prowess, defended himself, one against the whole army'.[68] Shapland shows that Henry of Huntingdon's account of events at Balsham can be fleshed out through landscape evidence. Balsham lies close to the strategically important crossing of Wool Street Roman road (part of the so-called Via Devana) and the Icknield Way, on the line of the linear earthwork known as Fleam Dyke, which also guards this crossing.[69] Whilst the Anglo-Saxon church is now gone, the planform of Balsham reveals the existence of a probable former manorial enclosure, in which it was originally sited. Further components of the defensive landscape can be reconstructed. On Fleam Dyke is an early medieval mound which was the location of Mutlow, probably once the meeting-place of a group of three Domesday hundreds,[70] a site which bears strong similarities to a class of military mustering sites known as 'hanging promontories'.[71] Intervisible with Mutlow and Balsham, and overlooking the main Viking approach from Thetford along Watling Street, is Wadloo, a place name containing Old English *weard* 'watch'.[72] Given this arrangement Shapland concludes that a system may have existed whereby the beacon warned the lord at Balsham of impending danger.[73] He then assembled the *fyrd* at the hundred meeting-place within sight of his tower, to which he could turn for refuge.[74] If Shapland's interpretation is correct, this is a rare documentary insight into the workings of a lookout and beacon system.

Significantly, the strategic purpose of Balsham would seem to be concerned with movement along the Icknield Way, a long-distance

Fig. 10.6 Map of the Avebury landscape, showing the relationship between beacons, strongholds and major thoroughfares. Elevation data source: SRTM.

routeway known to have been exploited by the Vikings on several occasions before 1010.[75] Other beacon systems appear similarly to have been reactive responses to well-used vectors of attack. What is striking about the evidence assembled by Hill and Sharp, on the other hand, is that most of it relates to coastal activity.[76] This may well be connected with the date of the sources, several of which belong to the last century of Anglo-Saxon rule. By that time, naval activity was a significant part of the more proactive Anglo-Saxon defensive arrangements,[77] but the *Anglo-Saxon Chronicle*'s account of 1006 seems to place the imagery of beacons very much in an inland context. Perhaps influenced by the role of that early modern beacon system, Hill and Sharp nevertheless seem to have interpreted even inland beacons as elements of a coastal system of defence – their role explicitly to convey the message of an approaching fleet from the sea to the West Saxon heartland and beyond.[78]

A series of studies has shown that strategically important roads might be deemed worthy of surveillance in their own right, and that surveillance sites can be linked specifically to nodal points on overland routeways.[79] These observations apply also to coastal regions; in fact, viewshed analysis suggests that lookout points were at least as interested in movement on land as at sea.[80] The Balsham example is important in demonstrating first, that beacons had a close association with major routeways, and second, that individual beacons were intervisible with other signalling sites and monuments.

Reynolds' study of the Yatesbury landscape serves as another important case study to put these two characteristics into context (Figure 10.6).[81] Excavations on the Yatesbury enclosure revealed evidence for a route, partially preserved in Ordnance Survey maps as Barrow Way/Yatesbury Lane leading south and eastwards to Avebury, where it forms the High Street of the regular and planned late Anglo-Saxon settlement on the western side of the great Neolithic henge monument. From Avebury the route continues, through the Avebury henge, exiting it by its eastern entrance before rising onto the high downland, crossing the Great Ridgeway and then turning to the south-east in the direction of Marlborough. This route is named as a 'herepath' (OE *herepæð* 'army road') in the bounds of an authentic charter of 939 for East Overton,[82] and appears to be a military route linking together the various military institutions across the Marlborough Downs: the thegnly enclosure of Yatesbury and the two strongholds (OE *byrg*) of Avebury and Marlborough.

Importantly, although Yatesbury and Avebury were linked by a *herepæð*, they are not intervisible, thereby rendering any signal from the beacon at Yatesbury only locally visible without further relays. Silbury

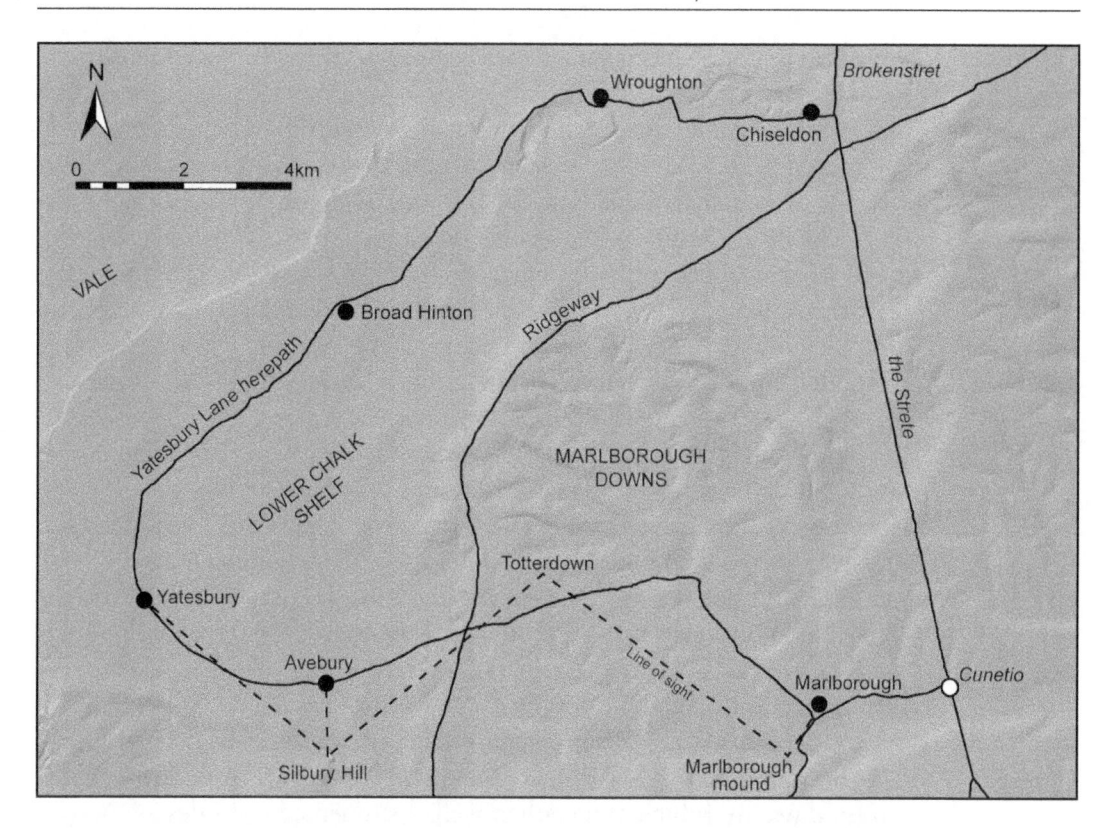

Hill provides the link between the two places, with the top of the hill just visible from the summit of the beacon mound at Yatesbury. Fragmentary archaeological evidence for a fortification – and in all likelihood also a beacon – has been identified from the summit of Silbury Hill, including the remains of a timber palisade and associated finds of early eleventh-century date.[83] Silbury Hill, in turn, is intervisible with Avebury, as well as Totterdown (OE *tōt-ærn-dūn*, 'lookout house hill') on the high downland between Avebury and Marlborough, a short distance north of the *herepæð* route linking the two.[84]

A number of comparable signalling systems of beacon chains have now been identified existing between major strongholds of the late Anglo-Saxon period, including that between the Isle of Wight, Winchester (via the beacon on Farley Mount) and the mustering point of Cuckhamsley;[85] between Chichester and London;[86] between Wallingford and the stronghold of *Wigingamere*[87] and linking together the Burghal Hidage strongholds of the Thames valley.[88] Taken as a whole, these suggest that dense networks of signalling existed which tied together specific military hard points in the late Anglo-Saxon landscape; but several observations are worth further comment. First, unlike the regular distribution of burghal forts, which appear to have been governed in

Fig. 10.7 Map of the south-east Midland lookouts along the Icknield Way. Elevation data source: SRTM.

part by issues of accessibility, the seemingly haphazard location of these beacons is determined primarily by intervisibility. Second, the pattern of beacons can be divided into two main types: the more common form – of which the Yatesbury system is an example – which involved short relays of less than 10 kilometres between lookouts lying alongside the principal routeways; and a second type, such as that identified by Hill and Sharp, which utilised much longer relays, roughly 40 kilometres apart, to link together two distant points.[89] It seems likely that the latter provides evidence for widespread warning systems, and was related to the mobilisation of a shire-level response. By contrast, the former suggests a concern with territorial control and the penetration, at a very localised level, of military structures. Whilst these two systems of signalling are not mutually exclusive, the relationship between the localised system, routeways and burghal strongholds strongly suggests this form of beacon system was a development of the late ninth to eleventh centuries.

The existence of the systems outlined in the foregoing discussion is crucial to any attempts to provide chronological context for lookouts preserved principally by onomastic evidence. The question of dating is an important one: while contemporary sources make clear that beacons were used in Anglo-Saxon England and early medieval Europe, many of the place names relating to lookouts are first recorded at a much later date, by which time other well-documented episodes of beacon use had taken place. Such dates only provide a *terminus ante quem* for the lookouts they describe – the names themselves may have been in existence for hundreds of years before first being written down. The element *ād*, for instance, seems to have become obsolete at a relatively early date, with the latest attestations dating to the early thirteenth century.[90] The late recording of a place name in which it occurs might therefore belie a much earlier period of coining, although, of course, the individual case might denote a limekiln rather than a beacon.

As Hill and Sharp demonstrated, context is everything. If some elements of a beacon system can be shown to have existed since the Anglo-Saxon period, there is a good chance that the rest of the network did too, already dotting the landscape, especially when those early recorded lookouts are key to the efficient working of the whole system. This, for example, seems to be the case with a group of intervisible lookout sites along the Icknield Way, in the vicinity of Luton: Totternhoe, Warden Hill, Ward's Hurst and Whorley Wood (Figure 10.7). Totternhoe, the earliest recorded of the names, is also the only lookout site to be intervisible with all the others, some of which would otherwise be entirely isolated. In other words, if this is a lookout system, it is Totternhoe that makes it so.[91] In northern

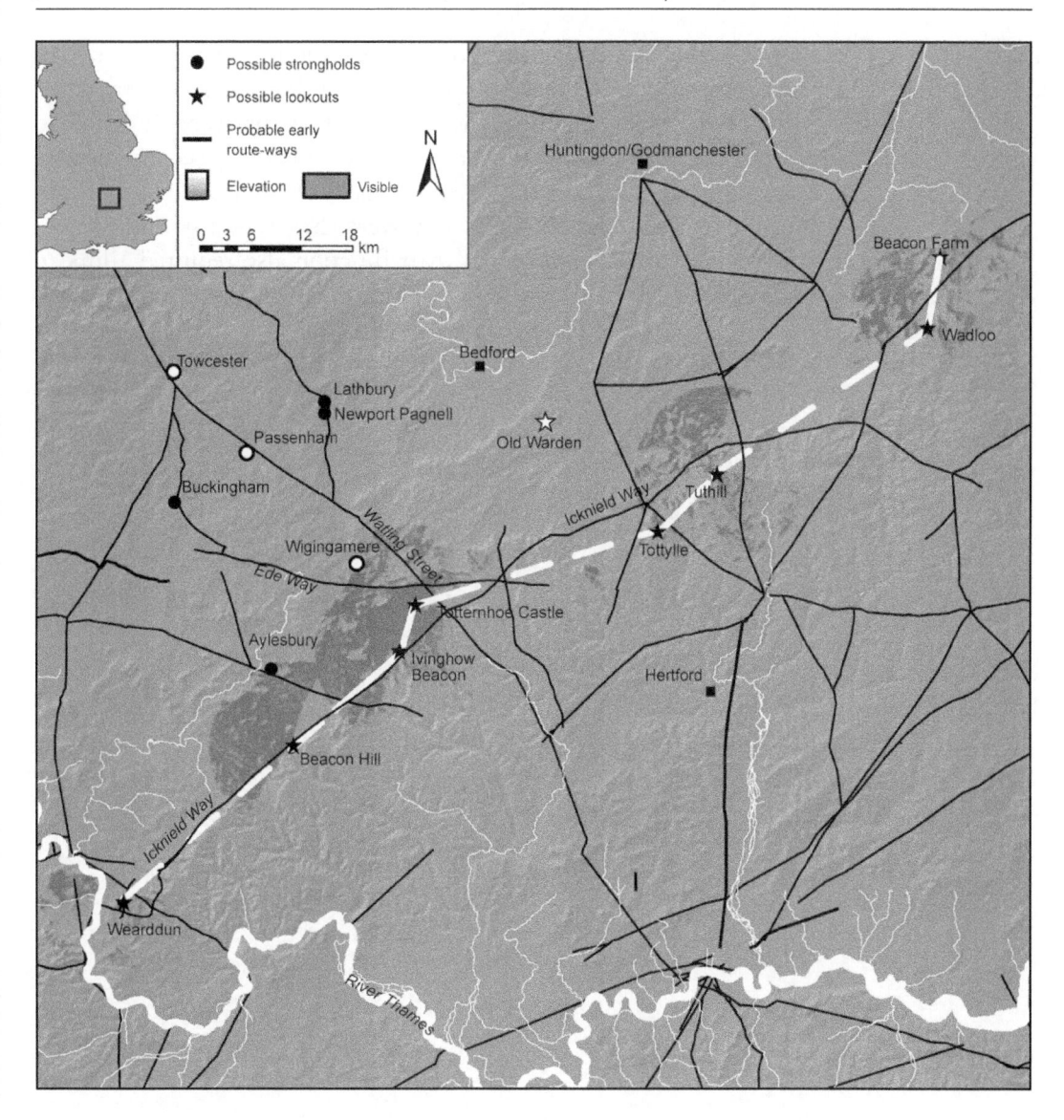

Wiltshire and Berkshire, on the other hand, a suggested system of communication seems to include lookouts at strongholds used during the late Anglo-Saxon period, again suggesting a pre-Conquest date for the system as a whole.[92]

Conclusion

There is sufficient evidence to be confident that beacons were used in Anglo-Saxon England, but their physical characteristics and their relationship to contemporary social organisation and infrastructure are less clearly understood. Partially, our understanding is hampered by the general lack of good archaeological evidence, but, more significantly, understanding how signalling and sighting systems were designed to work can only proceed with very detailed landscape reconstruction. Perhaps more than any other element of the built environment, beacons cannot be seen in isolation – not only were they typically one element in a wider network of signals, but their function also required a link to systems of mobilisation, movement and military defence.

Notes

Special thanks to Tiffany Conley for her assistance in editing the notes for this volume.

Introduction: *Gale R. Owen-Crocker*

1 Bede, *Historia Ecclesiastica*, in B. Colgrave and R.A.B. Mynors (eds), *Bede's Ecclesiastical History of the English People* (Oxford: Clarendon Press, 1969), book 2, ch. 16, p. 193.

2 Colgrave and Mynors note that similar stories 'were told about any powerful king in the Middle Ages'; ibid., pp. 192–93 n. 2.

3 My thanks to Dr Christopher Grocock for discussing this phrase with me.

4 For surviving Roman milestones in Britain, see R.G. Collingwood and R.P. Wright, *The Roman Inscriptions of Britain*, vol. 1, *The Inscriptions on Stone, Part Four: Milestones and Honorific Pillars*: http://www.roman-britain.org/epigraphy/rib_milestones.htm [accessed 3 August 2014].

5 Veronica Ortenberg, 'Archbishop Sigeric's Journey to Rome in 990', *Anglo-Saxon England* 19 (1990), pp. 197–246.

6 Simon Keynes, 'Church Councils, Royal Assemblies, and Anglo-Saxon Royal Diplomas', in Gale R. Owen-Crocker and Brian W. Schneider (eds), *Kingship, Legislation and Power in Anglo-Saxon England*, Publications of the Manchester Centre for Anglo-Saxon Studies 13 (Woodbridge: Boydell Press, 2013), p. 35.

7 For coppicing, see Christopher Grocock, 'Barriers to Knowledge: Coppicing and Landscape Usage in the Anglo-Saxon Economy', in Nicholas J. Higham and Martin J. Ryan (eds), *The Landscape Archaeology of Anglo-Saxon England*, Publications of the Manchester Centre for Anglo-Saxon Studies 9 (Woodbridge: Boydell Press, 2010), pp. 23–37; for woodland use, see Della Hooke, 'The Woodland Landscape of Early Medieval England', in Nicholas J. Higham and Martin J. Ryan (eds), *Place-Names, Language and the Anglo-Saxon Landscape*, Publications of the Manchester Centre for Anglo-Saxon Studies 10 (Woodbridge: Boydell Press, 2011), pp. 143–74. It is generally believed that horses were not used for heavy draught before the invention of the horse collar. The Bayeux Tapestry (c.1070–80) has what is probably the earliest depiction of this in western Europe; see David M. Wilson, *The Bayeux Tapestry* (London: Thames & Hudson, 1985), plates 10–11, lower border. The same artwork depicts men pulling a cart laden with a large barrel, helmets and spears (plates 38–39).

8 Debby Banham, '*Lectun* and *Orceard*: A Preliminary Survey for the Evidence for Horticulture in Anglo-Saxon England', in Gale R. Owen-Crocker and Brian W. Schneider (eds), *The Anglo-Saxons: The World through their Eyes*, British Archaeological Reports, British Series 595 (Oxford: Archaeopress, 2014), pp. 33–48.

9 See, for example, the West Heslerton study discussed in Dominic Powlesland, 'Reflections upon the Anglo-Saxon Landscape and Settlement of the Vale of Pickering, Yorkshire', in Gale R. Owen-Crocker and Susan D. Thompson (eds), *Towns and Topography: Essays in Memory of David H. Hill* (Oxford: Oxbow, 2014), pp. 111–23.

10 Michael Lewis, Andrew Richardson and David Williams, 'Things of This World: Portable Antiquities and their Potential', in Maren Clegg

Hyer and Gale R. Owen-Crocker (eds), *The Material Culture of Daily Living in the Anglo-Saxon World* (Exeter: University of Exeter Press, 2011), pp. 252–57.
11 *eald enta geworc*, l. 87; George Philip Krapp and Elliott van Kirk Dobbie (eds), *The Exeter Book*, Anglo-Saxon Poetic Records 3 (New York: Columbia University Press, 1936), p. 136.
12 *enta geweorc*, l. 2717; *Beowulf*, in Elliott van Kirk Dobbie (ed.), *Beowulf and Judith*, Anglo-Saxon Poetic Records 4 (New York: Columbia University Press, 1953), p. 84.

Chapter 1: *Christopher Grocock*
1 All quotations from *The Ruin* are taken from the edition in George Philip Krapp and Elliott van Kirk Dobbie (eds), *The Exeter Book*, Anglo-Saxon Poetic Records 3 (New York: Columbia University Press, 1936), pp. 227–29. See also R.F. Leslie, *Three Old English Elegies: The Wife's Lament, The Husband's Message, The Ruin* (Manchester: Manchester University Press, 1961). The translations given here are from R. Hamer, *A Choice of Anglo-Saxon Verse* (London: Faber, 1970), pp. 25–30, with some adaptations by the author.
2 Sîan Eckhard has a translation and text of the poem at her homepage, entitled 'The Ruin': http://faculty.arts.ubc.ca/sechard/oeruin.htm [accessed 13 August 2013].
3 Leslie, *Three Old English Elegies*, p. 1.
4 Hamer, citing W.C. Johnson, '"The Ruin" as Body-City Riddle', *Philological Quarterly* 59.4 (1980), p. 397; C. Abram, 'In Search of Lost Time: Aldhelm and *The Ruin*', *Quaestio (Selected Proceedings of the Cambridge Colloquium in Anglo-Saxon, Norse and Celtic)* 1 (2000), pp. 37–43: http://www.ucl.ac.uk/~ucmgcab/ruin-andaldhelm.pdf [accessed 13 August 2013]. See comments and translation by Roy Liuzza: http://web.utk.edu/~rliuzza/401/Elegies.pdf [accessed 7 August 2013].
5 Abram, 'In Search of Lost Time'; J.F. Doubleday, '"The Ruin": Structure and Theme', *Journal of English and Germanic Philology* 71.3 (July 1972), pp. 369–81: http://www.jstor.org/stable/27706243 [accessed 7 August 2013].
6 Leslie, *Three Old English Elegies*, pp. 2–3.

13 Margaret Gelling and Ann Cole, *The Landscape of Place-Names* (Stamford: Shaun Tyas, 2000), *passim*.
14 Debby Banham, '"In the Sweat of thy Brow Shalt thou eat Bread": Cereals and Cereal Production in the Anglo-Saxon Landscape', in Higham and Ryan, *Landscape Archaeology*, pp. 178–79; developing a connection between wheat bread and the Roman Empire and later Christianity first articulated by Martin Jones, *Feast: Why Humans Share Food* (Oxford: Oxford University Press, 2007), pp. 260–62, 269–70.

7 Extensive references in Abram, 'In Search of Lost Time', pp. 23–24, no. 2.
8 Leslie, *Three Old English Elegies*, p. 68.
9 Abram, 'In Search of Lost Time', pp. 35–36.
10 Leslie, *Three Old English Elegies*, p. 72; R. Cramp, *Wearmouth and Jarrow Monastic Sites*, 2 vols (Swindon: English Heritage, 2005), vol. 1, pp. 80, 85, 232–41, 323–29. It may be significant that in *Historia Abbatum* 5, Bede refers to the builders of Wearmouth recruited from Gaul as *cementarii*, as it is principally lime mortar which was used to bond pieces of stone; see the discussion below.
11 The ASPR text has a rune for this word.
12 See Tony Rook, *Roman Baths in Britain* (Princes Risborough: Shire, 2002), p. 25; Guy de la Bedoyère, *Architecture in Roman Britain* (Princes Risborough: Shire, 2002), pp. 39–43.
13 I am indebted to Maren Clegg Hyer for drawing my attention to this point; see also Chapter 3 of this volume.
14 Barry C. Burnham and John Wacher, *The Small Towns of Roman Britain* (Berkeley: University of California Press, 1990), p. 175.
15 Burnham and Wacher, *Small Towns*, pp. 175–76.
16 See the discussion in C.E. Fell, 'Perceptions of Transience', in M. Godden and M. Lapidge (eds), *The Cambridge Companion to Old English Literature* (Cambridge: Cambridge University Press, 1991), pp. 172–89; referenced by Abram, 'In Search of Lost Time', p. 23.
17 Abram, 'In Search of Lost Time', p. 29.
18 Leslie, *Three Old English Elegies*,

pp. 26–28; see also Abram, 'In Search of Lost Time,' pp. 31 ff., for a discussion of possible influences on *The Ruin* by Aldhelm and his circle, which would also place it in the eighth century.

19 Frank Stenton, *Anglo-Saxon England*, 3rd edn (Oxford: Clarendon Press, 1971), pp. 1–31.

20 Ibid., pp. xi, 30.

21 J. Morris, 'Anglo-Saxon Surrey', *Arthurian Sources*, vol. 4, *People and Places, and Saxon Archaeology* (Chichester: Phillimore, 1995), esp. pp. 97–100.

22 J. Morris, *The Age of Arthur* (London: Wiedenfeld & Nicholson, 1973); 'The Chronology of Early Anglo-Saxon Archaeology', *Medieval Archaeology* 18 (1974), pp. 225–32, reprinted in *Arthurian Sources*, vol. 4, pp. 73–79.

23 D.J.V. Fisher, *The Anglo-Saxon Age* (London: Longman, 1973), p. 28.

24 N.J. Higham, *Rome, Britain and the Anglo-Saxons* (London: Seaby, 1992), p. 209.

25 N.J. Higham, *The English Conquest: Gildas and Britain in the Fifth Century* (Manchester: Manchester University Press, 1994), p. 211.

26 M.E. Jones, *The End of Roman Britain* (Ithaca, NY: Cornell University Press, 1996), p. 103.

27 G. Halsall, *Worlds of Arthur: Facts and Fictions of the Dark Ages* (Oxford: Oxford University Press, 2013), pp. 250–51, Fig. 10. 4.

28 Higham, *Rome, Britain and the Anglo-Saxons*, p. 216.

29 A. Rogers, *Late Roman Towns in Britain: Rethinking Change and Decline* (Cambridge: Cambridge University Press, 2011), p. 112.

30 Ibid., p. 116.

31 T. Beaumont-James, *Winchester: From Prehistory to the Present*, rev. edn (Stroud: Tempus, 2007), p. 45. Also see the discussion in J. Wacher, *The Towns of Roman Britain*, 2nd edn (London: Batsford, 1995), pp. 299–301.

32 J.M. Zant, *The Brooks Winchester, 1987–88: The Roman Structural Remains* (Winchester: Winchester Museums Service, 1993), pp. 149–50.

33 B. Cunliffe (ed.), *Winchester Excavations, 1949–1960*, vol. I (Winchester: City of Winchester Museums and Libraries Committee, 1964), p. 24.

34 P. Booth, A. Simmonds, A. Boyle et al., *The Late Roman Cemetery at Lankhills, Winchester: Excavations, 2000–2005*, Oxford University School of Archaeology Monograph 10 (Oxford: Oxford University Press, 2010), p. 5, no. 10; Martin Biddle, 'The Study of Winchester: Archaeology and History in a British Town', *Proceedings of the British Academy* 69 (1983), pp. 93–135.

35 Beaumont-James, *Winchester*, p. 46.

36 On ironworking, see the discussion by P.J. Ottaway, in H. Rees, N. Crummy, P.G. Ottaway and G. Dunn, *Artefacts and Society in Roman and Medieval Winchester: Small Finds from the Suburbs and Defences, 1971–1986* (Winchester: Winchester Museums Service, 2008), pp. 391–93.

37 On bastions, see Biddle, 'The Study of Winchester', pp. 112–13.

38 Beaumont-James, *Winchester*, p. 46.

39 Ibid., p. 45.

40 Zant, *The Brooks Winchester*, p. 155.

41 Ibid.

42 Beaumont-James, *Winchester*, p. 46.

43 G. Clarke, J.L. Macdonald and M. Biddle, *Pre-Roman and Roman Winchester*, Part 2, *The Roman Cemetery at Lankhills*, Winchester Studies 3 (Oxford: Clarendon Press, 1979); Booth, Simmonds, Boyle et al., *The Late Roman Cemetery at Lankhills, Winchester*.

44 Booth, Simmonds, Boyle et al., *The Late Roman Cemetery at Lankhills, Winchester*, p. xv.

45 P.J. Ottaway, K.E. Qualmann, H. Rees and G.D. Scobie, *The Roman Cemeteries and Suburbs of Winchester: Excavations, 1971–86* (Winchester: Winchester Museums and English Heritage, 2012); pp. 345, 374–75.

46 Rees et al., *Artefacts and Society in Roman and Medieval Winchester*, p. 385.

47 Beaumont-James, *Winchester*, p. 46.

48 Ibid., p. 47.

49 Ibid., pp. 51–52.

50 P. Ottaway, *Archaeology in British Towns: From the Emperor Claudius to the Black Death* (London: Routledge, 1992), p. 135. See Chapter 9 of this volume for further discussion of *burhs* built by plan.

51 Beaumont-James, *Winchester*, p. 49.

52 M. Lapidge, 'Bede and Roman Britain', in M. Henig and N. Ramsay (eds), *Intersections:*

The Archaeology and History of Christianity in England, 400–1200: Papers in Honour of Martin Biddle and Birthe Kjølbye-Biddle, British Archaeological Reports, British Series 505 (Oxford: Archaeopress, 2010), p. 117; Bede, *Historia Ecclesiastica*, in B. Colgrave and R.A.B. Mynors (eds), *Bede's Ecclesiastical History of the English People* (Oxford: Clarendon Press, 1969) (hereafter, *HE*), book 3, ch. 28, pp. 316–17. Chad was consecrated by Bishop Wine of Winchester, who was assisted by two other bishops 'of the British race'. There were, evidently, other non-Anglo-Saxon bishops in the area whose services could be called on. Sadly, Bede does not say where their sees were.

53 Halsall, *Worlds of Arthur*, pp. 99–100, 286; see also Chapter 3 of this volume.

54 P. Barker, R. White, K. Pretty et al., *The Baths Basilica Wroxeter: Excavations 1966–90* (Swindon: English Heritage, 1997), pp. 15–19.

55 Wacher, *The Towns of Roman Britain*, p. 377.

56 Barker, White, Pretty et al., *The Baths Basilica Wroxeter*, pp. xvi; only this period of reconstruction is summarised in Rogers, *Late Towns in Roman Britain*, p. 88: 'the "Old Work" at Wroxeter indicates that at least part of the public bath building remained standing and probably in use, although not necessarily for its original purpose, into the late and post-Roman period'. There is a more detailed summary and discussion in C. A. Snyder, *An Age of Tyrants: Britain and the Britons AD 400–600* (Stroud: Sutton Publishing, 1988), pp. 158–60.

57 Barker, White, Pretty et al., *The Baths Basilica Wroxeter*, pp. xvi.

58 Ibid.

59 Ibid., pp. xvi–xvii.

60 Ibid., p. 248.

61 T. Eaton, *Plundering the Roman Past: Roman Stonework in Medieval Britain* (Stroud: Tempus, 2000), p. 67.

62 Barker, White, Pretty et al., *The Baths Basilica Wroxeter*, p. 245.

63 Higham, *Rome, Britain and the Anglo-Saxons*, p. 220.

64 Barker, White, Pretty et al., *The Baths Basilica Wroxeter*, p. 247.

65 Bede's *Life of St Cuthbert*, in B. Colgrave (trans. and ed.), *Two Lives of Saint Cuthbert* (Cambridge: Cambridge University Press, 1940), ch. 27, pp. 244–46.

66 J.F. Webb (trans.), in D.H. Farmer (ed.), *The Age of Bede*, revised edn (Harmondsworth: Penguin, 1988), p. 79.

67 For a good summary of the evidence from Carlisle, see M. McCarthy, *Roman Carlisle and the Lands of the Solway* (Stroud: Tempus, 2002), pp. 67–92.

68 Lapidge, 'Bede and Roman Britain', p. 107, citing *HE*, book 1, ch. 11, p. 2; Lapidge also comments that 'the wording of this sentence is Bede's own, and is not lifted from an earlier source such as Orosius, whose narrative Bede has been closely following up to this point' (p. 107, no. 3).

69 *HE*, book 1, ch. 5, pp. 24–27.

70 *HE*, book 2, ch. 12, pp. 44–45. See also D.J. Breeze, *J. Collingwood Bruce's Handbook to the Roman Wall*, 14th edn (Newcastle upon Tyne: Society of Antiquaries of Newcastle upon Tyne, 2006), p. 93.

71 Lapidge states that 'this description (i.e., of the Antonine Wall) evidently derives from personal observation', and the account of local place names seems also to imply local knowledge ('Bede and Roman Britain', p. 111).

72 A.M. Whitworth, *Hadrian's Wall: Some Aspects of its Post-Roman Influence on the Landscape*, British Archaeological Reports, British Series 296 (Oxford: Archaeopress, 2006), p. 10.

73 See T. Wilmott, *Birdoswald Roman Fort* (London: English Heritage, 2001).

74 Breeze, *J. Collingwood Bruce's Handbook to the Roman Wall*, p. 305.

75 Jones, *End of Roman Britain*, p. 106.

76 Book 3, ch. 25.

77 For details on Lyminge, see http://www.lymingearchaeology.org/ and http://www.reading.ac.uk/archaeology/research/lyminge/ [accessed 22 November 2014].

78 J. Hawkes, 'A Sculptural Legacy: Stones of the North from the "Age of Wilfrid"', in N.J. Higham (ed.), *Wilfrid: Bishop, Abbot, Saint. Papers from the 1300th Anniversary Conferences* (Donington: Shaun Tyas, 2013), p. 136. See Chapters 3 and 5 of this volume for additional discussion of wooden structures and wooden and stone churches, respectively.

79 Translation taken from C. Grocock and I. Wood (eds), *Abbots of Wearmouth and Jarrow*, Oxford Medieval Texts (Oxford: Oxford University Press, 2013). See also the detailed commentary on this section.

80 Cramp, *Wearmouth and Jarrow Monastic Sites*, vol. 1, p. 56. Professor Cramp discusses St Peter's Wearmouth in detail at vol. 1, pp. 56–72, 351–55 and the Anglo-Saxon sculpture at vol. 2, pp. 162–302; the nineteenth-century rebuilding is outlined at vol. 1, pp. 55–56, 123.

81 Stephanus, *Vita Wilfridi*, in B. Colgrave (ed.), *The Life of Bishop Wilfrid by Eddius Stephanus* (Cambridge: Cambridge University Press, 1927), chapters 16, 17, 22.

82 E. Cambridge, 'The Sources and Function of Wilfrid's Architecture at Ripon and Hexham', in Higham, *Wilfrid: Bishop, Abbot, Saint*, p. 140.

83 See F.J. Alvarez Lopez, 'The *Rule of St Benedict* in England', ibid., pp. 49–52.

84 For a general discussion of this point, see Halsall, *Worlds of Arthur*, pp. 99–100, and esp. H. Hamerow, *Rural Settlements in Anglo-Saxon Society* (Oxford: Oxford University Press, 2012), pp. 1–16, 67 ff.; see also Chapter 5 of this volume.

85 See S.S. Frere, 'The Bignor Villa', *Britannia* 13 (1982), pp. 135–95; E.W. Black, 'The Roman Villa at Bignor in the Fourth Century', *Oxford Journal of Archaeology* 2.1 (2007), pp. 93–107.

86 Hamerow, *Rural Settlements*, p. 34.

87 See B. Ward-Perkins, *The Fall of Rome and the End of Civilization* (Oxford: Oxford University Press, 2005), pp. 123–37, noted in Hamerow, *Rural Settlements*, p. 14.

88 Hamerow, *Rural Settlements*, p. 35.

89 J. Blair, *Anglo-Saxon Oxfordshire* (Stroud: Tempus, 1994), pp. 33–34, noted by Hamerow, *Rural Settlements*, p. 15.

90 C. Platt, *The Parish Churches of Medieval England* (London: Secker & Warburg, 1981), p. 17.

91 J. Blair, *The Church in Anglo-Saxon Society* (Oxford: Oxford University Press, 2005), p. 127.

92 See T. Bell, *The Religious Re-use of Roman Structures in Early Medieval England*, British Archaeological Reports, British Series 390 (Oxford: Archaeopress, 2005). On the possible location of mercenaries, see Halsall, *World of Arthur*, pp. 249–52 and Fig. 10.4.

93 Rogers, *Late Roman Towns in Britain*, p. 116.

94 Snyder, *An Age of Tyrants*, p. 249.

95 Leslie, *Three Old English Elegies*, pp. 26–28; see also note 18.

96 Leslie, *Three Old English Elegies*, p. 3. For Anglo-Saxon reverence for their *Christian* past, see Chapter 5 of this volume.

Chapter 2: *Paul Hindle*

1 *Beowulf*, in Elliott van Kirk Dobbie (ed.), *Beowulf and Judith*, Anglo-Saxon Poetic Records 4 (New York: Columbia University Press, 1953), p. 44, ll. 1408–10. Translation by Seamus Heaney, *Beowulf* (London: Faber, 1999), p. 46.

2 D.A.E. Pelteret, 'The Roads of Anglo-Saxon England', *Wiltshire Archaeological and Natural History Society Magazine* 79 (1985), pp. 155–63.

3 Gilbert Keith Chesterton, 'The Rolling English Road', *New Witness* (25 September 1914).

4 Turnpikes were effectively privatised toll roads, created in response to increased traffic and poor road maintenance. The first was created in 1663, but most were created in the 'turnpike mania' of the 1750s and 1760s. At first, existing roads were simply improved, but later completely new roads were built, especially in the hillier northern and western parts of the country. Most of the Turnpike Trusts which operated them were dissolved in the 1870s and 1880s. Enclosure roads were created by Act of Parliament mainly between 1760 and 1820 as part of the process of enclosing open fields; they are mostly minor rural roads allowing access to the newly enclosed fields, and they are usually straight to make planning them easier, and wide to allow people to be able to avoid any difficult areas on the road.

5 Paul Hindle, *Roads and Tracks for Historians* (Chichester: Phillimore, 2001), pp. 1–12.

6 H.W. Timperley and Edith Brill, *Ancient Trackways of Wessex* (Shipston-on-Stour: Drinkwater, 1983).

7 Drove roads were a largely separate network of tracks used to drive cattle and sheep

from Scotland and Wales to English towns; they usually avoided towns and villages and often kept to higher ground, especially after the creation of turnpike roads, which would charge for the passage of animals.

8 Hugh Davies, *Roman Roads in Britain* (Oxford: Shire, 2007).

9 Ivan D. Margary, *Roman Roads in Britain* (London: Baker, 1973), p. 23.

10 David Harrison, *The Bridges of Medieval England* (Oxford: Clarendon Press, 2004), pp. 32–33.

11 Christopher Taylor, *Roads and Tracks of Britain* (London: Dent, 1979), pp. 97–99.

12 C.T. Flower, 'Public Works in Medieval Law', *Selden Society* 40 (1915–23), p. xvi.

13 Sidney Webb and Beatrice Webb, *The Story of the King's Highway* (London: Longmans, 1913), p. 5.

14 Della Hooke, 'The Reconstruction of Ancient Routeways', *Local Historian* 12 (1977), pp. 212–20.

15 For discussion of these *burhs*, see Chapter 9 of this volume.

16 See n. 11, above.

17 Peter Barber and Christopher Board, *Tales from the Map Room* (London: BBC, 1993), pp. 44–45.

18 John Blair (ed.), *Waterways and Canal-Building in Medieval England* (Oxford: Oxford University Press, 2007).

19 D. Hill, *An Atlas of Anglo-Saxon England* (Oxford: Blackwell, 1981), p. 115.

20 Ibid., pp. 134–42.

21 B. Thorpe, *Ancient Laws and Institutions* (London: Record Commission, 1840), vol. 1, p. 115, Laws of Ine, 20; see also Frederick Levi Attenborough, *The Laws of the Earliest English Kings* (Cambridge: Cambridge University Press, 1922).

22 A.J. Robertson, *The Laws of the Kings of England from Edmund to Henry I* (Cambridge: Cambridge University Press, 1925), pp. 266–67.

23 L.J. Downer (ed.), *Leges Henrici Primi* (Oxford: Clarendon Press, 1972), pp. 248–49.

24 Nicholas Howe, *Writing the Map of Anglo-Saxon England* (London: Yale University Press, 2008), p. 41.

25 Michael Swanton, *Anglo-Saxon Prose* (London: Dent, 1975) pp. 11–13; A.S. Napier and W.H. Stevenson, *The Crawford Collection of Early Charters and Documents* (Oxford: Clarendon Press, 1895), pp. 1–3, 37–46.

26 Della Hooke, *The Anglo-Saxon Landscape: The Kingdom of the Hwicce* (Manchester: Manchester University Press, 1985), p. 58.

27 Della Hooke, *The Landscape of Anglo-Saxon England* (London: Leicester University Press, 1998), pp. 161, 216.

28 Nick Millea, *The Gough Map: The Earliest Road Map of Great Britain?* (Oxford: Bodleian Library, 2007).

29 The images and text can be viewed at http://www.fulltable.com/vts/m/map/ogilby/mna.htm [accessed 27 June 2014].

30 Ann Cole, 'Place-Names as Travellers' Landmarks', in N.J. Higham and M.J. Ryan (eds), *Place-Names, Language and the Anglo-Saxon Landscape* (Woodbridge: Boydell Press, 2011), pp. 51–67.

31 Heaney, *Beowulf*, p. 12.

32 Cole, 'Place-Names', p. 53.

33 Hooke, *Anglo-Saxon Landscape*, p. 121.

34 Heaney, *Beowulf*, p. 46.

35 Harrison, *Bridges of Medieval England*, pp. 24–29, 32–43.

36 Elliott van Kirk Dobbie (ed.), *The Anglo-Saxon Minor Poems*, Anglo-Saxon Poetic Records 6 (London: Routledge & Kegan Paul, 1942), p. 9, ll. 74–83.

37 Hill, *Atlas of Anglo-Saxon England*, p. 116.

38 Cole, 'Place-Names', pp. 57–61.

39 Della Hooke, 'The Droitwich Salt Industry: An Examination of the West Midland Charter Evidence', *Anglo-Saxon Studies in Archaeology and History* 2 (1981), pp. 123–69; Della Hooke, *The Landscape of Anglo-Saxon England* (London: Leicester University Press, 1998), pp. 4, 8.

40 Hooke, *Anglo-Saxon Landscape*, p. 126.

41 Ibid., p. 207.

42 Ibid., p. 215.

43 Taylor, *Roads and Tracks*, pp. 84–110.

44 A.E. Dodd and E.M. Dodd, *Peakland Roads and Trackways* (Ashbourne: Moorland, 1980), pp. 45–53.

45 Paul Hindle, *Medieval Roads and Tracks* (Oxford: Shire, 2009).

46 Taylor, *Roads and Tracks*, p. 110.
47 Richard Muir, *The New Reading the Landscape* (Exeter: University of Exeter Press, 2000), p. 112.

Chapter 3: *Kevin Leahy and Michael Lewis*

1 Bede, *Historia Ecclesiastica*, in B. Colgrave and R.A.B. Mynors (eds), *Bede's Ecclesiastical History of the English People* (Oxford: Clarendon Press, 1969), book 2, ch. 13.
2 Le Corbusier, *Vers une architecture* (Paris: Crès et Cie, 1924), p. ix.
3 P. Dark, *The Environment of Britain in the First Millennium AD* (London: Duckworth, 2000), pp. 19–28.
4 J. Hillam and C. Groves, 'Trees and Woodland in the Saxon Period: The Dendrochronological Evidence', in J. Rackham (ed.), *Environment and Economy in Anglo-Saxon England*, Council for British Archaeology Research Report 89 (York: Council for British Archaeology, 1994), pp. 12–22.
5 T.C. Lethbridge and C.F. Tebbutt, 'Huts of the Anglo-Saxon Period', *Cambridge Antiquarian Society's Communications* 33 (1933), p. 149.
6 Ibid.
7 H. Hamerow, 'Anglo-Saxon Timber Buildings and their Social Context', in H. Hamerow, D.A. Hinton and S. Crawford (eds), *The Oxford Handbook of Anglo-Saxon Archaeology* (Oxford: Oxford University Press, 2011), pp. 129–30.
8 See Michael Lewis, Andrew Richardson and David Williams, 'Things of This World: Portable Antiquities and their Potential', in Maren Clegg Hyer and Gale R. Owen-Crocker (eds), *The Material Culture of Daily Living in the Anglo-Saxon World* (Exeter: University of Exeter Press, 2011), pp. 231–57.
9 M.J. Lewis, *The Archaeological Authority of the Bayeux Tapestry*, British Archaeological Reports, British Series 404 (Oxford: John and Erica Hedges Ltd, 2005), pp. 17–18.
10 H. Hamerow, 'Anglo-Saxon Timber Buildings: The Continental Connection', in H. Sarfatij, W.J.H. Verwers and P.J. Woltering (eds), *Discussion with the Past: Archaeological Studies Presented to W.A. van Es* (Zwolle and Amersfoort: Stichting Promotie Archeologie, 1999), pp. 119–28.

11 Although, since it is apparent that these smaller timber buildings are similar to those that appear along the Frisian coast at the same time (H. Hamerow, *Rural Settlement and Society in Anglo-Saxon England* (Oxford: Oxford University Press, 2012), pp. 18–22), it is also possible other factors might be at play.
12 K.A. Leahy, *The Anglo-Saxon Kingdom of Lindsey* (Stroud: Tempus, 2007), pp. 82–83.
13 J. Tipper, *The Grubenhaus in Anglo-Saxon England: An Analysis and Interpretation of the Evidence from a Most Distinctive Building Type* (Yedingham: English Heritage, 2004).
14 S. West, *West Stow: The Anglo-Saxon Village*, East Anglian Archaeology 24 (Ipswich: Suffolk County Council, 1985).
15 Tipper, *Grubenhaus*, p. 147. Hamerow, 'Timber Buildings', p. 150.
16 H. Hamerow, 'Special Deposits in Anglo-Saxon Settlements', *Medieval Archaeology* 50 (2006), pp. 1–30.
17 Tipper, *Grubenhaus*.
18 G. Milne and J. Richards, *Two Anglo-Saxon Buildings and Associated Finds*, York University Archaeological Publication 9 (York: University of York, 1992).
19 S. Losco-Bradley and G. Kinsley, *Catholme: An Anglo-Saxon Settlement on the Trent Gravels in Staffordshire*, Nottingham Studies in Archaeology 3 (Nottingham: University of Nottingham, 2002).
20 D. Powlesland, 'The Anglo-Saxon Settlement at West Heslerton', in J. Hawkes and S. Mills (eds), *Northumbria's Golden Age* (Stroud: Sutton, 1999), p. 59.
21 West, *West Stow*, p. 120.
22 Tipper, *Grubenhaus*, p. 77.
23 P. Dixon, 'How Saxon is the Saxon House?', in P.J. Drury (ed.), *Structural Reconstruction*, British Archaeological Reports, British Series 30 (Oxford: British Archaeological Reports, 1982), pp. 275–88.
24 D. Garton and D. Riley, 'Dunston's Clump', *Current Archaeology* 7.2.85 (1982), pp. 43–48.

25 S. James, A. Marshall and M. Millett, 'An Early Medieval Building Tradition', *Archaeological Journal* 141 (1984), pp. 205–06.

26 M. Millett and S. James, 'Excavations at Cowdery's Down, Basingstoke, Hants: 1978–1981', *Archaeological Journal* 140 (1983), pp. 151–279.

27 P. Addyman, D. Leigh and M. Hughes, 'Anglo-Saxon Houses at Chalton, Hampshire', *Medieval Archaeology* 16 (1972), pp. 13–32.

28 Millet and James, 'Cowdery's Down', pp. 151–279.

29 Addyman, Leigh and Hughes, 'Anglo-Saxon Houses at Chalton'; West, *West Stow*.

30 *Beowulf*, trans. M. Alexander (Harmondsworth: Penguin, 1973), ll. 116, 146, 285, 658 and 935.

31 Millet and James, 'Cowdery's Down', pp. 227–46.

32 M. Pitts, 'Were Anglo-Saxon Halls Homes to Kings', *British Archaeology*, January–February 2014, pp. 6–7.

33 B. Hope-Taylor, *Yeavering: An Anglo-British Centre of Early Northumbria* (London: HMSO, 1977).

34 Millet and James, 'Cowdery's Down', microfiche M5/02.

35 *Beowulf*, trans. Alexander, ll. 67–70, 74–76, 78 and 86–91.

36 M.J. Swanton (trans. and ed.), *The Anglo-Saxon Chronicle* (London: Dent, 1996), pp. 46–47 n. 13.

37 *Beowulf*, trans. Alexander, ll. 141–42.

38 P. Rahtz, *The Saxon and Medieval Palaces at Cheddar: Excavations 1960–62*, British Archaeological Reports, British Series 65 (Oxford: British Archaeological Reports, 1979).

39 Tipper, *Grubenhaus*, p. 11.

40 R. Daniels, 'The Anglo-Saxon Monastery at Church Close, Hartlepool, Cleveland', *Archaeological Journal* 145 (1988), pp. 158–210.

41 C. Loveluck and R. Darrah, 'The Built Environment: The Buildings, Aspects of Settlement Morphology and the Use of Space', in C. Loveluck (ed.), *Rural Settlement, Lifestyle and Social Change in the Later First Millennium AD: Anglo-Saxon Flixborough in its Wider Context, Excavations at Flixborough 4* (Oxford: Oxbow, 2007), pp. 31–74.

42 P. Ottaway, L.M. Wastling, R. Cramp et al., 'Building Materials and Fittings', in D. Evans and C. Loveluck (eds), *Life and Economy at Early Medieval Flixborough, c.AD 600–1000, Excavations at Flixborough 2, The Artefact Evidence* (Oxford: Oxbow, 2009), pp. 143–64.

43 P. Rahtz and R. Meeson, *An Anglo-Saxon Watermill at Tamworth*, Council for British Archaeology Research Report 83 (London: Council for British Archaeology, 1992).

44 K.A. Leahy, *Anglo-Saxon Crafts* (Stroud: Tempus, 2003), pp. 16–24, Figs 2–9.

45 R. Darrah, 'Identifying the Architectural Features of the Anglo-Saxon Buildings at Flixborough and Understanding their Structures', in C. Loveluck, *Rural Settlement*, pp. 51–66.

46 W. Rodwell, 'Appearances Can Be Deceptive: Building and Decorating Anglo-Saxon Churches', *Journal of the British Archaeological Association* 165 (2012), pp. 24–25. See related discussion in Chapter 5 of this volume.

47 A. Selkirk, 'Bull Wharf, Queenhythe', *Current Archaeology* 158.14. 2 (1998), pp. 75–77.

48 G. Beresford, *Goltho: The Development of an Early Medieval Manor c.850–1150* (London: Historic Buildings and Monuments Commission for England, 1987).

49 G. Thomas, 'The Symbolic Lives of Late Anglo-Saxon Settlements: A Cellared Structure and Iron Hoard from Bishopstone, East Sussex', *Archaeological Journal* 165 (2008), pp. 334–98. See additional discussion of timbered towers in Chapter 5 of this volume

50 R. Hall, *Viking Age York* (London: Batsford Ltd/English Heritage, 1994).

51 A.J. Mainman, *Anglo-Scandinavian Pottery from 16–22 Coppergate, The Archaeology of York 16.5: The Pottery* (London: Council for British Archaeology for the York Archaeological Trust, 1990), p. 427 and Fig. 186. See also J. Young and A. Vince, *A Corpus of Anglo-Saxon and Medieval Pottery from Lincoln*, Lincoln Archaeological Studies 7 (Oxford: Oxbow, 2005), p. 54, Fig. 52.

52 Thomas, 'Symbolic Lives'.

53 Tipper, *Grubenhaus*, pp. 13–14.

54 J.D. Richards, *Viking Age England* (London: Batsford Ltd/English Heritage, 1994), p. 61, Fig. 32.

55 Hall, *Viking Age York*, p. 72.
56 B. Cunliffe, *Excavations at Portchester Castle*, vol. 2, *Saxon*, Reports of the Research Committee of the Society of Antiquaries of London 33 (London: Society of Antiquaries, 1976).
57 P. Wade-Martins and D. Yaxley, *Excavations in North Elmham Park*, 2 vols, East Anglian Archaeology 9 (Gressenhall: Norfolk Museums Service, 1980).
58 Hall, *Viking Age York*, pp. 66–68.
59 M.J. Lewis, G.R. Owen-Crocker and D. Terkla, *The Bayeux Tapestry: New Approaches* (Oxford: Oxbow 2011), facsimile, scene 3.
60 P.J. Huggins, 'The Excavation of an 11th-century Viking Hall and 14th-century Rooms at Waltham Abbey, Essex, 1969–71', *Medieval Archaeology* 20 (1976), pp. 75–133.
61 Ibid., pp. 85–93.
62 E. Coatsworth, 'Cushioning (Early) Medieval Life: Domestic Textiles in Anglo-Saxon England', *Medieval Clothing and Textiles* 3 (2007), pp. 1–12. See also the *Liber Confortatorius of Goscelin of Saint Bertin*, ibid., pp. 5–6, which discusses the decoration of walls.
63 Hall, *Viking Age York*, p. 64.
64 Beresford, *Goltho*, p. 59.
65 C. Loveluck and D. Atkinson, *The Early Medieval Settlement Remains from Flixborough, Lincolnshire: The Occupation Sequence, c.AD 600–1000, Excavations at Flixborough 1* (Oxford: Oxbow, 2007).
66 Lewis, Owen-Crocker and Terkla, *Bayeux Tapestry*, facsimile, scene 47.
67 *The Saga of the People of Vatnsdal*, trans. A. Wawn, in Ö. Thorsson (ed.), *The Sagas of Icelanders* (London: Penguin, 2001), pp. 190. The saga was written in the thirteenth century and chronicles events surrounding the family of Ingimund in Vatnsdal from the late ninth century to the late tenth century.
68 R. Bruce-Mitford, A. Care Evans et al., *The Sutton Hoo Ship Burial*, vol. 3, *Late Roman and Byzantine Silver, Hanging Bowls, Drinking Vessels, Cauldrons and other Containers, Textiles, the Lyre, Pottery Bottle and other Items* (London: British Museum Press, 1983), pp. 511–49.
69 P. Ottaway, 'Iron Domestic Fixtures, Fittings and Implements', in D. Evans and C. Loveluck (eds), *Life and Economy*, pp. 173–74, Fig. 5.5.
70 See PAS Records: LANCUM-9D53B5, -9D4811, -9D3313 and -9D2137.
71 Wade-Martins and Yaxley, *North Elmham*, pp. 69–71.
72 Lewis, Owen-Crocker and Terkla, *Bayeux Tapestry*, facsimile, scene 42.
73 N. Field and K. Leahy, 'Prehistoric and Anglo-Saxon Remains at Nettleton Top, Nettleton', *Lincolnshire History and Archaeology* 38 (1993), pp. 9–38.
74 Addyman, Leigh and Hughes, 'Anglo-Saxon Houses at Chalton', p.17.
75 Contemporary images exist for coppicing and harvesting wood; see the two eleventh-century Anglo-Saxon agricultural calendars discussed and illustrated in D. Hill, 'Agriculture through the Year', in Maren Clegg Hyer and Gale R. Owen-Crocker (eds), *The Material Culture of Daily Living in the Anglo-Saxon World* (Exeter: University of Exeter Press, 2011), pp. 14, 17. Coppicing is shown as a task for the month of June, wood-piling near the fire a task for the month of November. See also C. Grocock, 'Barriers to Knowledge: Coppicing and Landscape Usage in the Anglo-Saxon Economy', in N.J. Higham and M.J. Ryan (eds), *The Landscape Archaeology of Anglo-Saxon England*, Publications of the Manchester Centre for Anglo-Saxon Studies 9 (Woodbridge, Boydell Press, 2010), pp. 23–37.
76 R. Cramp, 'The Window Glass and Lead Canes', in D.H. Evans and C. Loveluck, *Life and Economy*, pp. 159–62.
77 Rodwell, 'Appearances Can Be Deceptive', pp. 43–44, Fig. 16.
78 B.N.J. Edwards, 'A Group of Pre-Conquest Metalwork from Asby Winderwath Common', *Transactions of the Cumberland and Westmorland Antiquarian and Archaeological Society* 2 (2002), pp. 111–43.
79 Tipper, *Grubenhaus*, p. 164.
80 See calendar images and discussion in Hill, 'Agriculture through the Year', pp. 17–18; threshing is listed as a task for the month of December.
81 Loveluck and Atkinson, *Early Medieval Settlement Remains*.

82 Hall, *Viking Age York*, p. 61.
83 Ibid., p. 66.
84 C. A. Morris, *Wood and Woodworking in Anglo-Scandinavian and Medieval York*, The Archaeology of York: The Small Finds 17/13, Craft, Industry and Everyday Life (York: Council for British Archaeology, 2000), p. 2271.
85 S.J. Sherlock, *A Royal Anglo-Saxon Cemetery at Street House, Loftus, North-East Yorkshire*, Tees Archaeology Monograph Series 6 (Hartlepool: Tees Archaeology, 2012), pp. 89–100.
86 C. Hills, *Spong Hill, Part IV, Catalogue of Cremations*, East Anglian Archaeology 34 (Gressenhall: Norfolk Archaeological Unit, 1987), p. 80, no. 3324, plate IX.
87 Museum of London Archaeology Service, *The Prittlewell Prince: The Discovery of a Rich Anglo-Saxon Burial in Essex* (London: Museum of London Archaeology Service, 2004).
88 Leahy, *Anglo-Saxon Crafts*, pp. 37–40.
89 M. Hoffmann, *The Warp-weighted Loom*, Studia Norvegica 14 (Oslo: Universitetsforlaget, 1964), p. 40.
90 Coatsworth, 'Cushioning', pp. 7–12.
91 Ibid., p. 8.
92 Ibid., p. 7, after D. Whitelock (ed.), *Anglo-Saxon Wills* (Cambridge: Cambridge University Press, 1930), Will no. 3, p. 12, ll. 12–13.
93 Coatsworth, 'Cushioning', p. 8, after D. Whitelock (ed.), *The Will of Æthelgifu* (Cambridge: Cambridge University Press, 1930), p. 7, l. 7, and p. 13, ll. 44–45 and 49.

94 *The Saga of the People of Vatnsdal*, p. 3.
95 Ottaway, 'Iron Domestic Fixtures', in D. Evans and C. Loveluck (eds), *Life and Economy*, pp. 187–95.
96 *Beowulf*, trans. Alexander, ll. 995–97.
97 Coatsworth, 'Cushioning', pp. 5–6.
98 See M. Budny, 'The Byrhtnoth Tapestry or Embroidery', in D.G. Scragg (ed.), *The Battle of Maldon, AD 991* (Oxford: Basil Blackwell, 1991), pp. 263–78.
99 Rodwell, 'Appearances Can Be Deceptive', pp. 22–60.
100 J.R. Fairbrother, *Faccombe Netherton: Excavation of a Saxon and Medieval Manorial Complex*, British Museum Occasional Paper 74 (London: British Museum, 1990).
101 K. Milek, 'The Roles of Pit Houses and Gendered Spaces on Viking Age Farmsteads in Iceland', *Medieval Archaeology* 56 (2012), pp. 85–130.
102 See Loveluck and Atkinson, *Early Medieval Settlement Remains*.
103 H. Hamerow, 'Anglo-Saxon Timber Buildings and their Social Context', p. 141.
104 *Egil's Saga*, trans. B. Scudder, in Ö. Thorsson (ed.), *The Sagas of Icelanders* (London: Penguin, 2001), pp. 66.
105 *Beowulf*, trans. Alexander, ll. 1239–40.
106 Beresford, *Goltho*, p. 59.
107 For discussion of civic planning and the later *burhs*, in particular, see Chapter 9 of this volume.

Chapter 4: *Damian Tyler*
1 Stephen of Ripon, *Vita Wilfridi*, in B. Colgrave (trans. and ed.), *The Life of Bishop Wilfrid by Eddius Stephanus* (Cambridge: Cambridge University Press, 1927) (hereafter, *VW*), 17, pp. 36–37.
2 It is unfortunate that this dedication cannot be dated with greater precision. It certainly took place after the death of Oswiu in 670, as Ecgfrith was now the senior Northumbrian ruler, and before Wilfrid's expulsion from his see, which Bede dates to 678; Bede, *Historia Ecclesiastica*, in B. Colgrave and R.A.B. Mynors (eds), *Bede's Ecclesiastical History of the English People* (Oxford: Clarendon Press, 1969) (hereafter, *HE*), book 5, ch. 24, p. 365. On Bishop Wilfrid, see, in the first instance, N.J. Higham (ed.), *Wilfrid: Bishop, Abbot, Saint. Papers from the 1300th Anniversary Conferences* (Donington: Shaun Tyas, 2013). On Wilfrid's church at Ripon, see E. Coatsworth, *Corpus of Anglo-Saxon Stone Sculpture*, vol. 8, *Western Yorkshire* (Oxford: Oxford University Press for the British Academy, 2008), pp. 13–15 and 67–68.
3 *VW*, 17, p. 37
4 For additional discussion of stone churches and their impact in the Anglo-Saxon landscape, see Chapter 5 of this volume.
5 *VW*, 17, pp. 36–37.

6 Ibid.
7 Ibid.
8 *HE*, book 3, ch. 24, p. 291.
9 *HE*, book 3, ch. 24, pp. 291–92.
10 *et reges Brittonum inerfecti sunt, qui exierant cum rege Pantha in expeditionem usque ad urbem quae vocatur Iudea* (J. Morris (trans. and ed.), *Historia Brittonum*, in *Nennius – British History and the Welsh Annals* (Chichester: Phillimore, 1980), 64, p. 79).
11 Who *cum exercitu suo evasit de nocte consurgens* (ibid., pp. 79–80).
12 *VW*, 20, pp. 32–33.
13 *The Anglo-Saxon Chronicle* records a battle fought between the forces of Æthelberht and those of the West Saxons under Ceawlin and Cutha in 568; M.J. Swanton (trans. and ed.), *The Anglo-Saxon Chronicle* (London: Dent, 1996) MSS A and E, *sub anno* 568, pp. 18–19. It now appears unlikely that Æthelberht became king of Kent before the 580s, which renders this annal suspect. For discussions of the probable date of the accession of Æthelberht, see N. Brooks, 'The Creation and Early Structure of the Kingdom of Kent', in S. Bassett (ed.), *The Origins of Anglo-Saxon Kingdoms* (London: Leicester University Press, 1989), pp. 66–67 and D. Kirby, *The Earliest English Kings* (Cambridge: Cambridge University Press, 1991), pp. 31–34.
14 For a discussion of the nature of Æthelberht's *imperium*, see N.J. Higham, *The Convert Kings: Power and Religious Affiliation in Early Anglo-Saxon England* (Manchester: Manchester University Press, 1997), pp. 53–119.
15 Bede's story about Imma, the Northumbrian thegn captured by the Mercians after the battle of the Trent in 679, who attempted to deceive his captors by pretending to be a peasant who had brought provisions for the army, is suggestive in this context; *HE*, book 4, ch. 22, pp. 401–05.
16 For these conflicts, see *HE*, book 2, ch. 2, pp. 140–43; book 2, ch. 12, pp. 180–81; book 3, ch. 24, pp. 290–91; book 4, ch. 21 (19), pp. 400–01.
17 See B. Hope-Taylor, *Yeavering: An Anglo-British Centre of Early Northumbria* (London: HMSO, 1977), pp. 129–30. For further, more extensive discussion of these and other wooden structures, see Chapter 3 in this volume.

18 *Beowulf*, in Elliott van Kirk Dobbie (ed.), *Beowulf and Judith*, Anglo-Saxon Poetic Records 4 (New York: Columbia University Press, 1953).
19 Swanton, *The Anglo-Saxon Chronicles*, *sub anno* 755, pp. 46–50.
20 *Beowulf and Judith*, ed. Dobbie, p. 22, ll. 662–65 and p. 7, ll. 138–40.
21 M. Millett and S. James, 'Excavations at Cowdery's Down, Basingstoke, Hants: 1978-1981', *Archaeological Journal* 140 (1983), pp. 151–279.
22 *HE*, book 2, ch. 15, pp. 190–91.
23 *frequenter ad eum [Oswiu of Northumbria] in provinciam Nordanhymbrorum venerit* (*HE*, book 3, ch. 22, pp. 280–83).
24 *HE*, book 3, ch. 21, pp. 278–81.
25 *HE*, book 4, ch. 13, pp. 372–73. Bede does not date this incident, but states that it took place *non multo ante* the arrival of Bishop Wilfrid in Sussex in 678. It must have occurred before 675, as Wulfhere died in that year; *HE*, book 5, ch. 24, pp. 564–65.
26 D. Binchy (ed.), *Críth Gablach*, Medieval and Modern Irish Series 11 (Dublin: Dublin Institute for Advanced Studies, 1941), l. 503. For a translation of *Críth Gablach*, see E. Mac Neill, 'Ancient Irish Law: The Law on Status or Franchise', *Proceedings of the Royal Irish Academy* 36 (1923), pp. 281–306.
27 See S. Keynes, 'Church Councils, Royal Assemblies and Royal Diplomas', in Owen-Crocker and Schneider, *Kingship, Legislation and Power in Anglo-Saxon England*, p. 19.
28 Hope-Taylor, *Yeavering*, pp. 119–22.
29 *HE*, book 3, ch. 21, pp. 278–81.
30 *Beowulf and Judith*, ed. Dobbie, ll. 1020–53. The implications of this treasure-giving scene in relation to the interior of Heorot are discussed in detail in G.R. Owen-Crocker, 'Furnishing Heorot', in Eric Cambridge and Jane Hawkes (eds), *Crossing Boundaries: interdisciplinary approaches to the art, material culture, language and literature of the early medieval world* (Oxford: Oxbow, forthcoming 2016).
31 *HE*, book 4, ch. 13, pp. 372–73.
32 *Beowulf and Judith*, ed. Dobbie, p. 68, l. 2195.
33 *HE*, book 2, ch. 10, pp. 170–71.
34 J.G. Dillon (trans. and ed.), *Lebor na*

Cert: The Book of Rights (Dublin: Educational County of Ireland for the Irish Texts Society, 1962), p. xvi.

35   *Pictorum quoque atque Scottorum gentes ... tributarias fecit* (*HE*, book 2, ch. 5, pp. 150–51).

36   *VW*, 20, pp. 42–43.

37   Only thirty-four hidations are given; Lindsey and Hatfield are assessed jointly. A facsimile of the earliest extant copy of this text, together with a transcription and a brief discussion of the relationships between the various recensions, is given by David Dumville in 'The Tribal Hidage: An Introduction to its Texts and their History', in Bassett, *The Origins of Anglo-Saxon Kingdoms*, pp. 225–30. For further discussions, see, *inter alia*, Frank Stenton, *Anglo-Saxon England*, 3rd edn (Oxford: Clarendon Press, 1971), pp. 43 and 196–97; C.R. Hart, 'The *Tribal Hidage*', *Transactions of the Royal Historical Society*, 5th series, 21 (1971), pp. 133–57; W. Davies and H. Vierck, 'The Contexts of the *Tribal Hidage*: Social Aggregates and Settlement Patterns', *Frühmittelalterliche Studien* 7 (1974), pp. 223–93; N.J. Higham, *An English Empire: Bede and the Early Anglo-Saxon Kings* (Manchester: Manchester University Press, 1995), pp. 74–99.

38   Wendy Davies has argued that many of the smaller peoples appearing in the *Tribal Hidage* should not be regarded as kingdoms; Davies and Vierck, 'The Contexts of the *Tribal Hidage*', *passim*, esp. pp. 236–42. This hypothesis has been challenged by James Campbell in 'Bede's *Reges* and *Principes*', Jarrow Lecture (Jarrow: Parish PCC, 1979), p. 6.

39   G. Mac Niocaill, *Ireland before the Vikings* (Dublin: Gill & Macmillan, 1972), p. 30.

40   Ryan Lavelle's recent discussion of the food renders in early Wessex may help illuminate the processes involved in collecting food stuffs to be rendered as tribute; Lavelle, 'Ine 70.1 and Royal Provision in Anglo-Saxon Wessex', in Owen-Crocker and Schneider, *Kingship, Legislation and Power in Anglo-Saxon England*, pp. 259–73.

41   Bede does not include any Mercian kings in his famous list of rulers wielding *imperium* over the southern English; *HE*, book 2, ch. 5. This is likely to be a reflection of his biases as the dominance of Mercia is clearly shown by his treatment of Penda and, to a lesser extent, Wulfhere and Æthelræd. On the overkingship of Penda, see D.J. Tyler, 'An Early Mercian Hegemony: Penda and Overkingship in the Seventh Century', *Midland History* 30 (2005), pp. 1–19. Bede does state that at the time he wrote the *Historia Ecclesiastica* all the kingdoms of the southern English were subject to the authority of the Mercian king Æthelbald; *HE*, book 5, ch. 23, pp. 538–39.

42   Accounts of the Synod of Whitby are given in *HE*, book 3, ch. 25, pp. 294–309 and *VW*, 10, pp. 20–23. For doubts as to the identification of *Streanæshealh* with Whitby, see P.S. Barnwell, L.A.S. Butler and C.J. Dunn, 'The Confusion of Conversion: Streanæshalch, Strensall and Whitby and the Northumbrian Church', in M. Carver (ed.), *The Cross Goes North: Processes of Conversion in Northern Europe, AD 300–1300* (Woodbridge: Boydell Press, 2003), pp. 311–26.

43   Bede is not entirely clear on this point, but it is strongly implied; *HE*, book 3, ch. 24, pp. 292–93.

44   *HE*, book 3, ch. 25, pp. 296–97.

45   *VW*, 10, pp. 20–21.

46   H. Mayr-Harting, *The Coming of Christianity to Anglo-Saxon England*, 3rd edn (London: Batsford, 1991), p. 106; Higham, *The Convert Kings*, p. 256.

47   Mayr-Harting, *The Coming of Christianity*, p. 106; Higham, *The Convert Kings*, p. 256.

48   *HE*, book 3, ch. 14, pp. 254–55.

49   Who, in 654, would have predicted that Oswiu would destroy the mighty Penda?

50   Oswiu became king in 642 as *iuuenis xxx circiter annorum* and died in 670; *HE*, book 3, ch. 14, pp. 254–55; book 5, ch. 25, pp. 264–65.

51   *VW*, 10, pp. 20–21.

52   *HE*, book 3, ch. 25, pp. 298–99.

53   E.g. the baptism of Edwin; *HE*, book 2, ch. 14, pp. 186–89; the dedication of Ripon; *VW*, 17, pp. 34–39.

54   *HE*, book 3, ch. 25, pp. 298–99.

55   *HE*, book 1, ch. 25, pp. 72–77.

56   *HE*, book 1, ch. 26, pp. 76–77.

57   *fecit rex Aedilberct in ciuitate Lundonia ecclesiam sancti Pauli apostoli* (*HE*, book 2, ch. 3, p. 142).

58 *HE*, book 2, ch. 3, pp. 142–43.
59 *VW*, 17, pp. 34–37.
60 For what else can we call the signed and witnessed lists Wilfrid read to the congregation?
61 In 693, a man describing himself as *Ego Oshere rex Hwiccorum* granted lands at *Penitanham* to an Abbess Cutsuida without reference to any other king; W. de G. Birch (ed.), *Cartularium Saxonicum*, 3 vols (London, 1885–93) (hereafter, *BCS*, charters cited by number), vol. 1, no. 85; P.H. Sawyer (ed.), *Anglo-Saxon Charters: An Annotated List and Bibliography* (London: Royal Historical Society, 1968) (hereafter, *S*, charters cited by number), no. 53. Sixty-six years later, in 759, three joint rulers of the Hwicce, describing themselves as *reguli*, issued a charter *cum licentia et permissione regis Offan Merciorum* (*BCS* 187; *S* 56). By 777/78 Offa was referring to *subregulo meo Aldredo videlicet duce propriae gentis Huiccorum* (*BCS* 223; *S* 113).
62 E.g. Frank Stenton, *Anglo-Saxon England*, p. 45 and Barbara Yorke, *Kings and Kingdoms of Early Anglo-Saxon England* (London: Routledge, 1990) p. 109. For my own reservations regarding this hypothesis, see D.J. Tyler, 'Kingship and Conversion: Constructing Pre-Viking Mercia', unpublished PhD thesis, University of Manchester, 2002, pp. 68–69.
63 *S* 1165. On Frithuwold's kingship, see J. Blair, 'Frithuwold's Kingdom and the Origins of Surrey', in Bassett, *The Origins of Anglo-Saxon Kingdoms*, pp. 97–107.
64 For a good, concise discussion of the reduction of Kentish independence, see Yorke, *Kings and Kingdoms*, pp. 28–32.
65 E.g. *S* 7, 8 and 9.
66 *BCS* 195; *S* 105.
67 *S* 34.
68 Ibid.
69 *BCS* 195; *S* 105.
70 I am indebted to Nicholas Higham for drawing my attention to this meeting, initially in a personal communication, but see also Higham, *The Convert Kings*, pp. 216–17.
71 *HE*, book 3, ch. 7, 232–33.

Chapter 5: *Michael Shapland*

1 Bede, *Historia Ecclesiastica*, in B. Colgrave and R.A.B. Mynors (eds), *Bede's Ecclesiastical History of the English People* (Oxford: Clarendon Press, 1969) (hereafter *HE*), book 1, ch. 30.
2 The nave, the long, central hall and public part of a church, commonly comprised its largest internal space. In contrast, the smaller chancel, or area around the altar, commonly lay at the east end of a church, and was reserved for the clergy.
3 See, for example, H.L.F. Guermonprez and P.M. Johnston, 'The "Barton": or "Manor" Farm, Nyetimber, Pagham', *Sussex Archaeological Collections* 46 (1903), pp. 145–54; A.W. Clapham, 'An Early Hall at Chilham Castle', *Antiquaries Journal* 8 (1928), pp. 350–53; P.C. Buckland, 'The "Anglian Tower" and the Use of Jurassic Limestone in York', in P.V. Addyman and V.E. Black (eds), *Archaeological Papers from York Presented to M.W. Barley* (York: York Archaeological Trust, 1984), pp. 51–57; D. Parsons, 'Odda's Chapel, Deerhurst: Place of Worship or Royal Hall?', *Medieval Archaeology* 44 (2000), pp. 225–28; Essex County Council, 'Prior's Hall, Widdington, Essex: Archaeological Monitoring' (Essex County Council Field Archaeology Unit, unpublished report, 2007). See also Chapter 3 in this volume.
4 R. Gem, 'The Anglo-Saxon and Norman Churches', in R. Gem (ed.), *St Augustine's Abbey, Canterbury* (London: B.T. Batsford, 1997), pp. 93–95.
5 The validity of drawing too distinct a line between Anglo-Saxon and Norman buildings is increasingly questioned (e.g. R. Gem, 'The English Parish Church in the Eleventh and Early Twelfth Centuries: A Great Rebuilding?', in J. Blair (ed.), *Minsters and Parish Churches: The Local Church in Transition 950–1200* (Oxford: Oxford University Committee for Archaeology, 1988), pp. 21–30; E. Fernie, 'Architecture and the Effects of the Norman Conquest', in D. Bates and A. Curry (eds), *England and Normandy in the Middle Ages* (London: Hambledon Press, 1994), pp. 105–16; J. Blair, *The Church in Anglo-Saxon Society* (Oxford: Oxford University Press, 2005), p. 412. The classic example is the gatehouse at Exeter Castle (*c.*1068), which merges Anglo-Saxon long-and-short quoins and triangular-headed

openings with characteristically Norman cushion capitals, billet ornaments and upper imposts (S. Blaylock, *Excavation and Fabric Recording at the Southern Corner of Exeter Castle, 1990*, Exeter Museums Archaeological Field Visit Report 91.29 (Exeter: Exeter Museums, 1991)).

6 J.T. Micklethwaite, 'Something about Anglo-Saxon Church Building', *Archaeological Journal* 63 (1896), pp. 293–351; G. Baldwin Brown, *The Arts in Early England: Anglo-Saxon Architecture*, 2nd edn (London: John Murray, 1925); A.W. Clapham, *English Romanesque Architecture before the Conquest* (Oxford: Oxford University Press, 1930); E.A. Fisher, *The Greater Anglo-Saxon Churches: An Architectural-Historical Study* (London: Faber and Faber, 1962); H.M. Taylor and J. Taylor, *Anglo-Saxon Architecture*, 2 vols (Cambridge: Cambridge University Press, 1965); R. Morris, *The Church in British Archaeology* (London: Council for British Archaeology, 1983), pp. 33–48.

7 Recent examples include Brixworth (D. Parsons and D.S. Sutherland, *The Anglo-Saxon Church of All Saints, Brixworth, Northamptonshire: Survey, Excavation and Analysis, 1972–2010* (Oxford: Oxbow, 2013)); Barton-upon-Humber (W. Rodwell and C. Atkins, *St. Peter's, Barton-upon-Humber, Lincolnshire: A Parish Church and its Community*, vol. 1, *History, Archaeology and Architecture* (Oxford: Oxbow, 2011)); Monkwearmouth/Jarrow (R. Cramp, *Wearmouth and Jarrow Monastic Sites* (Swindon: English Heritage, 2005)); Deerhurst (P. Rahtz and L. Watts, *St. Mary's Church, Deerhurst, Gloucestershire: Fieldwork, Excavations, and Structural Analysis, 1971–1984* (London: Society of Antiquaries, 1997)).

8 Examples of the literary and documentary approach include H.M. Taylor, 'The Architectural Interest of Aethelwulf's De Abbatibus', *Anglo-Saxon England* 3 (1974), pp. 163–73; R. Gem, 'Architecture of the Anglo-Saxon Church, 735 to 870: From Archbishop Ecgberht to Archbishop Ceolnoth', *Journal of the British Archaeological Association* 146 (1993), pp. 29–66.

9 E. Fernie, *The Architecture of the Anglo-Saxons* (London: B.T. Batsford, 1983); W. Rodwell, 'Anglo-Saxon Church Building: Aspects of Design and Construction', in L.A.S. Butler and R.K. Morris (eds), *The Anglo-Saxon Church: Papers on History, Architecture, and Archaeology in Honour of Dr H.M. Taylor* (York: Council for British Archaeology, 1986), pp. 156–75; Blair, *The Church in Anglo-Saxon Society*; S. Foot, *Monastic Life in England, c.600–900* (Cambridge: Cambridge University Press, 2006); H. Gittos, *Liturgy, Architecture, and Sacred Places in Anglo-Saxon England* (Oxford: Oxford University Press, 2013).

10 G. Bandmann, *Early Medieval Architecture as Bearer of Meaning*, new edn (New York: Columbia University Press, 2005 [1951]), pp. 3, 61, 160–61, 250. The word 'church' – *ekklēsia* – originally meant 'congregation' (L.M. White, *Building God's House in the Roman World: Architectural Adaptation Among Pagans, Jews, and Christians* (Baltimore, MD: Johns Hopkins University Press for the American Schools of Oriental Research, 1990), pp. 107–09).

11 White, *Building God's House*, pp. 107–20; S. Balderstone, *Early Church Architectural Forms: A Theologically Contextual Typology for the Eastern Churches of the 4th–6th Centuries* (Melbourne: Australian Institute of Archaeology, 2007), pp. 5–6; A. Doig, *Liturgy and Architecture from the Early Church to the Middle Ages* (Aldershot: Ashgate, 2008), pp. 17–18.

12 Discussed in Balderstone, *Early Church Architectural Forms*, pp. 6–7.

13 R. Krautheimer, *Early Christian and Byzantine Architecture*, 3rd edn (New Haven, CT: Yale University Press, 1986), p. 26; Balderstone, *Early Church Architectural Forms*, pp. 5–7. That Christian architecture could be symbolic of the divine is not apparent until the early fourth century (ibid., pp. 6–7).

14 Summarised in Doig, *Liturgy and Architecture*, pp. 21–52.

15 E.B. Smith, *Architectural Symbolism of Imperial Rome and the Middle Ages* (Princeton, NJ: Princeton University Press, 1956), p. 74; I. Lavin, 'The House of the Lord: Aspects of the Role of Palace Triclinia in the Architecture of Late Antiquity and the Early Middle Ages', *Art Bulletin* 44 (1962), pp. 16–17.

16 White, *Building God's House*, p. 18; Balderstone, *Early Church Architectural Forms*, pp. 8–11; Doig, *Liturgy and Architecture*, p. 18.

17 Doig, *Liturgy and Architecture*, pp. 22–24.

18 Smith, *Architectural Symbolism*, pp. 139, 166; G. Downey, *A History of Antioch in Syria: From Seleucus to the Arab Conquest* (Princeton, NJ: Princeton University Press, 1961), pp. 342–60; Lavin, 'The House of the Lord', pp. 16–21; Krautheimer, *Early Christian and Byzantine Architecture*, pp. 77–80; Balderstone, *Early Church Architectural Forms*, pp. 8–11.

19 *HE*, book 1, ch. 26.

20 Gem, 'The Anglo-Saxon and Norman Churches', pp. 93–95.

21 Debate on the re-use of Roman building materials – *spolia* – to evoke the Roman past is summarised in M.G. Shapland, 'Meanings of Timber and Stone in Anglo-Saxon Building Practice', in M.D.J. Bintley and M.G. Shapland (eds), *Trees and Timber in the Anglo-Saxon World* (Oxford: Oxford University Press, 2013), pp. 29–30.

22 T. Bell, *The Religious Reuse of Roman Structures in Early Medieval England* (Oxford: Archaeopress, 2005).

23 For further discussion of churches constructed or refurbished as 'kingly' meeting places, see Chapter 4 of this volume.

24 *Historiam Abbatum* 5, in C. Plummer (ed.), *Venerabilis Baedae Opera Historica* (Oxford: Oxford University Press, 1896), vol. 1, p. 368.

25 Fernie, *The Architecture of the Anglo-Saxons*, p. 72.

26 See T. Ó'Carragáin, *Churches in Early Medieval Ireland: Architecture, Ritual and Memory* (New Haven, CT: Yale University Press, 2010), p. 38.

27 Such as Silchester and Colchester.

28 M.O.H. Carver, 'Why That, Why There, Why Then? The Politics of Early Medieval Monumentality', in H. Hamerow and A. MacGregor (eds), *Image and Power in the Archaeology of Early Medieval Britain: Essays in Honour of Rosemary Cramp* (Oxford: Oxbow, 2001), p. 20.

29 T. Green, *Britons and Anglo-Saxons: Lincolnshire AD 400–650* (Lincoln: The History of Lincolnshire Committee, 2012), pp. 65–67 is the most recent assessment of the date and development of this church.

30 William of Malmesbury, *De Antiquitate Glastonie Ecclesie* in J. Scott (trans. and ed.), *The Early History of Glastonbury: An Edition, Translation, and Study of William of Malmesbury's* De Antiquitate Glastonie Ecclesie (Woodbridge: Boydell Press, 1981), p. 53 and *Gesta Regum Anglorum*, in R.M. Thomson and M. Winterbottom, *William of Malmesbury, Gesta Regum Anglorum: The History of the English Kings* (Oxford: Oxford University Press, 1998), vol. 1, pp. 804–05. Discussed in P. Rahtz, *The English Heritage Book of Glastonbury* (London: B.T. Batsford, 1993), pp. 72–74.

31 B. Yorke, *Kings and Kingdoms of Early Anglo-Saxon England* (London: Seaby, 1990), pp. 72–85.

32 P.S. Barnwell, L.A.S. Butler and C.J. Dunn, 'The Confusion of Conversion: Streahæshalch, Strensall, Whitby, and the Northumbrian Church', in M. Carver (ed.), *The Cross Goes North: Processes of Conversion in Northern Europe, AD 300–1300* (Woodbridge: Boydell Press, 2003), pp. 311–12; Nennius, *Historia Brittonum*, in J. Morris (trans. and ed.), *Nennius: British History and the Welsh Annals*, Arthurian Period Sources 8 (Chichester: Phillimore, 1980); *Annales Cambriae*, ibid., s.a. 626.

33 D. O'Sullivan and R. Young, *Lindisfarne: Holy Island* (London: B.T. Batsford, 1995), pp. 42–43; *HE*, book 3, ch. 25.

34 *HE*, book 3, ch. 7.

35 J. Hawkes, 'Iuxta Morem Romanorum: Stone and Sculpture in Anglo-Saxon England', in C.E. Karkov and G.H. Brown (eds), *Anglo-Saxon Styles* (Albany: State University of New York Press, 2003), pp. 74, 115–30.

36 R. Cramp, 'A Reconsideration of the Monastic Site of Whitby', in R.M. Spearman and J. Higgitt (eds), *The Age of Migrating Ideas: Early Medieval Art in Northern Britain and Ireland* (Edinburgh: National Museums of Scotland, 1993), pp. 65–66.

37 B. Hope-Taylor, *Yeavering: An Anglo-British Centre of Early Northumbria* (London: HMSO, 1977), pp. 276–77.

38 *HE*, book 3, ch. 4.

39 Ó'Carragáin, *Churches in Early Medieval Ireland*, pp. 15–17.

40 N. Venclová, 'The Venerable Bede, Druidic Tonsure and Archaeology', *Antiquity* 76 (2002), pp. 458–71.

41 R.H. Hutton, *The Pagan Religions of the Ancient British Isles: Their Nature and Legacy* (Oxford: Blackwell, 1991), pp. 268, 285–86.

42 *HE*, book 3, ch. 25; see also Ó'Carragáin, *Churches in Early Medieval Ireland*, p. 15. The evidence for early timber-built churches in Ireland is summarised by Ó'Carragáin, ibid., pp. 15–47. C.E. Karkov, *Text and Picture in Anglo-Saxon England*, Cambridge Studies in Anglo-Saxon England 31 (Cambridge: Cambridge University Press, 2001), p. 38 notes the great similarity between early medieval Northumbrian and Irish wooden architecture. Timber monastic buildings 'in the Irish manner' have been excavated at Iona, Hartlepool and Whitby (R. Cramp, 'Monkwearmouth and Jarrow in their European Context', in K.S. Painter (ed.), *Churches Built in Ancient Times: Recent Studies in Early Christian Archaeology* (London: Society of Antiquaries, 1994), pp. 280–81).

43 *HE*, book 5, ch. 21; *Historiam Abbatum* 5, in Plummer, *Venerabilis Baedae Opera Historica*, p. 368.

44 Hawkes, *Iuxta Morem Romanorum*, p. 74.

45 *HE*, book 2, ch. 14.

46 R. Daniels, *Anglo-Saxon Hartlepool and the Foundations of English Christianity: An Archaeology of the Anglo-Saxon Monastery* (Hartlepool: Tees Archaeology, 2007), pp. 68, 133, 198–99.

47 Fernie, *The Architecture of the Anglo-Saxons*, p. 59.

48 Blair, *The Church in Anglo-Saxon Society*, pp. 368–425.

49 Evidence summarised ibid., pp. 392, 413; Foot, *Monastic Life*, pp. 116–17; Gittos, *Liturgy, Architecture, and Sacred Places*, pp. 180–81.

50 Gittos, *Liturgy, Architecture, and Sacred Places*, p. 241.

51 Gem, 'The English Parish Church'; Blair, *The Church in Anglo-Saxon Society*, pp. 411–22. See Richard Morris ('Local Churches in the Anglo-Saxon Countryside', in H. Hamerow, D.A. Hinton and S. Crawford (eds), *The Oxford Handbook of Anglo-Saxon Archaeology* (Oxford: Oxford University Press, 2011), pp. 184–85) for a note of caution and a plea for regional variation on the 'great rebuilding' of Anglo-Saxon timber churches. The toponymic evidence for timber churches is summarised by Blair, *The Church in Anglo-Saxon Society*, p. 387 and J. Baker, 'References to Timber Building Materials in Old English Place-Names', in Bintley and Shapland, *Trees and Timber*, pp. 92–93.

52 D. Parsons, 'Review and Prospect: The Stone Industry in Roman, Anglo-Saxon and Medieval England', in D. Parsons (ed.), *Stone Quarrying and Building in England AD 43–1525* (Chichester: Phillimore, 1990), pp. 1–15.

53 See related discussion in Chapter 3 of this volume.

54 Shapland, 'Meanings of Timber and Stone'.

55 Yorke, *Kings and Kingdoms*, pp. 285–90; C. Senecal, 'Keeping up with the Godwinesons: In Pursuit of Aristocratic Status in Late Anglo-Saxon England', in J. Gillingham (ed.), *Anglo-Norman Studies XXIII: Proceedings of the Battle Conference* (Woodbridge: Boydell Press, 2001), pp. 251–66.

56 Ruling elites often underpin their legitimacy by using material culture to imply the permanence and inviolability of the social contract (M. Mann, *The Sources of Social Power*, vol. 1, *A History of Power from the Beginning to AD 1760* (Cambridge: Cambridge University Press, 1985); T. Earle, *How Chiefs Come to Power* (Stanford, CA: Stanford University Press, 1997)).

57 Comparable Norman disdain for old Anglo-Saxon churches by Abbot Aldelelm of Abingdon (1071–83) is recorded in the thirteenth century *de Abbatibus Abbendoniae*. For both, see R. Gem, 'England and the Resistance to Romanesque Architecture', in C. Harper-Bill, C.J. Holdsworth and J.L. Nelson (eds), *Studies in Medieval History Presented to Allen Brown* (Woodbridge: Boydell Press, 1989), pp. 134–35. On this topic, see also R. Plant, 'Innovation and Traditionalism in Writings on the English Romanesque', in J.A. Franklin, T.A. Heslop and C. Stevenson (eds), *Architecture and Interpretation: Essays for Eric Fernie* (Woodbridge: Boydell Press, 2012), pp. 278–79.

58 Limited exceptions include fragments of the west end of Sherborne Abbey (J.H.P. Gibb, 'The

Saxon Cathedral at Sherborne', *Archaeological Journal* 132 (1975), pp. 71–105).

59 Fernie, *The Architecture of the Anglo-Saxons*, pp. 155, 161, 176; H. Gittos, 'Architecture and Liturgy in England c.1000: Problems and Possibilities', in N. Hiscock (ed.), *The White Mantle of Churches: Architecture, Liturgy and Art around the Millennium* (Turnhout: Brepols, 2003), p. 93; Gittos, *Liturgy, Architecture, and Sacred Places*, pp. 90–94.

60 M. Winterbottom, *William of Malmesbury, Gesta Pontificum Anglorum: The History of the English Bishops* (Oxford: Oxford University Press, 2007), vol. 1, pp. 437–39.

61 R. Gem, 'Towards an Iconography of Anglo-Saxon Architecture', *Journal of the Warburg and Courtauld Institutes* 46 (1983), pp. 9–11.

62 R. Gem, 'Reconstructions of St Augustine's Abbey, Canterbury, in the Anglo-Saxon Period', in N. Ramsay, M. Sparks and T. Tatton-Brown (eds), *St Dunstan: His Life, Times and Cult* (Woodbridge: Boydell Press, 1992), p. 71; Gem, 'England and the Resistance to Romanesque Architecture', p. 134.

63 See introductory quotation. Some of the most famous early Christian churches were converted temples, not least Rome's Pantheon and the Parthenon in Athens. The putative Romano-British structure incorporated into the church at Stone-by-Faversham (Kent) may be an insular example (Fernie, *The Architecture of the Anglo-Saxons*, p. 44).

64 Summarised in Gem, 'The Anglo-Saxon and Norman Churches'.

65 Detailed by Rahtz, *The English Heritage Book of Glastonbury*, pp. 66–100. The extensive twentieth-century excavations at the abbey are presently undergoing comprehensive publication (R. Gilchrist, C. Allum and T. Astin, 'Glastonbury Abbey Chapter House', *Medieval Archaeology* 52 (2008), pp. 358–63).

66 M. Biddle, 'Excavations at Winchester, 1969: Eighth Interim Report', *Antiquaries Journal* 50 (1970), pp. 277–326; M. Biddle and B. Kjølbye-Biddle, 'Old Minster, St Swithun's Day 1093', in J. Crook (ed.), *Winchester Cathedral: Nine Hundred Years, 1093–1993* (Chichester: Phillimore, 1993), pp. 13–20.

67 Gittos, *Liturgy, Architecture, and Sacred Places*, p. 170. For an introduction to the Reform movement, see Blair, *The Church in Anglo-Saxon Society*, pp. 341–54.

68 D. Stocker, 'Fons et Origo: The Symbolic Death, Burial and Resurrection of English Font Stones', *Church Archaeology* 1 (1997), pp. 17–25.

69 On this topic, see D.A. Stocker and P. Everson, 'Rubbish Recycled: A Study of the Re-use of Stone in Lincolnshire', in D. Parsons (ed.), *Stone Quarrying and Building in England AD 43–1525* (Chichester: Phillimore, 1990), pp. 83–101; T. Eaton, *Plundering the Past: Roman Stonework in Medieval Britain* (Stroud: Tempus, 2000).

70 *HE*, book 3, ch. 17 (translated by Colgrave and Mynors at pp. 264–65).

71 Foot, *Monastic Life*, p. 115.

72 *HE*, book 3, ch. 25.

73 Rahtz, *The English Heritage Book of Glastonbury*, p. 72.

74 The chapel is thought to have stood at the entrance to the cathedral precinct, in the site of the later medieval church of St Michael-le-Belfry (C. Norton, 'The Anglo-Saxon Cathedral at York and the Topography of the Anglian City', *Journal of the British Archaeological Association* 151 (1998), pp. 1–42).

75 Alcuin, *Epistola* 226, quoted in Norton, 'The Anglo-Saxon Cathedral at York', p. 8 (my emphasis).

76 Cramp, 'Monkwearmouth and Jarrow in their European Context', pp. 281–89; Foot, *Monastic Life*, pp. 111–14.

77 R. Cramp, 'The Artistic Influence of Lindisfarne within Northumbria', in G. Bonner, D. Rollason and C. Stancliffe (eds), *St Cuthbert, His Cult and Community to AD 1200* (Woodbridge: Boydell Press, 1989), pp. 217–19.

78 Fernie, *The Architecture of the Anglo-Saxons*, pp. 32–46 and 73.

79 F. Herschend, *Journey of Civilisation: The Late Iron Age View of the Human World* (Uppsala: Uppsala University Department of Archaeology and Ancient History, 2001), p. 91.

80 Shapland, 'Meanings of Timber and Stone', pp. 27–28.

81 Cramp, *Wearmouth and Jarrow Monastic Sites*, p. 354.

82 H. Hamerow, *Rural Settlements and Society in Anglo-Saxon England* (Oxford: Oxford University Press, 2012), pp. 18–24, building on S. James, A. Marshall and M. Millet, 'An Early Medieval Building Tradition', *Archaeological Journal* 141 (1985), pp. 203–06.

83 W. Rodwell, 'Churches in the Landscape: Aspects of Topography and Planning', in M.L. Faull (ed.), *Studies in Late Anglo-Saxon Settlement* (Oxford: Oxford University Department for External Studies, 1984), pp. 1–23; J. Blair, 'Anglo-Saxon Minsters: A Topographical Review', in J. Blair and R. Sharpe (eds), *Pastoral Care before the Parish* (Leicester: Leicester University Press, 1992), pp. 226–66; Cramp, 'Monkwearmouth and Jarrow in Their European Context', p. 290.

84 F. Herschend, *The Idea of the Good in Late Iron Age Society* (Uppsala: Uppsala University Department of Archaeology and Ancient History, 1998), p. 176.

85 On this topic, see F. Herschend, 'The Origin of the Hall in South Scandinavia', *Tor* 25 (1993), pp. 175–99; Herschend, *The Idea of the Good*, pp. 49–51, 168–79; J. Walker, 'In the Hall', in M. Carver, A. Sanmark and S. Semple (eds), *Signals of Belief in Early England: Anglo-Saxon Paganism Revisited* (Oxford: Oxbow, 2010), pp. 83–102.

86 Herschend, *The Idea of the Good*, pp. 174–77; Herschend, *Journey of Civilisation*, pp. 90–91; J. Hines, 'No Place like Home? The Anglo-Saxon Social Landscape from Within and Without', in H. Sauer and J. Story (eds), *Anglo-Saxon England and the Continent*, Essays in Anglo-Saxon Studies 3/Medieval and Renaissance Texts and Studies 394 (Tempe: Arizona Center for Medieval and Renaissance Studies, 2011), pp. 25–27; Hamerow, *Rural Settlements*, p. 40.

87 Hope-Taylor, *Yeavering*, pp. 97–103; Morris, *The Church in British Archaeology*, p. 29.

88 S. Losco-Bradley and G. Kinsley, *Catholme: An Anglo-Saxon Settlement on the Trent Gravels in Staffordshire* (Nottingham: University of Nottingham, 2002), pp. 95–96; Hamerow, *Rural Settlements*, p. 39.

89 Of the type identified by John Blair ('Anglo-Saxon Pagan Shrines and their Prototypes', *Anglo-Saxon Studies in Archaeology and History* 8 (1995), pp. 1–28). See related discussion in Chapter 3 of this volume.

90 M.D.J. Bintley, 'Trees and Woodland in Anglo-Saxon Culture', unpublished PhD thesis, University College London, 2009; essays in Bintley and Shapland, *Trees and Timber*. See, for example, Post BX at Yeavering (Fig. 5.2).

91 For the incorporation of sacred trees into Christian practice, see Blair, *The Church in Anglo-Saxon Society*, pp. 374–83; Bintley, 'Trees and Woodland'; D. Hooke, *Trees in Anglo-Saxon England: Literature, Lore and Landscape* (Woodbridge: Boydell Press, 2010); essays in Bintley and Shapland, *Trees and Timber*.

92 D. Wilson, *Anglo-Saxon Paganism* (London: Routledge, 1992), p. 44; Herschend, *The Idea of the Good*, p. 13. Gregory's letter is quoted at the beginning of this chapter.

93 R. Daniels, 'The Church, the Manor and the Settlement: The Evidence from the Tees Valley, England', *Ruralia* 1 (1996), pp. 102–14; R. Faith, *The English Peasantry and the Growth of Lordship* (London: Leicester University Press, 1997), p. 167; T. Saunders, 'Class, Space and "Feudal" Identities in Early Medieval England', in W.O. Frazer and A. Tyrell (eds), *Social Identity in Early Medieval Britain* (London: Leicester University Press, 2000), pp. 222–24.

94 See, for example, David Parsons' discussion of the small excavated lordly chapel at Raunds, Northamptonshire ('Liturgical and Social Aspects', in A. Boddington (ed.), *Raunds Furnells: The Anglo-Saxon Church and Churchyard* (London: English Heritage, 1996), pp. 58–66). Peter Sawyer has estimated that Anglo-Saxon churches with a nave area of less than 45 m^2 should be considered private chapels for landowners (*Anglo-Saxon Lincolnshire* (Lincoln: The History of Lincolnshire Committee, 1998)): many small Anglo-Saxon churches fall into this category (H.M. Taylor, *Anglo-Saxon Architecture* (Cambridge: Cambridge University Press, 1978), vol. 3, p. 1033).

95 For tower-nave churches, see below, pp. 111–15. For private household chapels, see Shapland, 'Meanings of Timber and Stone', pp. 31–32.

96 See above, p. 100.

97 D. Bullough, 'Burial, Community and

Belief in the Early Medieval West', in P. Wormald, D. Bullough and R. Collins (eds), *Ideal and Reality in Frankish and Anglo-Saxon Society: Studies Presented to J.M. Wallace-Hadrill* (Oxford: Blackwell, 1983), p. 186. See Chapter 7 of this volume for broader discussion of landmarks of the dead. Here, I will discuss mausolea and related burial areas in their interrelationships with church buildings.

98 This was formalised by the Council of Nantes in 658.

99 *HE*, book 2, ch. 20.

100 Discussed in Cramp, 'Monkwearmouth and Jarrow in Their European Context', p. 289; Cramp, *Wearmouth and Jarrow Monastic Sites*, p. 352.

101 The evidence is summarised by Gittos, *Liturgy, Architecture, and Sacred Places*, pp. 98–100.

102 P. Hill, *Whithorn and St Ninian: Excavations of a Monastic Town, 1984–91* (Stroud: Whithorn Trust, 1997), pp. 164–70.

103 E. Cambridge and A.J.T. Williams, 'Hexham Abbey: Review of Recent Work and its Implications', *Archaeologia Aeliana* 5.23 (1996), pp. 76–80.

104 W. Rodwell, *Wells Cathedral: Excavations and Structural Studies, 1978–93* (London: English Heritage, 2001), vol. 1, pp. 75–83.

105 P.H. Sawyer, *Anglo-Saxon Charters: An Annotated List and Bibliography* (London: Royal Historical Society, 1968), no. 1185; S. Bassett, 'A Probable Royal Mausoleum at Winchcombe, Gloucestershire', *Antiquaries Journal* 65 (1985), p. 91.

106 Bassett, 'A Probable Royal Mausoleum'.

107 H.M. Taylor, 'St Wystan's Church, Repton, Derbyshire: A Reconstruction Essay', *Archaeological Journal* 144 (1987), pp. 205–45; M. Biddle and B. Kjølbye-Biddle, 'Repton and the Vikings', *Antiquity* 66 (1992), pp. 36–51.

108 Bassett, 'A Probable Royal Mausoleum'.

109 Biddle and Kjølbye-Biddle, 'Repton and the Vikings'.

110 C. Heighway and R. Bryant, *The Golden Minster: The Anglo-Saxon Minster and Later Medieval Priory of St Oswald at Gloucester* (York: Council for British Archaeology, 1999), pp. 62–67.

111 H.M. Taylor, 'The Anglo-Saxon Chapel at Bradford-upon-Avon', *Archaeological Journal* 130 (1973), pp. 141–71; D.A. Hinton., 'Recent Work at the Chapel of St Laurence, Bradford-on-Avon, Wiltshire', *Archaeological Journal* 166 (2009), pp. 193–209; D.A. Hinton, 'The Saxon Chapel at Bradford-on-Avon, Wiltshire', in S.L. Keefer, K.L. Jolly and C.E. Karkov (eds), *Cross and Cruciform in the Anglo-Saxon World: Studies to Honor the Memory of Timothy Reuter* (Morgantown: West Virginia University Press, 2010), pp. 319–39.

112 Hinton, 'Recent Work at the Chapel of St Laurence'.

113 R. Gem, 'A Recession in English Architecture during the Early Eleventh Century, and its Effect on the Development of the Romanesque Style', *Journal of the British Archaeological Association* 3.38 (1975), p. 37.

114 Their development has recently been surveyed (M.J. Johnson, *The Roman Imperial Mausoleum in Late Antiquity* (Cambridge: Cambridge University Press, 2009)). These structures profoundly influenced the architecture of Christian tombs of the highest possible status, including those of Mary and Jesus: see n. 18, above.

115 Johnson, *The Roman Imperial Mausoleum*, pp. 196–97. The late fourth-century 'Probus' mausoleum to the east of Old St Peter's in Rome is another early Christian example of this type (Gittos, *Liturgy, Architecture, and Sacred Places*, p. 64).

116 Gem, 'Towards an Iconography', p. 9; Krautheimer, *Early Christian and Byzantine Architecture*, pp. 76–80. For wider discussion of the profound influence of Carolingian royal practice on late Anglo-Saxon England, see R. Deshman, 'Kingship and Christology in Ottonian and Anglo-Saxon Art', *Frühmittelalterliche Studien* 10 (1976), pp. 367–405 and essays in D. Parsons (ed.), *Tenth Century Studies: Essays in Commemoration of the Millennium of the Council of Winchester and the Regularis Concordia* (Chichester: Phillimore, 1975) and D. Rollason, C. Leyser and H. Williams (eds), *England and the Continent in the Tenth Century: Studies in Honour of Wilhelm Levison* (Turhout: Brepols, 2011).

117 Gem, 'A Recession in English Architecture', p. 37.
118 Bullough, 'Burial, Community and Belief', p. 196; Blair, *The Church in Anglo-Saxon Society*, pp. 53, 57.
119 Carver, 'Why that? Why there? Why then?', pp. 6–9; Herschend, *Journey of Civilisation*, pp. 64–65.
120 Johnson, *The Roman Imperial Mausoleum*, p. 158.
121 E.A Fisher, *Anglo-Saxon Towers: An Architectural and Historical Study* (Newton Abbot: David and Charles, 1969). Gittos, *Liturgy, Architecture, and Sacred Places*, pp. 172–74 is a useful recent summary.
122 For example, N. Christie, 'On Bells and Bell-towers: Origins and Evolutions in Italy and Britain, AD 700–1200', *Church Archaeology* 5/6 (2004), pp. 13–30.
123 Summarised in R. Gem, 'Staged Timber Spires in Carolingian North-East France and Late Anglo-Saxon England', *Journal of the British Archaeological Association* 148 (1995), pp. 40–44.
124 T. Bell, 'A Roman Signal-station at Whitby', *Archaeological Journal* 155 (1998), pp. 303–22; M.G Shapland, 'In Unenvied Greatness Stands: The Lordly Tower-Nave Church of St Mary Bishophill Junior, York', *Church Archaeology* 14 (2010), pp. 1–15.
125 See full discussion of the poem, including this line, in Chapter 1 of this volume.
126 Bede's *Life of St Cuthbert*, in B. Colgrave (trans. and ed.), *Two Lives of Saint Cuthbert* (Cambridge: Cambridge University Press, 1940), ch. 40, mentions *specula Lindisfarnensis insulae*. Its foundations may have been identified through geophysical survey (O'Sullivan and Young, *Lindisfarne*, pp. 46–47).
127 According to William of Poitier's *Gesta Gvilleimi*, in R.H.C. Davis and M. Chibnall, *The Gesta Gvilleimi of William of Poitiers* (Oxford: Oxford University Press, 1998), pp. 144–45.
128 In the *Carmen de Hastingae Proelio* of Guy, Bishop of Amiens, dated 1068 (F. Barlow, *The Carmen de Hastingae Proelio of Guy, Bishop of Amiens* (Oxford: Oxford University Press, 1999), pp. 40–41).
129 K. Booth, 'The Roman *pharos* at Dover Castle', *English Heritage Historical Review* 2 (2007), pp. 8–21.
130 For what follows, see M.G. Shapland, 'Buildings of Secular and Religious Lordship: Anglo-Saxon Tower-nave Churches', unpublished PhD thesis, University College London, 2012. An additional thirteen tower-naves are known from high-status monastic contexts, where they functioned as high-status chapels, mortuary chapels and gate-towers, but they will not be considered here. On tower-naves more generally, see M. Audouy, B. Dix and D. Parsons, 'The Tower of All Saints' Church, Earls Barton, Northamptonshire: Its Construction and Context', *Archaeological Journal* 152 (1995), pp. 73–94; M.G. Shapland, 'St Mary's, Broughton, Lincolnshire: A Thegnly Tower-nave in the Late Anglo-Saxon Landscape', *Archaeological Journal* 165 (2008), pp. 471–519; Shapland, 'In Unenvied Greatness Stands'; Rodwell and Atkins, *St Peter's, Barton-upon-Humber*.
131 For Ælfric's remarkable tower, see C.R. Hart, *The Early Charters of Eastern England* (Leicester: Leicester University Press, 1966), p. 71 and R. Gem and L. Keen, 'Late Anglo-Saxon Finds from the Site of St Edmund's Abbey', *Proceedings of the Suffolk Institute of Archaeology and History* 35 (1984), p. 2.
132 Bishopstone, Sussex (G. Thomas, *The Later Anglo-Saxon Settlement at Bishopstone: A Downland Manor in the Making* (York: Council for British Archaeology, 2010)); West Cotton, Northamptonshire (A. Chapman, *West Cotton, Raunds: A Study of the Medieval Settlement Dynamics, AD 450–1450* (Oxford: Oxbow, 2010)); Bishops Waltham, Hampshire (E. Lewis, 'Excavations in Bishops Waltham 1967–78', *Proceedings of the Hampshire Fieldclub & Archaeological Society* 41 (1985), pp. 81–126) and a documented example at Bury St Edmunds, Suffolk (A. Williams, 'A Bell-house and a Burhgeat: Lordly Residences in England before the Norman Conquest', in A.C. Harper-Bill and R. Harvey (eds), *Medieval Knighthood IV: Papers from the Fifth Strawberry Hill Conference 1990* (Woodbridge: Boydell Press, 1992), pp. 225–26). The unpublished excavations at Ketton Quarry, Northamptonshire (I. Meadows, 'Ketton Quarry (SK 969 056)', Transactions of the Leicestershire

Archaeological and Historical Society 73 (1999), pp. 119–21) and St Mary's Hospital, Winchester (S. Roffey, 'Medieval Leper Hospitals in England: An Archaeological Perspective from St Mary Magdalen, Winchester', *Medieval Archaeology* 56 (2012), pp. 203–34) are further possible examples. A possible tenth-century timber tower at Springfield Lyons, Essex, may have functioned as a church (S. Tyler and H. Major, *The Early Anglo-Saxon Cemetery and Later Saxon Settlement at Springfield Lyons, Essex* (Chelmsford: Essex County Council, 2005)). Several towers, apparently of timber, are depicted on the Bayeux Tapestry, one of which is likely to have belonged to the important Godwine family residence of Bosham (D.M. Wilson, *The Bayeux Tapestry* (London: Thames & Hudson, 1985), plate 27; D.F. Renn, 'Burhgeat and Gonfanon: Two Sidelights from the Bayeux Tapestry', in M. Chibnall (ed.), *Anglo-Norman Studies XVI: Proceedings of the Battle Conference* (Woodbridge: Boydell Press, 1994), pp. 178–79). See also Chapter 3 of this volume.

133   G. Thomas, 'The Symbolic Lives of Late Anglo-Saxon Settlements: A Cellared Structure and Iron Hoard from Bishopstone, East Sussex', *Archaeological Journal* 165 (2008), pp. 334–98; Thomas, *The Later Anglo-Saxon Settlement at Bishopstone*.

134   D. Whitelock, *English Historical Documents c.500–1042*, 2nd edn (London: Eyre Methuen, 1979), pp. 468–69; Williams, 'A Bell-house and a Burh-geat'. In both his late eleventh-century *Glossary* (J. Zupitza (ed.), *Ælfrics Grammatik und Glossar* (Berlin: Weidmann, 1880), p. 314) and *Colloquy* (M. Voss, 'Altenglische Glossen aus MS British Library, Cotton Otho E.i', *Arbeiten aus Anglistik und Amerikanistik* 21 (1996), pp. 184–86), Ælfric translates *belhus* into Latin as *cloccarium*, 'bell/clock tower'.

135   P.H. Reaney, *The Place-Names of Essex* (Cambridge: Cambridge University Press, 1935), p. 24.

136   M. Dolley, 'Appendix II: The Numismatic Evidence', in H.M. Taylor, 'The Origin, Purpose and Date of Pilaster Strips in Anglo-Saxon Architecture', *North Staffordshire Journal of Field Studies* 10 (1970), pp. 21–48.

137   Tyler and Major, *The Early Anglo-Saxon Cemetery*.

138   Originally thought to have been copied from the Continent (debate summarised in M. Schapiro, 'A Note on the Wall Strips of Saxon Churches', *Journal of the Society of Architectural Historians* 18 (1959), pp. 123–25; Taylor, 'The Origin Purpose and Date of Pilaster Strips', pp. 21–48), they are now thought to be stone skeuomorphs of timber building (Taylor, *Anglo-Saxon Architecture*, vol. 3, pp. 915–27; Audouy et al., 'The Tower of All Saints' Church, Earls Barton', p. 89; Rodwell and Atkins, *St Peter's, Barton-upon-Humber*, p. 329). See also discussion in Chapter 3 of this volume.

139   Most recently by Bintley, 'Trees and Woodland', pp. 247–48.

140   Shapland, 'Meanings of Timber and Stone'.

141   The standard syntheses of Anglo-Saxon church towers remain Fisher, *Anglo-Saxon Towers* and Taylor, *Anglo-Saxon Architecture*, vol. 3, pp. 887–901, neither of whom satisfactorily tracks the towers' development.

142   See, for example, E. Tyrrell Green, *Towers and Spires: Their Design and Arrangement* (London: Wells Gardner, Darton and Co., 1908), pp. 21–23; R. Morris, *Churches in the Landscape* (London: J.M. Dent and Sons, 1989), p. 255; Christie, 'On Bells and Bell-towers', p. 26.

143   Taylor, *Anglo-Saxon Architecture*, vol. 3, p. 900. The Lincolnshire group of western towers are excluded due to their recent reinterpretation as a coherent Norman assemblage (D.A Stocker and P. Everson, *Summoning St Michael: Early Romanesque Towers in Lincolnshire* (Oxford: Oxbow Books, 2006)), as have the round towers of East Anglia due to the enduring confusion over their date and development (e.g. C.J.W. Messent, *The Round Towers to English Parish Churches* (Norwich: Fletcher and Sons, 1958); W.J. Goode, *East Anglian Round Towers and their Churches* (Lowestoft: Friends of the Round Tower Churches Society, 1982); S. Heywood, 'The Round Towers of East Anglia', in J. Blair (ed.), *Minsters and Parish Churches: The Local Church in Transition 950–1200* (Oxford: Oxford University Committee for Archaeology, 1988), pp. 169–77; S. Hart,

The Round Church Towers of England (Suffolk: Lucas Books, 2003)).

144 Based upon the analysis of settlement forms fossilised in First Edition Ordnance Survey maps. For a recent application of this method, see Stocker and Everson, *Summoning St Michael*, pp. 62–70.

145 R. Cramp, 'Anglo-Saxon Sculpture of the Reform Period', in Parsons, *Tenth Century Studies*, p. 192; Gem, 'Staged Timber Spires', p. 44.

146 Barnack's enclosure is clearly visible on early maps: at its centre, adjacent to the church, lies a manor house with a twelfth-century great hall (N. Pevsner, *Bedfordshire and the County of Huntingdon and Peterborough* (Harmondsworth: Penguin, 1968), p. 210).

Chapter 6: *Elizabeth Coatsworth*

1 *The Dream of the Rood*, in George Philip Krapp (ed.), *The Vercelli Book*, Anglo-Saxon Poetic Records 2 (New York: Columbia University Press, 1932), p. 64, ll. 95–100; translation by Gale R. Owen-Crocker.

2 An embroidered frieze, 68.5 metres (224 ft 8 in.) long.

3 Steles or stelai are upright stones or pillars.

4 This is still sometimes said of the small inscribed grave markers from Hartlepool, County Durham, but careful reading of the discovery reports offers no convincing evidence that they were meant to be below ground. See E. Okasha, 'The Inscribed Stones from Hartlepool', in J. Hawkes and S. Mills (eds), *Northumbria's Golden Age* (Stroud: Sutton Publishing, 1999), pp. 113–25.

5 See, for example, J.R. Allen, *Early Christian Symbolism in Britain and Ireland before the Thirteenth Century*, Rhind Lectures in Archaeology for 1885 (London: Whiting, 1887).

6 W.O. Stevens, *The Cross in the Life and Literature of the Anglo-Saxons*, Yale Studies in English 23 (New York: Henry Holt and Company, 1904), pp. 54–61.

7 R. Cramp, 'New Directions in the Study of Anglo-Saxon Sculpture', *Transactions of the Leicestershire Archaeological and Historical Society* 84 (2010), pp. 1–25.

8 Ibid., p. 11.

9 E. Coatsworth, *Corpus of Anglo-Saxon Stone Sculpture*, vol. 8, *Western Yorkshire* (Oxford: Oxford University Press for the British Academy, 2008).

10 C. Loveluck, 'The Archaeology of Post-Roman Yorkshire, AD 400 to 700: Overview and Future Directions for Research', in T.G. Manby, S. Moorhouse and P. Ottaway (eds), *The Archaeology of Yorkshire: An Assessment at the Beginning of the 21st Century*, Yorkshire Archaeological Society Occasional Paper No. 3 (Leeds: Yorkshire Archaeological Society, 2003), pp. 155–58 and Fig. 39; G.R.J. Jones, 'Early Territorial Organisation in Gwynedd and Elmet', *Northern History* 10 (1975), pp. 3–27.

11 M.L. Faull and S.A. Moorhouse (eds), *West Yorkshire: An Archaeological Survey to AD 1500*, 4 vols (Wakefield: West Yorkshire Metropolitan County Council, 1974), vol. 1, p. 24.

12 G.R.J. Jones, 'The Ripon Estate: Landscape into Townscape', *Northern History* 37 (2000), pp. 20–22.

13 M.S. Parker, 'The Province of Hatfield', *Northern History* 29 (1992), p. 42; N.J. Higham, 'Northumbria's Southern Frontier: A Review', *Early Medieval Europe* 14.4 (2006), pp. 391–418; Coatsworth, *Western Yorkshire*, pp. 46–49 and illus. 692–95. For Eyam, Bradbourne and Bakewell crosses, see R.E. Routh, 'A Corpus of the Pre-Conquest Carved Stones of Derbyshire', *Archaeological Journal* 94 (1937), pp. 1–42, plates IIa, VIIIa and b and XIV.

14 M.L. Faull and M. Stinson, *Domesday Book 30, Yorkshire*, 2 vols (Chichester: Phillimore, 1985), vol. 1, 316c, 9W 64.

15 Coatsworth, *Western Yorkshire*, pp. 14–15, for a summary of the literature on this topic.

16 Loveluck, 'The Archaeology of Post-Roman Yorkshire', Figs 37, 39–40; R.A. Hall, 'Yorkshire AD 700–1066', in T.G. Manby, S. Moorhouse and P. Ottaway (eds), *Archaeology of Yorkshire*, pp. 171–80 and Fig. 44.

17 Faull and Moorhouse, *West Yorkshire*, vol. 1, pp. 216–18.

18 Ibid., vol. 4, map 15.
19 Faull and Stinson, *Domesday Book*, vol. 1, Dewsbury: 299d, 1Y 17; Thornhill: 317d, 9W 115; Wakefield: 299d, IY 15.
20 Ibid., vol. 1, 299d, Wakefield: IY 15.
21 Ibid., vol. 1, 299d, Dewsbury: 1Y 17.
22 Faull and Moorhouse, *West Yorkshire*, vol. 4, map 19.
23 F. Thorp (ed.), 'The Yorkshire Archaeological Register, 1974', *Yorkshire Archaeological Journal* 47 (1976), pp. 1–14.
24 Faull and Moorhouse, *West Yorkshire*, vol. 1, pp. 203–09.
25 For summaries of current thinking, see H. Gittos, 'Christian Sacred Spaces and Places', in H. Hamerow, D.A. Hinton and S. Crawford (eds), *The Oxford Handbook of Anglo-Saxon Archaeology* (Oxford: Oxford University Press, 2011), pp. 824–42; T. Pickles, 'Church Organisation and Pastoral Care', in P. Stafford (ed.), *A Companion to the Early Middle Ages* (Chichester: Wiley-Blackwell, 2009), pp. 161–70. For a more detailed analysis, see J. Blair, *The Church in Anglo-Saxon Society* (Oxford: Oxford University Press, 2006), pp. 2–5, 75, 118–21, 182–227, 440–51.
26 Bede, *Historia Ecclesiastica*, in B. Colgrave and R.A.B. Mynors (eds), *Bede's Ecclesiastical History of the English People* (Oxford: Clarendon Press, 1969) (hereafter, *HE*), book 3, ch. 26.
27 Blair, *The Church in Anglo-Saxon Society*, pp. 72 n. 245; pp. 88–90, 214; *HE*, book 4, ch. 23.
28 T. Pickles, 'Anglo-Saxon Monasteries as Sacred Places: Topography, Exegesis and Vocation', in J. Sterrett and P. Thomas (eds), *Sacred Text – Sacred Space* (Leiden: Brill, 2011), pp. 35–55.
29 Faull and Moorhouse, *West Yorkshire*, vol. 1, pp. 148, 226.
30 Faull and Stinson, *Domesday Book*, vol. 2, SW M13 (note) and 373d, CW 23.
31 Ibid., vol. 1, 299d, Wakefield: IY 15.
32 W.G. Collingwood, *Northumbrian Crosses of the Pre-Norman Age* (London: Faber and Gwyer, 1927), Figs 13 (6), 90, 91.
33 Coatsworth, *Western Yorkshire*, pp. 129–39, 141–42, illus. 195, 199–201, 207, 218–19.
34 Ibid., p. 53.
35 G. Schiller, *Iconography of Christian Art*, vol. 1, *Christ's Incarnation, Childhood, Baptism, Temptation, Transfiguration, Work and Miracles*, trans. J. Seligman (London: Lund Humphries, 1971), plate 257. See also M. Clayton, *The Cult of the Virgin Mary in Anglo-Saxon England* (Cambridge: Cambridge University Press, 1990), pp. 143; also E. Kitzinger, 'The Coffin-Reliquary', in C.F. Battiscombe (ed.), *The Relics of St Cuthbert* (Durham: The Dean and Chapter of Durham Cathedral, 1956), pp. 248–64 for a discussion of the early Insular depictions, and Coatsworth, *Western Yorkshire*, p. 34 for a summary of views on the development of the theme.
36 Coffin of St Cuthbert: Coatsworth, *Western Yorkshire*, illus. 861; Book of Kells, Dublin, Trinity College Library MS 58 (A.I.6), fol. 7v: J.J.G. Alexander, *Insular Manuscripts, 6th to the 9th Century: A Survey of Manuscripts Illuminated in the British Isles*, vol. 1 (London: Harvey Miller, 1978), cat. 52, illus. 233; Franks Casket: L. Webster, 'The Iconographic Programme of the Franks Casket', in J. Hawkes and S. Mills, *Northumbria's Golden Age* (Stroud: Sutton Publishing, 1999), p. 232 and Fig. 19.2.
37 J. Hawkes, 'The Non-Crucifixion Iconography of the Pre-Viking Sculpture in the North of England', 2 vols, unpublished PhD thesis, University of Newcastle, 1989, vol. 1, p. 293; R.E. Routh, 'A Corpus of the Pre-Conquest Carved Stones of Derbyshire', plate XIVB.
38 Coatsworth, *Western Yorkshire*, pp. 117–19, illus. 166.
39 Ibid., pp. 135–39; *Vita Sancti Cuthberti Auctore Anonymo*, chap. 4, pp. 82–84, and *Vita Sancti Cuthberti Auctore Beda*, chap. 11, pp. 192–95 in B. Colgrave (trans. and ed.), *Two Lives of St Cuthbert* (Cambridge: Cambridge University Press, 1940); D.A. Bullough, 'A Neglected Early-Ninth-Century Manuscript of the Lindisfarne *Vita S. Cuthberti*', *Anglo-Saxon England* 27 (1998), pp. 105–38.
40 R. Cramp, 'The Evangelist Symbols and their Parallels in Anglo-Saxon Sculpture', in R.T. Farrell (ed.), *Bede and Anglo-Saxon England. Papers in honour of the 1300th anniversary of the birth of Bede, given at Cornell University in 1973 and 1974* (British Archaeological Reports, British Series 46) (Oxford: British Archaeological Reports, 1978), p. 118 and plate VIII.

41 Stockholm, Kungliga Biblioteket MS A.135, fol. 9v: D.M. Wilson, *Anglo-Saxon Art from the Seventh Century to the Norman Conquest* (London: Thames & Hudson, 1984), illus. 102.

42 London, British Library, Cotton MS Nero D.IV, fol. 25v: T.D. Kendrick, T.J Brown, R.L.S. Bruce-Mitford et al. *Evangeliorum Quattuor Codex Lindisfarnensis*, 2 vols (Olten and Lausanne: Urs Graf, 1956–60), vol. 2, pp. 149–51, 158–61, plate 22c.

43 M.P. Brown, *The Lindisfarne Gospels: Society, Spirituality and the Scribe* (London: British Library, 2003), p. 359.

44 J. Hawkes, 'Gregory the Great and Angelic Mediation: The Anglo-Saxon Crosses of the Derbyshire Peaks', in A. Minnis and J. Roberts (eds), *Text, Image, Interpretation: Studies in Anglo-Saxon Literature and its Insular Context in Honour of Eamonn Ó Carragáin* (Turnhout: Brepols, 2007), pp. 445–47 and Fig. 30.

45 Coatsworth, *Western Yorkshire*, p. 142.

46 Otley 1, ibid., pp. 215–19 and illus. 554–67, 575–76.

47 J.T. Lang, *Corpus of Anglo-Saxon Stone Sculpture*, vol. 6, *Northern Yorkshire* (Oxford: Oxford University Press, 2001), pp. 168–71, illus. 91–95.

48 Coatsworth, *Western Yorkshire*, pp. 129–33 and illus. 190–97; Hawkes, 'The Non-Crucifixion Iconography', vol. 1, pp. 91–95. For comparative examples outside England, see G. Schiller, *Ikonographie der Christlichen Kunst*, vol. 3, *Die Auferstehung und Erhöhung*, 2nd edn (Gütersloh: Gerd Mohn, 1986), pp. 202–10, 216–22 and plates 577, 580, 582–83, 616.

49 Kitzinger, 'The Coffin-Reliquary', pp. 248–64.

50 Wilson, *Anglo-Saxon Art*, plate 93.

51 For fuller discussions of this topic, see Coatsworth, *Western Yorkshire*, pp. 130–32; J. Hawkes, *The Sandbach Crosses: Sign and Significance in Anglo-Saxon Sculpture* (Dublin: Four Courts Press, 2002), pp. 56–62.

52 Coatsworth, *Western Yorkshire*, pp. 140–41 and illus. 215–17; J.T. Lang and S. Wrathmell, 'A Fragment of Anglian Sculpture from Dewsbury, West Yorkshire', *Antiquaries Journal* 77 (1997), pp. 375–80.

53 Coatsworth, *Western Yorkshire*, pp. 183–88 and illus. 416–24.

54 E. Coatsworth, 'The Iconography of the Crucifixion in Pre-Conquest Sculpture in England', 2 vols, unpublished PhD thesis, University of Durham, 1979, vol. 1, pp. 200–07; R. Cramp, *Corpus of Anglo-Saxon Stone Sculpture*, vol. 1, *County Durham and Northumberland* (Oxford: Oxford University Press, 1984), pp. 217–21.

55 Collingwood, *Northumbrian Crosses*, p. 40, Fig. 51.

56 C.R. Dodwell, *The Pictorial Arts of the West, 800–1200* (New Haven, CT: Yale University Press, 1993), p. 211, plate 203.

57 Coatsworth, *Western Yorkshire*, pp. 198–202, Fig. 16 and illus. 478–86, 488–92.

58 Ibid., p. 184; Leeds cross, illus. 489–90; Coatsworth, 'The Iconography of the Crucifixion', vol. 1, pp. 83–107.

59 Coatsworth, *Western Yorkshire*, p. 139 and illus. 208–11.

60 Ibid., pp. 142–45; D. Parsons, 'The Inscriptions', ibid., pp. 80–81; J. Higgitt, '*Inscription*', ibid., pp. 143–44.

61 Parsons, 'The Inscriptions', pp. 79–84 and 258–62; Higgitt, 'Inscription', pp. 256–57.

62 See related discussion of mausolea and similar churchyard grave sites in Chapter 5 of this volume. Discussion of the full range of landmarks associated with the dead is found in Chapter 7 of this volume.

63 Coatsworth, *Western Yorkshire*, pp. 147–48 and illus. 237–39.

64 R. Cramp, 'Schools of Mercian Sculpture', in A. Dornier (ed.), *Mercian Studies* (Leicester: Leicester University Press, 1977), pp. 91–233, Fig. 57c.

65 Coatsworth, *Western Yorkshire*, pp. 38, 147–48.

66 J.T. Lang, 'The Hogback: A Viking Colonial Monument', in S.C. Hawkes, J. Campbell and D. Brown (eds), *Anglo-Saxon Studies in Archaeology and History*, 3 (Oxford: Oxford University Committee for Archaeology, 1984), pp. 85–176, esp. pp. 101, 130; R. Cramp, *Grammar of Anglo-Saxon Ornament: A General Introduction to the Corpus of Anglo-Saxon Stone Sculpture* (Oxford: Oxford University Press, 1991), Fig. 6i.

67 J.T. Lang, 'Hogbacks in North-Eastern England', unpublished MA thesis: University of Durham, 1967; Lang, 'The Hogback: A Viking Colonial Monument'.

68 Coatsworth, *Western Yorkshire*, p. 214 and illus. 546–51; J.T. Lang, *Corpus of Anglo-Saxon Stone Sculpture*, vol. 3, *York and Eastern Yorkshire* (Oxford: Oxford University Press, 1991), illus. 133, 138.

69 Faull and Moorhouse, *West Yorkshire*, p. 218.

70 Blair, *The Church in Anglo-Saxon Society*, pp. 72–73, 84–85.

71 For additional discussion of these landmarks of the dead, see Chapter 7 in this volume.

72 Coatsworth, *Western Yorkshire*, pp. 267–68 and illus. 773–76.

73 R.N. Bailey and R. Cramp, *Corpus of Anglo-Saxon Stone Sculpture*, vol. 2, *Cumberland, Westmorland, and Lancashire-North-of-the-Sands* (Oxford: Oxford University Press, 1988), illus. 5, 8, 584–85.

74 Lang, *Northern Yorkshire*, illus. 311–14; Lang, *York and Eastern Yorkshire*, illus. 457, 563.

75 Coatsworth, *Western Yorkshire*, pp. 103–04.

76 Ibid., Appendix A, p. 284.

77 Ibid., pp. 146–47 and illus. 235–36.

78 I.D. Margary, *Roman Roads in Britain*, rev. edn (London: J. Baker, 1967).

79 Coatsworth, *Western Yorkshire*, Fig. 3.

80 Ibid., pp. 43, 48, 54, 103–04, 147, 162–64, 229–30, 284.

81 Blair, *The Church in Anglo-Saxon Society*, p. 152.

82 Coatsworth, *Western Yorkshire*, pp. 251–52, illus. 704–07. See also R.N. Bailey, *Corpus of Anglo-Saxon Stone Sculpture*, vol. 9, *Cheshire and Lancashire* (Oxford: Oxford University Press, 2010), pp. 172–73.

83 Coatsworth, *Western Yorkshire*, pp. 266–67 and illus. 769–72.

84 Ibid., Stansfield: p. 253 and illus. 717–20; Otley 3: p. 221 and illus. 579–82; Ilkley 3: pp. 171–72 and illus. 361–64; Brompton 3 and Kirklevington 3: Lang, *Northern Yorkshire*, illus. 361–64, 579, 581.

85 The following is largely based on Parsons, 'The Inscriptions', pp. 79–84.

86 Ibid., p. 84.

87 Other examples are sculptures from Urswick, Lancashire, and Alnmouth, Northumberland (Bailey and Cramp, *Cumberland, Westmorland and Lancashire-north-of-the-Sands*, pp. 148–50 and illus. 565; Cramp, *Durham and Northumberland*, vol. 1, pp. 161–62, and vol. 2, plate 157.

88 See, for example, J. Hawkes, 'Reading Stone', in C.E. Karkov and F. Orton (eds), *Theorizing Anglo-Saxon Stone Sculpture* (Morgantown: West Virginia University Press, 2003), pp. 5–30, plates 1–4.

89 Cramp, 'New Directions', p. 19.

90 Cramp, *Durham and Northumberland*, Hexham 1, pp. 174–76, plates 167–71, and plate 172, illus. 909.

91 C. Neuman de Vegvar, 'Converting the Anglo-Saxon Landscape: Crosses and their Audiences', in A.J. Minnis and J. Roberts (eds), *Text, Image, Interpretation: Studies in Anglo-Saxon Literature and its Insular Context in Honour of Éamonn Ó Carragáin* (Turnhout: Brepols, 2007), pp. 407–30.

92 For the impact of Rogation-tide rituals on the laity, see Joyce Hill, 'The Liturgy and the Laity', in Gale R. Owen-Crocker and Brian W. Schneider (eds), *The Anglo-Saxons: The World through their Eyes*, British Archaeological Reports, British Series 595 (Oxford: Archaeopress, 2014), pp. 61–63.

93 Cramp, 'New Directions', p. 19; R. Cramp, *Corpus of Anglo-Saxon Stone Sculpture*, vol. 5, *South-west England* (Oxford: Oxford University Press, 2006), pp. 42–48, 71–72.

94 Cramp, *Durham and Northumberland*, pp. 3–5.

95 Michael Hare, 'Hemming's Crosses', in Gale R. Owen-Crocker and Susan D. Thompson (eds), *Towns and Topography (Essays in Memory of David H. Hill)* (Oxford: Oxbow Books, 2014), pp. 26–36.

96 Coatsworth, *Western Yorkshire*, pp. 73–74.

97 For this and other relevant references, see Blair, *The Church in Anglo-Saxon Society*, p. 227.

98 Ibid., pp. 478–80.

Chapter 7: *Sarah Semple and Howard Williams*

1 *Beowulf*, in Elliott van Kirk Dobbie (ed.), *Beowulf and Judith*, Anglo-Saxon Poetic Records 4 (New York: Columbia University Press, 1953), pp. 96–97, ll. 3137–49; translation from M. Alexander, *Beowulf: A Verse Translation* (Harmondsworth: Penguin, 1973).

2 See, for example, papers in D. Hooke, *The Landscape of Anglo-Saxon England* (Leicester: Leicester University Press, 1989); N. Higham and M. Ryan (eds), *The Landscape Archaeology of Anglo-Saxon England* (Martlesham: Boydell and Brewer, 2010).

3 Such as S. Lucy and A. Reynolds (eds), *Burial in Early Medieval England and Wales*, Society for Medieval Archaeology 17 (London: Society for Medieval Archaeology, 2002); S. Semple and H. Williams (eds), *Early Medieval Mortuary Practices: New Perspectives*, Anglo-Saxon Studies in Archaeology and History 14 (Oxford: Oxford University Press, 2007).

4 See W.J. Blair, *The Church in Anglo-Saxon Society* (Oxford: Oxford University Press, 2005); D. Hadley, 'The Garden Gives Up its Secret: The Developing Relationship between Rural Settlements and Cemeteries c.800–1100', *Anglo-Saxon Studies in Archaeology and History* 14 (2007), pp. 194–203; G. Astill, 'Anglo-Saxon Attitudes: How Should Post-AD 700 Burials Be Interpreted?', in D. Sayer and H. Williams (eds), *Mortuary Practices and Social Identities in the Middle Ages* (Exeter: University of Exeter Press, 2009), pp. 222–36; see also papers in J. Buckberry and A. Cherryson (eds), *Burial in Later Anglo-Saxon England c.650–100 AD* (Oxford: Oxbow Books, 2010).

5 See S. Semple, 'Burials and Political Boundaries in the Avebury Region, North Wiltshire', *Anglo-Saxon Studies in Archaeology and History* 12 (2003), pp. 72–91; S. Semple, 'Polities and Princes AD 400–800: New Perspectives on the Funerary Landscape of the South Saxon Kingdom', *Oxford Journal of Archaeology* 27.4 (2008), pp. 407–29; H. Williams, 'Ancient Landscapes and the Dead: The Reuse of Prehistoric and Roman Monuments as Early Anglo-Saxon Burial Sites', *Medieval Archaeology* 41 (1997), pp. 1–32; H. Williams, 'Placing the Dead: Investigating the Location of Wealthy Barrow Burials in Seventh Century England', in M. Rundkvist (ed.), *Grave Matters: Eight Studies of First Millennium AD Burials in Crimea, England and Southern Scandinavia*, British Archaeological Reports, International Series 781 (Oxford: Archaeopress, 1999), pp. 57–86; H. Williams, *Death and Memory in Early Medieval Britain* (Cambridge: Cambridge University Press, 2006).

6 See, for example, M.O.H. Carver (ed.), *A Seventh-Century Princely Burial Ground and its Context* (London: British Museum, 2005); H. Williams, 'Death, Memory and Time: A Consideration of the Mortuary Practices at Sutton Hoo', in C. Humphrey and W.M. Ormrod (eds), *Time in the Medieval World* (Woodbridge: York Medieval Press, 2001), pp. 35–72.

7 Williams, 'Ancient Landscapes'; S. Semple, *Perceptions of the Prehistoric in Anglo-Saxon England: Ritual, Religion and Rulership in the Landscape* (Oxford: Oxford University Press, 2013), pp. 13–62.

8 Hadley, 'The Garden Gives up its Secrets', pp. 200–01.

9 See discussions in Williams, *Death and Memory*.

10 J.Y. Akerman, 'Report on Researches in an Anglo-Saxon Cemetery at Long Wittenham, Berkshire, in 1859', *Archaeologia* 38 (1860), p. 327.

11 J.Y. Akerman, 'An Account on Researches in Anglo-Saxon Cemeteries at Filkins, and at Broughton Poggs, Oxon.', *Archaeologia* 37 (1857), p. 145.

12 J.M. Kemble, 'Notices of Heathen Interment in the Codex Diplomaticus', *Archaeological Journal* 14 (1857), p. 122.

13 R.C. Neville, *Saxon Obsequies Illustrated by Ornaments and Weapons: Discovered by the Hon. R.C. Neville in a Cemetery near Little Wilbraham, Cambridgeshire, during the Autumn of 1851, with Coloured Lithographic Plates* (London: J. Murray, 1852), p. 5; J.Y. Akerman, *Remains of Pagan Saxondom* (London: J.R. Smith, 1855).

14 See, for example, E.T. Leeds, *The Archaeology of the Anglo-Saxon Settlements* (Oxford: Clarendon Press, 1913); E.T. Leeds,

Early Anglo-Saxon Art and Archaeology (Oxford: Clarendon Press, 1936); J.N.L. Myres, *Anglo-Saxon Pottery and the Settlement of England* (Oxford: Clarendon Press, 1969).

15 Such as Myres, *Pottery and Settlement*.

16 J.N.L. Myres and B. Green, *The Anglo-Saxon Cemeteries of Caistor-by-Norwich and Markshall, Norfolk* (London: Society of Antiquaries, 1973).

17 Myres, *Pottery and Settlement*.

18 D.J. Bonney, 'Pagan Saxon Burials and Boundaries in Wiltshire', *Wiltshire Archaeological and Natural History Magazine* 61 (1966), pp. 25–30.

19 A. Goodier, 'The Formation of Boundaries in Anglo-Saxon England: A Statistical Study', *Medieval Archaeology* 28 (1984), pp. 1–21.

20 See, for example, E. O'Brien, *Post-Roman Britain to Anglo-Saxon England: Burial Practices Reviewed*, British Archaeological Reports, British Series 289 (Oxford: British Archaeological Reports, 1999); A. Reynolds, *Anglo-Saxon Deviant Burial Customs* (Oxford: Oxford University Press, 2009); Semple, 'Burial and Boundaries'; Williams, 'Placing the Dead'.

21 See, for example, S.J. Brookes, 'Walking with Anglo-Saxons: Landscapes of the Dead in Early Anglo-Saxon Kent', in Semple and Williams, *Early Medieval Mortuary Practices*, pp. 143–53; S. Lucy, *The Early Anglo-Saxon Cemeteries of East Yorkshire*, British Archaeological Reports, British Series 272 (Oxford: British Archaeological Reports, 1998); Williams, *Death and Memory*; M. Chester-Kadwell, *Early Anglo-Saxon Communities in the Landscape of Norfolk*, British Archaeological Reports, British Series 481 (Oxford: Archaeopress, 2009).

22 See M. Lewis, A. Richardson and D. Williams, 'Things of this World: Portable Antiquities and their Potential', in M. Clegg Hyer and G.R. Owen-Crocker (eds), *The Material Culture of Daily Living in the Anglo-Saxon World* (Liverpool: Liverpool University Press, 2011), pp. 231–57.

23 For example, for Norfolk, see Chester-Kadwell, *Anglo-Saxon Communities*; for finds north of the Humber, see R. Collins, 'Recent Discoveries of Early Anglian Material Culture in the North East', *Medieval Archaeology* 54 (2010), pp. 386–90.

24 R. Morris, *Churches in the Landscape* (London: J.M. Dent and Sons, 1989); Blair, *The Church in Anglo-Saxon Society*; Hadley, 'The Garden Gives up its Secrets', pp. 193–204; R. Morris, 'Local Churches in the Anglo-Saxon Countryside', in H. Hamerow, D.A. Hinton and S. Crawford (eds), *The Oxford Handbook of Archaeology* (Oxford: Oxford University Press, 2011), pp. 172–97.

25 Reynolds, *Deviant Burial Customs*; Semple, *Perceptions of the Prehistoric*, pp. 193–223.

26 For a full discussion, see Chapter 6 in this volume.

27 M.O.H. Carver, 'Why That, Why There, Why Then? The Politics of Early Medieval Monumentality', in H. Hamerow and A. MacGregor (eds), *Image and Power in Early Medieval British Archaeology: Essays in Honour of Rosemary Cramp* (Oxford: Oxbow Books, 2001), pp. 1–22; M.O.H. Carver, 'Reflections on the Meaning of Anglo-Saxon Barrows', in Lucy and Reynolds, *Burial in Early Medieval England and Wales*, pp. 132–43.

28 See, for example, S. Turner, *Making a Christian Landscape: The Countryside in Early Medieval Cornwall, Devon and Wessex* (Exeter: University of Exeter Press, 2006).

29 See N. Edwards, 'Rethinking the Pillar of Eliseg', *Antiquaries Journal* 89 (2009), pp. 143–78; H. Williams, 'Remembering Elites: Early Medieval Stone Crosses as Commemorative Technologies', in S. Kleingärtner, S. Pedersen and L. Matthes (eds), *Archäologie in Schleswig: 'Det 61. Internationale Sachsensymposion 2010'*, Haderslev, Denmark (Neumünster: Wachholtz/Museum Sønderjyllands, 2011), pp. 13–32.

30 S. Semple, 'A Fear of the Past: The Place of the Prehistoric Burial Mound in the Ideology of Middle and Later Anglo-Saxon England', *World Archaeology* 30.1 (1998), pp. 109–26; Semple, 'Burials and Boundaries'; Semple, *Perceptions of the Prehistoric*.

31 Carver, *Princely Burial Ground*; Williams, 'Death, Memory and Time'; Williams, *Death and Memory*.

32 H. Härke, 'Cemeteries as Places of Power', in M. De Iong, F. Theuws and C. van

Rhijn (eds), *Topographies of Power in the Early Middle Ages* (Leiden: Brill, 2001), pp. 9–10.

33 N. Price, 'Passing into Poetry: Viking-Age Mortuary Drama and the Origins of Norse Mythology', *Medieval Archaeology* 54 (2010), pp. 123–56.

34 Williams, *Death and Memory*, pp. 55–65, 158–62.

35 Williams, 'Ancient Landscapes'; H. Williams, 'Assembling the Dead', in A. Pantos and S. Semple (eds), *Assembly Places and Practices in Medieval Europe* (Dublin: Four Courts Press, 2004), pp. 109–34; J. Blair, 'Anglo-Saxon Pagan Shrines and their Prototypes', *Anglo-Saxon Studies in Archaeology and History* 8 (1995), pp. 1–28.

36 A. Down and M. Welch, *Chichester Excavations*, vol. 7, *Apple Down and the Mardens* (London: Phillimore, 1990).

37 A.C. Hogarth, 'Structural Features in Anglo-Saxon Graves', *Archaeological Journal* 130 (1973), pp. 104–19.

38 A. Wessman and H. Williams, 'Building for the Cremated Dead', in J.I. Cerezo-Román, A. Wessman and H. Williams (eds), *Archaeologies of Cremation: Death and Fire in Europe's Past* (forthcoming).

39 Down and Welch, *Chichester Excavations*, p. 29.

40 Ibid., p. 15.

41 M. Gardiner, 'The Sophistication of Anglo-Saxon Timber Buildings', in M.D.J. Bintley and M.G. Shapland (eds), *Trees and Timber in the Anglo-Saxon World* (Oxford: Oxford University Press, 2013), pp. 45–77.

42 J. Shephard, 'The Social Identity of the Individual in Isolated Barrows and Barrow Cemeteries in Anglo-Saxon England', in B. Burnham and J. Kingsbury (eds), *Space, Hierarchy and Society: Interdisciplinary Studies in Social Area Analysis*, British Archaeological Reports, International Series 59 (Oxford: British Archaeological Reports, 1979), pp. 47–79.

43 P. Struth and B. Eagles, 'An Anglo-Saxon Barrow Cemetery in Greenwich Park', in P. Pattison, D. Field and S. Ainsworth (eds), *Patterns of the Past: Essays in Landscape Archaeology for Christopher Taylor* (Oxford: Oxbow Books, 1999), pp. 37–52.

44 Williams, 'Death, Memory and Time'.

45 J.R. Mortimer, *Forty Year's Researches in British and Saxon Burial Mounds of East Yorkshire* (London: A. Brown and Sons, 1905); Lucy, *Cemeteries of East Yorkshire*, p. 118.

46 S.C. Hawkes and G. Grainger, *The Anglo-Saxon Cemetery at Finglesham, Kent* (Oxford: School for Archaeology, 2006).

47 D. Sayer, 'Laws, Funerals and Cemetery Organisation: The Seventh-Century Kentish Family', in H. Williams and D. Sayer (eds), *Mortuary Practice and Social Identities in the Middle Ages* (Exeter: University of Exeter Press, 2009), pp. 141–66.

48 Sayer, 'Laws, Funerals and Cemetery', pp. 160–66.

49 Ibid., p. 169.

50 Ibid.; D. Sayer, 'Death and the Family: Developing a Generational Chronology', *Journal of Social Archaeology* 10.1 (2010), pp. 59–91.

51 Sayer, 'Laws, Funerals and Cemetery'; Sayer, 'Death and the Family'.

52 B. Brugmann, 'Buckland Cemetery Chronology', in K. Parfitt and T. Anderson, *Buckland Anglo-Saxon Cemetery, Dover: Excavations 1994* (Canterbury: Canterbury Archaeological Trust, 2012), pp. 323–66; K. Parfitt and T. Anderson, *Buckland Anglo-Saxon Cemetery, Dover: Excavations 1994* (Canterbury: Canterbury Archaeological Trust, 2012), p. 372.

53 What follows is drawn and based upon the following publications: S. Sherlock and M. Simmons, 'A Seventh-Century Royal Cemetery at Street House, North-East Yorkshire, England', *Antiquity* 82.316 (2008), Project Gallery, June 2008; S. Sherlock, *A Royal Anglo-Saxon Cemetery at Street House, Loftus, North-East Yorkshire*, Tees Archaeology Monograph Series 6 (Hartlepool: Tees Archaeology, 2012).

54 H. Gittos, 'Resting in Peace: Churchyard Consecration and Sacred Spaces in Anglo-Saxon England', in Lucy and Reynolds, *Burial in Early Medieval England and Wales*, pp. 195–208; H. Gittos, *Liturgy and Architecture in Anglo-Saxon England* (Oxford: Oxford University Press, 2013).

55 H. Williams, 'Cemeteries as Central Places: Landscape and Identity in Early

Anglo-Saxon England', in B. Hardh and L. Larsson (eds), *Central Places in the Migration and Merovingian Periods*, Papers from the 52nd Sachsen Symposium (Lund: Almqvist, 2002), pp. 341–62; Williams, 'Assembling the Dead'; C. Hills and S. Lucy, *Spong Hill, Part IX, Chronology and Synthesis*, McDonald Institute Monographs (Cambridge: English Heritage, 2013).

56 Williams, 'Assembling the Dead'.

57 Hills and Lucy, *Spong Hill, Part IX*; contra R. Hoggett, 'Charting Conversion: Burial as a Barometer of Belief', in Semple and Williams, *Early Medieval Mortuary Practices*, pp. 28–37.

58 A. Sanmark, 'Living On: Ancestors and the Soul', in M.O.H. Carver, A. Sanmark, and S. Semple (eds), *Signals of Belief in Early England: Anglo-Saxon Paganism Revisited* (Oxford: Oxbow Books, 2010), pp. 158–80; see also Williams, *Death and Memory*.

59 H. Glass, P. Booth, T. Champion et al., *Tracks Through Time: The Archaeology of the Channel Tunnel Rail Link* (Oxford: Oxford Archaeology, 2011); S. Brooks and J. Baker, 'Folk Territories, Assembly and Territorial Geography in Early Anglo-Saxon England', in J. Carroll, A. Reynolds and B. Yorke (eds), *Power and Place in Later Roman and Early Medieval Europe* (London: British Academy, forthcoming).

60 Brookes and Baker, 'Folk Territories'.

61 C.J. Arnold, *The Anglo-Saxon Cemeteries of the Isle of Wight* (London: British Museums Publications, 1982), pp. 89–96.

62 Brookes and Baker, 'Folk Territories'.

63 A. Pantos, 'Assembly Places in the Anglo-Saxon Period: Aspects of Form and Location', unpublished DPhil thesis, University of Oxford, 2002; Semple, *Perceptions of the Prehistoric*, pp. 193–223.

64 B. Hope-Taylor, *Yeavering: An Anglo-British Centre of Early Northumbria*, Department of the Environment Archaeological Reports 7 (London: HMSO, 1977).

65 Ibid., Fig. 79; S. Lucy, 'Early Medieval Burial at Yeavering: A Retrospective', in P. Frodsham and C. O'Brien (eds), *Yeavering: People, Power and Place* (Stroud: Tempus, 2005), pp. 127–44.

66 I. Smith, 'Sprouston, Roxburghshire: An Early Anglian Centre of the Eastern Tweed Basin', *Proceedings of the Society of Antiquaries of Scotland* 121 (1991), pp. 261–94.

67 G. Hey, *Yarnton: Saxon and Medieval Settlement and Landscape: Results of Excavations 1990–96*, Thames Valley Monograph 20 (Oxford: Oxford Archaeology, 2004).

68 S. Crawford, 'Special Burials, Special Buildings? An Anglo-Saxon Perspective on the Interpretation of Infant Burials in Association with Rural Settlement Structures', in Krum Bacvarov (ed.), *Babies Reborn: Infant/Child Burials in Pre- and Protohistory*, British Archaeological Reports, International Series 1832 (Oxford: Archaeopress, 2008), pp. 197–204.

69 C. Scull, 'Foreign Identities in Burials at the Seventh-Century English Emporia', in S. Brookes, S. Harrington and A. Reynolds (eds), *Studies in Early Anglo-Saxon Art and Archaeology: Papers in Honour of Martin G. Welch*, British Archaeological Reports, British Series 527 (Oxford: Archaeopress, 2011).

70 See J. Lang, *York and Eastern Yorkshire: Corpus of Anglo-Saxon Stone Sculpture*, vol. 3 (Oxford: Oxford University Press, 1991). See also the findings in Chapter 6 of this volume.

71 B. Gilmour and D. Stocker, *St Mark's Church and Cemetery*, The Archaeology of Lincoln 13.1 (London: Council for British Archaeology for the Trust for Lincoln Archaeology, 1986).

72 Z. Devlin, 'Putting Memory in its Place: Sculpture, Cemetery Topography and Commemoration', in M.F. Reed (ed.), *New Voices on Early Medieval Sculpture in Britain and Ireland*, British Archaeological Reports, British Series 542 (Oxford: Archaeopress, 2011), pp. 32–41.

73 See Chapter 6 in this volume.

74 Carver, *Princely Burial Ground*.

75 O'Brien, *Post-Roman Britain*.

76 Williams, 'Remembering Elites'.

77 L. Webster, 'Taplow', in H. Beck, D. Geuenich and H. Steuer (eds), *Reallexikon der Germanischen Altertumskunde* (Berlin: De Gruyter, 2007), pp. 69–72.

78 Semple, 'Polities and Princes'.

79 S.J. Brookes, *Economics and Social Change in Anglo-Saxon Kent AD 400–900:*

Landscapes, Communities and Exchange, British Archaeological Reports, British Series 431 (Oxford: Archaeopress, 2007); see, too, discussion of roads in the Anglo-Saxon landscape in Chapter 2 of this volume.

80 T.M. Dickinson, 'The Formation of a Folk District in the Kingdom of Kent: Eastry and its Early Anglo-Saxon Archaeology', in R. Jones and S. Semple (eds), *Sense of Place in Anglo-Saxon England* (Donington: Shaun Tyas, 2012), pp. 147–67; T.M. Dickinson, C. Fern and A. Rogerson, 'Early Anglo-Saxon Eastry: Archaeological Evidence and the Development of a District Centre in the Kingdom of Kent', *Anglo-Saxon Studies in Archaeology and History* 17 (2011), pp. 1–86.

81 D. Rollason, *Northumbria 500–1100: The Creation and Destruction of a Kingdom* (Cambridge: Cambridge University Press, 2003).

82 Rollason, *Northumbria*, pp. 46–47

83 For further discussion of these movements and 'kingly meetings', see Chapter 4 of this volume.

84 J. Musty, 'The Excavation of Two Barrows, One of Saxon Date, at Ford, Laverstock, near Salisbury, Wiltshire', *Antiquaries Journal* 49.1 (1969), pp. 98–117.

85 G. Speake, *A Saxon Bed Burial on Swallowcliffe Down* (London: Historic Buildings and Monuments Commission for England, 1989).

86 Williams, 'Death, Memory and Time'.

87 Ibid.; Semple, 'Burials and Political Boundaries'; Semple, 'Polities and Princes'.

88 See refined dating put forward for elite female burials in J. Hines et al., *Anglo-Saxon Graves and Grave-Goods of the 6th and 7th Centuries AD: A Chronological Framework* (London: Society for Medieval Archaeology, 2013).

89 Speake, *Saxon Bed Burial*.

90 T.M. Dickinson, *Cuddesdon and Dorchester-upon-Thames, Oxfordshire: Two Early Saxon 'Princely' Sites in Wessex*, British Archaeological Reports, British Series 1 (Oxford: British Archaeological Reports, 1974).

91 H. Härke, 'A Context for the Saxon Barrow [on *Lowbury* Hill]', *Archaeological Journal* 151 (1994), pp. 158–211.

92 Härke, 'Saxon Barrow'; Williams, 'Ancient Landscapes'; Williams, 'Placing the Dead'; Williams, 'Death, Memory and Time'; Semple, 'Burials and Political Boundaries'.

93 For a discussion of churches and church architecture, see Chapter 5 in this volume.

94 R. Hall and M. Whyman, 'Settlement and Monasticism at Ripon, North Yorkshire, from the 7th to the 11th Centuries AD', *Medieval Archaeology* 40 (1996), pp. 62–150.

95 M. Biddle and B. Kjølbye-Biddle, 'Repton and the Vikings', *Antiquity* 66.250 (1992), pp. 36–51.

96 Hall and Whyman, 'Settlement and Monasticism', pp. 141–42, Fig. 36.

97 Turner, *Making a Christian Landscape*.

98 A. Coles, '"Tuns" by the Wayside', in R. Jones and S. Semple (eds), *Sense of Place in Anglo-Saxon England* (Donington: Shaun Tyas, 2012), pp. 243–59.

99 J. Montgomery, A. Evans, D. Powlesland and C.A. Roberts, 'Continuity or Colonization in Anglo-Saxon England? Isotope Evidence for Mobility, Subsistence Practice, and Status at West Heslerton', *American Journal of Physical Anthropology* 126 (2005), pp. 123–38; J. Montgomery, 'Passports from the Past: Investigating Human Dispersals Using Strontium Isotope Analysis of Tooth Enamel', *Annals of Human Biology* 37.3 (2010), pp. 325–46.

100 Montgomery, Evans, Powlesland et al., 'Continuity or Colonization'.

101 R. Brettell, J. Evans, S. Marzinzik, A. Lamb and J. Montgomery, '"Impious Easterners": Can Oxygen and Strontium Isotopes Serve as Indicators of Provenance in Early Medieval European Cemetery Populations?', *European Journal of Archaeology* 15 (2012), pp. 117–45.

102 G. Bonner, D. Rollason and C. Stancliffe, *St Cuthbert, His Cult and His Community to AD 1200* (Woodbridge: Boydell Press, 1989).

103 Ibid., pp. 103–22, 387–95, 437–46.

104 Bede, *Historia Ecclesiastica*, in B. Colgrave and R.A.B. Mynors (eds), *Bede's Ecclesiastical History of the English People* (Oxford: Clarendon Press, 1969), book 3, ch. 9–12; A. Thacker, 'Membra Disjecta: the Division of the Body and the Diffusion of

the Cult', in C. Stancliffe and E. Cambridge, *Oswald: Northumbrian King to European Saint* (Stamford: Paul Watkins, 1995), pp. 97–127.

105   Bede, *Historia Ecclesiastica*, book 3, ch. 9.

106   V. Thompson, *Dying and Death in Later Anglo-Saxon England* (Woodbridge: Boydell Press, 2004).

107   See Chapter 6 in this volume.

108   R. Cramp, *County Durham and Northumberland: Corpus of Anglo-Saxon Stone Sculpture*, vol. 1 (Oxford: British Academy, 1984).

109   J.L. Buckberry and D.M. Hadley, 'An Anglo-Saxon Execution Cemetery at Walkington Wold, Yorkshire', *Oxford Journal of Archaeology* 26 (2007), pp. 309–29.

110   Reynolds, *Deviant Burials*, pp. 243–47.

111   Ibid., p. 155.

112   Semple, *Perceptions of the Prehistoric*, pp. 195–207.

113   Reynolds, *Deviant Burials*, pp. 248–49; Semple, *Perceptions of the Prehistoric*, pp. 191–223. See related discussion of the perceptions of Roman ruins in Chapter 1 of this volume.

114   Semple, *Perceptions of the Prehistoric*, pp. 204–07.

115   Reynolds, *Deviant Burials*, p. 119.

116   N.G. Hill, 'Excavations on Stockbridge Down 1935–36', *Proceedings of the Hampshire Field Club* 13 (1937), pp. 247–59, plate 3; Reynolds, *Deviant Burials*, pp. 118–20.

117   D.M. Liddle, 'Excavations at Meon Hill', *Proceedings of the Hampshire Field Club* 12 (1933), p. 155.

118   H.P. Blackmore, 'On a Barrow near Old Sarum', *Salisbury Field Club Transactions* 1 (1894), pp. 49–51; Reynolds, *Deviant Burials*, p. 147.

119   B. Yorke, *Wessex in the Early Middle Ages* (Leicester: Leicester University Press, 1995).

120   S. Lucy, *The Anglo-Saxon Way of Death* (Stroud: Sutton Publishing, 2000), pp. 72–87; G.R. Owen-Crocker, *Dress in Anglo-Saxon England: Revised and Enlarged Edition* (Woodbridge: Boydell Press, 2004); P. Walton Rogers, *Cloth and Clothing in Early Anglo-Saxon England, AD 450–700* (York: Council for British Archaeology, 2007).

121   H. Williams, 'Transforming Body and Soul: Toilet Implements in Early Anglo-Saxon Graves', in Semple and Williams, *Early Medieval Mortuary Practices*, pp. 66–91.

122   B. Colgrave (trans. and ed.), *Felix's Life of St. Guthlac* (Cambridge: Cambridge University Press, 1956), ch. 18.

123   Ibid., ch. 20.

124   Thompson, *Dying and Death*, pp. 20–21.

125   Ibid., pp. 113–14.

126   A. Klevnäs, *Whodunnit? Grave Robbery in Anglo-Saxon England and the Merovingian Kingdoms*, British Archaeological Reports, International Series 2582 (Oxford: Archaeopress, 2013).

127   Semple, *Perceptions of the Prehistoric*, p. 127.

128   See overview in R.J. Bartlett, *Why Can the Dead do such Great Things? Saints and Worshippers from the Martyrs to the Reformation* (Princeton, NJ: Princeton University Press, 2013), ch. 8.

129   Ibid., p. 239.

130   See John Blair, 'The Dangerous Dead in Early Medieval England', in S. Baxter, C.E. Karkov, J.L. Nelson and D. Pelteret, *Early Medieval Studies in Memory of Patrick Wormald* (Aldershot: Ashgate, 2009), pp. 539–60.

131   Ibid.; R.J. Bartlett (trans. and ed.), *Geoffrey of Burton: The Life and Miracles of St Modwenna* (Oxford: Oxford University Press, 2002), pp. 196–99.

132   A. Meaney, *Anglo-Saxon Amulets and Curing Stones*, British Archaeological Reports, British Series 96 (Oxford: British Archaeological Reports, 1981), p. 138.

133   Ibid., p. 14.

134   Ibid., pp. 106–13, 131–47.

135   J.H.G. Grattan and C. Singer, *Anglo-Saxon Magic and Medicine* (London: Oxford University Press, 1952).

136   M. Jarvis, 'Baston, Hall Farm: Lincolnshire', *Medieval Settlement Research Group Annual Report* 8 (1993), p. 61.

Chapter 8: *Margaret Worthington Hill and Erik Grigg*

1 *Beowulf*, in Elliott van Kirk Dobbie (ed.), *Beowulf* and *Judith*, Anglo-Saxon Poetic Records 4 (New York: Columbia University Press, 1953), p. 97, ll. 3160–62. Translation by Gale R. Owen-Crocker.

2 P. Smith and P. Cox, *The Past in the Pipeline: Archaeology of the Esso Midline* (Salisbury: Trust for Wessex Archaeology, 1986); T. Malim, K. Penn, B. Robinson, G. Wait and K. Welsh, 'New Evidence on the Cambridgeshire Dykes and Worsted Street Roman Road', *Proceedings of the Cambridge Antiquarian Society* 85 (1996), pp. 27–122; K. Nurse, 'New Dating for Wat's Dyke', *History Today* 49.8 (1999), pp. 3–4; S. Bates, R. Hoggett and J. Schwenninger, 'An Archaeological Excavation at Devil's Ditch, Riddlesworth and Garboldisham, Norfolk', Norfolk Archaeological Unit, Norwich (unpublished excavation report 1436, 2008); L. Hayes and T. Malim, 'The Date and Nature of Wat's Dyke: A Reassessment in the Light of Recent Investigations at Gobowen, Shropshire', *Anglo-Saxon Studies in Archaeology and History* 15 (2008), pp. 147–79.

3 D.H. Hill and M. Worthington, *Offa's Dyke* (Stroud: Tempus, 2003; rev. 2009).

4 S. Keynes and M. Lapidge (trans. and eds), *Alfred the Great: Asser's Life of King Alfred and other Contemporary Sources* (Harmondsworth: Penguin, 1983), p. 71.

5 Bede, *Historia Ecclesiastica*, in B. Colgrave and R.A.B. Mynors (eds), *Bede's Ecclesiastical History of the English People* (Oxford: Clarendon Press, 1969), book 1, ch. 4.

6 M. Winterbottom (trans. and ed.), *Gildas: The Ruin of Britain and other Works* (London: Phillimore, 1978), ch. 15.

7 Reported in the Society of Antiquaries online newsletter SALON, issue 318 (April 2014).

8 A. Reynolds and A. Langlands, 'Social Identities on the Macro Scale: A Maximum View of Wansdyke', in W. Davies, G. Halsall and A. Reynolds (eds), *People and Space in the Middle Ages, 300–1300*, Studies in the Early Middle Ages 15 (Turnhout: Brepols, 2006), pp. 13–44; D. Tyler, 'Offa's Dyke: A Historiographical Appraisal', *Journal of Medieval History* 37 (2011), pp. 145–61.

9 A. Reynolds, *Later Anglo-Saxon England: Life and Landscape* (Stroud: Tempus, 1999), p. 82.

10 Note that other scholars give a higher percentage, but include major rivers that flow between the disconnected sections, whereas this figure only includes the built earthwork.

11 M. Worthington, 'Wat's Dyke: An Archaeological and Historical Enigma', *Anglo-Saxon Texts and Contexts*, ed. Gale R. Owen-Crocker, *Bulletin of the John Rylands University Library of Manchester* 79.3 (1997), pp. 177–96.

12 Hill and Worthington, *Offa's Dyke*.

13 J. Bradford and J. Morris, 'Notes and News', *Oxoniensia* 6 (1941), pp. 84–91; O.G.S. Crawford, *Archaeology in the Field* (London: Phoenix House, 1953), p. 240; J. Hunn, 'Kingston Bagpuize with Southmoor Bypass', *South Midlands Archaeology* 22 (1992), pp. 48–49; J. Hunn, 'A Note on the Excavation of Some Parish Boundaries in the Vale of the White Horse, Oxfordshire', *Oxoniensia* 58 (1993), pp. 309–13.

14 G. Grundy, 'Berkshire Charters', *Berks, Bucks and Oxon Archaeological Journal* 29 (1925), pp. 106–08. When a charter is cited within this chapter, the Sawyer number is given, named after the numbering system devised by Peter Sawyer (P. Sawyer, *Anglo-Saxon Charters: An Annotated List and Bibliography* (London: Offices of the Royal Historical Society, 1968)).

15 A. Russell, 'Hundred of Ock', in W. Page and P. Ditchfield (eds), *The Victoria County History of Berkshire*, vol. 4 (London: Dawsons, 1924), pp. 349–50.

16 G. Grundy, 'Berkshire Charters', p. 88.

17 D. Mattingly, *An Imperial Possession: Britain in the Roman Empire 54BC–AD409* (London: Penguin, 2006), p. 553.

18 R. White and P. Barker, *Wroxeter: Life and Death of a Roman City* (Stroud: Tempus, 1998).

19 See related discussion in Chapter 1 of this volume.

20 N.J. Higham, 'An Introduction' and S. Rippon, 'Landscape Changes in the Long Eighth Century', in N.J. Higham and M.J. Ryan (eds), *Landscape Archaeology of Anglo-Saxon*

England (Woodbridge: Boydell Press, 2010), pp. 1–21 and pp. 39–64, respectively.

21   H. Hamerow, 'Settlement Mobility and the "Middle Saxon Shift": Rural Settlements and Settlement Patterns in Anglo-Saxon England', *Anglo-Saxon England* 20 (1991), pp. 1–17.

22   D. Hill and A. Rumble, *The Defence of Wessex: The Burghal Hidage and the Anglo-Saxon Fortifications* (Manchester: Manchester University Press, 1996).

23   J. Baker, S. Brookes and A. Reynolds (eds), *Landscapes of Defence in the Viking Age: Anglo-Saxon England and Comparative Perspectives* (Turnhout: Brepols, 2013); J. Haslam, 'Daws Castle, Somerset, and Civil Defence Measures in Southern and Midland England in the Ninth to Eleventh Centuries', *Archaeological Journal* 168 (2011), pp. 195–226; Margaret Worthington Hill site visits and discussion with David Hill.

24   For further discussion of these later, planned *burhs*, see Chapter 9 of this volume.

25   For further discussion of burial areas within church enclosures, see Chapter 5 of this volume. For a discussion of the landscape of burial areas more generally, see Chapter 7 of this volume.

26   D. Farwell and T. Mollison, *Poundbury*, vol. 2, *The Cemeteries* (Dorchester: Dorset Natural History and Archaeology Society, 1993).

27   S. Lucy, *The Early Anglo-Saxon Cemeteries of East Yorkshire: An Analysis and Reinterpretation* (Oxford: J. and E. Hedges, 1998).

28   D. Bonney, 'Pagan Saxon Burials and Boundaries in Wiltshire', *Archaeological Magazine* 61 (1966), pp. 25–30.

29   S. Semple, 'Burials and Political Boundaries in the Avebury Region, North Wiltshire', *Anglo-Saxon Studies in Archaeology and History* 12 (2003), pp. 72–91.

30   C. Hollinrake and N. Hollinrake, 'The Abbey Enclosure Ditch and a Late-Saxon Canal: Rescue Excavations at Glastonbury 1984–1988', *Somerset Archaeology and Natural History* 136 (1992), pp. 73–94.

31   R. Cramp, 'Monastic Sites', in D.M. Wilson (ed.), *The Archaeology of Anglo-Saxon England* (Cambridge: Methuen, 1976), p. 204.

32   G.F. Bryant, *The Early History of Barton-upon Humber* (Barton-upon-Humber: Workers' Educational Association, 1994).

33   O. Rackham, 'Trees and Woodland in Anglo-Saxon England: The Documentary Evidence', in J. Rackham (ed.), *Environment and Economy in Anglo-Saxon England* (York: Council of British Archaeology, 1994), p. 8.

34   W.G. Hoskins, *The Making of the English Landscape* (London: Hodder and Stoughton, 1977 [1955]), p. 130; J. Barnatt and K. Smith, *English Heritage Book of the Peak District: Landscapes through Time* (London: Batsford/English Heritage, 1997), p. 80.

35   W.G. Hoskins, *Fieldwork in Local History* (London: Faber and Faber, 1967: repr. 1982), pp. 118–19; E. Pollard, M. Hooper and N. Moore, *Hedges* (London: Collins, 1974).

36   D. Whitelock (ed.), *English Historical Documents*, vol. 1, *c.500–1042* (London: Eyre & Spottiswoode, 1955), pp. 364–72; F.L. Attenborough, *The Laws of the Earliest English Kings* (New York: Russell and Russell, 1963), p. 49.

37   F. Liebermann (ed.), *Die Gesetze der Angelschsen*, vol. 1 (Halle: Max Niemeyer, 1903), pp. 444–53; trans. M. Swanton, *Anglo-Saxon Prose* (London: Dent, 1975), pp. 21–25.

38   D. Bonney, 'Early Boundaries in Wessex', in P. Fowler (ed.), *Archaeology and the Landscape: Essays for L.V. Grinsell* (London: John Baker, 1972), pp. 168–84; Rackham, 'Trees and Woodland in Anglo-Saxon England'.

39   Hoskins, *The English Landscape*, p. 30; Hoskins, *Fieldwork*, p. 124; W.G. Hoskins, *English Landscapes* (London: BBC, 1973), p. 43.

40   Hoskins, *The English Landscape*, pp. 24–25; P. Fowler, 'Agriculture and Rural Settlement ', in Wilson, *The Archaeology of Anglo-Saxon England*, p. 25.

41   S. Bassett, 'How the West Was Won: The Anglo-Saxon Takeover of the West Midlands', *Anglo-Saxon Studies in Archaeology and History* 11 (2000), pp. 107–18.

42   C. Taylor, *Dorset* (London: Hodder and Stoughton, 1970), pp. 72–75; Fowler, 'Agriculture and Rural Settlement', pp. 39–42; M. Wood, *Domesday: A Search for the Roots of England* (London: BBC, 1986), pp. 59–63; D.A. Hinton,

Discover Dorset: Saxons and Vikings (Wimborne: Dovecote Press, 1998), p. 20.

43   Wood, *Domesday*, pp. 57–59.

44   Hoskins, *The English Landscape*, p. 54; Hoskins, *Fieldwork*, pp. 140–42; Hoskins, *English Landscapes*, p. 38; Fowler, 'Agriculture and Rural Settlement', p. 26.

45   These reports and details of the project can be found at: http://humanities.exeter.ac.uk/archaeology/research/projects/title_84580_en.html [accessed 12 August 2014].

46   Fowler, 'Agriculture and Rural Settlement', pp. 32–34. See also Chapter 2 of this volume for a discussion of roads.

47   Hamerow, 'Settlement Mobility and the "Middle Saxon Shift"'.

48   P. Murphy, 'The Anglo-Saxon Landscape and Rural Economy: Some Results from Sites in East Anglia and Essex', in J. Rackham (ed.), *Environment and Economy in Anglo-Saxon England* (York: Council for British Archaeology, 1994), p. 24; J.E. Davey, *The Roman to Medieval Transition in the Region of South Cadbury Castle, Somerset* (Oxford: Archaeopress, 2005), pp. 122–23.

49   K. Steedman, 'Excavation of a Saxon Site at Riby Cross Roads, Lincolnshire', *Archaeological Journal* 151 (1994), pp. 212–306.

50   Hamerow, 'Settlement Mobility and the "Middle Saxon Shift"'; Barnatt and Smith, *English Heritage Book of the Peak District*, p. 57; H. Hamerow, *Early Medieval Settlements: The Archaeology of Rural Communities in Northern Europe, 400–900* (Oxford: Oxford University Press, 2002).

51   Hoskins, *Fieldwork*, p. 39; M. Green, *A Landscape Revealed: 10,000 Years on a Chalkland Farm* (Stroud: Tempus, 2000), p. 139.

52   Taylor, *Dorset*, pp. 51–54.

53   C. Grocock, 'Barriers to Knowledge: Coppicing and Landscape Usage in the Anglo-Saxon Economy', in N.J. Higham and M.J. Ryan (eds), *Landscape Archaeology of Anglo-Saxon England* (Woodbridge: Boydell Press, 2010), p. 37.

54   MWH personal experience in Shropshire.

55   Whitelock, *English Historical Documents c.500–1042*, p. 369.

56   Contemporary images exist for each of these activities, from pasturing of pigs in the forest to coppicing and harvesting wood for fences and fires; see the two eleventh-century Anglo-Saxon agricultural calendars discussed and illustrated in D. Hill, 'Agriculture through the Year', in Maren Clegg Hyer and Gale R. Owen-Crocker (eds), *The Material Culture of Daily Living in the Anglo-Saxon World* (Exeter: University of Exeter Press, 2011), pp. 14–15, 17. Coppicing is shown as a task for the month of June, grazing swine a task for September and fence-making or wood-piling near the fire a task for the month of November.

57   H. Braun, 'Some Earthworks of North-West Middlesex', *Transactions of the London and Middlesex Archaeological Society* 13 (1937), pp. 374–76.

58   P. Westgate, *Buckenham Castle: A Monograph* (Norwich: Mackley and Bunn, 1937), p. 23; N. Pevsner and B. Wilson, *The Buildings of England, Norfolk 1: Norwich and North-East* (Harmondsworth: Penguin, 1997), p. 102; L. Butler, 'Dark Age Archaeology', in M. Beresford and G. Jones (eds), *Leeds and its Region* (Leeds: Committee of the British Association for the Advancement of Science, 1967), pp. 97–100; T. Darvill, 'Landscapes – Myth or Reality', in M. Jones and I. Rotherham (eds), *Landscapes – Perception, Recognition and Management: Reconciling the Impossible?* (Sheffield: Wildtrack Publishing, 1998), pp. 11–13.

59   P. Remfry, *Buckenham Castles 1066 to 1649* (Worcester: SCS Publishing, 1997).

60   L. Cantor and J. Hatherley, 'The Medieval Parks of England', *Geography* 64.2 (1979), p. 71; Rackham, 'Trees and Woodland in Anglo-Saxon England', pp. 9–10.

61   C. Fox, *Offa's Dyke: A Field Survey of the Western Frontier-Works of Mercia in the Seventh and Eighth Centuries AD* (London: Oxford University Press, 1955).

62   Offa's Dyke Project, University of Manchester Extra-Mural Department; no longer active, archive with MWH.

63   Worthington, 'Wat's Dyke: An Archaeological and Historical Enigma', pp. 177–96.

64   H. Hannaford, 'An Excavation on Wat's Dyke at Mile Oak, Oswestry, Shropshire', *Transactions of the Shropshire Archaeological and Historical Society* 73 (1998), pp. 1–7.

65 Conversation between excavator and MWH.
66 Malim, 'Date and Nature of Wat's Dyke'.
67 Hill and Worthington, *Offa's Dyke*, pp. 117–18.
68 T. Lethbridge, 'Anglo-Saxon Remains', in L. Salzman (ed.), *The Victoria History of the County of Cambridgeshire and the Isle of Ely*, vol. 1 (London: Oxford University Press, 1938), p. 309; C. Phillips, 'Ancient Earthworks', in L. Salzman (ed.), *The Victoria County History of Cambridgeshire and the Isle of Ely*, vol. 2 (London: Oxford University Press, 1948), p. 9; Malim, Penn, Robinson, Wait and Welsh, 'New Evidence on the Cambridgeshire Dykes', pp. 65–67.
69 C. Fox and W. Palmer, 'Excavations in the Cambridgeshire Dykes', *Proceedings of the Cambridge Antiquarian Society* 24 (1921–22), pp. 21–53.
70 C. Fox and W. Palmer, 'Excavations in the Cambridgeshire Dykes', *Proceedings of the Cambridge Antiquarian Society* 27 (1924–25), p. 31.
71 T. Lethbridge and W. Palmer, 'Excavations in the Cambridgeshire Dykes', *Proceedings of the Cambridge Antiquarian Society* 30 (1927–28), pp. 78–96.
72 D. Hill, 'The Cambridgeshire Dykes: II: The Bran Ditch', *Proceedings of the Cambridge Antiquarian Society* 66 (1975–76), pp. 126–28.
73 J. Erskine, 'The West Wansdyke: An Appraisal of the Dating, Dimensions and Construction Techniques in the Light of Excavated Evidence', *Archaeological Journal* 164 (2007), pp. 80–108; P. Fowler, 'Wansdyke in the Woods: An Unfinished Roman Military Earthwork for a Non-event', in P. Ellis (ed.), *Roman Wiltshire and After: Papers in Honour of Ken Annable* (Devizes: Wiltshire Archaeological and Natural History Society, 2001), pp. 179–98.
74 G. Grundy, 'The Saxon Land Charters of Wiltshire (First Series)', *Archaeological Journal* 76 (1919), pp. 159–64; C. Fox and A. Fox, 'Wansdyke Reconsidered', *Archaeological Journal* 115 (1958), p. 14; D. Bonney, 'The Pagan Saxon Period c.500–c.700', in E. Crittall (ed.), *The Victoria County History of Wiltshire*, vol. 1, Part 2 (London: Oxford University Press, 1973), p. 478.
75 Grundy, 'The Saxon Land Charters of Wiltshire', pp. 190, 213–14, 241; J.E.B. Gover, A. Mawer and F.M. Stenton, *The Place-Names of Wiltshire*, English Place-Name Society 16 (Cambridge: Cambridge University Press, 1939), p. 17.
76 Smith, *The Past in the Pipeline*.
77 Fox, 'Wansdyke Reconsidered', pp. 19–20.
78 A. Burne, 'Ancient Wiltshire Battlefields', *Wiltshire Archaeological and Natural History Magazine* 53 (1950), p. 403.
79 Hill and Worthington, *Offa's Dyke*, pp. 139–41.
80 Whitelock, *English Historical Documents c.500–1042*, pp. 514–16.
81 Offa's Dyke Project archive with MWH.
82 L. Alcock, 'Aberford Dykes: The First Defence of the Brigantes?', *Antiquity* 28.111 (1954), pp. 147–54; S. Coffin, 'Linear Earthworks in the Froxfield, East Tisted and Hayling Wood District', *Proceedings of the Hampshire Field Club* 32 (1975), pp. 77–81; A. Fleming, 'Swadal, Swar (and Erechwydd?): Early Medieval Polities in Upper Swaledale', *Landscape History* 16 (1994), pp. 17–30.
83 R. Hankinson and A. Caseldine, 'Short Dykes of Powys and their Origins', *Archaeological Journal* 163 (2006), pp. 264–69.

Chapter 9: *Jeremy Haslam*
1 S. Keynes and M. Lapidge (trans. and eds), *Alfred the Great: Asser's Life of King Alfred and other Contemporary Sources* (New York: Penguin, 1983), para. 91.
2 Keith Lilley, 'Urban Landscapes and the Cultural Politics of Territorial Control in Anglo-Norman England', *Landscape Research* 24.1 (1999), p. 9.
3 Ibid.
4 *Lordship and Military Obligation in Anglo-Saxon England* (London: British Museum Publications, 1988), pp. 80–92; 'The Costs and Consequences of Anglo-Saxon Civil Defence, 878–1066', in J. Baker, S. Brookes and A. Reynolds (eds), *Landscapes of Defence in Early Medieval Europe* (Turnhout: Brepols, 2013), pp. 195–222.

5 'The North-west Frontier', in N.J. Higham and D. Hill (eds), *Edward the Elder* (London: Routledge, 2001), pp. 181–82. The political context of the formation of the *burhs* of the Burghal Hidage is emphasised by S. Keynes, 'Edward, King of the Anglo-Saxons', in Higham and Hill, *Edward the Elder*, pp. 58–60. See also G. Williams, 'Military and Non-military Functions of the Anglo-Saxon *burh*', in Baker, Brookes and Reynolds, *Landscapes of Defence in Early Medieval Europe*, pp. 134–35. The term '*burh*' here is used in the sense of a late Saxon fortified enclosure which has a strategic and administrative function within a particular historical context, whether on a new site or on one which reused earlier defences. Many (but not all) of these in the late ninth and early tenth centuries are argued in this chapter as having been new planted settlements which were urban by the standards of the time. The term has antecedents in earlier periods, and a complex set of variable meanings. Baker and Brookes have preferred to call these 'strongholds' ('From Frontier to Border: The Evolution of Northern West Saxon Territorial Delineation in the Ninth and Tenth Centuries', *Anglo-Saxon Studies in Archaeology and History* 17 (2011), pp. 104–19; *Beyond the Burghal Hidage: Anglo-Saxon Civil Defence in the Viking Age*, History of Warfare 84 (Leiden: Brill, 2013)); however, this term avoids any acknowledgement that these were founded within this historical context as new settlements. Baker and Brookes have, however, usefully discussed the issues involved in the use of this and other terms (*Beyond the Burghal Hidage*, pp. 37–41).

6 Lilley, 'Urban Landscapes', p. 10.

7 J. Haslam, *Urban–Rural Connections in Domesday Book and Late Anglo-Saxon Royal Administration*, British Archaeological Reports, British Series 571 (Oxford: Archaeopress, 2012), pp. 133–37; Haslam, 'The *burh* of Wallingford and its Context in Wessex', in J. Christie, O. Creighton, M. Edgeworth and H. Hamerow (eds), *Transforming Townscapes from Burh to Borough: The Archaeology of Wallingford, AD 800–1400*, Society for Medieval Archaeology 35 (London: Society for Medieval Archaeology, 2013), pp. 400–07; J. Haslam, 'The Burghal Hidage and the West Saxon *burhs*: A Reappraisal', forthcoming.

8 For a diametrically opposite view, see the recent publications of John Baker and Stuart Brookes, and comments thereon below (listed in n. 5).

9 M. Blackburn, 'The London Mint in the Reign of Alfred', in M.A.S. Blackburn and D.N. Dumville (eds), *Kings, Currency and Alliances: History and Coinage in Southern England in the Ninth Century* (Woodbridge: Boydell Press, 1998); M. Blackburn, 'Alfred's Coinage Reforms in Context', in T. Reuter (ed.), *Alfred the Great: Papers from the Eleventh-centenary Conferences* (Aldershot: Ashgate, 2003); Williams, 'Military and Non-military Functions', pp. 135–41.

10 E.g. M. Biddle and D. Hill, 'Late Saxon Planned Towns', *Antiquaries Journal* 51 (1971), pp. 70–85; M. Biddle, 'Towns', in D.M. Wilson (ed.), *The Archaeology of Anglo-Saxon England* (London: Methuen, 1976), pp. 99–150; M. Biddle, 'The Evolution of Towns: Planned Towns before 1066', in M.W. Barley (ed.), *The Plans and Topography of Medieval Towns in England and Wales*, Council for British Archaeology Research Report 14 (London: Council for British Archaeology, 1976).

11 Biddle, 'Towns', pp. 126–27.

12 Ibid., pp. 127–31.

13 D. Hill, 'Gazetteer of Burghal Hidage Sites', in D. Hill and A.R. Rumble (eds), *The Defence of Wessex: The Burghal Hidage and Anglo-Saxon Fortifications* (Manchester: Manchester University Press, 1996), pp. 189–231.

14 D. Whitelock, *English Historical Documents*, vol. 1, *c.500–1042*, 2nd edn (London: Eyre Methuen, 1979). In M.J. Swanton (trans. and ed.), *The Anglo-Saxon Chronicle* (London: Dent, 1996), Swanton lists the events as occurring in 913 (912), 920 (919) and 921 (920) (A) and 913 (D). However, the dates in Whitelock cited here are also those accepted by Frank Stenton, *Anglo-Saxon England*, 3rd edn (Oxford: Clarendon Press, 1971), pp. 327–29.

15 This model of the early development of Maldon will be more fully analysed and discussed at a later date. Middle Saxon occupation along the line of High Street is attested at 77–79 High

Street (Essex Historic Environment Records 46097). Significant middle and late Saxon settlement, which includes evidence of middle Saxon craft and industrial production, has been located at St Mary's (see Essex Historic Environment Records, Sites and Monuments Record Nos. 14743 and 46749). There are grounds for suggesting that St Mary's church could well have been a pre-Viking minster, and that the waterside area around it would have functioned as a minor *wic* (a middle Saxon trading centre). The archaeological work at 62–64 High Street has been summarised in S. Bassett, 'Final Interim Report on the Archaeological Investigation of the Site of 62–64 High Street, Maldon', unpublished report, 1972; typescript as Essex Historic Environment Records 7725. For summaries of the archaeological and other evidence relating to the *burhs*, see M.R. Eddy and M.R. Petchy, *Historic Towns in Essex* (Essex: Essex County Council, 1983), pp. 63–64; P. Brown, *The Maldon Burh Jigsaw* (Maldon: Maldon Archaeological Group Internal Publication, 1986); O. Bedwin, 'Early Iron-Age Settlement in Maldon: The Maldon *burh* and Excavations at Beacon Green', *Essex Archaeology and History* 23 (1992), pp. 10–24 and M. Medlycot, *Extensive Urban Survey: Maldon Historic Towns Assessment Report* (English Heritage and Essex County Council, 1999): http://archaeologydataservice.ac.uk/archiveDS/archiveDownload?t=arch-681-1/dissemination/pdf/Maldon/fulltext/Maldon_1999_Historic_Towns_Assessment_Report.pdf [accessed 31 August 2014]. The ditches on the northern side of the *burh* are discussed in R. Isserlin and P. Connell, 'A Previously Unknown Medieval Earthwork in Maldon: Excavation Behind the Moot Hall, 39 High Street, Maldon, 1991', *Essex Archaeology and History* 28 (1997), pp. 133–41.

16 I have pointed out elsewhere that *burhs* were often built and manned in sometimes remarkably short spaces of time: J. Haslam, 'King Alfred and the Vikings: Strategies and Tactics, 876–886AD', *Anglo-Saxon Studies in Archaeology and History* 13 (2005), pp. 132–33; see also comments on this point in Abels, 'The Costs and Consequences', pp. 201–02.

17 Haslam, *Urban–Rural Connections*, esp. pp. 70–81; Haslam, 'The Burghal Hidage and the West Saxon *burhs*', forthcoming. There is late evidence of heterogeneous tenure at Maldon; this will be discussed elsewhere.

18 This concept of the functional complementarity of different elements in the townscape as an ensemble has been used by the writer in relation to the analysis of the development of late ninth-century London by King Alfred (J. Haslam, 'The Development of London by King Alfred: A Reassessment', *Transactions of the London and Middlesex Archaeological Society* 61 (2010), pp. 109–43), as well as at Worcester (J. Haslam, 'Planning in Late Saxon Worcester', *Anglo-Saxon Studies in Archaeology and History* 19 (2014), pp. 153–72). A related call to recognise features of the urban landscape as an 'integrated entity' and as an 'ensemble' is made by Jeremy Whitehand ('Urban Landscapes as Ensembles', *Urban Morphology* 14.1 (2010), pp. 3–4).

19 Biddle, 'Evolution of Towns', p. 20.

20 J. Haslam, 'The Towns of Devon', in J. Haslam (ed.), *Anglo-Saxon Towns in Southern England* (Chichester: Phillimore, 1984), pp. 262–67; J. Haslam, 'The Development of Late Saxon Christchurch, Dorset, and the Burghal Hidage', *Medieval Archaeology* 53 (2009), pp. 103–04.

21 S. Keynes, 'King Alfred and the Mercians', in M. Blackburn and D. Dumville (eds), *Kings, Currency and Alliances: History and Coinage in Southern England in the Ninth Century* (Woodbridge: Boydell Press, 1998), pp. 1–45. These arguments are discussed more fully by the writer elsewhere: Haslam, 'King Alfred and the Vikings'; J. Haslam, 'Daws Castle, Somerset, and Civil Defence Measures in Southern and Midland England in the Ninth to Eleventh Centuries', *Archaeological Journal* 168 (2011), pp. 196–227; Haslam, *Urban–Rural Connections*, pp. 124–25, 133–37; Haslam, 'Burghal Hidage and the West Saxon *burhs*', forthcoming.

22 Baker and Brookes, *Beyond the Burghal Hidage*. Baker and Brookes have adopted a developmental model for the *burhs* of Wessex in which burghal formation is seen as extending over more than half a century in the late ninth and early tenth centuries in response solely to changing military circumstances. In doing this, they have lost sight of the formation of the *burhs* of the Burghal Hidage as a system brought into being

within the context of a particular set of historical and political circumstances, or as the outcome of broadly based political, economic or social agendas of King Alfred. For comments on the *burhs* of the Burghal Hidage as a system, which also contradict this series of assumptions, see Abels, 'Costs and Consequences', pp. 200–09. This series of arguments will be analysed in detail elsewhere (Haslam, 'Burghal Hidage and the West Saxon *burhs*', forthcoming).

23 This is based on a detailed analysis of the hidages of all the burghal territories in central Wessex in Haslam, *Urban–Rural Connections* (see references in the caption).

24 This evidence also directly contradicts the notion espoused by Baker and Brookes that the river Thames acted as a boundary in the later ninth century and into the tenth (Baker and Brookes, *Beyond the Burghal Hidage*, pp. 269–333, 397–403). This ignores the fact of the absorption of western Mercia to the north of the river under King Alfred's hegemony from c.880 (among other political considerations), and the development of London as a *burh* from this time. See further discussion in J. Haslam, 'King Alfred, Mercia and London, 874–86: A Reassessment', *Anglo-Saxon Studies in Archaeology and History* 17 (2011), pp. 120–46.

25 S. Keynes, 'Edward, King of the Anglo-Saxons', pp. 40–66.

26 For a convenient summary of this way of analysing diverse characteristics, see the entry in Wikipedia under 'Family resemblance'; see also C.J. Van Rijsbergen, *The Geometry of Information Retrieval* (Cambridge: Cambridge University Press, 2004), ch. 3 (http://www.dcs.gla.ac.uk/Keith/Chapter.3/Ch.3.html#REF.14) [accessed 31 August 2014].

27 This is in spite of assertions to the contrary by Baker and Brookes, who see the 'de novo' rectilinear *burhs* as forming later additions in the early tenth century to an earlier system of 'emergency *burhs*' (Baker and Brookes, *Beyond the Burghal Hidage*, pp. 123–28 and Fig. 24, pp. 397–403). The distinction implied by these arguments between the class of *burhs* described as 'de novo' and 'emergency' is, however, somewhat artificial and ultimately meaningless. It is a fundamental conclusion from the evidence examined in this paper that the *burhs* with a linear plan-form (the High Street type), as well as those with more rectilinear plan-form, were *all* 'de novo' at the time they were first laid out. The conclusion that the *burhs* of the Burghal Hidage and their interlocking and contiguous burghal territories were set out as a complete and contemporaneous system, demonstrated by the evidence discussed in this chapter, divests any meaning from the commonly used term 'emergency *burh*' as a distinct class. Either all the *burhs* were 'emergency *burhs*', or none of them was, and all of them were 'de novo' in terms of their function as part of a system, whether they were built on earlier defensive footprints or not.

28 Whitelock, *English Historical Documents*, p. 216.

29 These have been derived from Edina Digimap1:2500 maps of various dates prior to the 1920s (http://edina.ac.uk/digimap). Crown Copyright and Landmark Information Group Limited (2014). All rights reserved. The areas of the *burhs* as shown represent a 'maximum view' and include the areas occupied by the defensive banks as well as a zone occupied by a berm or berms (the space between bank and ditch, or between ditches) and a ditch or ditches (see Chapter 8 of this volume for further discussion of dykes and ditches). These are presented as topographical hypotheses which it should be the business of archaeologists to test. The archaeological and historical evidence relating to these places is in most cases summed up in the recent Extensive Urban Surveys, and in other sources. For a list of these EUS, and for links to those appearing online, see https://www.english-heritage.org.uk/professional/research/landscapes-and-areas/characterisation/townscape-character/. The English Heritage web site www.pastscape.org.uk also contains useful detailed information which supplements these sources. See also the gazetteer of Burghal Hidage sites given by Hill, 'Gazetteer of Burghal Hidage Sites', though the interpretation of the topography offered here is in many cases at variance to his. Many of the places are discussed in various chapters in Haslam, *Anglo-Saxon Towns in Southern England*, though none of the chapters in this volume is referenced in Hill's gazetteer.

Selected references and other comments on the topographical and archaeological evidence are given below in the Appendix.

30 For a discussion of 'ensembles' in town plans, see n. 18, above.

31 Haslam, *Urban–Rural Connections*, esp. pp. 72–81; see also a discussion of some of these points in Williams, 'Military and Non-military Functions'.

32 Haslam, 'Planning in Late Saxon Worcester', pp. 57–60.

33 A. Reynolds, 'Archaeological Correlates for Anglo-Saxon Military Activity in Comparative Perspective', in J. Baker, S. Brookes and A. Reynolds (eds), *Landscapes of Defence in Early Medieval Europe* (Turnhout: Brepols, 2013), p. 21. Reynolds goes on to entertain the possibility that Viking incursions retarded the emergence of towns in Wessex, rather than stimulated it (p. 22). The evidence in the chapter would suggest, however, that the opposite is the case.

34 G. Astill, 'Community, Identity and the Later Anglo-Saxon Town: The Case of Southern England', in W. Davies, G. Halsall and A. Reynolds (eds), *People and Space in the Middle Ages, 300–1300*, Studies in the Early Middle Ages 15 (Tournhout: Brepols, 2006), p. 236; see also G. Astill, 'Towns and Town Hierarchies in Saxon England', *Oxford Journal of Archaeology* 10 (1991), pp. 95–117.

35 Astill, 'Community, Identity and the Later Anglo-Saxon Town', p. 245. This general trend of interpretation is discussed in detail by Martin Carver in relation to the development of Stafford (*The Birth of a Borough: An Archaeological Study of Anglo-Saxon Stafford* (Woodbridge: Boydell Press, 2010), pp. 127–45). Carver sees Stafford in the early tenth century as little more than a barracks with a command economy. This general interpretation is also followed by Baker and Brookes, *Beyond the Burghal Hidage*, pp. 89–90.

36 A. Vince, 'The Economic Basis of Anglo-Saxon London', in R. Hodges and B. Hobley (eds), *The Rebirth of Towns in the West*, CBA Research Report 68 (London: Council for British Archaeology, 1988), pp. 83–92; A. Vince, 'The Urban Economy in Mercia in the 9th and 10th Centuries', *Arkeologiske Skrifter* 5 (Bergen: Historisk Museum, 1989).

37 Haslam, 'The Development of Late Saxon Christchurch, Dorset, and the Burghal Hidage', p. 104. It will be argued by the writer in another publication that new urban *burhs* were also constructed at Arundel and Steyning, Sussex, to replace the hill fort *burh* at Burpham. The former has been lost to post-Conquest development associated with the building of the castle. The latter, with a similar plan-form to others of the High Street type discussed here, is still recognisable in the present townscape.

38 For the example of the new *burh* at Cambridge, see J. Haslam, 'The Development and Topography of Saxon Cambridge', *Proceedings of the Cambridge Antiquarian Society* 72 (1984), pp. 13–29.

39 M. Biddle (ed.), *Winchester in the Early Middle Ages*, Winchester Studies 1 (Oxford: Clarendon Press, 1976), pp. 349–69; Haslam, *Urban–Rural Connections*, p. 73 and Fig. 16.

40 Haslam, *Urban–Rural Connections*, pp. 70–81.

41 R. Higham, *Making Anglo-Saxon Devon: Emergence of a Shire* (Exeter: Mint Press, 2008), p. 187. This is, however, a large subject with a number of important issues, which can only be touched upon here.

42 Some examples in Winchester, Oxford, Wallingford, Gloucester and other places are given in Haslam, *Urban–Rural Connections*. Many if not most of these tended to become (or to have been initially formed as) sokes with their own jurisdiction, and to have been originally appurtenant to the rural estates of their holders.

43 For a useful, recent general source for the development of earlier Saxon urbanism and urban places, a portal for exploring all recent literature, see R.A. Hall, 'Burhs and Boroughs: Defended Places, Trade, and Towns: Plans, Defences and Civic Features', in H. Hamerow, D.A. Hinton and S. Crawford (eds), *The Oxford Handbook of Anglo-Saxon Archaeology* (Oxford: Oxford University Press, 2011), pp. 600–21.

44 For Cambridge, see Haslam, 'The Development and Topography of Saxon Cambridge', pp. 13–29; for Langport, see

J. Haslam, 'The Late Saxon *burhs* of Somerset – A Review', in G.R. Owen-Crocker and S.D. Thompson (eds), *Towns and Topography: Essays in Memory of David H. Hill* (Oxford: Oxbow, 2014), pp. 51–52. The canalisation of the river Cam at Cambridge, to facilitate and channel water-borne trade to the *burh*, is another infrastructure development which can be associated with the initial formation of the new *burh* of 921 by King Edward the Elder. This is also another strand of evidence which supports the hypothesis that this site was founded as an urban place.

45 Haslam, 'The Development of Late Saxon Christchurch, Dorset, and the Burghal Hidage', p. 110.

46 These 'Portfields' have not been systematically studied, but examples are given, for instance, in F.W. Maitland, *Township and Borough* (Cambridge: Cambridge University Press, 1898); Haslam, 'The Development and Topography of Saxon Cambridge'; J. Dewey, 'The Origins of Wallingford: Topography, Boundaries and Parishes', in K.S.B. Keats-Rohan and D.R. Roffe, *The Origins of the Borough of Wallingford*, British Archaeological Reports, British Series 494 (Oxford: British Archaeological Reports, 2009), p. 23; Haslam, 'The Development of Late Saxon Christchurch, Dorset, and the Burghal Hidage', p. 99, Fig. 2, p. 110; Haslam, 'The Late Saxon *burhs* of Somerset' (in particular in relation to Langport). In all cases, however, these fields are associated with places which had been *burhs*.

47 This aspect is extensively discussed in Baker and Brooks, *Beyond the Burghal Hidage*.

48 It is hoped to explore this theme at a later date. This topographical evidence supplies an important corrective to the prevailing notion, based on documentary evidence alone, that bridges were not an important part of the landscape until well into the tenth century (C. Gillmor, 'The Logistics of Fortified Bridge Building on the Seine under Charles the Bald', *Anglo-Norman Studies* 11 (1988), pp. 87–105 and A.R. Cooper, *Bridges, Law and Power in Medieval England, 700–1400* (Woodbridge: Boydell Press, 2006)). See further comments on this subject in relation to Langport and Axbridge, Somerset, in Haslam, 'The Late Saxon *burhs* of Somerset – A Review', pp. 47–52, 56–60, 63–67.

49 These aspects are discussed in detail in Haslam, *Urban–Rural Connections*: for Wessex, chs 3 and 4; for Berkshire, Oxfordshire and Buckinghamshire, chs 10, 11 and 12; for Mercia, chs 5, 6, 7 and 8. An alternative view of the development of the burghal territories of Wiltshire put forward by Baker and Brookes (*Beyond the Burghal Hidage*, pp. 265–67) is based on several basic premises or assumptions which in my view can be falsified. See further comments on this issue in Haslam, *Urban–Rural Connections*, pp. 19–27; J. Haslam, 'A Probable Late Saxon *burh* at Ilchester', *Landscape History* 34.1 (2013), pp. 7–11.

50 N.J. Baker and R. Holt, 'The City of Worcester in the Tenth Century' in N. Brooks and C. Cubitt (eds), *St. Oswald of Worcester: Life and Influence* (Leicester: Leicester University Press, 1996), pp. 132–34; N.J. Baker and R. Holt, *Urban Growth and the Medieval Church: Gloucester and Worcester* (Aldershot: Ashgate, 2004), pp. 127–29, 133; R. Holt, 'The Urban Transformation in England, 900–1100', *Anglo-Norman Studies* 32 (2009), pp. 65–66.

51 Holt, 'The Urban Transformation in England', pp. 65–66.

52 Haslam, 'Planning in Late Saxon Worcester'; Haslam, *Urban–Rural Connections*, pp. 51–59, 70–81. I have also argued, contrary to received opinion, that the charter of Æthelred and Æthelflæd granting rights to the bishop (S.223) should not be considered as a foundation charter for the initial setting up of the *burh*, but rather as confirming the redistribution of rights between the king and the bishop which were already associated with an urban *burh*.

53 E.g. Astill, 'Community, Identity and the Later Anglo-Saxon Town', p. 240; R.A. Hall, 'Burhs and Boroughs: Defended Places, Trade and Towns, Plans, Defences and Civic Features', in H. Hamerow, D.A. Hinton and S. Crawford (eds), *The Oxford Handbook of Anglo-Saxon Archaeology* (Oxford: Oxford University Press, 2011), p. 606; Baker and Brookes, *Beyond the Burghal Hidage*, pp. 64–65. See further comments on 'emergency *burhs*' in Haslam, 'The Late Saxon *burhs* of Somerset – A Review'.

54 Williams, 'Military and Non-military Functions', pp. 131–35; Abels, *Lordship and Military Obligation*, p. 204; Baker and Brookes, *Beyond the Burghal Hidage*, pp. 64–65.

55 Holt, 'The Urban Transformation in England', p. 61.

56 A significant parallel to the kingly power manoeuvres involving earlier built environments, as discussed in Chapter 4 of this volume.

57 Biddle, 'Towns', p. 134.

58 Haslam, 'The Late Saxon *burhs* of Somerset', pp. 57–60.

59 Not shown in Figure 9.4, but see the *burh* in its landscape context in Haslam, 'The Late Saxon *burhs* of Somerset', Fig.8.8.

60 L. Keen, 'The Towns of Dorset', in J. Haslam (ed.), *Anglo-Saxon Towns in Southern England* (Chichester: Phillimore, 1984), pp. 234–35; see also K.J. Penn, *Historic Towns in Dorset*, Dorset Natural History and Archaeological Society Monograph Series 1 (Dorchester: Dorset Natural History and Archaeological Society, 1980).

61 Extensive Urban Survey Buckingham (hereafter, EUS) (2008): http://www.buckscc.gov.uk/media/130388/A_HT_Buckingham_Report_Part_3.pdf (pp. 16, 35–39) [accessed 31 August 2014].

62 W. Page, *Victoria History of the County of Buckingham* (London: A. Constable, 1925), vol. 3, p. 476 (hereafter, *VCH*). See further comments under Newport Pagnell, below, and Haslam, *Urban–Rural Connections*, pp. 117–22.

63 Haslam, 'The Development of Late Saxon Christchurch, Dorset, and the Burghal Hidage'.

64 Haslam, 'The Late Saxon *burhs* of Somerset', pp. 47–52.

65 For further discussion of such potential beacon sites, see Baker and Brookes, Chapter 10 of this volume.

66 R.B. Harris, 'Lewes Historic Character Assessment Report', English Heritage and West Sussex County Council, 2005: http://www.westsussex.gov.uk/living/planning/the_county_plan/west_sussex_character_project/extensive_urban_surveys_eus.aspx [accessed 31 August 2014].

67 Haslam, 'The Towns of Devon', pp. 256–59.

See also comments on Lydford, as well as the other Devon *burhs*, in Higham, *Making Anglo-Saxon Devon*, pp. 167–88.

68 Haslam, 'The Late Saxon *burhs* of Somerset', pp. 52–56.

69 J. Haslam, 'The Towns of Wiltshire', in J. Haslam (ed.), *Anglo-Saxon Towns in Southern England* (Chichester: Phillimore, 1984), pp. 111–17.

70 EUS Malmesbury (2004): http://archaeologydataservice.ac.uk/archiveDS/archiveDownload?t=arch-906-1/dissemination/pdf/EUS_Texts/Malmesbury.pdf (p. 16) [accessed 31 August 2014].

71 T. Longman, 'Iron-Age and Later Defences at Malmesbury, Wilts: Excavations 1998–2000', *Wiltshire Archaeological Magazine* 99 (2006), pp. 104–64.

72 Keen, 'The Towns of Dorset', pp. 221–24; J. Chandler, *A Higher Reality: The History of Shaftesbury's Royal Nunnery* (Salisbury: Hobnob Press, 2003); S. Keynes, 'Alfred the Great and Shaftesbury Abbey', in L. Keen (ed.), *Studies in the Early History of Shaftesbury Abbey* (Dorchester: Dorset County Council, 1998), pp. 17–72.

73 E.g. Biddle, 'Towns', p. 127; D. Hill, 'The Burghal Hidage – Southampton', *Proceedings of the Hampshire Field Club* 24 (1967), pp. 59–61; Hill, 'Gazetteer of Burghal Hidage Sites', pp. 85, 217–18.

74 N.P. Brooks, 'The Administrative Background of the Burghal Hidage', in Hill and Rumble, *Defence of Wessex*, pp. 129–33.

75 Haslam, *Urban–Rural Connections*, pp. 217–21.

76 See further discussion in Haslam, 'Daws Castle, Somerset, and Civil Defence Measures' and 'The Late Saxon *burhs* of Somerset', pp. 60–62.

77 Haslam, 'The Towns of Wiltshire', pp. 122–28.

78 P. Andrews, L. McPhain and R.S. Smith, 'Excavations at Wilton 1995–96: St John's Hospital and South Street', *Wiltshire Archaeological Magazine* 93 (2000), pp. 181–204.

79 Haslam, *Urban–Rural Connections*, pp. 9–18.

80 Haslam, 'The Development of Late Saxon

Christchurch, Dorset, and the Burghal Hidage', pp. 103–04.

81 Haslam, 'The Towns of Devon', pp. 251–56; see also Higham, *Making Anglo-Saxon Devon*, pp. 167–88.

82 M. O'Connell and R. Poulton, 'The Towns of Surrey', in Haslam, *Anglo-Saxon Towns in Southern England*, pp. 43–46.

83 Haslam, 'The Towns of Devon', pp. 271–75. See also further comments in P. Luscombe, 'Charters, Place-names and Anglo-Saxon Settlement in South Devon', *Report of the Transactions of the Devon Association for the Advancement of Science* 137 (2005), pp. 89–138.

84 Haslam, 'The Towns of Wiltshire', pp. 94–102.

85 EUS Marlborough (2004): http://archaeologydataservice.ac.uk/archiveDS/archiveDownload?t=arch-906-1/dissemination/pdf/EUS_Texts/Marlborough.pdf (p. 20, para. 6.10) [accessed 31 August 2014]; Baker and Brookes, *Beyond the Burghal Hidage*, e.g. pp. 129, 215–67.

86 Haslam, 'The Towns of Devon', pp. 259–62; M. Dyer and J. Allen, 'An Excavation on the Defences of the Anglo-Saxon *burh* and Medieval Town of Totnes', *Proceedings of the Devon Archaeological Society* 62 (2004).

87 T.R. Slater, 'Controlling the South Hams: The Anglo-Saxon Burh at Halwell', *Report of the Transactions of the Devonshire Association for the Advancement of Science* 123 (1991), pp. 57–78; Luscombe, 'Charters, Place-names and Anglo-Saxon Settlement'; Higham, *Making Anglo-Saxon Devon*, pp. 167–88.

88 Haslam, 'The Late Saxon *burhs* of Somerset'; see further discussion and detailed plans in Baker and Holt, 'The City of Worcester in the Tenth Century'.

89 J. Haslam, 'The Two Anglo-Saxon *burhs* of Oxford', *Oxoniensia* 75 (2010), pp. 15–34.

90 Royal Commission on Historical Monuments, *The Town of Stamford* (London: Royal Commission on Historical Monuments, 1977); M. Mahany, A. Burchard and G. Simpson, *Excavations in Stamford, Lincolnshire 1963–69* (London: Society for Medieval Archaeology, 1982), pp. 1–10; C. Mahany and D. Roffe, 'Stamford: The Development of an Anglo-Scandinavian Borough', in R.A. Brown (ed.), *Anglo-Norman Studies 5: Proceedings of Battle Conference 1982* (Woodbridge: Boydell Press, 1983), pp. 199–219 (reprinted with updated references in D.A.E. Pelteret (ed.), *Anglo-Saxon History: Basic Readings*, Garland Reference Library of the Humanities (New York: Garland, 2000), pp. 387–417); Blair, 'Stamford', p. 428.

91 Contra W. Rodwell, *The Origins and Early Development of Witham, Essex*, Oxbow Monograph 26 (Oxford: Oxbow, 1993), p. 79, Fig. 44, whose analysis of the topography is somewhat misleading.

92 J. Haslam, 'The Location of the *burh* of Wigingamere – A Reappraisal', in A.R. Rumble and A.D. Mills (eds), *Names, People and Places* (Stamford: Watkins, 1977), pp. 124–26; Haslam, *Urban–Rural Connections*, pp. 125–26.

93 EUS Newport Pagnell (2010): http://www.bucksc.gov.uk/media/130580/newport_pagnell_consultation_report.pdf (pp. 45–47) [accessed 31 August 2014].

Chapter 10: *John Baker and Stuart Brookes*

1 M.J. Swanton (trans. and ed.), *The Anglo-Saxon Chronicle* (London: Dent, 1996), Version E, 1006.

2 D. Hill and S. Sharp, 'An Anglo-Saxon Beacon System', in A.R. Rumble and A.D. Mills (eds), *Names, Places and People: An Onomastic Miscellany for John McNeal Dodgson* (Stamford: Paul Watkins, 1997), pp. 157–65.

3 *Rect.* 1 and 3.4, in F. Liebermann (ed.), *Die Gesetze der Angelsachsen*, vol. 1 (Halle: M. Niemayer, 1903, repr. 1960), pp. 444, 446.

4 S 832; Anglo-Saxon charters are annotated with reference to the numbering outlined in P. Sawyer, *Anglo-Saxon Charters: An Annotated List and Bibliography*, Guides and Handbooks 8 (London: Royal Historical Society, 1968): http://www.esawyer.org.uk [accessed 12 August 2014].

5 Swanton, *Anglo-Saxon Chronicle*, Version A, 789.

6 R. Latouche (trans. and ed.), Richer, *Histoire de France (888–995)* (Paris: H. Champion, 1930), §3, pp. 130–31.

7 S 895.

8 H. Kurath et al., *Middle English Dictionary*

(Ann Arbor: University of Michigan, 1956–2001), s. *bēken*; *Oxford English Dictionary*, online, s. beacon, sense 3: http://www.oed.com/ [accessed 12 August 2014].

9 *Dictionary of Old English: A to G*, online, s. *bēacen*: http://www.doe.utoronto.ca/pages/pub/fasc-a-g-web.html.

10 Hill and Sharp, 'An Anglo-Saxon Beacon System', p. 157.

11 A.D. Healey (ed.), *Dictionary of Old English Web Corpus* (2011): http://www.doe.utoronto.ca/pages/pub/web-corpus.html [accessed 12 August 2014].

12 Swanton, *Anglo-Saxon Chronicle*, Version C; Version E gives *beacna*, and D reads *here beacna*.

13 T.N. Toller (ed.), *An Anglo-Saxon Dictionary Based on the Manuscript Collections of the Late Joseph Bosworth* (Oxford: Clarendon Press, 1898).

14 R. Forsberg, 'On Old English *ād* in English Place-Names', *Namn och Bygd* 58 (1970), pp. 66–69. For glosses of *farus*, see Healey, *Dictionary of Old English Web Corpus*.

15 H.T. White, 'The Beacon System in Hampshire', *Papers and Proceedings of the Hampshire Field Club and Archaeological Society* 10 (1931), pp. 252–78; H.T. White, 'The Beacon System in Kent', *Archaeologia Cantiana* 46 (1934), pp. 77–79; P. Russell, 'Fire Beacons in Devon', *Report and Transactions of the Devonshire Association for the Advancement of Science, Literature and Art* 87 (1955), pp. 250–302; P. Ottaway, *Romans on the Yorkshire Coast* (York: York Archaeological Trust and English Heritage, 1996); J.F. Verbruggen, *The Art of Warfare in Western Europe During the Middle Ages, from the Eighth Century to 1340*, trans. R.W. Southern, 2nd edn (Woodbridge: Boydell Press, 1997), p. 326; J. Baker and S. Brookes, *Beyond the Burghal Hidage: Anglo-Saxon Civil Defence in the Viking Age* (Leiden: Brill, 2013), pp. 179–99.

16 A.H. Smith, *English Place-Name Elements* (Cambridge: Cambridge University Press, 1956), vol. 1, p. 21; D. Parsons, T. Styles and C. Hough, *The Vocabulary of English Place-Names: Á–BOX* (Nottingham: Centre for English Name Studies, 1997), p. 68.

17 Forsberg, 'On Old English *ād*'; Parsons, Styles and Hough, *Vocabulary*, pp. 5–6.

18 Baker and Brookes, *Beyond the Burghal Hidage*, pp. 184–89.

19 Hill and Sharp, 'An Anglo-Saxon Beacon System', pp. 161–64. A slightly different version of this beacon chain, derived from sixteenth-century evidence, is suggested by P.C. Beauchamp, 'Appendix IV: The Beacons that Summoned Oxfordshire in 1545', in P.C. Beauchamp (ed.), *The Oxfordshire Muster Rolls 1539, 1542, 1569*, Oxfordshire Record Society 60 (Oxford: Oxfordshire Record Society, 1996), pp. xxxvi–xxxvii.

20 J. Shemming and K. Briggs, 'Anglo-Saxon Communication Networks': http://keithbriggs.info/AS_networks.html [accessed: 17 May 2008].

21 For example, B. Cox, 'The Pattern of Old English *burh* in Early Lindsey', *Anglo-Saxon England* 23 (1994), pp. 35–56; B. Cox, *The Place-Names of Rutland* (Nottingham: English Place-Name Society, 1994); G. Gower, 'The Place-Name "Totterdown" and the Early History of Tooting', *Journal of the Wandsworth Historical Society* 65 (1992), pp. 1–6; G. Gower, 'A Suggested Anglo-Saxon Signalling System between Chichester and London', *London Archaeologist* 10.3 (2002), pp. 59–63; M.G. Shapland, 'Towers of Strength: The Role of Churches in the Defence of the Late Anglo-Saxon Landscape', unpublished BA dissertation, University College London, 2005; J. Baker, 'Warriors and Watchmen: Place-Names and Anglo-Saxon Civil Defence', *Medieval Archaeology* 55 (2011), pp. 258–67; Baker and Brookes, *Beyond the Burghal Hidage*, pp. 189–99, 259–62, 312–27, 358–69.

22 Cameron et al., *Dictionary of Old English*, s. *ād*; R.E. Latham, *Revised Medieval Latin Word-List from British and Irish Sources* (London: Oxford University Press, 1965), s. *rogus*; C.T. Lewis and C. Short, *A Latin Dictionary* (Oxford: Clarendon Press, 2002), s. *rogus*, 'a funeral pile'.

23 S 412; Forsberg, 'On Old English *ād*', pp. 44–51, 73.

24 S. Brookes, 'Mapping Anglo-Saxon Civil Defence', in J. Baker, S. Brookes and A. Reynolds (eds), *Landscapes of Defence in Early Medieval Europe* (Turnhout: Brepols, 2013), pp. 39–64.

25 Beauchamp, 'The Beacons that Summoned Oxfordshire in 1545', p. xxxvi.

26 Ibid.

27 Use of spies and scouts is discussed by Baker and Brookes, *Beyond the Burghal Hidage*, pp. 179–80, and seems to be depicted in the Bayeux Tapestry. In a scene shortly after Harold's accession, he appears to receive news from a messenger (D.M. Wilson, *The Bayeux Tapestry* (London: Thames & Hudson, 1985), plate 33). Between this and the following scene the upper border shows a man obviously gazing out at a distance, perhaps indicating his role as a spy gathering intelligence. This watchman appears to be signalling the news of Harold's accession to the Normans in some way. What appears below him is a ship urgently sailing across to Normandy and then a messenger giving William and Odo the news. The authors are very grateful to Gale R. Owen-Crocker for drawing our attention to these scenes.

28 P. Southern, 'Signals versus Illumination on Roman Frontiers', *Britannia* 21(1990), pp. 233–42.

29 Richer, *Histoire*, §3, pp. 130–31.

30 J. Rider (ed.), *Galbertus Notarius Brugensis: De Multro, Traditione, et Occisione Gloriosi Karoli Comitis Flandriarum* (Turnhout: Brepols, 1994), p. 121; Verbruggen, *The Art of Warfare in Western Europe*, p. 326.

31 Hill and Sharp, 'An Anglo-Saxon Beacon System', p. 160.

32 Wilson, *The Bayeux Tapestry*, plate 50.

33 The possibility of a compositional borrowing from Roman art was pointed out to the authors by Gale R. Owen-Crocker (personal communication), and the grounds for her interpretation are outlined in her 'Stylistic Variation and Roman Influence on the Bayeux Tapestry', in G.R. Owen-Crocker, *The Bayeux Tapestry: Collected Papers* (Farnham: Ashgate, 2012), pp. 30–31: http://peregrinations.kenyon.edu/vol2_3/current/fb4.pdf [accessed 10 April 2014].

34 Beauchamp, 'The Beacons that Summoned Oxfordshire in 1545', p. xxxvi.

35 A. Reynolds, 'Avebury, Yatesbury and the Archaeology of Communications', *Papers from the Institute of Archaeology* 6 (1995), pp. 21–30; A. Reynolds and S. Brookes, 'Anglo-Saxon Civil Defence in the Localities: A Case Study of the Avebury Region', in A. Reynolds and L. Webster (eds), *The Northern World in the Early Middle Ages: Studies in Honour of James Graham-Campbell* (Turnhout: Brepols, 2013), pp. 561–606.

36 A. Reynolds, *Life and Landscape in Later Anglo-Saxon England* (Stroud: Tempus, 1999), p. 93; A. Williams, 'A Bell-House and a Burh-Geat: Lordly Residences in England before the Norman Conquest', in C. Harper-Bill and R. Harvey (eds), *Medieval Knighthood IV: Papers from the Fifth Strawberry Hill Conference, 1990* (Woodbridge: Boydell Press, 1992), pp. 221–40; J. Baker, 'The Language of Anglo-Saxon Defence', in J. Baker, S. Brookes and A. Reynolds (eds), *Landscapes of Defence in the Viking Age: Anglo-Saxon England and Comparative Perspectives* (Turnhout: Brepols, 2013), pp. 65–90.

37 Hill and Sharp, 'An Anglo-Saxon Beacon System', pp. 161–62.

38 *Tattle Street* 1710: J.K. Wallenberg, *The Place-Names of Kent* (Uppsala: A.-B. Lundequistska Bokhandeln, 1934), p. 79; P. Cullen, 'The Place-Names of the Lathes of St Augustine and Shipway, Kent', unpublished PhD thesis: University of Sussex, 1997, p. 533.

39 White, 'The Beacon System in Kent', p. 79; Baker and Brookes, *Beyond the Burghal Hidage*, p. 364.

40 J. Bradley and M. Gaimster, 'Medieval Britain and Ireland in 1999', *Medieval Archaeology* 44 (2000), p. 338.

41 Ibid. In this instance, the place name itself may preserve a tradition of lookouts. The first edition Ordnance Survey 1:2500 (1882) shows Ward Hill and a house nearby called Warthill. The first element of these names may well derive from ON *varða, varði*, the basic meaning of which is 'a cairn, a heap of stones', which Smith suggested was probably used as a lookout place (A.H. Smith, *English Place-Name Elements, Part I: Á–ÍW*, English Place-Name Society 25 (Cambridge: Cambridge University Press, 1956), p. 229).

42 Baker, 'Warriors and Watchmen', p. 263.

43 A long-distance 'Ridgeway' and Roman road, respectively. For discussion of roads, see Chapter 2 of this volume.

44 C.F.C. Hawkes, 'The Exhibition', *Archaeological Journal* 103 (1947), pp. 89–90; A. Meaney, *A Gazetteer of Early Anglo-Saxon Burial Sites* (London: Allen & Unwin, 1964), p. 153.

45 Although several scholars have believed that it was once a beacon, including W. Johnson, *Byways in British Archaeology* (Cambridge: Cambridge University Press, 1912), p. 131; P. Rahtz, 'Glastonbury Tor', in G. Ashe (ed.), *The Quest for Arthur's Britain* (London: Pall Mall Press, 1968), pp. 147–48; P. Rahtz, 'Excavations on Glastonbury Tor, Somerset, 1964–66', *Archaeological Journal* (1970), pp. 11, 21; P. Rahtz and L. Watts, *Glastonbury Myth and Archaeology* (Stroud: Tempus, 1993), pp. 30–31, 67–78, 71–78.

46 K. Booth, 'The Roman *Pharos* at Dover Castle', *English Heritage Historical Review* 2 (2007), pp. 5–17.

47 G.G. Scott, 'The Church on the Castle Hill, Dover', *Archaeologia Cantiana* 5 (1864), pp. 1–18.

48 Booth, 'The Roman *Pharos* at Dover Castle', p. 12.

49 T. Tatton-Brown, 'The Churches of Canterbury Diocese in the 11th Century', in J. Blair (ed.), *Minsters and Parish Churches: The Local Church in Transition 950–1200* (Oxford: Oxford University Committee for Archaeology, 1988), p. 110; J. Coad, *Dover Castle* (London: Batsford, 1995), pp. 15–20.

50 Baker and Brookes, *Beyond the Burghal Hidage*, p. 376.

51 See M. Biddle and B. Kjølbye-Biddle, 'Old Minster, St Swithun's Day 1093', in J. Crook (ed.), *Winchester Cathedral: Nine Hundred Years, 1093–1993* (Chichester: Dean and Chapter of Winchester Cathedral in association with Phillimore, 1993), pp. 13–20. We are grateful to Michael Shapland for suggesting this idea.

52 *Annales regni Francorum*, 811, in F. Kurze (ed.), *Annales regni Francorum (741–829)* (Hannover: Impensis Bibliopolii Hahniani, 1895). At a line-of-sight distance of only 48.2 km, the two *pharos* are likely to have been intervisible with towers of at least 10 metres height at Dover and 30 metres at Bolougne.

53 Baker and Brookes, *Beyond the Burghal Hidage*, pp. 266–67; later medieval examples of this practice are listed by Johnson, *Byways in British Archaeology*, pp. 127–31.

54 S 895; S. Keynes, 'King Æthelred's Charter for Sherborne Abbey, 998', in K. Barker, D.A. Hinton and A. Hunt (eds), *St Wulfsige and Sherborne: Essays to Celebrate the Millennium of the Benedictine Abbey, 998–1998* (Oxford: Oxbow, 2005), p. 12

55 S. Batson, *Terrier and Inventory of Church Possessions in the Parish of Welford, Berkshire* (Newbury: G.J. Cosburn, 1892), pp. 41–42; M.G. Shapland, 'Buildings of Secular and Religious Lordship: Anglo-Saxon Tower-nave Churches', unpublished PhD thesis, University College London, 2012, pp. 717–38.

56 S 491.

57 D.E. Greenway (trans. and ed.), *Historia Anglorum: The History of the English People* (Oxford: Oxford Medieval Texts, 1996), pp. 348–49; Shapland, 'Buildings of Secular and Religious Lordship', pp. 190–93.

58 Baker and Brookes, *Beyond the Burghal Hidage*, pp. 366–67.

59 Cox, *The Place-Names of Rutland*, pp. xxxiii–xxxvii; B. Cox, 'Yarboroughs in Lindsey', *Journal of the English Place-Name Society* 28 (1995–96), pp. 53–55.

60 Gower, 'A Suggested Anglo-Saxon Signalling System', pp. 59–62.

61 See n. 21, above.

62 For discussion of roads, see Chapter 2 of this volume.

63 See Chapter 8 of this volume for a discussion of these great dykes.

64 A.H. Smith, *The Place-names of Gloucestershire, Part 3* (Cambridge: Cambridge University Press, 1964), p. 234.

65 A.T. Bannister, *The Place-Names of Herefordshire, their Origin and Development* (Cambridge: Cambridge University Press, 1916), pp. 186, 225.

66 It is so named on the Ordnance Survey (1st edn, County Series 1:10560, 1889–91): http://digimap.edina.ac.uk/ancientroam/historic [accessed 8 November 2013], and is recorded as *Worsel Wood* on the Ordnance Survey Unions map of 1830: http://visionofbritain.org.uk/iipmooviewer/iipmooviewer_new.html?map=os_unions_1830s_1840_sw/Radnor_1830_1840

[accessed 8 November 2013]. The authors would like to thank Emily Pennifold for providing information relating to this place name.

67 Shapland, 'Buildings of Secular and Religious Lordship', pp. 190–93.

68 Greenway, *Historia Anglorum*, pp. 348–49.

69 See discussion of Cambridgeshire dykes in Chapter 8 of this volume.

70 O.S. Anderson, *The English Hundred-Names* (Lund: Lunds Universitets, 1934), p. 100; A. Meaney, 'Gazetteer of Hundred and Wapentake Meeting-Places of the Cambridgeshire Region,' *Proceedings of the Cambridge Antiquarian Society* 82 (1993), p. 83.

71 J. Baker and S. Brookes, 'Monumentalising the Political Landscape: A Special Class of Anglo-Saxon Assembly-sites', *Antiquaries Journal* 94 (2013), pp. 1–16.

72 *Ward(e)lou(h)(e)feld* in c.250, P.H. Reaney, *Place-Names of Cambridgeshire* (London: Cambridge University Press/English Place-Name Society, 1943), pp. 122–23.

73 It is possible that this was carried out by local officials. In a recent survey of some 800 personal names listed in the 1279 hundred rolls of Ewelme hundred – at the southern Oxfordshire end of the Chilterns beacon chain – appeared individuals with the bynames 'Wardein' (at Latchford), 'Weyte' (watchman) at Berrick Salome and Totere ('watchman, lookout') at Warborough.

74 Shapland, 'Buildings of Secular and Religious Lordship', p. 193.

75 E.g. AD 870, 875, 1006. Cf. discussion of the Icknield Way in Baker and Brookes, *Beyond the Burghal Hidage*, pp. 140–52.

76 Hill and Sharp, 'An Anglo-Saxon Beacon System'.

77 N. Hooper, 'Some Observations on the Navy in Late Anglo-Saxon England', in C. Harper-Bill, C.J. Holdsworth and J.L. Nelson (eds), *Studies in Medieval History Presented to R. Allen Brown* (London: Boydell Press, 1989), pp. 203–14; R. Lavelle, *Alfred's Wars: Sources and Interpretations of Anglo-Saxon Warfare in the Viking Age* (Woodbridge: Boydell Press, 2010), pp. 141–76; Baker and Brookes, *Beyond the Burghal Hidage*, pp. 403–06.

78 Hill and Sharp, 'An Anglo-Saxon Beacon System', pp. 163–64.

79 Gower, 'A Suggested Anglo-Saxon Signalling System', p. 59; Baker, 'Warriors and Watchmen', pp. 263–64; Baker and Brookes, *Beyond the Burghal Hidage*, pp. 193–97.

80 J. Baker and S. Brookes, 'Overseeing the Sea: Some West Saxon Responses to Waterborne Threats in the South-East', in S. Klein, S. Lewis and B. Shipper (eds), *The Maritime World of the Anglo-Saxons*, Medieval and Renaissance Texts and Studies Volume 448, Essays in Anglo-Saxon Studies Volume 5 (Tempe, AZ: Arizona Centre for Medieval and Renaissance Studies, 2014), pp. 37–58.

81 Reynolds, 'Avebury, Yatesbury and the Archaeology of Communications'; J. Pollard and A. Reynolds, *Avebury: The Biography of a Landscape* (Stroud: Tempus, 2002; repr. 2012), pp. 224–26; Reynolds and Brookes, 'Anglo-Saxon Civil Defence in the Localities'; Baker and Brookes, *Beyond the Burghal Hidage*, pp. 215–67.

82 S 449. For discussion of 'herepaths', see Chapter 2 of this volume.

83 Pollard and Reynolds, *Avebury*, pp. 226–28; Reynolds and Brookes, 'Anglo-Saxon Civil Defence in the Localities', pp. 584–86.

84 J.E.B. Gover, A. Mawer and F.M. Stenton, *The Place-Names of Wiltshire*, English Place-Name Society 16 (Cambridge: Cambridge University Press, 1939), p. 296; M. Gelling, *Signposts to the Past*, 3rd edn (Chichester: Phillimore, 1997), p. 147.

85 Hill and Sharp, 'An Anglo-Saxon Beacon System', pp. 159, Fig. 11, and pp. 162–64.

86 Gower, 'A Suggested Anglo-Saxon Signalling System'.

87 Baker, 'Warriors and Watchmen', p. 264.

88 Baker and Brookes, *Beyond the Burghal Hidage*, pp. 312–33.

89 Brookes, 'Mapping Anglo-Saxon Civil Defence', pp. 46–47.

90 *Middle English Dictionary*, s.v.; *Oxford English Dictionary*, online, s.v.

91 Baker, 'Warriors and Watchmen', p. 263.

92 Baker and Brookes, *Beyond the Burghal Hidage*, pp. 269–333.

Suggested Reading

Chapter 1
T. Eaton, *Plundering the Roman Past: Roman Stonework in Medieval Britain* (Stroud: Tempus, 2000).

C.E. Fell, 'Perceptions of Transience', in M. Godden and M. Lapidge (eds), *The Cambridge Companion to Old English Literature* (Cambridge: Cambridge University Press, 1991).

G. Halsall, *Worlds of Arthur: Facts and Fictions of the Dark Ages* (Oxford: Oxford University Press, 2013).

H. Hamerow, *Rural Settlements in Anglo-Saxon Society* (Oxford: Oxford University Press, 2012).

N. Higham, *Rome, Britain and the Anglo-Saxons* (London: Seaby, 1992).

A. Rogers, *Late Roman Towns in Britain: Rethinking Change and Decline* (Cambridge: Cambridge University Press, 2011).

R. White and P. Barker, *Wroxeter: Life and Death of a Roman City* (Stroud: Tempus, 1988).

Chapter 2
A. Cole, 'Place-Names as Travellers' Landmarks', in N.J. Higham and M.J. Ryan (eds), *Place-names, Language and the Anglo-Saxon Landscape* (Woodbridge: Boydell Press, 2011), pp. 51–67.

D. Harrison, *The Bridges of Medieval England* (Oxford: Clarendon Press, 2004).

D. Hill, *An Atlas of Anglo-Saxon England* (Oxford: Blackwell, 1981).

P. Hindle, *Roads and Tracks for Historians* (Chichester: Phillimore, 2001).

—— *Medieval Roads and Tracks* (Oxford: Shire, 2009).

D. Hooke, *The Anglo-Saxon Landscape: The Kingdom of the Hwicce* (Manchester: Manchester University Press, 1985).

—— *The Landscape of Anglo-Saxon England* (London: Leicester University Press, 1998).

I.D. Margary, *Roman Roads in Britain* (London: Baker, 1973).

Chapter 3
G. Beresford, *Goltho: The Development of an Early Medieval Manor, c.850–1150* (London: Historic Buildings and Monuments Commission for England, 1987).

R. Darrah, 'Identifying the Architectural Features of the Anglo-Saxon Buildings at Flixborough and Understanding their Structures', in C. Loveluck (ed.), *Rural Settlement, Lifestyles and Social Change in the Later First Millennium AD: Anglo-Saxon Flixborough in its Wider Context* (Oxford: Oxbow, 2007), pp. 51–56.

R. Hall, *Viking Age York* (London: Batsford/English Heritage, 1994).

H. Hamerow, 'Anglo-Saxon Timber Buildings and their Social Context', in H. Hamerow, D.A. Hinton and S. Crawford (eds), *The Oxford Handbook of Anglo-Saxon Archaeology* (Oxford: Oxford University Press, 2011), pp. 128–55.

K.A. Leahy, *Anglo-Saxon Crafts* (Stroud: Tempus, 2003).

S. Losco-Bradley and G. Kinsley, *Catholme: An Anglo-Saxon Settlement on the Trent Gravels in Staffordshire*, Nottingham Studies in Archaeology 3 (Nottingham: University of Nottingham, 2002).

C. Loveluck and R. Darrah, 'The Built Environment: The Buildings, Aspects of Settlement Morphology and the Use of Space', in C. Loveluck (ed.), *Rural Settlement, Lifestyle and Social Change in the Later First Millennium AD: Anglo-Saxon Flixborough in its Wider Context, Excavations at Flixborough* 4 (Oxford: Oxbow, 2007), pp. 31–74.

M. Millett and S. James, 'Excavations at Cowdery's Down, Basingstoke, Hants: 1978–1981', *Archaeological Journal* 140 (1983), pp. 151–279.

J. Tipper, *The Grubenhaus in Anglo-Saxon England: An Analysis and Interpretation of the Evidence from a Most Distinctive Building Type* (Yedingham: English Heritage, 2004).

S. West, *West Stow: The Anglo-Saxon Village*, East Anglian Archaeology 24 (Ipswich: Suffolk County Council, 1985).

Chapter 5

J. Blair, *The Church in Anglo-Saxon Society* (Oxford: Oxford University Press, 2005).

E. Fernie, *The Architecture of the Anglo-Saxons* (London: B.T. Batsford, 1983).

R. Gem, 'Towards an Iconography of Anglo-Saxon Architecture', *Journal of the Warburg and Courtauld Institutes* 46 (1983), pp. 1–18.

H. Gittos, *Liturgy, Architecture, and Sacred Places in Anglo-Saxon England* (Oxford: Oxford University Press, 2013).

R. Morris, *Churches in the Landscape* (London: J.M. Dent and Sons, 1989).

M.G. Shapland, 'Meanings of Timber and Stone in Anglo-Saxon Building Practice', in M.D.J. Bintley and M.G. Shapland (eds), *Trees and Timber in the Anglo-Saxon World* (Oxford: Oxford University Press, 2013), pp. 21–44.

H.M. Taylor and J. Taylor, *Anglo-Saxon Architecture*, 2 vols (Cambridge: Cambridge University Press, 1965).

L.M. White, *Building God's House in the Roman World: Architectural Adaptation among Pagans, Jews, and Christians* (Baltimore, MD: Johns Hopkins University Press for the American Schools of Oriental Research, 1990).

Chapter 7

J. Blair, *The Church in Anglo-Saxon Society* (Oxford: Oxford University Press, 2005).

J. Buckberry and A. Cherryson (eds), *Burial in Later Anglo-Saxon England, c.650–100 AD* (Oxford: Oxbow Books, 2010).

S. Lucy and A. Reynolds (eds), *Burial in Early Medieval England and Wales*, Society for Medieval Archaeological Monograph 17 (London: Society for Medieval Archaeology, 2002).

A. Reynolds, *Anglo-Saxon Deviant Burial Customs* (Oxford: Oxford University Press, 2009).

S. Semple, *Perceptions of the Prehistoric in Anglo-Saxon England: Ritual, Religion and Rulership in the Landscape* (Oxford: Oxford University Press, 2013).

S. Semple and H. Williams (eds), *Early Medieval Mortuary Practices: New Perspectives*, Anglo-Saxon Studies in Archaeology and History 14 (Oxford: Oxford University Press, 2007).

V. Thompson, *Dying and Death in Later Anglo-Saxon England* (Woodbridge: Boydell Press, 2004).

H. Williams, *Death and Memory in Early Medieval Britain* (Cambridge: Cambridge University Press, 2006).

Chapter 8

D. Griffiths, A. Reynolds and S. Semple, 'Boundaries in Early Medieval Britain', *Anglo-Saxon Studies in Archaeology and History* 12 (2003).

D. Hill and M. Worthington, *Offa's Dyke: History and Guide* (Stroud: Tempus, 2003).

D. Hooke (ed.), *Anglo-Saxon Settlement* (Oxford: Blackwell, 1988).

O. Rackham, *Ancient Woodland of England: The Woods of South-East Essex* (Rochford: Rochford District Council, 1986).

Chapter 10

J. Baker, 'Warriors and Watchmen: Place-names and Anglo-Saxon Civil Defence', *Medieval Archaeology* 55 (2011), pp. 258–67.

J. Baker and S. Brookes, *Beyond the Burghal Hidage: Anglo-Saxon Civil Defence in the Viking Age* (Leiden: Brill, 2013).

B. Cox, 'The Pattern of Old English *burh* in Early Lindsey', *Anglo-Saxon England* 23 (1994), pp. 35–56.

D. Hill and S. Sharp, 'An Anglo-Saxon Beacon System', in A.R. Rumble and A.D. Mills (eds), *Names, Places and People: An Onomastic Miscellany for John McNeal Dodgson* (Stamford: Paul Watkins, 1997), pp. 157–65.

R. Lavelle, *Alfred's Wars: Sources and Interpretations of Anglo-Saxon Warfare in the Viking Age* (Woodbridge: Boydell Press, 2010).

A. Reynolds and S. Brookes, 'Anglo-Saxon Civil Defence in the Localities: A Case Study of the Avebury Region', in A.J. Reynolds and L. Webster (eds), *The Northern World in the Early Middle Ages: Studies in Honour of James Graham-Campbell* (Turnhout: Brepols, 2013), pp. 561–606.

Index

Special thanks to Emily Rothman for her assistance in compiling the index for this volume. Places are located to modern countries and British counties.

Aachen, Germany; imperial chapel of Charlemagne (St Mary's) 93, 110
Abels, Richard 181, 209
Abercorn, West Lothian, Scotland, monastery 29
Aberford Dykes, West Yorkshire 180
Abram, Christopher 14, 16, 20
Acca's Cross, Hexham Abbey, Northumberland 134
Ælfric, abbot of Eynsham, *Glossary* 255n.134
Ælfric, earl 112, 254n.131
Ælfrith's Ditch/Dyke, Oxfordshire 166
Ælfwine (Aelfwini), king of the Deiri 76, 81, 89
Ælfwold, king of Northumbria 109
Æthelbald, king of Mercia 109, 246n.41
Æthelberht, king of Kent 80, 82, 88, 95, 108, 245nn.13,14
Æthelberht, St, king of East Anglia 42
Æthelflæd, 'Lady of the Mercians' 110, 184, 191, 274n.52
Æthelfrith king of the Bernicians, king of the Northumbrians 81
Æthelgifu, testatrix 72
Æthelhere, king of the East Angles 79
Æthelræd, king of Mercia, son of Penda 81, 246n.41
Æthelred II, 'the Unready', king of England 110
Æthelred, ealdorman of Mercia 110, 191, 274n.52
Æthelwalh, king of the South Saxons 83–4

Æthelwold, St, abbot of Abingdon, bishop of Winchester 43
Æthelwold's hedge, Herefordshire 180
Æthelwulf, under-king of Kent, king of Wessex 179
Agilbert, bishop of the West Saxons 86
Aidan, St, bishop of Lindisfarne 97–9
Aire river, Aire valley, Yorkshire 122
Airedale, Yorkshire 120
Akerman, John Yonge 140
Alban, St, martyr 42
Alcester, Warwickshire 48, 171
Alcuin of York 105, 160; *Bishops, Kings and Saints of York* 20
Aldborough, North Yorkshire 40
Aldhelm, abbot of Malmesbury, bishop of Sherborne 36, 237n.18
Aldred, subking to Offa 247n.61
Alfred 'the Great', king of the West Saxons 5, 25, 36, 167, 189, 191, 205, 271n.18, 272nn.22, 24
Alhfrith, king of the Deiri 86–8, 120
Almondbury, West Yorkshire 122
Amish culture 54
Ancyra, now Ankara, Turkey 84
Aneirin, *Gododdin* 36
Anglo-Saxon Chronicle 20, 60, 66, 82, 183–4, 186–9, 201, 214, 217–18, 221, 230, 245n.13
Antioch, now Turkey; Golden Octagon church 94
Antonine Wall, Scotland 29, 164, 238n.71
Apple Down, West Sussex 143, 146

Index

Arrow, river 179, 229
Asby Winderwath, Cumbria 70
Ashdown, East Sussex 216
Asser, bishop of Sherborne 164–5
Astill, Grenville 203–4
Athelstan, king of the English 43, 158, 217, 221
Athens, Greece, Parthenon 251n.63
Atherton, Jill 92, 96
Augustine, St, missionary to Kent, archbishop of Canterbury 42, 88, 95–6, 103, 106, 108, 115
Augustus, Caesar Divi Filius Augustus, Roman Emperor 110–11
Avebury, Wiltshire 46, 168, 230–1
Avon, river 48, 171, 178
Axbridge, Somerset 192, 194, 202, 205, 207, 211
Axe, river 207, 211

Baker, David 92, 112
Baker, John xvi, 10, 189, 213, 225, 270nn.5, 8, 271n.22, 272nn.24, 27
Baker, Nigel 208
Bakewell, Derbyshire 49, 120, 256n.13
Balsham, Cambridgeshire 218, 227, 229–30
Bamburgh, Northumberland 97–8, 104
Banham, Debby 7
Bard, character in *Egil's Saga* 73
Barnack, Northamptonshire 114, 256n.146
Barnstaple, Devon 189, 192, 197, 202, 204–5
Barton-upon-Humber, Lincolnshire 63, 114–15, 169, 248n.7
Barwick in Elmet, West Yorkshire 120
Basingwerk, Flintshire, Wales 176–7
Bassett, Stephen 187
Baston, Lincolnshire 160
Bath, Somerset 15, 18–19, 35, 178, 184, 193
Battle of Maldon, The, Old English poem 47, 72
Bayeux, city of 68; Tapestry 53, 66–9, 72, 117, 221, 235n.7, 255n.132, 278n.27
Beacon Hill, Hampshire 224
Beacon Hill, Lincolnshire 225
Beaumont-James, Tom 23–5
Beccles, Suffolk 193, 200, 202, 215; Ravensgate 215
Bede, St, 'the Venerable' 2, 20, 25, 29, 33, 36, 53, 59, 79, 83, 87–8, 95, 98, 104, 108, 111, 123, 126, 128, 136, 155–6, 164, 236n.10, 238nn.52, 68, 244n.2, 245nn.15, 25, 246nn.41, 43; *Historia Abbatum* 31, 33; *Historia Ecclesiastica* 25, 31, 79, 82, 95; *Vita Cuthberti* 29
Bedwyn Dyke, Wiltshire 179
Belgae, Celtic people 25
Belstead Hall, Broomfield, Essex 113
Benedict Biscop, founder of Jarrow and Monkwearmouth monasteries 31
Benedictine Reform 104
Benwell, Newcastle upon Tyne 30
Beowulf, hero of Old English poem *Beowulf* 84–5, 162, 168
Beowulf, Old English poem 5, 46, 59, 61, 72–3, 81–2, 84, 168, 217
Berinsfield, Oxfordshire 146
Berkshire 190, 207, 216, 218, 220, 222, 233, 274n.49
Bernicia 96
Bewcastle, Cumbria 133
Bica's Dyke, Oxfordshire 166–7
Biddle, Martin 182–3, 188, 204, 210
Bignor, West Sussex 33
Birdoswald, Cumbria 30, 167
Birinus, bishop of the West Saxons 90–1
Birstall, West Yorkshire 123–4, 131–2
Bishops Waltham, Hampshire 254n.132
Bishopstone, East Sussex 63–4, 70, 72, 113, 254n.132
Blair, John 34, 92, 132, 136
Bokerley Dyke, Dorset 163
Boniface V, pope 84
Bonney, Desmond 140
Booth, Paul 23
Boroughbridge, North Yorkshire 40
Boulogne, France, lighthouse 221, 226
Boulton, Meg 92
Bowcombe Down, Isle of Wight 148
Boxford, Berkshire 69
Bradbourne, Derbyshire 120, 256n.13
Bradford on Avon, Wiltshire 6, 110
Bradford, West Yorkshire 121–2, 124, 134
Bradnor Hill, Herefordshire 229
Bran Ditch, Cambridgeshire 163, 165, 177
Bransty, Cumbria 46
Braun, Hugh 175
Bridport, Dorset 192, 194, 202, 205, 211
Brigantes, British people 120
Briggs, Keith 220
Bristol 47

Britain 1–2, 5, 16, 18, 20–22, 25, 29, 36, 51–2, 54, 56, 74, 76, 79, 83, 85–6, 97, 106, 139, 154, 163, 167–8, 218, 235n.4
Brixworth, Northamptonshire 34, 248n.7; the Friends of Brixworth 34
Broadstairs, Kent 143
Broadway, Worcestershire 46
Brookes, Stuart xvi, 10, 148, 151, 189, 213, 270nn.5, 8, 271n.22, 272nn.24, 27
Broughton Poggs, Oxfordshire 140
Brycgstow see Bristol
Buckenham Park, Norfolk 175
Buckingham 189, 191–2, 194, 202, 207, 211, 215; church in Prebend End 211
Buckinghamshire 190, 207, 274n.49
Buckland, Dover, Kent 146
Bunns Bank, Norfolk 175
Burghal Hidage 168, 177, 183–4, 189–90, 192–3, 202, 207, 209, 211–13, 231, 270n.5, 271n.22, 272nn.27, 29
Burghclere, Hampshire 224
Burgred, king of Mercia 174
Burnham, Barry C. 19
Burnley, Lancashire 132
Bury St Edmunds, Suffolk 110, 112, 254n.132
Byrhtnoth, ealdorman of Essex 72
Byzantine Empire 134

Cadafael, king of Gwynedd 80
Caistor St Edmund, Norfolk 140
Caistor-by-Norwich, Norfolk 167
Calder river; Calder Valley, Yorkshire 121–2
Calderdale, West Yorkshire 120
Calne, Wiltshire 66
Cam, river 274
Cambridge 273nn.38, 44; King's Ditch 206; King's Mill 206
Cambridge, Eric 33
Cambridgeshire 48; Cambridgeshire Dykes 10, 163, 165, 177
Cana, wedding at, biblical event 126
Canterbury, Kent 42, 88–9, 101, 104, 106, 167; church of St Martin 88, 93, 95; church of St Mary 101; church of SS Peter and Paul 96, 101, 106; St Augustine's Abbey 96, 101–2, 108
Carlisle, Cumbria 29–30, 36, 238n.67
Catholme, Staffordshire 53, 56, 58, 61, 63, 69, 74

Cedd, bishop of the East Saxons 86
Cenwalh, king of Wessex 103–4
Cenwulf, king of Mercia 177
Chad, bishop of the Northumbrians, bishop of the Mercians 238n.52
Chalton, Hampshire 58–9, 69, 106
Chandler, John 212
Charlemagne, king of the Franks, Holy Roman Emperor 93, 110, 221, 226
Cheddar, Somerset 61, 66–7, 74, 171
Cheriton Bishop, Devon 170
Chertsey, Surrey, Abbey 89
Cheshire 118, 176
Chester 16, 81, 113, 131; Lower Bridge Street 64
Chester-le-Street, Co. Durham 42, 105, 155
Chesters, Northumberland, Roman fort 16
Chesterton, G.K. 37, 41
Chichester, West Sussex 42, 193, 228, 231
Chisbury, Wiltshire 189
Christchurch, Dorset 192, 195, 202, 205–6, 211, 213; Port Mill 206
Cirencester, Gloucestershire 34
Clausentum, Roman site 212
Clegg Hyer, Maren xv, 236n.13
Cnut, king of England, Denmark and Norway 110
Coatsworth, Elizabeth xvi, 9, 71
Coenwulf, king of Mercia 109
Colchester, Essex 186, 249n.27
Coles, Ann 154
Colgrave, Bertram 2, 29
Collingham, West Yorkshire 125
Collingwood, W.G. 125
Colne, Lancashire 132
Compton Beauchamp, Oxfordshire 166–7
Constantine I, 'the Great', Flavius Valerius Aurelius Constantinus Augustus, Roman Emperor 92, 94, 110
Cornwall 163, 171
Cotswolds (Gloucestershire, Oxfordshire, Somerset, Warwickshire, Wiltshire and Worcestershire) 46
Cowdery's Down, Hampshire 57–9, 61, 82, 106–7
Cox, Barrie 228
Cramp, Rosemary 32, 118, 134–5, 239n.80
Craven, Romano-British district, North Yorkshire 120

Cricklade, Wiltshire 184, 193
Cuckhamsley Hill (also called Cwichelm's Barrow or Scutchamer Knob), Oxfordshire 231
Cuddesdon, Oxfordshire 153
Cumbria 120, 131–2
Cunliffe, Barry 23
Cuthberht, ealdorman of Mercia 109
Cuthbert, St, bishop of Lindisfarne 29, 36, 42, 105, 154–6; *Anonymous Life of St Cuthbert* 126; Bede's *Vita Cuthberti* 29; reliquary coffin of St Cuthbert 125, 127, 257n.36
Cutsuida, abbess 247n.61
Cwichelm's Barrow (also called Cuckhamsley Hill or Scutchamer Knob), Oxfordshire 216
Cynegisl, king of the West Saxons 90–1
Cyneheard, West Saxon prince 82
Cynewulf, king of the West Saxons 61, 82
Cynhelm, St, prince of Mercia 109

Danelaw 43, 204
Danes 189, 229
Darrah, Richard 63
Davies, Wendy 246n.38
Dee, river 81, 176
Deerhurst, Gloucestershire 6, 248n.7, cover illustration
Deira 86–7, 96–7, 120, 151
Denmark 54
Derbyshire 118
Derwent, river 151
Detraymond, Wikimedia Commons 226
Devil's Ditch, Cambridgeshire 163, 165–6
Devil's Dyke, Cambridgeshire 177
Devizes, Wiltshire 178
Devlin, Zöe 150
Devon 48, 171, 214
Dewsbury, West Yorkshire 9, 118–136
Ditchedge Lane, Oxfordshire 44
Ditchley, Oxfordshire 171
Dodd, A.E. and E.M. 48
Domesday Book 54, 120, 122–3, 132, 148, 165, 176, 190, 202–3, 205, 213, 229
Doon Hill, East Lothian, Scotland 30
Dorchester-on-Thames, Oxfordshire 90–1
Dorset 171
Doubleday, J.F. 14

Dover, Kent 42, 111, 225; church of St Mary-in-Castro 111, 225–6; Dover Castle 225; Roman *pharos*, 5, 11, 111–12, 279n.52; *see also* Buckland
Driffield, East Yorkshire 151
Droitwich, Worcestershire 47, 171
Dryham, Battle of 19
Dunbar, East Lothian, Scotland 30
Dunstable, Bedfordshire, Marina Drive 160
Dunstan, St, archbishop of Canterbury 66
Dunstan's Clump, Nottinghamshire 56
Durham 42, 155
Durham, Old English poem 20

Eadberht, bishop of Lindisfarne 105
Eadgifu, beneficiary 71
Ealhstan, minister of King Edgar 180
Eanbald II, archbishop of York 105
Eanflæd, queen of the Northumbrians, wife of Oswiu 87
Eardwulf, bishop of Rochester 89–90
Earls Barton, Northamptonshire 6, 63, 114
Eashing, Surrey 189
East Anglia 8, 55, 86, 150, 165, 184, 186, 188, 191, 193, 202, 204, 207, 255n.143
East Hampshire Dykes 180
East Overton, Wiltshire 230
East Riding, historic subdivision of Yorkshire 118
Eastry, Kent 151
Ecgberht II, king of Kent 90
Ecgburh, abbess of Repton 158
Ecgfrith, king of the Bernicians, king of the Northumbrians 76, 85, 89, 95, 244n.2
Eckhard, Sîan 14, 236n.2
Edgar, king of Mercia and Northumbria, king of Wessex, king of the English 44, 180
Edington, battle at 189
Edmund, St, king of East Anglia 42, 110
Edward II, king of England 224
Edward III, king of England 224
Edward, 'the Confessor', king of England 101, 122
Edward, 'the Elder', king of the West Saxons 36, 113, 181, 184, 186–7, 191, 193, 214, 274n.44
Edward, 'the Martyr', king of England 110
Edwin, king of the Northumbrians 1–2, 5, 50, 53, 84, 87, 97, 108, 120, 246n.53

Egil Skallagrimsson, *Egil's Saga* 73
Elmet, British kingdom 120
Ely, Cambridgeshire, Cathedral 72
English Channel 42, 217, 222, 225
Eoforwic see York
Eostre ('Easter'), pagan goddess 98
Ermine Street, Roman road from London to Lincoln and York 40, 43
Ermine Way, Roman road from London to Gloucester 226
Escomb, Co. Durham 99, 106
Essex 47, 175, 193
Exeter Book 14, 20
Exeter, Devon 193; Castle 247n.5; University 171
Eyam, Derbyshire 120, 125, 256n.13

Faccombe Netherton, Hampshire 73
Farley Mount, Hampshire 231
Farningham, Kent 171
Faull, Margaret 120, 122–3, 131–2
Feddersen Wierde, Germany 54
Felix of Crowland, *Life of St Guthlac* 158
Feltwell, Norfolk 171
Fens, The, Norfolk, Lincolnshire, Cambridgeshire and Suffolk 3, 171, 177
Finan, St, bishop of Lindisfarne 31, 97–8, 105
Finglesham, Kent 145–6
Fisher, D.J.V. 21
Flanders 221
Fleam Dyke, Cambridgeshire 163, 165, 177, 229
Flixborough, Lincolnshire 34, 42, 51, 61–3, 67–73
Ford, Laverstock, Wiltshire 152
Foss, river 66
Fosse Way, Roman road from Exeter to Lincoln 43–4, 46
Fox, George 26
Fox, Sir Cyril 176–7
France 2
Franks Casket 125, 257n.36
Frisia 5
Frithuwold, king of Surrey 89, 247n.63
Fyfield, Oxfordshire 46

Galbert of Bruges, chronicler 221–2
Gaul 32, 95, 236n.10
Geats, fictional people in *Beowulf* 84, 137

Gem, Richard 92, 96
Germany 5, 54
Geþyncðo, Old English legal text 113, 222
Gildas, *De Excidio Britanniae* 20, 29, 36, 164
Gilmour, Brian 150
Glastonbury, Somerset 96, 101, 104; abbey 169; chapel/gatehouse of St John 103; church of St Mary 96, 103, 105; church of St Peter 103, 108
Glastonbury Tor, Somerset 225
Gloucester 205, 273n.42; St Oswald's Priory 110; Vales of Gloucester 172
Gloucestershire 46, 48
Gobowen, Shropshire 177
Goltho, Lincolnshire 8, 63–4, 66–7, 73–4
Gomersal, West Yorkshire 123
Goodier, Ann 140
Goodmanham, East Yorkshire 151
Goscelin of St Bertin, monk, hagiographer 72, 101
Gough Map 45
Great Bedwyn, Wiltshire 179
Great Ridgeway, trackway from Wiltshire to East Anglia 38, 230
Greensted, Essex 31, 34
Gregory I, 'the Great', pope 92, 95, 101, 107, 126, 252n.92
Grendel, monster in *Beowulf* 59, 61, 82, 84
Griffiths, David 182
Grigg, Erik xvi, 10, 163, 165–6, 178
Grimsby, Lincolnshire 225
Grocock, Christopher xvi, 7, 15–16, 21–2, 26, 28, 30–1, 33, 174, 235n.3
Guildford, Surrey 189, 192, 198, 202, 204–5
Guthlac, St, hermit 158

Hackness, North Yorkshire 123, 131, 135
Hadrian's Wall, Cumbria and Northumberland 13, 16, 22, 29–30, 47, 164, 167
Hadstock, Essex 34
Hæberht, Kentish king 90
Hakon, 'the Good', king of Norway 217
Halifax, West Yorkshire 122
Halsall, Guy 21, 26
Halwell, Devon 189, 213
Hamer, R.F.S. 14
Hampshire 25, 158, 190, 216, 218, 220; East Hampshire Dykes 180

Hamwic, Southampton 42, 150, 206
Harold I, 'Harefoot', king of England 159
Harold II, 'Godwinson', king of England 43, 221, 278n.27
Harris, Roland 212
Harrison, David 40, 47
Harrow Way, trackway in Southern England 38
Harthacnut, king of England 159
Hartlepool, Co. Durham 61, 99, 156, 250n.42, 256n.4
Hartshead, West Yorkshire 121, 124, 132
Haslam, Jeremy xvii, 8
Hastings, battle of 221
Hayes, Laurence 177
Heane, Kent, Domesday Hundred 148
Heaney, Seamus 46
Heathy Fields, Herefordshire 180
Hedda Stone, Peterborough Cathedral 127, 130
Henry I, king of England 43
Henry of Huntingdon, chronicler 227, 229
Heorot, royal hall in *Beowulf* 59, 72, 81, 245n.30
Hereford 42, 164, 180
Herefordshire 179; Herefordshire Plain 179
Hergest Ridge, Herefordshire 229
Hexham, Northumberland 33, 108, 134; mausoleum of St Andrew 108
Higgitt, John 129
High Ditch, Cambridgeshire 177
Higham Ferrers, Northamptonshire 34
Higham, Nicholas 21–2, 28, 87, 247n.70
Higham, Robert 205, 214
Highclere, Hampshire 224
Hild, abbess of Whitby 86–8
Hill, David 43, 176, 184, 217, 267
Hill, Margaret Worthington xvii, 10, 176
Hindle, Paul xvii, 10, 40–1
Hinton-on-the-Green, Worcestershire 48
Historia Brittonum (commonly attributed to Nennius) 80
Hoddom, Dumfriesshire, Scotland 128
Hoffmann, Marta 71
Holme-next-the-Sea, Norfolk 171
Holt, Richard 204, 208–9
Holy Land 42
Hooper, Max 169
Horsecombe Brook, Bath, Somerset 178
Hoskins, William 170–1

Hrothgar, king of the Danes in *Beowulf* 59, 73, 81, 84–5
Huddersfield, West Yorkshire 122
Hwicce, Anglo-Saxon people 247n.61

Ibn Fadlan, Arab traveller 142
Iceland 60, 73
Icknield Way, trackway from Norfolk to Wiltshire 38, 43, 177, 218, 225–6, 229, 232, 280n.75
Idle, river, battle of 81, 97
Ilbert de Laci, Norman landholder 122
Ilkley, West Yorkshire 132, 135
Ine, king of the West Saxons 43
Ingimund, character in *The Saga of the People of Vatnsdal* 72, 243n.67
Inkpen Beacon, Berkshire 226
Iona, Isle of, Scotland 250n.42
Ipswich, Suffolk 42
Ireland 83, 85, 97, 125, 250n.42
Isle of Wight 84, 148, 231
Italy 2, 106
Ivinghoe Beacon, Buckinghamshire 225

James, Simon 61
Jarrow, Tyne and Wear, monastery 13, 17, 31, 69, 106, 123, 248n.7
Jerusalem, church of the Holy Sepulchre 94
Jesus Christ 94, 98, 125–30, 253n.114
John, St, 'the Evangelist', Gospel of 126
Johnson, William 14
Jokul, character in *The Saga of the People of Vatnsdal* 72
Jones, Michael 21

Kapelle, The Netherlands 221
Keen, Laurence 211–12
Kemble, John 140
Kent 44, 77, 86–7, 89, 108, 151, 159, 224–5
Kenyon, Dame Kathleen 26
Kerry Ridgeway, path bordering mid-Wales and southern England 180
Ketil, 'the Large', character in *Egil's Saga* 68
Ketton Quarry, Northamptonshire 254n.132
Keynes, Simon 83, 191, 212
Kingsbridge, Devon 189, 192, 198, 202, 204–5, 213
Kingsholm, Gloucester, royal palace 110
Kingston Bagpuize, Oxfordshire 166

Kirkburton, West Yorkshire 121, 124, 128–9, 132–3, 135; All Hallows Church 128
Kirkdale, North Yorkshire 131, 135
Kirkheaton, West Yorkshire 121, 124, 132–5
Klevnäs, Alison 159
Kneen, Maggie 82, 84, cover

Lacnunga, Old English medical texts and prayers 160
Lake District 38
Lambarde, William, cartographer 224–5, 227
Lancashire 118
Lang, J.T. 130
Langport, Somerset 192, 194, 202, 205–7, 211, 273n.44, 274nn.46, 48
Lapidge, Michael 25, 29, 238nn.68, 71
Lavelle, Ryan 246n.40
Le Corbusier, Charles-Édouard, architect 50, 74
Lea Green, North Yorkshire 68, 70
Leahy, Kevin xviii, 7–8, 51, 62–3
Leckhampstead, Buckinghamshire 227
Leeds 81, 123, 128, 131
Leicester 18, 28; Jewry Wall Baths 28
Leofsige, beneficiary 72
Leslie, R.F. 14–15, 20
Lester-Makin, Alexandra 119
Lethbridge, Tom 52, 55
Lewes, East Sussex 192, 195, 202, 207, 212
Lewis, Michael xviii, 7–8
Lichfield, Staffordshire 43, 171
Life of St Willibald 136
Lilley, Keith 181–2
Lincoln 40, 64, 96, 150, 167; church of St Paul in the Bail 95; Wigford, church of St Mark 150
Lincolnshire 40, 45, 54, 118, 255n.143
Lindisfarne (Holy Island), Northumberland 31, 42, 96–7, 99, 105, 111, 123, 126, 128, 136, 154, 156; Church of St Peter 31; *Lindisfarne Gospels* 126
Lindsey, Lincolnshire 54, 228, 246n.37
Little Bedwyn, Wiltshire 179
Little Oakley, Essex 34
Little Wilbraham, Cambridgeshire 140
London 40, 42–3, 64, 70, 72, 74, 88, 111, 151, 167, 206, 208, 231; Bull Wharf 63; church of St Paul 88; Greenwich Park 144; Westminster Abbey 101, 159

Long Wittenham, Oxfordshire 140
Loveden Hill, Lincolnshire 147
Lowbury Hill, Oxfordshire (formerly Berkshire) 153
Lower Short Ditches, Shropshire 180
Luguvalium (Carlisle), Cumbria 29
Luscombe, Paul 214
Luton, Bedfordshire 232
Lydd, Kent, basilica 95
Lydford, Devon 168, 183, 192, 195, 202, 212, 275n.67
Lyminge, Kent 31, 59, 238n.77
Lyng, Somerset 192, 196, 202, 212

Maesbury, Shropshire 176
Maesknoll, Somerset 178
Magi, biblical figures 125–6
Maldon, Essex 8, 184, 187–8, 193, 201–2, 205, 207, 270n.15, 271n.17; St Mary's church 187, 201, 271n.15; St Peter's church 187, 201
Malim, Tim 177
Malmesbury, Wiltshire 192, 196, 202
Manchester 131; Deansgate 47; University 176
Manuscripts: England, Cambridge, Cambridge University Library, MS Ll. 1.10 (*Book of Cerne*) 126; London, British Library Additional 62935,9 (map of beacons) 224–5; British Library Cotton MS Nero D. iv (*Lindisfarne Gospels*) 126; London, British Library, Cotton Tiberius B. v 2; France, Amiens, Bibliothèque Municipale, MS 18 (*Corbie Psalter*) 126; Paris, Bibliothèque Nationale, MS. Lat. 11550, f.6 (*Psalter Hymnal, St Germain-des-Prés*) 128; Ireland, Dublin, Trinity College Library, MS A.I. (58) (*Book of Kells*) 125; Sweden, Stockholm, National Library of Sweden, MS A.35 (*Codex Aureus*) 126
Margary, Ivan D. 39, 131, 226
Marlborough, Wiltshire 43, 46, 189, 193, 198, 202, 204, 213, 230–1; Marlborough Downs 230
Mary, St, Virgin 101, 110, 127, 253n.114
Maserfeld (? Oswestry), Shropshire 155
Masham, North Yorkshire 127
Matthew of Paris 42
Matthew, St 126
Mayr-Harting, Henry 87

Medway, river 89
Mellitus, missionary to Kent, bishop of the East Saxons, archbishop of Canterbury 88–9, 92
Melrose, Scottish Borders, Scotland; monastery 97
Meon Hill, Hampshire 157
Meonware, Anglo-Saxon people 84
Mercia 8, 85–6, 120, 171, 176–7, 181–4, 186, 189, 191–3, 202, 204, 207–10, 214, 228, 246n.41, 272n.24, 274n.49
Merovingia 159
Merton, estate in Anglo-Saxon Wessex 82
Middlesex, former county, area now in Greater London and Berkshire 175
Middlewich, Cheshire 47
Mill Hill, Deal, Kent 146, 148
Mill names (King's Mill, Port Mill, Town Mill) 203, 206
Millett, Martin 61
Minchinhampton Bulwarks, Gloucestershire 175
Mirfield, West Yorkshire 124, 130, 133
Modwenna, St, *Life and Miracles of St Modwenna* 159
Monkwearmouth [Wearmouth], Sunderland, Tyne and Wear, monastery 13, 17, 31, 108, 123, 236n.10, 248n.7; church of St Peter 31–3, 239n.80
Moorhouse, Stephen 120, 122–3, 131–2
Morgan's Hill, Wiltshire 178
Morris, John 20
Mucking, Essex 56, 172
Muir, Richard 49
Mutlow, Cambridgeshire 229
Mynors, R.A.B. 2, 235n.2

Nantwich, Cheshire 47
Nene, river 40
Nettleton Top, Lincolnshire 69
Neuman de Vegvar, Carol 134
Neville, Richard Cornwallis 140
Newcastle-on-Clun, Shropshire 165
Newcastle upon Tyne 30
Newport Pagnell, Buckinghamshire 193, 200, 202, 205, 207, 214, 275n.62
Ninian, St 97–8
Norham, Northumberland 42, 105
North Elmham, Norfolk 65, 68, 74

North Riding, historic subdivision of Yorkshire 118
North Sea 5, 42, 150
Northamptonshire 48, 81, 190
Northumbria 83, 85–9, 97, 106, 116, 120, 132–3
Northwich, Cheshire 47
Norway 60, 72, 217
Norwich 150
Nottingham 43, 49
Nottinghamshire 118

O'Brien, Elizabeth 150
Ock, river 166
Odell, Bedfordshire 71
Offa, king of the Mercians 89–90, 164, 247n.61
Offa's Dyke 10, 162–6, 176–7, 179, 228–9
Ogilby, John 45
Old Dairy Cottage, Winchester, Hampshire 157
Old Sarum, Wiltshire 41, 157
Orton Hall Farm, Essex 34
Oshere, king of the Hwicce 247n.61
Oswald, St, bishop of Worcester, archbishop of York 101
Oswald, St, king of the Northumbrians 90, 97, 108, 110, 155
Oswestry, Shropshire 155; Maesbury Road 177
Oswiu, king of the Bernicians, king of the Northumbrians 81, 83, 85–8, 97, 244n.2, 245n.23, 246nn.49, 50
Otley, West Yorkshire 120, 125–6, 132, 135
Ottaway, P.J. 25
Overton Downs, Wiltshire 46
Owen-Crocker, Gale R. 221, 256n.1, 266n.1, 278nn.27, 33
Oxford 189, 193, 199, 202, 205, 207, 214
Oxfordshire 44, 48, 166, 190, 207

Painsthorpe Wold, East Yorkshire 152–3
Palmer, William 177
Parisi, British people 120
Park Pale, near Topcliffe, North Yorkshire 175
Patrick, St 97
Paul, St 127
Paulinus, St, missionary to Kent and Northumbria, bishop of Rochester 97
Peada, king/princeps of the Middle Angles 83
Peak District 48, 169, 173

Pega, St, hermit, sister of Guthlac 159
Pembridge, Herefordshire 179
Penda, king of the Mercians 79–81, 83, 104, 155, 246nn.41, 49
Pennine Hills 119, 122, 132
Peter, St 32, 109, 127
Peterborough, Cambridgeshire 90, 127, 130
Picts 85
Piddletrenthide, Dorset 173
Piercebridge, Co. Durham 22
Pilton, Somerset 189
Pitfield Farm, Herefordshire 179
Platt, C. 34
Portable Antiquities Scheme (PAS) 53, 67, 70, 75, 141
Portchester, Hampshire 65–6, 71
Portfield names 203, 206, 274n.46
Portway, route name found in various places 46, 49
Poundbury, Dorset 168
Powys, Wales 180
Prestatyn, Denbighshire, Wales 163
Prittlewell, Essex 71, 106, 142
Procopius of Caesarea, historian 20
Puddlehill, Bedfordshire 56

Rædwald, king of the East Angles 81–2
Rastrick, West Yorkshire 121, 124, 131–2
Raunds, Northamptonshire 252n.94
Readan Dyke, Oxfordshire 167
Reading, Berkshire 41, 216
Rectitudines Singularum Personarum, Anglo-Saxon text on estate management 170, 217
Reculver, Kent, basilica 106
Repton, Derbyshire 109–10, 153; St Wystan's church 109
Reynolds, Andrew 92, 157, 203–4, 222–3, 230
Rhunn, son of King Urien of Rheged 97
Riby, Lincolnshire 173
Richborough, Kent 21, 28
Richer of Reims, historian 217, 221–2
Ringlemere, Kent 154
Ripon, North Yorkshire 33, 76–7, 79, 81, 88–90, 97, 99, 108, 119–20, 153–4, 244n.2, 246n.53; Ailcy Hill 154
Rippon, Stephen 171
Robert le Frison (Robert the Frisian), count of Flanders 221

Rochester, Kent 47
Rodwell, Warwick 73
Rogers, Adam 22, 35
Rome, Italy 2, 23, 42, 86, 94, 98, 100, 116; Pantheon 251n.63; 'Probus' mausoleum 253n.115; Old St Peters 253n.115; tomb of St Peter 109
Rothbury, Northumberland 128
Roundway Down, Wiltshire 153
Rowe Ditch, Herefordshire 179–80
Ruin, The, Old English poem 7, 13–36, 111, 237n.18
Rus, Viking people 142
Rushock Hill, Herefordshire 164–5, 179
Ruthwell Cross, Dumfries and Galloway, Scotland 117, 126, 133
Rutland 228
Ryknield Way/Street, Staffordshire, Roman road 44, 48

Sæberht, king of the East Saxons 88
Saga of the People of Vatnsdal, The, Icelandic text 68, 72, 243n.67
Salt Street, route name found in various places 47
Saltersford, Cheshire 47
Saltwood, Kent 148
Sandbach, Cheshire, crosses 125, 127
Sandwich, Kent 111
Sashes (island and *burh* near Cookham), Berkshire 207
Savernake Forest, Wiltshire 178–9
Sawyer, Peter 252n.94, 266n.14
Sayer, Duncan 145–6
Scandinavia 5
Scots 85
Scyldingas, legendary Danish people in *Beowulf* 217
Semple, Sarah xviii, 9, 153, 157
Severn, river 163, 176
Severus, Lucius Septimius, Roman Emperor 164
Shaftesbury, Wiltshire 192, 196, 202; Abbey 110
Shapinsay, Orkney Islands, Scotland 224
Shapland, Michael xviii, 8, 97, 102–3, 107, 109, 115, 227, 229, 279n.51
Sharp, Sheila 217–18, 221, 224, 230, 232
Sheffield, South Yorkshire, cross 120

Index

Shemming, Jake 220
Sherborne, Dorset, Abbey 217, 226, 250n.58
Sherburn in Elmet, North Yorkshire 120
Short Dyke, Oxfordshire 166
Shropshire 176, 180, 268n.54; Shropshire County Council 177
Sigeberht, king of the East Saxons 83
Sigeric, archbishop of Canterbury 2
Silbury Hill, Wiltshire 230–1
Silchester, Hampshire 41, 95, 157, 167, 249n.27
Slater, Terry 214
Snyder, Christopher 36
Solent, strait between the Isle of Wight and England 220
Somerset 48; Somerset Levels 207, 211
South Shields, Co. Durham 30
Southampton, Hampshire 192, 197, 202, 212; see also Hamwih
Spong Hill, Norfolk 71, 147
Springfield Lyons, Essex 63, 113, 255n.132
Sprouston, Roxburghshire, Scotland 149
St Albans, Hertfordshire 42
Stamford, Lincolnshire 40, 42, 48, 193, 199, 202, 207, 214; Stamford Ware pottery 187
Stanbury, West Yorkshire 122, 124, 132, 134
Stansfield, West Yorkshire 122, 124, 132–6
Stanway, Gloucestershire 46
Staunton on Arrow, Herefordshire 180
Steenberg, Axel and Sophie 154
Stenton, Sir Frank 20, 270n.14
Stephen of Ripon (formerly known as Eddius Stephanus), *Vita Sancti Wilfrithi* 79–80, 87–9
Stevens, W.O. 118
Stocker, David 92, 150
Stockbridge Down, Hampshire 157
Stone-by-Faversham, Kent 251n.63
Stratford place names 40, 46
Stratford-upon-Avon, Warwickshire 40, 48, 171
Streanæshealh (probably Whitby, North Yorkshire) 86, 88, 246n.42
Street House, Loftus, North Yorkshire 146–7
Stye Head, Cumbria 46
Sussex 221, 245n.25
Sutton Courtenay, Oxfordshire 52

Sutton Hoo, Suffolk 68, 106, 142, 150
Swaledale Dykes, Yorkshire 180
Swallowcliffe Down, Wiltshire 142, 152
Swithun, St, bishop of Winchester 42, 103
Switzerland 2

Tadcaster, North Yorkshire 131
Tamworth, Staffordshire 42, 48, 61; Tamworth Mill 67
Tanshelf, West Yorkshire 120
Taplow, Buckinghamshire 144, 150–1
Taylor, Arnold 114
Taylor, Christopher 40, 42, 48–9
Tebbutt, Fred 52, 55
Thames, river 48, 140, 150–1, 166, 189, 191, 208, 224, 231, 272n.24
Thanet, Kent 88
Theodore, archbishop of Canterbury 31; *Penitential* 105
Thetford, Norfolk 229; Brandon Road 64
Thompson, Victoria 159
Thorestein, character in *The Saga of the People of Vatnsdal* 72
Till, river 149
Tipper, Jess 55
Todmorden, West Yorkshire 122, 124, 132, 134
Tothill Terrace, Minster-in-Thanet, Kent 224
Totnes, Devon 189, 193, 201–2, 204–5, 207, 213–24
Totnor, Herefordshire 228
Totterdown, Wiltshire 231
Totternhoe, Bedfordshire, lookout site 232
Tour d'Odre, Boulogne, France, *pharos* 225
Trent and Peak Archaeological Trust 53, 58
Trent, river 81, 245n.15
Treuddyn, near Mold, Flintshire, Wales 163, 165
Trewhiddle Style 122
Tribal Hidage 85
Turner, Sam 154
Tutt, The, Hewelsfield parish, Gloucestershire, look-out place 228
Tweed, river 149
Tyler, Damian xix, 8

Uncleby, East Yorkshire 145
Upper Short Ditch, Shropshire 180
Ure, river 40

Vale of York 151
Vallet Covert, Herefordshire 179
Venta Belgarum (Winchester), Hampshire 23–5
Via Devana, Roman road from Colchester to Chester 229
Vikings 3, 5, 7, 25, 47, 66, 74, 110, 130, 154, 158, 167, 182, 184, 186, 188–9, 208–10, 213, 217–18, 222, 230
Vindolanda, Northumberland 30
Volga, river 142
Vyrnwy, river 176

Wacher, John 19, 26
Wadloo, West Wratting, Cambridgeshire 229
Wakefield, West Yorkshire 118, 120–4, 131–6; Cathedral 122; Manor of 129, 131–2
Wales 45, 47, 53, 163, 173, 228–9, 240
Wallingford, Oxfordshire 42, 168, 193, 205, 207, 216, 231, 273n.42
Wallsend, Tyne and Wear 30
Waltham Abbey, Essex 66
Wanderer, The, Old English poem 5
Wansdyke, Wiltshire and Somerset 163, 165, 178–9
Wansford, Cambridgeshire 40
Wantsum Channel, Kent 224
Wantyn Dyke, Powys, Wales 180
Ward's Hurst, Buckinghamshire, lookout site 232
Warden Hill, Bedfordshire, lookout site 232
Wardhill, Shapinsay, Orkney Islands, Scotland 224, 278n.41
Wareham, Dorset 42, 193
Warrendown Row, Leckhampstead, Buckinghamshire 227
Warwick 48
Warwickshire 44, 48, 175
Wat's Dyke 10, 162, 165, 176–7
Watchet, Somerset 168, 192, 197, 202
Water Newton, Cambridgeshire 40
Watling Street, Roman road from the Kent coast to London and Wroxeter 43–4, 225, 229
Watson, Aaron 142
Wealhtheow, queen of Denmark, wife of Hrothgar, in *Beowulf* 82

Wearmouth *see* Monkwearmouth
Webster, Graham 26
Webster, Leslie 151
Welland, river 40
Welsh Marches 176
Werferth, bishop of Worcester 159
Wessex 8, 38, 158, 165, 167, 182–4, 186, 189–192, 204, 207, 209–10, 213, 217, 246n.40, 271n.22, 272n.23, 273n.33
West Ardsley, West Yorkshire 123
West Cotton, Northamptonshire 254n.132
West Heslerton, North Yorkshire 56, 154, 172, 235n.9
West Riding, historic subdivision of Yorkshire 118–20, 126
West Stow, Suffolk 55–6, 59, 63, 167, 172
West, Stanley 55
Whalley, Lancashire 132
Wharfedale, West Yorkshire 120
Wharram Percy, North Yorkshire 56, 167
Whitby, North Yorkshire 97, 123, 250n.42; Synod of 8, 86–9, 98–9, 246n.42
Whithorn, Dumfries and Galloway, Scotland 31, 108; St Ninian's church 98
Whittington, Gloucestershire, Roman villa 34
Whitworth, A.M. 29
Whorley Wood, Buckinghamshire, lookout site 232
Wickham, Welford, Berkshire, church of St Swithun 226
Wiferd and Alta, tomb of, in Worcester Cathedral 109
Wigingamere, possibly Essex 231
Wiglaf, king of Mercia 109
Wijster, The Netherlands 54
Wilfrid, St, bishop of York 33, 77–8, 81, 89, 99, 120, 134, 151, 244n.2, 245n.25, 247n.60
William I, 'the Conqueror', duke of Normandy, king of England 43, 49, 111, 221–2, 278n.27
William of Malmesbury, historian 101
Williams, Gareth 209
Williams, Howard xix, 9, 92, 109, 144
Wilton 192, 197, 202, 205
Wiltshire 158, 190, 233, 274n.49; Herepath 46
Winchcombe, Gloucestershire; church of St Pancras 109–10

Winchester, Hampshire 13, 23–5, 42–3, 48, 101, 103–4, 157, 168, 183–4, 193, 204, 208, 231, 273n.42; Lankhills Cemetery 24; Old Minster 103; St George's Street 23; St Martin's Close 24; St Mary's Hospital 255n.132; The Brooks 23–5; tower of St Martin 103; tomb of St Swithun 103; *see also Venta Belgarum*
Wine, bishop of Winchester 238n.52
Winwæd, river, battle at 79, 81
Wirksworth, Derbyshire 49
Withington, Gloucestershire 171
Woden, Norse god 179
Wollaston, Northamptonshire 171
Woodbridge, Suffolk 193, 200, 202, 215
Woodkirk, West Yorkshire 123–4, 131–2
Woodnesborough, Kent 151
Wool Street, Cambridgeshire, Roman road 229
Worcester 46, 193, 199, 202, 208, 214, 271n.18; Cathedral 101, 109
Worsell Wood, Radnorshire, Wales 229
Wright, Duncan 92
Wright, Thomas 26
Wroxeter, Shropshire 13, 18, 26–8, 167, 171, 238n.56; church of St Andrew 28
Wulfhere, king of the Mercians, son of Penda 80, 83–4, 89, 245n.25, 246n.41

Wulfric, abbot of St Augustine's, Canterbury 101, 103
Wulfstan II, bishop of Worcester 101
Wulfwynn, beneficiary 72
Wynflæd, testatrix 71
Wystan, St, prince of Mercia 109

Yarnton, Oxfordshire 149
Yarwell, Northamptonshire 171
Yatesbury, Wiltshire 222–3, 227, 230–2; Yatesbury Lane 230
Yeavering, Northumberland, royal palace site 59, 61, 81–4, 97–9, 106–7, 149
York 8, 33, 43, 53, 67, 70–2, 74, 96, 99, 105, 108, 119–20, 131, 135, 150–1; Archaeological Trust 65; archbishopric 120; church of St Michael-le-Belfry 251n.74; Coppergate 64–5; *Eoforwic* 42; King Edwin's baptistery 5; Micklegate 47; Minster 130; Skeldergate 65
Yorkshire 45, 48, 118, 120, 122, 125, 130–3, 151; Yorkshire Dales 119; Yorkshire Wolds 151–2; *see also* East Riding, North Riding, West Riding

Zant, John M. 23–4